PROSECUTING DOMESTIC VIOLENCE

Prosecuting Domestic Violence

A Philosophical Analysis

MICHELLE MADDEN DEMPSEY

OXFORD
UNIVERSITY PRESS

OXFORD

UNIVERSITY PRESS

Great Clarendon Street, Oxford OX2 6DP

Oxford University Press is a department of the University of Oxford.
It furthers the University's objective of excellence in research, scholarship,
and education by publishing worldwide in

Oxford New York

Auckland Cape Town Dar es Salaam Hong Kong Karachi
Kuala Lumpur Madrid Melbourne Mexico City Nairobi
New Delhi Shanghai Taipei Toronto

With offices in

Argentina Austria Brazil Chile Czech Republic France Greece
Guatemala Hungary Italy Japan Poland Portugal Singapore
South Korea Switzerland Thailand Turkey Ukraine Vietnam

Oxford is a registered trade mark of Oxford University Press
in the UK and in certain other countries

Published in the United States
by Oxford University Press Inc., New York

British Library Cataloguing in Publication Data

Data available

Library of Congress Cataloging in Publication Data

Dempsey, Michelle Madden.
  Prosecuting domestic violence : a philosophical analysis / Michelle
Madden Dempsey.
     p. cm.
  Includes bibliographical references and index.
  ISBN 978–0–19–956216–9
  1. Family violence—Law and legislation—United States.
2. Prosecution—United States—Decision making. 3. Prosecution—
United States—Social aspects. I. Title.
KF9322.D46 2009
345.73′02555—dc22   2009002655

Typeset by Newgen Imaging Systems (P) Ltd., Chennai, India
Printed in Great Britain
on acid-free paper by
the MPG Books Group in the UK

ISBN 978–0–19–956216–9

1 3 5 7 9 10 8 6 4 2

For B

General Editor's Preface

This is a closely argued and richly textured monograph around two principal themes—domestic violence, a major crime of our times; and prosecutorial discretion, a significant element in many criminal justice systems. The richness of the book comes from its foundations in legal theory and its focus on what the author terms 'feminist practical reasoning'. Through this lens, Dr Madden Dempsey develops a ground-breaking analysis of what prosecutors are and do, what the value of public prosecution is, the relationship between the wrongs involved in domestic violence and the community, and the implications for how prosecutors ought to reason. In relation to domestic violence specifically, there is an exploration of the influence of patriarchy, sex discrimination and structural inequality; and then the author defends the practice of continuing with the prosecution when the victim requests dismissal of the charges, and sets out the proper role of victims in prosecutions. The result is a challenging and intellectually sophisticated examination of some major yet under-researched themes in criminal justice, and a significant addition to this series of monographs.

Andrew Ashworth

Preface

The main question which motivates the inquiry undertaken in this book is: what should public prosecutors do when victims withdraw support for domestic violence prosecutions? The answer defended herein can be summarized as follows: within the realm of justified (permissible) action, prosecutors should respond *effectively*; which is to say that, *ceteris paribus*, domestic-violence prosecutors should respond as feminists. This claim is intended as a provocative formulation of the proposition that domestic violence prosecutors should act for reasons generated by the value of reconstituting their states (and communities) as less patriarchal. This book defends that claim in two steps: first, it sets out a general theory of prosecutorial practical reasoning and second, it considers the prosecution of domestic-violence offences in particular. Along the way, this book provides an original account of the nature of prosecutorial action, the values that can be realized through such action, and the relationship between these values and the practical reasoning of criminal prosecutors. Moreover, it provides analyses of two key concepts, domestic violence and patriarchy, and explains the relevance of the latter to a proper understanding of the former. The book then puts the preceding insights to work in answering the motivating question stated above, providing answers both in terms of what prosecutors would be *justified* in doing and what prosecutors should do in order to be *effective*. Chapter 9 applies this general framework in addressing the rights and duties of domestic-violence victims to participate in criminal prosecutions. In the final chapter, the book examines and responds to some general objections that might be raised to the arguments herein, ultimately defending the role of the domestic-violence prosecutor-as-feminist.

In its former life, this book (or most of it anyway) was submitted as my doctoral thesis at the University of Oxford. It is now my first published book and indeed, one of my first published academic works. For both reasons, perhaps, its aims are somewhat modest. Principally, it seeks to clarify some issues that perplexed me during my years as a domestic violence prosecutor, and some further issues that only became perplexing to me once I had the benefit of time and academic distance to reflect on my experiences as a prosecutor.

The central thought motivating this book is that domestic-violence prosecutors may have a legitimate role to play in creating more feminist states and communities. No doubt, this thought will strike some as clearly wrong. Indeed, I confess to some sympathy with this view; although (obviously) I think there is at least something to be said in support of the role of prosecutor-as-feminist. While the book certainly does not aim to answer every question it raises, it does, I hope, provide a clear account of some important issues faced by those attempting to use the criminal justice system to address the problem of domestic violence specifically, and to further the aims of feminism more generally. Thus, to the extent any of my arguments are clearly wrong, I hope at least to have displayed something of what HLA Hart characterized as a 'sovereign virtue in jurisprudence' by being wrong *clearly*.[1]

There is no denying that this book targets an unusual audience. I suspect its ideal reader is a philosophically curious feminist-domestic-violence-criminal-prosecutor-turned-academic. (Not surprisingly, perhaps, its author fits that description.) Readers with an interest in criminal prosecution generally, but no particular interest in domestic violence or feminism, may find profitable discussions in Part II, whilst readers concerned with domestic violence and feminism more generally may find Part III of particular interest. Readers should be warned, however, that the book's argument develops throughout each chapter and thus, it would be difficult to pick up the thread of argument by jumping in at say, Chapter 5 or Chapter 8 (both of which tie together various threads set forth in previous chapters).

I have accumulated a huge number of debts in writing this book. First and foremost, I would like to thank my husband, Liam Dempsey, to whom this book is dedicated. In the eleven years since I first began thinking about this project, Liam has spent countless hours helping me to develop and articulate the ideas that inform this work. On a professional note, I am particularly grateful for the insights and practical expertise Liam has lent this project based on his own experience working in criminal-law enforcement. On a more personal note, I am deeply thankful to Liam for his unfailing support, encouragement, love, and good humour.

To my doctoral supervisors, Professor John Gardner and Dr Carolyn Hoyle, I owe tremendous intellectual debts, both for their professional writings and personal guidance. Throughout the writing of the thesis upon which this book is based, I often found myself thinking, 'Oh my . . . the confusions I would avoid if only I could borrow John's brain! The thesis would write itself!' Well, I never convinced John to lend me his brain, but he did the next best thing by spending four years training me how to think. I cannot recall how my brain worked before John got his hands on it, but I am sure that it works far better now than it did then, and for that I am deeply grateful. Carolyn Hoyle's encyclopaedic knowledge and sophisticated understanding of the criminal justice system's response to domestic violence saved me from making numerous mistakes throughout the writing of this book. As a work of applied moral philosophy, it was crucial that this book connect theory with reality, and it is here where I am most grateful to Carolyn. With her expert assistance and guidance, I hope that this book bridges at least some of the many gaps between theory and practice.

---

[1] HLA Hart, 'Positivism and the Separation of Law and Morals' (1958) 71 Harvard LR 593.

It was my good fortune to have the support and generosity of my colleagues at the University of Oxford Faculty of Law while writing this book. In particular, I would like to thank Dr. Mary Bosworth, Cathryn Costello, Professor Judith Freedman Dr. Benjamin Goold, Michelle Grossman, Jonathan Herring, Dr. Dori Kimel, Dr. Grant Lamond, Dr. Patricia Londono, Donal Nolan, Professor Julian Roberts, Dr Shlomit Wallerstein, Dr. Rebecca Williams, and Professor Lucia Zedner for serving as mentors and friends throughout the writing of this book. I would also like to thank Professor Andrew Ashworth, who served as my official co-supervisor in the first year of my doctoral studies and generously continued to provide assistance as an unofficial supervisor and mentor throughout this project. I cannot overstate the value of having worked with Professor Ashworth as my first professional mentor in academic life. His remarkable productivity, intellect, and dedication to excellence have set clearly in my mind the benchmarks for professional success, and I will undoubtedly continue to be inspired by his example. Finally, and most deeply, I am indebted to my doctoral examiners, Professor Antony Duff and Professor Jeremy Horder, whose work has long inspired much of my own thinking regarding the proper function of the criminal justice system and will surely continue to do so in the future. Their insightful comments on my thesis and challenging questions in my *viva voce* helped to refine and clarify many of the arguments in this book.

In the transition from thesis to book, I accumulated additional debts of gratitude to numerous colleagues who were kind enough to read and comment on earlier drafts. In particular, I am tremendously appreciative of the time and comments offered to me by Professor Denise Réaume, whose advice prompted a much-needed restructuring of Chapter 7. I am also especially indebted to the helpful critique offered by Professor Michael Steven Green, who helped me avoid some mistakes in Chapter 2. Undoubtedly, many errors remain, for which I take sole responsibility.

The incredibly professional team at Oxford University Press UK have my sincere thanks for their hard work in bringing this project to completion. In particular, I am grateful to Alex Flach and Lucy Page for their support and patience throughout the production process. Special thanks are due to Jeremy Langworthy, the book's copy-editor, whose tremendous attention to detail caught an embarrassing number of errors in the original draft and corrected them with expert efficiency.

I would like to thank my parents for their love and support, both during the writing of this book and throughout my life. Especially, I thank my mother for setting such an excellent example of hard work and commitment in the pursuit of post-graduate studies (having herself obtained a master's degree whilst raising five young children and working full-time). I would like to thank my father for instilling in me a great love of law and philosophy, and a passion for pursuing the kinds of arguments to which these disciplines give rise.

Last but not least, I would like to thank my daughter, Katy, for filling my everyday of the last five years with joy, and to thank my son, Charlie, for bringing even greater love and happiness to our family. I love you both more than words can express.

Chapter 6 has been published (with some alterations) as 'What counts as domestic violence? A conceptual analysis' (2006) 12 William and Mary Journal of Women and the Law 301. Parts of the book's central argument is summarized in 'Toward a feminist state: What does 'effective' prosecution of domestic violence mean?' (2007) 70 Modern Law Review.

Contents

Table of Cases and Statutes

STATUTES

CASES

PART I

SOME PRELIMINARY
CONSIDERATIONS

1

Introduction

A central claim of this book is that domestic-violence prosecutors should be feminists, *ceteris paribus*. This claim is intended as a provocative formulation of the proposition that domestic-violence prosecutors should, other things being equal, act for reasons generated by the value of reconstituting their communities as less patriarchal. The book defends this claim in a two-part argument. Chapters 3–5 set out a general theory of prosecutorial discretion, whilst Chapters 6–9 consider the prosecution of domestic-violence offences in particular, applying the insights gained from the previous chapters in considering how prosecutors should manage such cases.

This introductory chapter explains the context in which I became intrigued by the moral questions raised by domestic-violence prosecution and the tools I employ in this book to explore such questions. In addition to unpacking some underlying assumptions which animate my approach, this chapter explains and defends the methodology of feminist practical reasoning which I have adopted in writing this book. Importantly, this chapter sets out the central question that has long motivated my concern with this topic and inspired the writing of this book (what should public prosecutors do when victims withdraw their support for the prosecution of domestic violence cases?). Moreover, this chapter provides an analysis of victim withdrawal from prosecutions and provides a brief introduction to the debates surrounding so-called 'victimless' prosecution of domestic violence.

A. Why Domestic-violence Prosecution?

In the interest of being upfront about the motivations which inform my approach in this work, I should confess that I personally served as a domestic-violence prosecutor in the US during the early stages of my legal career.[1] To some extent, admittedly, this project can be understood as an attempt to justify the policies I implemented as a prosecutor; although it must be said that upon reflection I have found justification lacking in many instances.

---

[1] Champaign County State's Attorneys Office, Urbana, Illinois (1996–8).

When I first began prosecuting these cases, US domestic-violence prosecutorial policies were in the midst of radical transformation from a traditional approach (wherein such cases are typically dismissed unless the victim insists upon prosecution) to what was has been coined a 'pro-prosecution' or 'mandatory prosecution' approach (wherein the victim's request for dismissal is disregarded in prosecutorial decision-making).[2] Pursuant to grant funding obtained under the US Violence Against Women Act,[3] I was appointed to the position of prosecuting attorney in a newly established Domestic-violence prosecution Unit (DV Unit). In this position, I was given relatively free reign to determine which cases fell under the authority of the DV Unit[4] and to establish new policies for prosecuting these cases.[5] In the main, the policies I implemented reflected an aggressive pro-prosecution policy: the scope of domestic-violence cases was defined broadly; charging decisions were taken irrespective of the victims' wishes; witness subpoenas were routinely issued for victims to testify in court; and charges were not dismissed pursuant to the victims' requests.[6] Whilst these aggressive policies were supported by the local domestic abuse refuge, they sparked a heated backlash both by the defence bar and judiciary, as well as by many victims themselves.[7] Indeed, the vast majority of threats I received during this period were issued not by defendants I had prosecuted, but rather by victims who were enraged at my refusal to dismiss their partners' cases.

At any given time, up to 85 per cent of the named victims in my caseload requested dismissal of charges against their alleged batterers, and nearly all such requests were refused.[8] Such refusals led to a huge surge in the number of jury

---

[2] For a review of the traditional approach, see J Zorza, 'The criminal law of misdemeanor violence (1970–1990)' (1992) 83 J of Crim L and Criminology 46; for a quick review of pro-prosecution policies, see Editors, 'New State and Federal responses to domestic violence' (1993) 106 Harvard L Rev 1528, 1540–2. See n 52 below for more detailed consideration of the differences between pro-prosecution and mandatory prosecution approaches.

[3] This Act was specifically intended 'to establish projects in local communities... to coordinate intervention and prevention of domestic violence'. US Violence Against Women Act of 1994 42 USC 10418.

[4] Illinois law defined domestic violence quite broadly, including 'spouses, former spouses, parents, children, stepchildren and other persons related by blood or by present or prior marriage, persons who share or formerly shared a common dwelling, persons who have or allegedly have a child in common, persons who share or allegedly share a blood relationship through a child, persons who have or have had a dating or engagement relationship, persons with disabilities and their personal assistants'. Illinois Domestic Violence Act of 1986 750 ILCS 60/103(6) (as effective in 1996–9).

[5] Illinois does not have any general prosecutorial policies akin to the Code for Crown Prosecutors. In smaller jurisdictions, prosecutorial policies are often unwritten and vary considerably according to the discretion of the individual prosecutor placed in charge of a particular caseload.

[6] M Schenk, 'Aggressively pursuing abuse cases at issue' *News-Gazette* (Urbana, Illinois, 13 July 1997) <http://www.news-gazette.com/search/archives/aggressively pursuing abuse cases at issue. htm> accessed 24 August 2008.

[7] Ibid.

[8] The rate of victim withdrawal was not always so high, and the percentage cited sticks in my mind simply because it was, admittedly, a very bad month (and so, out of curiosity, I calculated the total percentage of withdrawals). Notably, this all-time high rate of victim withdrawal came

trials required to resolve these cases, which in turn generated a tremendous backlog of charges waiting to be tried. It soon became apparent that applying a blanket no-drop policy to all cases that fell under the statutory definition of domestic violence was untenable in light of the practical necessity to resolve cases prior to violating speedy trial dictates.[9] Choices had to be made: if we did not take it upon ourselves to turn down the heat selectively, we would risk having quite serious cases dismissed simply for lack of time and resources to bring them to trial under the terms of the Speedy Trial Act.

In light of these concerns, I developed policies that limited the scope of domestic-violence cases that would be prosecuted by the DV Unit,[10] and from amongst these cases, further prioritized only particular kinds of domestic violence for the most aggressive prosecutions. Whilst never reduced to writing, these policies ran something like this:

1. Domestic-violence cases will be selected for prosecution by the DV Unit based on their similarity to what is perceived to be the paradigm of domestic violence: wife battering. As such, cases involving violence amongst siblings, cousins, platonic room-mates, or by carers of vulnerable adults will rarely if ever be treated as cases of domestic violence for these purposes.

2. Domestic-violence cases will be prioritized for aggressive prosecution by the DV Unit when the violence tends to sustain or perpetuate gendered power disparities. As such, the following types of case will be prioritized: those in which the relationship between the named victim and defendant bear hallmarks of stereotypical gender expectations (eg, he works while she attends to childcare and housework, he controls the finances, etc); those in which the socially disempowered partner is degraded and/or denied basic requirements of living an autonomous life (eg, she is not permitted to have her own friends, independent access to money, or to travel away from home unattended, etc);

approximately two to three months after I became responsible for making charging decisions in non-arrest cases (ie, cases where the police had been notified of a possible domestic battery, but in which no arrest had been made either due to the inability to locate the suspect, or because the police exercised their discretion not to arrest at the time). Undoubtedly, the high rate of victim withdrawal was due in part to the fact that a much wider range of cases had been charged. Under the previous administration, such cases would not have been charged and thus the issue of victim withdrawal would not have arisen. This dynamic relationship between aggressive charging and victim withdrawal should be taken into account in evaluating studies which purport to demonstrate quite low levels of victim withdrawal. See for example, studies cited in A Jones, *Next Time She'll be Dead* (Boston: Beacon Press, 2000) 143.

[9] Defendants held in custody pending trial were entitled to a trial within 120 days, whilst defendants on recognizance were entitled to be tried within 160 days. Violation of these provisions resulted in dismissal of charges on procedural grounds. Illinois Code of Criminal Procedure of 1963 (Speedy Trial Act) 725 ILCS 5/103–5.

[10] The fact that a given case would not be prosecuted by the DV Unit did not, of course, automatically result in non-prosecution. Rather, such cases were referred to general subject matter prosecution units.

and/or those in which the violence evinces a sadistic desire to make the socially disempowered partner suffer.[11]

Although I likely would not have articulated these points in quite the same way during my years as a prosecutor, the above formulations capture the gist of the reformulated policies.[12] At the time, these policies were characterized in the local media as 'prosecutorial discretion run amok':[13] a characterization I resisted at the time and continue to resist, albeit for somewhat different and more considered reasons. This book is motivated in part by a desire to further articulate the precise meaning of these policies and to defend them as an appropriate exercise of prosecutorial discretion.

Aside from all of this, the writing of this book has also been driven by an academic desire to develop a general account of prosecutorial decision-making. As Lucia Zedner has noted, prosecution has not been the subject of extensive scholarly debate.[14] Indeed, prosecutors seem to have gotten lost somehow in the academic chasm between criminology on the one hand (which is typically more concerned with the exercise of police discretion) and analytic jurisprudence on the other hand (which is notable for its 'longstanding obsession...with the judicial branch of government').[15] This project is therefore an attempt to rescue prosecutors from this chasm and to provide an account of what they do (and why it matters) which is informed by both sides of the criminological/jurisprudential divide.

The choice to focus my inquiry regarding prosecutorial discretion on the prosecution of a particular *kind* of criminal offence (ie, domestic violence) was also inspired by the personal experiences explained above and further academic considerations. Principally, I chose to focus on a specific offence rather than providing a more generalized account of prosecutorial discretion due to my belief that very little of interest can be said about the proper function of the criminal justice system without having regard to the particular wrongdoing being targeted. As John Gardner has noted, 'we need to begin by asking which particular actions are wrongful and only then ask whether some supervisory...doctrines should constrain or inform our attempt to criminalize them'.[16] Without an adequate account of the wrongdoing targeted by the criminal justice systems' bureaucratic mechanisms, we will be at a loss to develop a full account of the considerations which should guide its response. Since different crimes are covered by different

---

[11] A side-constraint operated to allow dismissal in cases where continued prosecution was deemed to present a significant risk of death or serious injury to the victim.

[12] Schenk (n 6 above).

[13] Ibid.

[14] L Zedner, *Criminal Justice* (Oxford: Clarendon, 2004) 146.

[15] D Husak, 'Why criminal law? A question of content' (2008) 2 Criminal Law and Philosophy 99, 116–17.

[16] J Gardner, 'On the general part of criminal law' in R Duff (ed), *Philosophy and the Criminal Law: Principle and Critique* (Cambridge: Cambridge University Press, 1998) 249.

moral maps,[17] it is necessary to develop one's account of prosecutorial discretion with an eye toward the particular moral map at issue. Thus, while I hope the analysis I have developed here is productive of clear thinking regarding prosecutorial discretion in a variety of settings (eg, theft offences, etc), I remain convinced that substantial further work would have to be done in order to develop an account of prosecutorial discretion in alternative settings.

None of this, however, explains why I have chosen domestic violence (as opposed to some other particular offence) as my focus. This move is grounded both in feminist concerns regarding the way in which violence against women tends to sustain and perpetuate gendered social injustice, and a concern regarding the way domestic violence offences in particular have traditionally been featured (or not) in the criminal-law literature.

The vast majority of academic criminal-law literature focuses on violent offences as opposed to regulatory offences, property crimes, etc.[18] Given that 'domestic violence forms the largest single category of violent crime',[19] one might reasonably expect that domestic violence would feature prominently in this literature. Yet traditionally, domestic violence has either been entirely absent from this literature or has featured as a mere sideline in discussions of criminally violent conduct: a special case that is frequently dismissed with a cursory mention.[20] I call this latter tendency 'domestic violence amnesia': a syndrome in which infected criminal-law academics briefly note that the majority of violent crime is domestic violence and then promptly forget this fact when making empirical claims and reaching normative conclusions.

A prime example of domestic violence amnesia is found in Herbert Packer's discussion of aggravated assaults in *The Limits of the Criminal Sanction*. Notably, especially for an author writing in 1968, Packer explicitly recognizes that such offences usually take place within the family.[21] Inexplicably, however, he goes on to hypothesize that 'we can be reasonably confident that a substantial proportion of those who commit these offences are actually being apprehended, tried, convicted and punished' and that '[s]ubstantial prison terms are served by persons

---

[17] J Gardner, 'Crime: In proportion and perspective' in A Ashworth and M Wasik (eds), *Fundamentals of Sentencing Theory: Essays in honour of Andrew von Hirsch* (Oxford: Clarendon, 1998) 48.

[18] Notable exceptions include the work of John Braithwaite and Keith Hawkins regarding regulatory offences. Eg, J Braithwaite, *Markets in Vice, Markets in Virtue* (New York: OUP, 2005); J Braithwaite, *Restorative Justice and Responsive Regulation* (New York: OUP, 2005); K Hawkins, *Law as Last Resort: Prosecution decision-making in a regulatory agency* (Oxford: OUP, 2002); and Stuart Green's work regarding white-collar crime. S Green, *Lying, Cheating, and Stealing: A moral theory of white-collar crime* (Oxford: OUP, 2006).

[19] A Cretney and G Davis, 'Prosecuting domestic assault' [1996] Crim LR 162, 165.

[20] For a recent example of specifically exempting domestic violence from a general theory of prosecutorial discretion, see T Meares, 'Rewards for good behavior: Influencing prosecutorial discretion and conduct with financial incentives' (1995) 64 Fordham L Rev 851, 876, n 87.

[21] H Packer, *The Limits of the Criminal Sanction* (Stanford: Stanford University Press, 1968) 298.

convicted of these crimes'.[22] In fact, at the time Packer was writing and still today, the vast majority of those committing such offences in a domestic context are neither convicted nor subjected to substantial prison terms. Packer's domestic-violence amnesia features again in his normative claim that there is 'no reasonable alternative to the use of the criminal sanction' in such cases: '[n]o other kind of legal control is even remotely relevant... [a]nd the alternative of laissez-faire is unthinkable.'[23] This claim borders on the bizarre given that the overwhelming tenor of the criminal justice response to domestic violence in 1968 was precisely the type of laissez-faire approach Packer deems 'unthinkable'.

In terms of academic goals then, this book marks an attempt to reverse the process of domestic-violence amnesia that has gripped the majority of criminal-law scholarship and to rescue the topic of prosecutorial discretion from being overlooked in the academic divide between criminology's focus on policing discretion and legal philosophy's focus on judicial discretion. By developing a general theory of prosecutorial discretion, with an eye toward applying this theory to the specific issue of domestic-violence cases, I hope to provide an account of prosecutorial discretion that is illuminating *in virtue of*, rather than despite, its particularity.

B. Some Assumptions

I have made various limiting choices in the course of my research and writing of this book. As with any manageable academic project, one must set limits within which the inquiry will proceed. While reasonable minds may differ as to whether these limitations are justifiable, I would at least like to make them clear and explicit. (I will leave it to the reader to evaluate whether they are justifiable.)

First, I have grounded my considerations in the context of common-law legal systems within modern, liberal democratic states (particularly the United States and England). This choice is due in part to my personal experience of having prosecuted in such a jurisdiction within the US and having served as an expert consultant in domestic violence cases in England; but it is further motivated by a desire to limit my inquiry to a manageable scope. Two key distinctions arise when considering prosecutorial discretion in common-law systems such as the US and England as compared to many of the European civil-law systems such as Germany and Austria, which threatened to expand the scope of my inquiry to an unmanageable degree. The first distinction is that common-law systems are generally governed by the 'principle of opportunity', whilst civil-law systems are generally governed by the 'principle of legality'.[24] Under the principle of legality,

---

[22] Ibid 299.　　　[23] Ibid 299–301.
[24] A Ashworth and M Redmayne, *The Criminal Process: An evaluative study* (3rd edn, New York: OUP, 2005) 147.

in theory at least, 'all those who commit offences are brought before the courts for an open determination of guilt and...there is no broad discretionary power to avoid prosecution'; whereas under the principle of opportunity, the discretion not to prosecute (or to discontinue a pending prosecution) is officially acknowledged.[25] The principle of legality raises the question of whether prosecutorial discretion is itself justifiable, and thus risks diverting attention from the central question under consideration in this book: assuming that the existence of prosecutorial discretion is itself justifiable (or at least unavoidable), *how should it be exercised?* In order to bracket (as far as possible) the issue of whether prosecutorial discretion should exist, I have chosen to limit my focus to jurisdictions governed by the principle of opportunity.[26]

The second distinction regards the way in which the doctrine of *partie civile* in civil-law criminal justice systems such as France has informed an understanding of the role of the prosecutor in a way that has not, by and large, arisen in the US or England. Where a lawyer represents a *partie civile*, he serves in the role of prosecutor within the context of a *public* prosecution. One may deduce from this practice that directly representing the interests of a particular victim is not fundamentally in tension with the role of a public prosecutor in France. In comparison, however, prosecutors in the US and England are generally understood to represent the public interest—representing 'the People' as a whole rather than any particular victim.[27] Whilst private prosecutions are generally permitted in these jurisdictions (and in such cases, the victims and their counsel serve as 'prosecutors'), these actions are maintained separately from the public prosecution of crime in common-law jurisdictions; and indeed private prosecutions are not permitted by common-law courts if they undermine the functioning of the public criminal justice system.[28]

Another choice I have made in researching and writing this book is to limit the extent to which I consider cases of same-sex intimate partner domestic violence. This choice is grounded in my belief that the paradigm of domestic violence is properly understood as involving male violence against a female partner.[29] My

[25] Ibid. I will consider the coherence of the principle of legality briefly below in Chapter 2 at n 10 and surrounding text. There is some question as to whether the principle of legality applies to the type of non-fatal domestic-violence cases that concern us here. HH Jeschenk, 'The discretionary powers of the prosecuting attorney in West Germany' (1970) 18 American Journal of Comparative Law 508, 513, explains that the general principle of legality does not apply to '[n]umerous petty offences and a few isolated more serious cases as well, in which intimate relationships have been disturbed...In such cases, the prosecutor files a public complaint only if it lies in the public interest.'

[26] See Ashworth and Redmayne (n 24 above) 147 for consideration of whether this distinction in principle realizes any significant differences in prosecutorial practice.

[27] P Krug, 'Prosecutorial discretion and its limits' (2002) 50 American Journal of Comparative Law 643, 660; see also, T Hetherington, *Prosecution and the Public Interest* (London: Waterlow, 1989) 201, characterizing the victim's interest as relevant to prosecutorial decision-making only insofar as it constitutes part of the public interest.

[28] L Leigh, 'Private prosecutions and diversionary justice' [2007] Crim LR 289.

[29] I explain and defend an account of domestic violence consistent with this paradigm case in Chapter 6.

choice to focus primarily upon heterosexual domestic violence is not intended to convey a belief that domestic violence in same-sex relationships is any less serious than that in heterosexual relationships. Moreover, it is not intended to suggest that same-sex intimate relationships are best understood in terms of male-female gender dynamics, nor even that abused partners in violent same-sex intimate relationships are best understood as socially gendered as female. However, my focus does suggest sympathy with the view that in at least some cases of same-sex batterering, salient features can be illuminated within an account of domestic violence which takes male violence against women as its paradigm. As Ruthann Robson has (correctly) observed, any account of same-sex domestic violence that supposed one partner is necessarily 'the man' and the other is necessarily 'the woman' would seriously misapprehend the nature of such relationships;[30] likewise, however, any account of domestic violence that denied the relevance of patriarchy to understanding domestic violence would seriously misapprehend the nature of such violence.

I will not, however, explore these issues further here. The discussion in Chapter 6 goes some way toward considering some of these issues (namely, the relevance of patriarchy to understanding domestic violence). While the specific issues raised by same-sex domestic violence are certainly deserving of attention, the scope of the project undertaken herein does not allow for their adequate consideration. As such, although I do not limit my account of domestic violence strictly to male–female relationships, this book does not purport to consider in full the particular range of the issues raised by same-sex domestic violence.

C. On Methodology

The methodological approach of this book is grounded in a concern with both practical reasoning and feminist legal theory. The term 'feminist legal theory' is understood to mean a group of related theses that offer explanatory and/or normative accounts of law, legal practice, or legal systems from a stance which is self-consciously critical of existing patriarchal structural inequality. The methodology adopted herein can be understood as feminist insofar as it is particularly concerned to examine the function of patriarchal social forms in sustaining and perpetuating women's subordinate social status, and to highlight the role that prosecutors might play in transforming these social conditions. This approach has been characterized by Kathleen Bartlett as 'asking the woman question'; and by combining this approach with an emphasis on practical reason, the general

---

[30] R Robson, 'Lavender bruises' (1990) 20 Golden Gate University L Rev 567, 586. In making this point, Robson interprets Catharine MacKinnon's work as endorsing such a view, citing C A MacKinnon, *Toward a Feminist Theory of the State* (Cambridge: Harvard University Press, 1989) 178. However, I suggest the better interpretation of MacKinnon's claim renders it largely consistent with the revised view stated above.

methodological approach of this book can be characterized as 'feminist practical reasoning'.[31]

If patriarchy is a structural inequality that systematically limits valuable options which are critical to the success of women's lives (and I shall argue that is it),[32] then the existence of patriarchy generates reasons for its own avoidance, repudiation, curtailment, denunciation, and cessation. In principle there is nothing particularly feminist about recognizing that such reasons exist. The reasons exist in virtue of the wrong (patriarchy) which generates them. All rational beings in principle have access to appreciating the rational force of these reasons—which is simply to say that they are not *basically* feminist reasons. However, in light of the fact that traditional artefacts of practical reasoning have largely obscured, discounted, or actively ignored such reasons, it clarifies the methodology adopted herein to characterize it as a particularly feminist mode of practical reasoning. By adopting a self-consciously feminist approach to practical reasoning, I do not suggest a basic change in what the methodology of practical reason requires; I merely note the traditional failure of its artefacts to satisfy the requirements of the method (ie, to attend to all reasons which bear rational force, without arbitrary or unjustified limitation).

I do not take the methodology of feminist practical reasoning to be an oxymoron, which is simply to say that I do not perceive any necessary conflict between engaging in practical reasoning and engaging in feminist theory. Emphasizing this point signals my rejection of two premises: (1) that rationality is antithetical to feminism; and (2) that feminist theory 'fails as rational discourse'.[33] I take the first point to be uncontroversial.[34] As noted above, the central concern of feminism is the avoidance, repudiation, curtailment, denunciation, and cessation of patriarchy. The wrongness of patriarchy generates reasons to address these concerns. Attending to these reasons requires *engaging* practical reason, not rejecting it. The claim that one's reaction to patriarchy should not be based upon nor judged according to standards of rationality is a dangerously misguided mistake of thought; but perhaps this mistake is excusable when understood as a reaction to the dominant tradition within practical reasoning—a tradition that has consistently obscured, discounted, and ignored the wrongness of patriarchy and the reasons it generates. If you live, think, hope, dream, feel, and reason in a world that systematically obscures, discounts, and ignores the reasons which

---

[31] K Bartlett, 'Feminist legal methods' (1990) 103 Harvard L Rev 829, 854–5, defining feminist practical reasoning as a methodological approach that 'builds upon the traditional mode of practical reasoning by bringing to it the critical concerns and values reflected in other feminist methods, including the woman question'.

[32] See Chapter 7.

[33] L Alexander, 'What we do and why we do it' (1993) 45 Stanford L Rev 1885, 1896.

[34] Hence, I agree that feminist critiques of reason (eg, that 'reason is male') often have been misinterpreted as 'reaffirmation of female irrationality or as a misleadingly literal claim of exclusion from the practices of professional philosophy'. G Lloyd, 'Rationality' in A Jaggar and IM Young (eds), *Blackwell's Companion to Feminist Philosophy* (Oxford: Blackwell, 2000) 165, 166.

appear most salient to you—signalling that these reasons, in fact, have little or no rational force—you may justifiably come to feel that this system of rationality is to be rejected. Insofar as this feeling is justifiable, the anti-rationalist feminists' rejection of practical reason may be excusable. But, nonetheless, the rejection of practical reason itself is not justifiable: it is a mistake which confuses the substance of the message with the sins of the messenger. Rationality itself does not obscure, discount, or ignore reasons generated by the wrongness of patriarchy; rather, this process has been accomplished by those (fallible) people who have been empowered to speak on behalf of rationality.[35] Thus, I share Genevieve Lloyd's resistance 'to move beyond the diagnosis of reason's maleness to any positive reconstruction of either a new feminized reason or a new feminine alternative to reason'.[36] That rationality has been deemed a particularly male facility is a mistake of thought which should be rejected outright, not accommodated through a rejection of rationality in the name of feminism.

The second premise rejected above was Larry Alexander's claim that feminist theory 'fails as rational discourse'.[37] One aspect of Alexander's complaint is grounded in his belief that the 'moral and empirical claims of [feminist theories] are rarely stated with clarity [or], more importantly, defended'.[38] 'For example', he continues, 'many feminist articles contain an implicit normative premise that women and men as groups should possess equal amounts of power... [and this] premise needs to be made explicit.'[39] Alexander is right to observe that feminist

---

[35] For an illuminating study of this phenomenon, see G Lloyd, *The Man of Reason: 'Male' and 'Female' in Western Philosophy* (Minneapolis: University of Minnesota Press, 1984).

[36] Ibid 7.

[37] Alexander (n 33 above) 1896. Specifically, Alexander levels this critique against feminist theory which 'addresses explicitly how women fare as a group' and adopts as one of its 'pet issues' the subordination of women as a group. Notably, all of the authors identified by Alexander as subject to this critique endorse a dominance theory of gender as hierarchy. Ibid 1890 fn 14, citing C A MacKinnon, *Feminism Unmodified* (Cambridge: Harvard University Press, 1987) 37–45; C Littleton, 'Reconstructing sexual equality' (1987) 75 California Law Review 1279; A Scales, 'The emergence of feminist jurisprudence: An essay' (1986) 95 Yale LJ 1373; P Smith, 'Discrimination and disadvantage in feminist legal theory: A review of Deborah Rhode's *Justice and Gender*' (1992) 11 Law and Philosophy 431. MacKinnon undoubtedly endorses such a view and indeed is widely credited with having developed this genre of feminist theory. Littleton endorses a similar view, identifying it as a core project of feminist theory to 'loosen the grip that hierarchical ordering by sex has kept on our lives and on our imaginations'. Littleton, 'Reconstructing sexual equality', 1336. Scales explicitly endorses MacKinnon's dominance theory of gender (Scales, 'The emergence of feminist jurisprudence', 1374), whilst Smith endorses a substantively identical claim offered by Deborah Rhode (ie, that gender is better understood as a matter of disadvantage rather than difference). Smith, 'Discrimination and disadvantage', discussing D Rhode, *Justice and Gender* (Cambridge: Harvard University Press, 1989). It is this category of feminist theory which Alexander takes as his target, and which informs the methodology of this book. For further elaboration and critique of Alexander's argument on this point, see MM Dempsey, *Prosecution, Reason and Value: Considering domestic violence* (D Phil thesis, University of Oxford, 2007) 16–24.

[38] Alexander (n 33 above) 1892.

[39] Ibid.

scholarship is typically grounded in this normative premise.[40] He is also right to maintain that scholarship in general fares better qua rational discourse when its normative premises are made explicit and defended.[41] However, there appears to be no reason to deny the status of rational discourse to feminist theories simply in virtue of their (perceived) failure to articulate clearly and defend this premise. When faced with a perceived deficiency in another's theory, we can choose a number of responses: eg, we can present a generous interpretation of the author's meaning so that it is more explicit, rationally coherent, and intuitively attractive; or we can choose not to defend the author's theory and simply offer critique without reconstruction. Interestingly, Alexander chooses a different response: excluding the theories from the realm of rational discourse altogether.

The more pressing issue, of course, is whether this premise, once articulated, can be defended. To resolve this issue, we must first determine what the premise is meant to do and what principles it relies upon. Clearly, the premise that women and men as groups should possess equal amounts of power is meant to invoke the concept of equality, but it does not seem to rely on what Joseph Raz has identified as strictly egalitarian principles.[42] As such, the premise is perhaps best understood as a rhetorical device meant to assert the basic principle of women's humanity.[43] This interpretation of the equality premise is not intended to critique or detract from the force of feminist theories which rely upon notions of equality. Indeed, there are good reasons to craft arguments from premises which assert women's basic humanity,[44] and if 'resort to fashionable egalitarian formulations makes them more attractive, so much the better.'[45]

Still, if Alexander's complaint is interpreted as an objection to the intellectual confusion created by the vague use of equality premises, then he may have a point.[46] Specifically, I agree that a failure to clarify whether one's use of an equality premise is meant to invoke strictly egalitarian principles (or is merely intended as a rhetorical device invoking a more basic claim regarding women's moral status

---

[40] Contra Alexander, however, MacKinnon's sex inequality theory does articulate this premise explicitly. Whilst she does not adopt verbatim the words Alexander uses, her point is nonetheless clear. MacKinnon (n 37 above) 40.

[41] I will attempt to meet the demands of normative clarity in Chapter 7, by providing a detailed account of what I take to be feminist theory's principle concern: the wrongness of patriarchy.

[42] J Raz, *The Morality of Freedom* (Oxford: OUP, 1986) 217–44.

[43] Ibid 228.

[44] On the need for such arguments, see C A MacKinnon, *Are Women Human? And Other International Dialogues* (London: Harvard University Press, 2006).

[45] Raz (n 42 above) 228.

[46] It is worth noting, however, that the feminist equality premise Alexander critiques shares logical form with Ronald Dworkin's principle of 'equal concern and respect' (a pointed noted in Raz (n 42 above) 228) and thus Dworkin should be liable to the same criticism Alexander levels against feminist theorists. Yet, notably, Alexander does not accuse Dworkin of failing to engage in rational discourse. Instead, Alexander characterizes Dworkin's work as the paradigm of what he calls 'scholarly legal advocacy'. Alexander (n 33 above) 1898. This is not to say that Alexander is uncritical of Dworkin—but his critique is limited to the claim that Dworkin's scholarship is 'philosophically untenable': he never suggests that Dworkin's theories fail as rational discourse.

as human beings) invites some degree of intellectual confusion.[47] In order to avoid giving rise to any similar confusion in this book, it should be noted that my arguments do not rely on strictly egalitarian principles. Moreover, because I agree that rhetorical equality premises can be somewhat confusing, I will avoid invoking the notion of equality where possible.[48] In other words, the argument to be defended in this book will not be phrased in terms such as 'domestic violence is wrong because it leads to inequality' or 'domestic-violence prosecutions should enhance equality', nor will it be claimed that acting for feminist reasons means affirming or supporting either 'gender equality' (a concept I take to be oxymoronic, since I take gender to be a hierarchy) or 'sex equality' (a concept which I take to reflect a rhetorical use of equality).[49]

D. A Motivating Question

A fundamental question motivating this book is: what should public prosecutors do when victims withdraw their support for the prosecution of domestic-violence cases? For example, should prosecutors dismiss charges against alleged abusers when faced with victims' requests to dismiss? Or should they continue such prosecutions without the victims' support, engaging in so-called 'victimless prosecutions'? These questions have captured the attention of academic legal scholars in the US since the late 1980s, soon after the introduction of pro-prosecution and mandatory-prosecution policies in many state and local jurisdictions.[50] Increasingly, these issues have been played out in the UK academic literature, inspired by similar changes to policing and prosecutorial policy in England.[51]

---

[47] However, feminist theory is hardly the principal or sole source of such confusion. See (n 46).

[48] I do not believe that such confusion is alleviated by distinguishing between formal and substantive equality. See Chapter 7, nn 58–61.

[49] In unpacking the concept of patriarchy (see Chapter 7), I do employ the concept of structural inequality, but this reference to equality should be read as a rhetorical use.

[50] Amongst the earliest offerings on this topic in the US legal literature were K Waites, 'The criminal justice system's response to battering: Understanding the problem, forging the solutions' (1985) 60 Washington L Rev 267; NL Clark, 'Crime begins at home: Let's stop punishing victims and perpetuating violence' (1987) 28 William and Mary L Rev 263; E Buzawa and C Buzawa, *Domestic Violence: The criminal justice response* (Newbury Park: Sage, 1990); M Asmus, T Ritmeester, and E Pence, 'Prosecuting domestic abuse cases in Duluth: Developing effective prosecution strategies from understanding the dynamics of abusive relationships' (1991) 15 Hamline L Rev 115; Zorza (n 2 above); and Editors of Harvard L Rev (n 2 above).

[51] The earliest offerings in the UK literature tended to focus upon police responses to domestic violence, debating the wisdom of pro-arrest and mandatory-arrest policies, rather than focusing specifically on prosecutorial issues. See T Faragher, 'The police response to violence against women in the home' in J Pahl (ed), *Private Violence and Public Policy* (London: Routledge, 1985); A Sanders, 'Personal violence and public order: Prosecution of domestic violence in England and Wales' [1988] Intl J of Sociology of Law 359; S Edwards, *Policing 'Domestic' Violence: Women, the law and the state* (London: Sage, 1989); S Edwards and A Halpern, 'Protection for the victim of domestic violence: Time for a radical revision?' [1991] J of Social Welfare and Family Law 94; R Morley and A Mullender, 'Hype or hope: The importation of pro-arrest policies and batterers'

The literature on both sides of the Atlantic centres on a debate between those who endorse aggressive prosecution policies in such cases (pro-prosecution and mandatory-prosecution policies) and those who oppose such policies in favour of victim-led and victim-oriented prosecution policies.[52] Although I will discuss the considerations which arise in the context of these debates in more depth in Chapter 8, for now it will suffice to clarify the question under debate, define a number of key terms that arise in these debates, and then present the arguments in broad outline.

It is important to distinguish between two questions that often arise in thinking about the prosecution of domestic violence without victim support: (1) *can* such cases be prosecuted? (2) *should* such cases be prosecuted? Roughly, the first question arises under what the Crown Prosecution Service (CPS) refers to as the Evidential Sufficiency Test, whilst the latter arises under its Public Interest Test.[53] Often these two questions become conflated in prosecutors' thinking: the perceived difficulty of prosecuting cases without victim support, well grounded or not, promotes a culture in which the question of whether such cases *should* be pursued often fails to arise. Carolyn Hoyle's landmark study of the Thames Valley Police response to domestic violence documented this phenomenon. Hoyle found that, in practice, prosecutors 'never attempted a prosecution when the victim withdrew her statement, even when there was corroborative evidence', due to the perception that such cases would necessarily suffer from adequate evidence at trial.[54] However, despite this perception, 'it is not necessarily true that victim withdrawal has to mark the end of a case'.[55] Indeed, as Louise Ellison has

programmes from North America to Britain as key measures for preventing violence against women in the home' (1992) 6 Intl J of Law and the Family 265.

[52] The distinction between victim-led prosecution, victim-oriented prosecution, mandatory-prosecution, and pro-prosecution policies will be understood as follows: under victim-led prosecution policies, cases are always discontinued pursuant to a victim's request to dismiss; under victim-oriented prosecution policies, cases are generally discontinued when the victims request dismissal, unless strong reasons weigh in favour of continuing prosecution; under pro-prosecution policies, cases are generally *not* discontinued when victims request dismissal (although requests may be taken into account in deciding whether to continue prosecution); and under mandatory-prosecution policies, a victim's request to dismiss is deemed wholly irrelevant to the prosecutor's decision of whether to continue the prosecution.

[53] CPS, *Code for Crown Prosecutors* (2004).

[54] Moreover, pending prosecutions were almost always discontinued when victims withdrew their support. C Hoyle, *Negotiating Domestic Violence: Police, criminal justice and victims* (Oxford: OUP, 1998) 152, 155, 159, 175. In the quote above, Hoyle was specifically considering the charging decisions of police officers; however, as discussed in Chapter 3, I contend that the charging decision is best understood as prosecutorial action. So, in Hoyle's example, the police officers are best understood as acting *qua* prosecutors. This mixed role was consistent with the procedural rules in effect when Hoyle conducted her research, under which police were empowered to make initial charging decisions. Under current law, however, '[t]he initial decision whether or not to charge...is now formally the responsibility of the Crown Prosecution Service'. A Ashworth, *Principles of Criminal Law* (5th edn, Oxford: OUP, 2005) 12. See also ID Brownlee, 'The statutory charging scheme in England and Wales: Towards a unified prosecution system' [2004] Crim LR 896.

[55] Hoyle (n 54 above) 175.

argued, evidential initiatives like those which drove victimless prosecution in the US during the 1980s and 1990s may avoid many of the perceived difficulties in prosecuting such cases.[56] Indeed, since Ellison advanced her case on this point, the evidential laws in England and Wales regarding the admission of hearsay evidence have expanded dramatically under the Criminal Justice Act 2003,[57] so that so-called 'victimless prosecutions' are now far more feasible than was previously thought.[58]

Further, it is crucial to define some of the key terms used in the debates regarding the prosecution of domestic violence. For example, what exactly is meant by the phrase which features in our motivating question: that 'victims *withdraw* their support for the prosecution of domestic-violence cases'? This particular phrasing is the British government's preferred choice for identifying a set of cases in which the victims are unsupportive of prosecutorial pursuit action against the alleged abusers.[59] The language of 'withdrawal', however, is somewhat misleading insofar as it implies that at some prior time, the victim *did* support the prosecution (and now she's withdrawn that support). Often this is not the case: frequently victims decline to support state intervention from the very start; and so there is no prior support to be withdrawn. This terminology is, however, so widely used in the literature that I will use it here, without intending to imply anything about whether a victim's lack of support reflects a change in her attitude toward prosecution. Another phrase that pops up in debates regarding the prosecution of domestic violence is what I have referred to as 'so-called victimless prosecution'.[60] The somewhat haughty use of 'so-called' as a qualifier here is meant to underscore my view that it can be misleading and disrespectful to conceptualize such

[56] L Ellison, 'Prosecuting domestic violence without victim participation' (2003) 65 MLR 834.

[57] Criminal Justice Act 2003 ss 116, 119, 120. At the time Ellison wrote on this issue, the applicable hearsay law was far more restrictive, insofar as it required the prosecution to establish either that the victim was being kept away by fear or that the victim's refusal to testify was based on her fear. Criminal Justice Act 1988 s 23(3)(b).

[58] Ironically, given the dramatic restrictions on the admission of hearsay evidence in the US under *Crawford v Washington* 541 US 36 (2004) and its progeny, as compared to the expansive approach to hearsay taken in England and Wales under the Criminal Justice Act 2003, victimless prosecutions now appear far more likely to succeed in England than in the US. See also *Davis v Washington* 126 S Ct 2266 (2006) and D Tuerkheimer, '*Crawford*'s Triangle: Domestic violence and the right of confrontation' (2006) 85 North Carolina L Rev 1; A King-Reis, '*Crawford v Washington*: The end of victimless prosecution?' (2005) 28 Seattle U L Rev 301. For analysis of post-*Davis* developments in US hearsay law, see M Raeder, 'Domestic-violence cases after Davis: Is the glass half empty or half full?' Crawford and Beyond Symposium, *Brooklyn Journal of Law and Policy*, 2007, available at SSRN: <http://ssrn.com/abstract=952077>, accessed 24 August 2008.

[59] HMCPSI, *Violence at Home* (2004); M Hester and N Westmarland, *Tackling Domestic Violence: Effective Interventions and Approaches* (Home Office, 2005); CPS, *Policy for Prosecuting Cases of Domestic Violence* (2005).

[60] This phrase is employed extensively in the literature, eg, A King-Reis, 'Crawford v. Washington: The end of victimless prosecution?' (2005) 28 Seattle University L Rev 301; S Choudhry and J Herring, 'Righting domestic violence' (2006) 20 Intl J of Law and the Family 95; L Ellison, 'Responding to victim withdrawal in domestic-violence prosecutions' [2003] Crim LR 760; C Adams, 'Deterring domestic violence: Prospects for heightened success in the "victimless" prosecution of domestic-violence cases' (2000) 11 J of Contemporary Legal Issues 51.

prosecutions as victimless—as if those who decline to support state intervention are somehow undeserving of recognition as victims. Nonetheless, since the relevant literature typically frames the issue in terms of 'victimless' prosecution, I will adopt the phrase here despite its problematic implications.

E. Four Types of Domestic-violence Case

The labels, 'victim withdrawal' and 'victimless prosecution', tend to blur important distinctions between four types of cases:

1. Cases in which victims request dismissal. This type of case is sometimes inaccurately referred to as the victim 'dropping the charges'.[61] It consists simply of victims asking prosecutors to drop the charges.

2. Cases in which the victim's testimony contradicts the prosecution's case: eg, she testifies on behalf of the defendant, recants her prior inculpatory statements, etc.

3. Cases in which the victims fail to testify: eg, a victim attends court but refuses to testify or refuses to attend the trial altogether.

4. Cases of what I refer to as 'performative victim withdrawal'. In these cases, victims make a public showing of requesting dismissal and/or recanting their statements of abuse in order to appease their abusers, whilst covertly acknowledging to the prosecutors the truth of their original statements of abuse and their continued desire to see their abusers prosecuted.

Obviously, there is quite a lot of overlap amongst these types of cases. Notably, cases of performative withdrawal (type 4) necessarily imply that the victim has made a show of requesting dismissal (type 1), recanting (type 2), or refusing to testify (type 3). It is only in virtue of the victim's covert acknowledgement to the prosecutor that she indeed wants the case to proceed that such cases can be distinguished from those involving sincere withdrawal. While I make no empirical claims regarding the relative frequency with which such cases arise in pro-prosecution jurisdictions, I can report anecdotally that I regularly encountered cases of performative while prosecuting domestic-violence cases.[62]

---

[61] MA Case, 'Reflections on constitutionalizing women's equality' (2002) 90 California L Rev 765, 790 fn 154; E Sack, 'Battered women and the state: The struggle for the future of domestic violence policy' [2004] Wisconsin L Rev 1657, 1667 fn 51. In both the US and England, of course, victims are not empowered to drop charges in public prosecutions, so the phrase 'the victim dropped the charges' is a bit of a sloppy fiction which refers to a situation in which a victim requested dismissal and the prosecutor agreed to drop the charges on that basis.

[62] Whether more rigorous and verifiable evidence is available to identify the percentage of cases which fall into type (4) is, I suspect, unlikely, given that any attempt to acquire reliable empirical data on this issue would be stymied by the likelihood that some substantial number of victims'

Occasionally victims in performative withdrawal cases displayed extreme fear of their batterers and were clearly terrified that the defendants might learn the victims' true wish for the case to proceed. Indeed, such was the case in one of the first performative withdrawal cases I encountered. The issue of victim withdrawal in this case first arose when the defendant asked the court to quash the no-contact order which had been set as a condition of his bond. If the no-contact order were quashed, the defendant (assuming he posted bond), would have been permitted to have contact with the victim and thus return to live in the apartment they shared. According to defence counsel, the victim supported the defendant's motion to quash the no-contact order, but when I spoke to her privately, she told a very different story. As we stepped into the court hallway to discuss whether she supported the motion, she began visibly shaking. Her eyes filled with tears as she stepped close to me and whispered, 'Please don't drop the no-contact order. He'll kill me, I know it.' The history of violence by the defendant against the victim was extensive, with the defendant having been previously convicted of aggravated battery in connection with previous beatings. She explained to me that leaving him was too dangerous and that he'd be furious if he found out that she didn't want contact with him.

Somewhat taken aback and being relatively new to this kind of thing, I was uncertain as to how to proceed. I explained to her that I would do everything I could to keep the no-contact order in place but that ultimately decision was made by the judge. 'Can't you object to the motion? Won't that do it?' she asked. I explained that I could object to the motion, but that doing so might raise some questions since usually, when the victim wanted contact with the defendant, the prosecution would not object. She stared me straight in the eyes as if pleading for her life, 'I don't want contact with him, but he can't know that. He'll kill me, I know it.' Then and there I decided to embark upon my first (but not last) instance of collusion with a victim. 'Okay', I said, 'here's what we can do. I'll object to the motion. The judge will be a little confused, but if we're lucky he'll see this is an exceptional case. I won't tell anyone what you said, so no one ever has to find out. Okay?' She nodded, wiped her tears, and collected herself as we re-entered the courtroom. Luckily, the judge kept the no-contact order in place and never inquired as to whether the victim actually desired contact, thus allowing me to keep her secret safe.[63]

---

self-reports would be affected by their fear of reprisal by the defendant if they are seen to have supported the prosecution.

[63] The judge's decision was lucky for me as well, since it meant that I was never faced with the choice of how to respond if asked what the victim had said to me in the hallway. My plan was to refuse to answer any such question, so that I might keep my promise to the victim and avoid making any misrepresentation to the court. Still, if I had refused to answer the judge's inquiry, the defendant might easily have guessed the secret, and I might have faced being held in contempt. This case illustrates the importance of insightful and responsible judicial decision-making taken independently on the merits of each case. I was fortunate to have practiced before judges who regularly displayed high levels of insightfulness and responsible independence.

Not all cases of performative withdrawal arose in such emotionally powered contexts. More typically in my experience, defence counsel would simply request dismissal and inform me that the victim supported the request. I would then meet with the victim and explain our policy not to dismiss cases solely on the basis of the victim's request. Many times during such meetings, the victims' responses upon hearing our policy demonstrated relief. They would explain to me that in fact they thought it would probably be a good idea for their partners to go to court, face up to what they had done, and be placed under a court order to attend batterers' treatment classes.[64] The thing that made these cases examples of performative withdrawal, therefore, was that the victim asked me not to tell the defendant that she in fact supported the prosecution. I routinely honoured such requests out of concern for the victims' safety and the belief that, ultimately, the responsibility for deciding whether to proceed with the prosecution was on the state, not on the victim.[65] I believed then, and continue to believe, that prosecutors who routinely abdicate their decision-making responsibility by universally deferring to victim's requests for dismissal do a disservice not only to the individual victims, but they violate their obligation to execute the duties of their office in good faith.[66]

In order to ameliorate the concern that a victim's apparent withdrawal was actually merely performative withdrawal, it was standard operating procedure in the domestic violence unit to meet face-to-face with each victim who claimed that she wanted the charges against her alleged batterer dismissed.[67] Thus, while our policy was not to refuse such requests outright, we did routinely require assurance that the request was a sincere reflection of the victim's wishes rather than a case of performative withdrawal for the defendant's benefit. For, as experience had taught, sometimes the story we heard from the victim in private did not match up with the story the victim wanted the defendant to hear.

These accounts of performative withdrawal are not meant to suggest that all cases of victim withdrawal are merely performative, nor even that performative withdrawals constitute a substantial percentage of all cases of withdrawal in domestic-violence cases.[68] They are, however, meant to illustrate the important

---

[64] As most of the cases prosecuted by the DV Unit were misdemeanours, it was relatively rare for defendants to be subjected to long terms of imprisonment.

[65] Fortunately, I was able to honour these requests without making any false representations to the court, in light of the fact that the judiciary (at times grudgingly) respected the prosecution's policy to proceed irrespective of the victims' requests. Given its legal irrelevance, the question of what the victim 'really' wanted did not arise in the courtroom.

[66] Moreover, as this book argues, such prosecutors also miss the opportunity to reconstitute their communities as less patriarchal *ceteris paribus*.

[67] Specifically, we would ask that the victim come to the courthouse, unaccompanied by the defendant, to speak with a prosecutor and the victim-witness liaison of the State's Attorney's Office. Often, victims would arrive at the courthouse accompanied by the defendants, who sat in the lobby during our meeting. Disproportionately (but perhaps not surprisingly), such victims often reported that they did not actually want the cases dismissed but were simply making the request to keep the peace with their abusive partners.

[68] As noted above, I believe it would be impossible to measure adequately such percentages given the victim's need for secrecy.

differences between sincere victim withdrawal and performative withdrawal. In my experience, the majority of victims who withdrew support were, to my belief and understanding, entirely sincere in their request that the charges be dismissed.

Occasionally I came across victims who sincerely requested dismissal (type 1) but, upon being informed that the case would proceed despite their requests, agreed to testify consistently with their prior statements. Such cases constituted withdrawal, but with no attendant loss of evidence. More typically, however, victims who requested dismissal (type 1) also recanted their prior statements (type 2) or refused to testify (type 3). A typical pattern seems to emerge in pro-prosecution jurisdictions as domestic-violence cases progress through the court system: a victim's request to dismiss (type 1) will turn into a refusal to testify (type 3), and when the prosecution proceeds regardless, the victim appears at trial and testifies for the defence (type 2).

Indeed, such was the course of events in the very first 'victimless' trial I prosecuted. Having recently established a dedicated domestic-violence prosecution unit and adopted a strong pro-prosecution policy in such cases, the unit received a report that David Williams had been arrested for pushing his wife, Linda, over a couch, choking her around the neck with his hands and causing bruising to her neck.[69] The history of violence by David against Linda went back some years, according to numerous police reports. On one occasion in the past, David had been arrested and charged with battering Linda, only to have the charges dismissed at her request. So when the Williams report hit my desk, it occurred to me that this case might be the first real test of whether our new prosecution policies could result in conviction despite victim withdrawal. Of course, at the time, I had no way of knowing whether Linda would withdraw (and certainly no way of knowing the consequences—both positive and negative—that would flow from this case[70]), but given the history of abuse and Linda's prior withdrawal of support for a previous prosecution, I strongly suspected that this case might present an opportunity to try-out so-called 'victimless' prosecution.

In anticipation of the possibility that Linda might withdraw support for the prosecution, I obtained a copy of her 911 emergency phone call reporting the battery, which she made from a neighbour's house after fleeing her home. In that call, an agitated Linda reported that David had been 'jumping on' her, and had choked her so tightly that she had his finger prints on her neck. She also informed the 911 operator that she wanted David arrested. In addition to securing the 911 tape, I asked the arresting officer to re-interview Linda on audio tape and take photographs of her injuries. In this audio-taped interview, obtained nine days

---

[69] The names of the parties have been changed to protect the victim's safety. I use the word 'choke' to reflect the language used by Linda to describe David's attack, although it should be noted that in placing his hands around her neck and applying pressure, it may be more accurate to characterise his conduct as 'strangling' her.

[70] See Chapter 10, section C.1 ('How good cases go bad').

after the battery, Linda explained the incident in more detail: she confirmed that David had choked her, and added that he had pushed her over the arm of a couch as well, 'knocking the baby straight out of my hands'.[71] Consistent with what the initial police report had indicated, Linda also recounted how David had openly threatened to kill her in front of the arresting officers as he was being taken into custody after the incident.

As the trial date approached, I arranged for Linda to be served with a subpoena to testify. In the event that Linda refused to appear at trial or went missing, it would be necessary under the relevant evidence laws at the time to establish that the prosecution had made a good faith effort to secure her attendance.[72] If we could not prove such efforts, there would be no basis for admitting her prior statements as substantive evidence of David's guilt and, since Linda was the only witness to the battery, the case would fail for lack of evidence. Thus, issuing the subpoena was a necessary step to laying the evidential foundation which would be required if the Williams case became a type (3) case.

In the event, the Williams case tracked the path outlined above from type (1) to type (3) to type (2). First, after receiving her subpoena, Linda telephoned the prosecutors' office and requested dismissal of the charges. After being informed by the domestic-violence victim-witness counsellor that charges would not be dismissed, Linda stated that she would refuse to testify at trial. When it was explained to Linda that the prosecution would proceed to trial even if she refused to testify, she promptly hung up. As the trial date drew closer, we continued efforts to secure Linda's testimony at trial by calling her home, and calling for her at her mother's and neighbour's houses.

On the day of trial, Linda failed to appear and was declared unavailable by the court, thus opening the door to the prosecution's use of her prior statements as substantive evidence of David's guilt. No sooner had Linda been declared unavailable, however, than she was in fact quite available (and quite angry), having heard that the trial was proceeding without her presence. She had come to the courthouse to demand an end to the prosecution. After being informed that the case would proceed with or without her testimony, Linda took the witness stand and recanted all of her prior statements. She claimed in her testimony that in fact *she* had been abusive to David on the morning in question, she had pushed him, and that he had not choked her. She explained her prior statements as lies, motivated by her anger at David for not helping to care for their baby. Despite her testimony, the jury convicted David on all counts.

The *Williams* case illustrates all three forms of sincere victim withdrawal and the way a single case can morph through each type at different stages in the prosecution. Further, it illustrates well the distinction between whether a case *can* be

[71] Transcript of audiotaped victim interview in *People v Williams*, on file with author.
[72] 725 ILCS 5/115–10.2, which created a statutory hearsay exception in cases where the declarant is unavailable.

prosecuted and whether a case *should* be prosecuted. As noted, whether a case *can* be prosecuted is principally a question of evidence and procedural law. Provided victim withdrawal does not generate a procedural bar to prosecution, then the issue of whether such cases *can* be prosecuted rests squarely on the adequacy of the evidence in each type of case. Where the victim simply requests dismissal, there is no loss of evidence whatsoever, and so the question of whether a case *can* be prosecuted is unaffected by this form of victim withdrawal. However, the remaining types of withdrawal each involve some form of evidence loss, which may complicate the continued prosecution of such cases.[73] Where hearsay exceptions or alternative sources of evidence provide adequate grounds for prosecuting, the question of whether the case can be prosecuted will be resolved affirmatively. This resolution, however, does not begin to answer the more interesting question of whether the case *should* be prosecuted.

F. Victimless Prosecution: Framing the Debate

The debate regarding whether such cases *should* be prosecuted has generated heated debate and a voluminous academic literature. Like every good debate, this one has two starkly opposed sides: the 'pros' and the 'antis'. The pro side is generally in favour of policies that mandate aggressive prosecution of domestic violence irrespective of victims' requests for dismissal.[74] Moreover, they are in favour of aggressive evidential and procedural tactics, such as routinely summoning reluctant victims to testify, calling child witnesses, etc. The justifications claimed for such practices are grounded in the perceived need 'to hold batterers accountable',[75] to take the responsibility of prosecution 'off the victim's shoulders',[76] and to 'protect victims'.[77] On the other side are the 'antis', who are generally opposed to prosecuting domestic violence without the victims' support,

---

[73] However, as noted above, given the expansive hearsay exceptions under the Criminal Justice Act 2003, there is now little reason to believe that such prosecutions face insurmountable evidential difficulties in England and Wales. See text surrounding nn 57–8 above. Expert testimony may also prove helpful in explaining the victim's perplexing behaviour to the fact-finder, although courts in England and Wales have as yet been unwelcoming of such innovations. See MM Dempsey, *The Use of Expert Witness Testimony in Domestic-violence Cases* (CPS, 2004).

[74] Eg, C Hanna, 'No right to choose: Mandated victim participation in domestic-violence prosecutions' (1996) 109 Harvard L Rev 1849.

[75] DRH Ogden, 'Prosecuting domestic violence crimes: Effectively using Rule 404(B) to hold batterers accountable for repeated abuse' (1998–9) 34 Gonzaga L Rev 361.

[76] D Wills, 'Mandatory prosecution in domestic-violence cases: The case for aggressive prosecution' (1997) 7 UCLA Women's LJ 173, 173.

[77] S Choudhry and J Herring, 'Righting Domestic Violence' (2006) 20 Intl J of Law and the Family 95, 101, arguing that the need to protect victims' rights under Arts 3 and 8 of the European Convention on Human Rights justifies pro-prosecution policies.

claiming that such prosecutions constitute a form of state violence against the victims, causing 'the state to replicate...the behaviour of the batterer'.[78]

As the 'antis' are keen to point out, some of the earlier offerings from the pro camp were grounded in an unjustified paternalism toward victims of domestic violence, based on the mistaken assumption that victims were often 'blind to the serious nature of the violence' they faced.[79] As the debates matured, however, both sides came to realize that victims who withdraw support are often in the best position to weigh the risks and benefits for their own lives, and thus in fact their decisions to withdraw support for prosecutions typically represent entirely rational choices.[80]

G. Conclusion

This introduction has attempted to provide some background to the issues under consideration in this book: to explain why I have chosen this topic, what assumptions I have made regarding its nature and scope, and how I intend to approach this topic in terms of methodology. Moreover, this chapter has set forth a motivating question which will guide our considerations throughout the book (what should public prosecutors do when victims withdraw their support for the prosecution of domestic violence cases?), and provided a brief account of how others have answered this question. In the next chapter, I will examine two initially attractive (but ultimately unsatisfying) frameworks within which to seek an answer to this motivating question: legal formalism and the public/private distinction. After considering and rejecting these approaches to answering our motivating question, I make a fresh start in Part II of the book, where I develop a general account of prosecutorial action and value, and use this account to generate a general theory of prosecutorial practical reasoning. I return directly to the question of domestic-violence prosecutions in Part III, where I spend some time developing an account of domestic violence and patriarchy, provide an account of prosecutorial practical reasoning in domestic-violence cases, and consider the rights and duties of domestic-violence victims to participate in the criminal prosecutions of their batterers.

---

[78] Eg, L Mills, 'Killing her softly: Intimate abuse and the violence of state intervention' 113 Harvard L Rev 550, 595.

[79] Clark (n 50 above) 268.

[80] C Hoyle and A Sanders, 'Police response to domestic violence: From victim choice to victim empowerment?' (2000) 40 British J of Criminology 14, 21, 29. For detailed accounts of the reasons why victims stay in abusive relationships, see S Buel, 'Obstacles to leaving, aka, why abuse victims stay' [1999] Colorado Lawyer 19; JM Cruz, '"Why doesn't he just leave?" Gay male domestic violence and the reasons victims stay' (2003) 11 *J Men's Studies* 309; H Hendy and others, 'Decision to leave scale: Perceived reasons to stay in or leave violent relationships' (2003) 27 *Psych Women Q* 167.

2

Wrong Turns on the Way to an Answer

This chapter examines two possible ways of answering our motivating question: what should public prosecutors do when victims withdraw their support for the prosecution of domestic-violence cases? The first way one might answer this question is to say 'prosecutors should do whatever the law requires of them'. Such an answer is inadequate for at least two reasons: first, it assumes a degree of ruliness in prosecutorial decision-making which is inconsistent with the principle of opportunity that governs the type of legal systems under consideration in this book; and second, it evidences a mistaken assumption that legal rules provide fully determined answers to legal questions. The second way one might answer the motivating question is to draw upon the framework provided by the distinction between the public and private spheres. For example, one might claim that prosecutors should continue to prosecute cases in which the wrongs done are public in nature, but discontinue cases in which the wrongs at issue are merely private. This approach (while significantly more promising than the previous one) proves inadequate as well; for as I shall argue below, the public/private dichotomy tends to obscure rather than illuminate the very values upon which it is grounded.

A. Legal Formalism: How Far Does Law Get Us?

It is tempting to believe that legal formalism provides a quick and easy answer to our motivating question. We might think that the laws governing public prosecution do (or at least can) fully determine what a prosecutor should do when faced with a victim's request to dismiss. This line of thought is appealing in its simplicity: prosecutors should simply do whatever the law directs them to do. However, for at least two reasons, legal formalism is inadequate to the task of finding an answer to our motivating question.

First, the answer to this question is not found in the positive law of any modern criminal-law jurisdiction. When faced with victims' requests to dismiss domestic-violence cases, prosecutors are not required by law to continue (or discontinue) such prosecutions.[1] Whilst CPS guidelines such as the *Code for Crown*

---

[1] This is clearly the case in jurisdictions that adopt the principle of opportunity in prosecutorial decision-making. See Chapter 1, text to nn 25–6.

Prosecutors[2] and the *Policy for Prosecuting Cases of Domestic Violence*[3] offer some guidance to public prosecutors in reaching their decisions, these guidelines do not have the status of law. That is to say, the guidelines do not claim the authority to direct prosecutors' actions: rather, they merely claim to identify particular first-order reasons that already feature on the prosecutors' rational horizons and to render some of these reasons particularly salient to prosecutorial decision-making.[4]

1. How far can law get us?

Can the positive law be amended so that the answer we seek is fully determined by legal sources? It is easy enough to imagine several types of law that remove prosecutors' discretion in responding to victims' requests to dismiss domestic-violence cases. For example, a law might require prosecutors to abide by the victim's request for dismissal in every case. Under such a law, it seems the answer we seek would be straightforwardly determined: do what the victim has asked, ie, dismiss the case. Alternately, we can imagine a law that prohibits the prosecutor from taking the victim's request into account whatsoever. Again, the legal answer seems thereby easily identified: carry on with the prosecution regardless, as if the victim had never made such a request. However, of course, even these directives would require some interpretation by prosecutors in determining, for example, what counts as a victim's request to dismiss (ie, what should be determinative under the first example and totally ignored under the second?). We might avoid this complication by imagining a law that directs prosecutors faced with victim withdrawal to refer the decision to some third party or entity such as judge, tribunal, or legislature. Thus, whilst the decision would remain discretionary (as to the tribunal or legislature), it would no longer be a matter for the exercise of *prosecutorial* discretion.[5] In principle then, it appears that legal formalism might be able to provide an easy answer to our question.

But if we suspect this is so, we should pause to consider what damage this answer does to our concept of the prosecutor's role in the criminal justice system. Consider again the hypothetical of a law that directs prosecutors to refer out all

---

[2] CPS, *Code for Crown Prosecutors* (2004).

[3] CPS, *Policy for Prosecuting Cases of Domestic Violence* (2005).

[4] In terms borrowed from Joseph Raz, the guidelines do not claim to provide prosecutors with 'protected reasons'. J Raz, *The Authority of Law* (Oxford: OUP, 1979) 18, 21–3. The accounts of law and the authority of law adopted throughout this book are based broadly on Raz's work, especially Raz, *The Authority of Law*; J Raz, *Ethics in the Public Domain* (Oxford: OUP, 1994); and J Raz, 'Incorporation by law' (2004) 10 Legal Theory 1. On first and second-order reasons generally, see J Raz, *Practical Reason and Norms* (2nd edn, New York: OUP, 1999) Chapter 1, especially 39–40 and postscript. See also n 30 below.

[5] We could further imagine that any concerns regarding potential ambiguity in determining whether a victim is requesting dismissal (so as to trigger the referring-out) could itself be resolved in favour of referral, so that prosecutors could avoid any risk of exercising discretion in answering our motivating question.

cases of victim withdrawal for decision-making by other bodies. This hypothetical parallels Raz's discussion of a legal system which exists despite lacking a feature which he takes as common, indeed central, to most legal systems: judicial discretion.[6] Raz conceives of a legal system in which judges are directed not to adjudicate whenever they are faced with 'a case for which the law does not provide a uniquely correct solution'.[7] By engaging in this thought experiment, Raz demonstrates that such systems are a conceptual possibility. But since the law does not provide (nor even claim to provide) a uniquely correct way of understanding the facts which give rise to legal cases, we should suppose that the conceptual category Raz has identified is an empty category; for the application of general laws to specific factual scenarios will rarely (if ever) generate a case in which the law does provide a uniquely correct solution.[8] Rules, of which legal rules are one kind, are by their nature general: they apply across more than one factual scenario.[9] In applying necessarily general rules to specific, one-off, factual scenarios, it is not to be expected that the rules will provide uniquely correct solutions; for their generality makes them ill-suited to providing fully determined answers to questions which arise in specific legal cases.[10] For this reason, it is the function of judges to span the gap between the general and the specific: to apply (general) rules to (specific) factual scenarios. In other words, it is the function of judges to adjudicate. The notion of a judge who refuses to adjudicate is fundamentally inconsistent with the concept of being a judge.[11] Whatever else they do, judges must adjudicate (render judgment), or else they are no longer functioning in the role of judge.[12]

In the same way, prosecutors who refuse to make decisions about whether to file charges or (dis)continue prosecutions are abdicating their responsibilities qua

---

[6] J Raz, 'Legal principles and the limits of law' in M Cohen (ed), *Ronald Dworkin and Contemporary Jurisprudence* (London: Duckworth, 1984) 75.

[7] Ibid.

[8] The example of rape law demonstrates this point well. The fact that a rape law prohibits non-consensual sexual penetration does not begin to resolve the question of whether any given case of sexual penetration is correctly understood as consensual or non-consensual. Thus, mechanical application of the law to the facts will itself not provide a uniquely correct solution, since the law does not assist in achieving a correct understanding of the facts.

[9] J Gardner, 'The Virtue of Justice and the Character of Law' [2001] Current Legal Problems 1, 14; and F Schauer, *Playing by the Rules* (Oxford: Clarendon, 1991; reprint 2002) ch 2.

[10] In this respect, I question whether the principle of legality discussed previously is coherent; for surely even in those jurisdictions, prosecutors are nonetheless exercising some degree of discretion in determining which specific factual scenarios fall under the scope of the general criminal-law rules.

[11] Gardner (n 9 above) 18–20.

[12] This point assumes nothing about how judges come to decide cases and render judgment: they can consider the law, principles, arguments of counsel, etc; or they can decide by throwing darts at the wall. Either way, as long as they make decisions, they are still functioning qua judges. (Although, of course, if they opt for the latter method of decision-making, they violate a legal duty. See Raz, n 6 above, 76). My point here is simply that if judges throw up their hands and say 'I refuse to decide this case' then they are abdicating their fundamental responsibility qua judges.

prosecutors. By failing to make these decisions and choosing instead to pass these decisions along to some other decision-making body, the prosecutors are (in that instance) not acting as prosecutors but as buck-passers. In such a situation, the decision-making body to which the buck is passed takes on the (temporary) role of prosecutor for the purpose of making these decisions.[13] Thus, this solution does not help avoid the problem of prosecutorial discretion.

2. How far should law get us?

It should be clear from the foregoing that I do not think legal formalism has the conceptual resources to answer our motivating question. But even if legal formalism *could* answer our question, *should it?* If the academic literature on prosecutorial ethics is any indication, the answer promised by legal formalism is appealing to many. The predominant theme in this literature is a concern to 'confine, structure and check' prosecutorial discretion.[14] This concern seems to stem from the assumption that any gap in the positive law allows space for prosecutors to exercise 'unfettered moral discretion'.[15] This assumption, I shall argue, is grounded in two confusions of thought.

First, it is based on a confused account of discretion, according to which any gap in the confinement, structuring and checking of prosecutorial discretion allows prosecutors to exercise discretion completely unbounded by any standards. As we shall see, the notion of exercising discretion completely unbounded by any standards is itself incoherent. My starting point in elaborating this claim will be Ronald Dworkin's correct observation that discretion is 'like the hole in a doughnut': it is a 'relative concept' that only makes sense when we understand it as existing within 'an area left open by a surrounding belt of restriction'.[16] Thus, Dworkin is correct in claiming that in order to gain a proper understanding of discretion it 'only makes sense to ask, "[d]iscretion under which standards?" or "[d]iscretion as to which authority?"'[17]

This initially promising observation was, however, quickly followed by Dworkin's more problematic distinction between strong and weak discretion, and the claim that strong discretion exists only where the decision-maker 'simply is not bound by standards set by the authority in question'.[18] Dworkin makes this

---

[13] Unlike judges, however, prosecutors are not essential to the existence of legal systems. Gardner (n 9 above) 20. My point is simply that if prosecutors *do* exist in a legal system, then they cannot routinely abdicate responsibility by passing the buck. Note that this is a conceptual point about the nature of prosecutorial action, not a normative point about whether legal systems should have prosecutors. For more on the nature of prosecutorial action, see Chapter 3.

[14] K Davis, *Discretionary Justice: A preliminary inquiry* (Baton Rouge: Louisiana State University, 1969). See Chapter 3, n 8 and surrounding text for further discussion.

[15] L Griffin, 'The prudent prosecutor' (2001) 14 Georgetown J of Legal Ethics 259, 262.

[16] R Dworkin, *Taking Rights Seriously* (London: Duckworth, 1978) 31.

[17] Ibid.

[18] Ibid 32.

distinction in the course of defending his famous conclusion that judges never exercise strong discretion.[19] In elaborating his conception of weak discretion, Dworkin supposes that there are only two forms: exercising judgement in the application of standards, and serving as the final arbiter of a decision.[20] This distinction, however, fails to account for the variety of forms discretion may take. Discretion may consist not only in exercising judgement in the application of standards, but also in determining what the applicable standards are, interpreting vague language used in articulating the standards, reconciling apparently inconsistent standards, assessing the weight to be given to conflicting standards, determining what if any action to take in a particular case according to the generally applicable standards, and determining what if any action to take, all things considered. Additionally, whilst Dworkin was correct to note that one form of discretion consists in being the final arbiter of a decision, this observation ignores the discretion exercised in being a co-author of a decision, having a vote in a decision, being an influential contributor to the making of a decision, and being consulted in the course of a decision's being made. Finally, as Neil MacCormick has observed, Dworkin's explanation fails to account for 'the reality of the difference between disagreeing over what to do and disagreeing about what is the case'.[21] For simplicity and clarity, we will drop Dworkin's distinction between strong and weak discretion in what follows and simply refer to discretion as a singular concept, which we will be understood as decision-making bounded by standards.

In all of its forms, prosecutorial discretion is bounded by standards to a greater or lesser degree.[22] Not only do degrees of discretion exist in virtue of factors relating to the application of standards (eg, how much uncertainty exists in determining the relevant standards, how vague is the language of the standards being applied, how much inconsistency or conflict exists between standards, etc); but degrees of discretion also exist in virtue of factors relating to the time that passes before the discretionary decision comes under effective review by a higher authority. For example, *ceteris paribus*, a prosecutor usually has a greater degree of discretion in making a charging decision than in deciding to submit a given piece of evidence at trial, because the amount of time that typically passes before

---

[19] On whether the claim that judges never exercise discretion in its strong sense is a conclusion of Dworkin's argument or an assumed premise, see Raz (n 6 above) 84.

[20] Dworkin (n 16 above) 31–2.

[21] N MacCormick, *Legal Reasoning and Legal Theory* (Oxford: Clarendon, 1978) 248. For an illuminating study of discretion in determining what is the case in the context of criminal prosecution, see generally M McConville, A Sanders, and R Leng, *The Case for the Prosecution* (London: Routledge, 1991); especially noteworthy is the authors' discussion of the manner in which domestic-violence case constructions shift in light of actual or anticipated victim non-cooperation (34, 106–7).

[22] As MacCormick has correctly observed, discretion is a matter of degree: '"Discretions" come not in differences of kind (as Dworkin supposes Hart to suppose) but in differences of degree (as Hart supposes in fact).' N MacCormick, *HLA Hart* (London: Edward Arnold, 1981) 130. A similar point is observed in D Galligan, *Discretionary Powers: A legal study of official discretion* (Oxford: Clarendon, 1986) 14–20.

charging decisions come under effective review by a higher authority is considerably longer than the time that passes before evidence submission decisions come under review by a higher authority. In the case of charging, the decision may not be reviewed for days, weeks, or months (eg, until the time of preliminary hearing in the United States or trial in England), whilst in the case of evidence submission, the decision is likely to be reviewed instantaneously in the course of trial (eg, when opposing counsel states an objection and the trial judge rules upon the admissibility of the submitted evidence).

The second confusion of thought which has led some to believe that any gap in the positive law allows space for prosecutors to exercise 'unfettered moral discretion' has already been foreshadowed. To review, there is a conceptual confusion in the notion of 'unfettered discretion'. As explained above, there is simply no such thing as unfettered discretion of any sort. Discretion is decision-making bounded by standards. To be unfettered is to be unbounded. That which is (conceptually) bounded cannot be unbounded. Thus, as a conceptual point, discretion cannot be unfettered.

Nonetheless, those affected by this second confusion remain undeterred. Indeed, they take the above confusion regarding the concept of discretion and apply it in the context of moral discretion to come up with the confused notion of 'unfettered moral discretion'. There is no such thing: rather, moral discretion (if the concept is a helpful one at all) is best understood as decision-making bounded by moral standards. Thus, if a prosecutor faces a gap in the positive law and turns to moral standards (ie, standards of practical reason) to further determine her decision, this does not mean that she is exercising 'unfettered moral discretion'. Rather, it means that she is engaged in practical reasoning bounded by all of the standards that apply to her (legal, moral, and otherwise).[23]

We can see now that the assumptions underpinning legal formalism's answer to our motivating question are misguided. We need not eliminate prosecutorial discretion on pain of prosecutors exercising the hobgoblin of 'unfettered moral discretion'.[24] As Raz has observed with respect to judicial discretion, so too with prosecutorial discretion:

> [It] is not a matter of arbitrary judgment. [Prosecutors] are never allowed to act arbitrarily. Even when discretion is not limited or guided in any specific direction the [prosecutors] are still legally bound to act as they think is best ... If they do not, if they give arbitrary judgment by tossing a coin, for example, they violate a legal duty.[25]

Perhaps, however, the complaint against prosecutors exercising 'unfettered moral discretion' is not grounded in the conceptual mistake regarding the nature

---

[23] While I do draw a distinction between legal and moral standards (insofar as I take legal standards to be valid according to their sources and not their merits), I will not attempt to draw any further distinctions between moral standards and other non-legal standards, for I remain unconvinced that there is a deep distinction worth making. J Raz, *Engaging Reason* (New York: OUP, 1999) 247–72.

[24] Contra Griffin (n 15 above).   [25] Raz (n 6 above) 76.

of discretion outlined above, so much as it simply points to a concern that prosecutorial decision-making should be bounded (to the appropriate extent) by legally posited standards. Presumably, those who voice concerns regarding 'unfettered moral discretion' believe that there is a greater role for such standards to play in appropriately confining, structuring and checking prosecutorial decision-making. Undoubtedly, there is strong appeal to this view: it explains why we do not simply hand prosecutors stacks of indictments and send them off to prosecute wrongful conduct, but instead delimit prosecutorial decision-making through the drafting of substantive criminal laws and legal ethics directives which prohibit, for example, vindictive or racially biased prosecutions.

It would be a mistake, however, to take this concern too far by attempting to eliminate prosecutorial discretion entirely in fashioning a response to our motivating question. Due to their general nature as rules, substantive criminal laws create categories which risk smoothing over salient distinctions between cases. One function of prosecutorial discretion is to salvage important distinctions from this smoothing over process: to allow for the sort of fine-grained, first-order reasoning which takes into account the variety of considerations that arise in different cases, even when those cases justifiably fall under the same general legal category.[26]

While significant values can be realised by enacting positive laws which remove (or substantially restrict) prosecutorial discretion,[27] it is often the case that significant values can be realised by prosecutors making the sort of fine-grained distinctions which generalised legal categories obscure. By eliminating prosecutorial discretion, we make it impossible for prosecutors to realise these values, and thus compromise the criminal justice system's ability to respond appropriately when rationally salient distinctions exist between cases which fall into the same legal category. Where significant values can be realised through recognising and acting on such distinctions, eliminating discretion will sacrifice this value in preference for certainty. It is this move in the argument against 'unfettered moral discretion' which I resist, for while certainty in the application of law is to be welcomed, its value is contingent upon the otherwise just application of law.[28]

In dealing with factual scenarios where salient distinctions are few and far between (eg, parking violations), there is little value to be realised by allowing prosecutors discretion over which cases to pursue and how aggressively to pursue them.[29] However, as we shall see in Chapters 6 and 7, domestic violence presents

---

[26] For further discussion of this point, see Chapter 10, section B ('Criminal Law: A Blunt Instrument?')

[27] The sorts of values I have in mind are those tied up in the ideal of the rule of law: eg, certainty, protection of expectations, etc. It goes without saying that restrictions on prosecutorial discretion can also realise value where prosecutors exercise their discretion unjustifiably, eg, through racist decision-making.

[28] I take these reflections to be broadly consistent with Raz's observations regarding the ideal of the rule of law in J Raz, 'The Rule of Law and its Virtue' in Raz, *The Authority of Law* (n 4 above) 225–6.

[29] For this reason, it is common (and commonly justifiable) for parking violations to be managed administratively, without the exercise of any substantive prosecutorial discretion.

factual scenarios which are rife with rationally salient distinctions. These distinctions generate good reasons why, normally, we should not enact positive laws that attempt to remove prosecutorial discretion when victims request dismissal in domestic violence cases, for the reasonable course of action to take in such cases is highly fact-sensitive to the particular context. In other words, the first-order reasons which apply to the prosecutors' decision will vary considerably from case to case. Imposing legal rules to mandate uniform prosecutorial responses in such cases would purport to exclude consideration of at least some of these first-order reasons.[30] Since in some cases, these first-order reasons are likely to weigh in favour of continuing the prosecution, whilst in others, they are likely to weigh in favour of dismissal, it is unlikely that a general rule would assist a prosecutor in conforming to the first-order reasons that apply to her.[31] In other words, positive laws which attempt to mandate a one-size-fits-all response by prosecutors when victims request dismissal in domestic-violence cases are unlikely to be justifiable.[32]

With this in mind, we would perhaps do better to concern ourselves less with confining, structuring, and checking prosecutorial discretion and more with *guiding* prosecutorial discretion. That is to say, we should focus on identifying, clarifying, and weighing up the first-order reasons that should guide domestic-violence prosecutors in deciding how to respond in the face of victims' requests for dismissal.

B. Does it Help to Think in Terms of Public/Private?

In attempting to identify the reasons that should guide domestic-violence prosecutors in deciding what to do in the face of victim withdrawal, one may be drawn to thinking in terms of a distinction between 'the public' and 'the private'. It may be helpful to ask, for example, whether domestic violence constitutes a public wrong, and if so, it might be reasonable to conclude that criminal justice

---

[30] This account assumes a Razian framework regarding the distinction between first and second-order reasons: first-order reasons are simply reasons to do (or not to do) something; whereas second-order reasons are either reasons to act for a reason (aka, positive second-order reasons, or 'self-reflexive' reasons) or reasons *not* to act for a reason (aka, negative second-order reasons, or 'exclusionary' reasons). Raz, *Practical Reason and Norms* (n 4 above) 39–40 and postscript. Legal rules which mandate a uniform response in cases of victim withdrawal (eg, rules requiring a mandatory prosecution response) claim to provide prosecutors with a 'protected reason' for prosecution: a first-order reason to continue the prosecution and a negative second-order reason which excludes acting on reasons grounded in the victim's request to dismiss. On protected reasons, see Raz, *The Authority of Law* (n 4 above) 18, 21–3.

[31] The law would not, in other words, satisfy Raz's normal justification thesis, according to which 'the normal and primary way to establish' that authoritative directives are justified 'involves showing that the ... subject is likely better to comply with the reasons which apply to [him] ... if he accepts the directives ... as authoritatively binding, and tries to follow them, than if he tries to follow the reasons which apply to him directly.' Raz, *Ethics in the Public Domain* (n 4 above) 214.

[32] For a possible exception, see Chapter 5, section E ('The Impact of Justified Authoritative Directives and Principles on Prosecutorial Reasons') and Chapter 8, section A.3 ('Reasons for domestic violence prosecutors').

intervention is justified. If the public character of this wrong survives a victim's request to dismiss the criminal charges, then it might be reasonable to conclude that the prosecution should continue despite the victim's request to dismiss.[33]

Thinking about the proper functions of the criminal law in terms of the public/private divide has a long and distinguished intellectual history. Blackstone famously observed a distinction in the common law between private and public wrongs, which he based upon an understanding of those who suffered wrongdoing: if the public suffered wrongdoing, it was a public wrong; if a private individual suffered wrongdoing, it was a private wrong.[34] Austin also utilized the public/private distinction, but his analysis turned on the identity of the person issuing the command: commands issued by the sovereign or his delegates were deemed public in nature, whilst commands issued by 'subjects as private persons' were private in nature.[35] More recently, Sandra Marshall and Antony Duff have adopted the public/private distinction based on their understanding that some wrongs gain their public character through being shared by one's community.[36]

These approaches may prove helpful in answering our motivating question (what should public prosecutors do when victims withdraw their support for the prosecution of domestic-violence cases?) and I will return to the Marshall/Duff account in more detail below.[37] But first I will examine one way to think in terms of the public/private divide which is clearly *not* helpful in answering the motivating question. As Andrew Ashworth has correctly observed, most serious crimes constitute both public wrongs and private wrongs.[38] So asking whether a wrong constitutes a public wrong should not be thought to set up a false choice between deciding whether a particular instance of wrongdoing is *either* public *or* private; for it may very well be both. The questions addressed below, therefore, are simply whether domestic violence can be understood to have a public character, how it gains that public character, and whether that public character survives a victim's request to dismiss the charges. None of what follows is intended to question the characterization of domestic violence as a private wrong as well as (potentially) a public wrong.

In order to evaluate the usefulness of the public/private divide as a conceptual tool, I will attempt to start with a clear understanding of what is meant by this distinction. Ruth Gavison has helpfully identified the various meanings reflected

---

[33] Here I am using the term 'character' quite loosely, as in the public nature or quality of a wrong. In subsequent chapters, I will consider further the concept of character and its relationship to both acts of domestic violence and prosecutorial responses to domestic violence.

[34] RM Kerr (ed), *Blackstone's Commentaries on the Laws of England* (London: John Murray, 1862) Book iv, 5–6.

[35] J Austin, *The Province of Jurisprudence Determined* (Indianapolis: Hackett, 1832, reprint 1998) 136–9.

[36] S Marshall and RA Duff, 'Sharing wrongs' (1998) 11 Canadian J of Law and Jurisprudence 7.

[37] See Chapter 5, nn 39–52 and surrounding text.

[38] A Ashworth, 'Punishment and compensation' (1986) 6 OJLS 86, 111.

by public and private.[39] The key to making sense of this distinction lies in differentiating descriptive uses of public/private from the normative judgements reflected by use of these terms.

[T]he terms 'private' and 'public' occur in various senses, which are distinct though interrelated, and...these terms typically have both descriptive and normative meanings which, if not carefully distinguished, can lead to confusion or equivocation. A term used descriptively in a premise, for example, often acquires a different normative sense when used to yield a conclusion.[40]

As Gavison correctly observes, the public/private distinction is typically invoked to reflect the difference between that which is accessible/inaccessible, in the sense of being knowable/unknowable or known/unknown (as in 'one's own private thoughts'), or observable/unobservable or observed/unobserved (as in 'the privacy of what is done behind closed doors'). In a different sense of public/private, however, the distinction is meant to reflect a difference between group/individual. In this sense, 'public' refers to a large group of people, and 'private' refers either to the self-regarding conduct of an individual or to conduct involving a small group.[41] Another meaning of the public/private distinction is used to reflect the difference between interference/non-interference, in which the 'public sphere' is subject to interference and the 'private sphere' is not. Finally, we might tease out another meaning of the public/private distinction which draws upon the latter two distinctions above. In this final sense, 'private' is used to refer to one's freely chosen behaviour, as when such behaviour is described as self-regarding and thus typically not subject to interference,[42] whilst 'public' is used to refer to conduct that is not freely chosen and is thus subject to interference.[43]

Each of these uses of the public/private distinction admits of complex meanings, overlapping descriptive/normative senses, and matters of degree. Moreover, each sense of private/public operates in different ways within practical reasoning: (1) to describe facts which generate reasons, (2) to reflect the existence of prima facie or pro tanto reasons to interfere or not interfere,[44] and (3) to reflect

---

[39] R Gavison, 'Feminism and the public/private distinction' (1992) 45 Stanford L Rev 1.

[40] Ibid 4.

[41] Ibid 6–7.

[42] J Feinberg, *Harm to Self* (Oxford: OUP, 1984) 176–7.

[43] Unlike the other distinctions discussed above, this one is not purely descriptive, since the concepts of freely chosen and not freely chosen each consist of both empirical and normative criteria. Cf Raz, *The Morality of Freedom* (Oxford: OUP, 1986) 80–8, 148–57, examining the related concepts of consent and coercion.

[44] Prima facie and pro tanto reasons are reasons that are capable, respectively, of being cancelled or defeated. Prima facie ('at first sight, on the face of it') reasons can be cancelled (in which case they no longer bear rational force). Pro tanto ('so far, to that extent') reasons can be defeated (in which case they continue to bear rational force). S Kagan, *The Limits of Morality* (Oxford: OUP, 1991) 17. The difference between these types of reason (so far as I can tell) is only relevant in considering the moral residue which remains when one fails to do what a reason would have one do. In such cases, we have no reason to regret failures to do what cancelled prima facie reasons would have us do, but we do have reason to regret (or do the second-best thing) with respect to defeated pro tanto reasons.

all-things-considered judgements regarding the justifiability of interference or non-interference.[45] For example, one might observe that 'the family home is private' simply to make a descriptive claim that what happens within the family home typically is not easily observed by those physically situated outside the home. This descriptive account is based on the empirical fact that family homes typically consist of four solid walls and a roof, with limited windows through which those physically situated outside the home can observe the goings-on inside its walls and under its roof. It follows that if families began living in the open air or in glass houses, the accuracy of this descriptive account of the family home as private would lose its purchase. One might also claim that 'the family home is private' as a means of asserting the existence of reasons to refrain from interfering in events occurring within the home, whilst acknowledging that such reasons may be cancelled or defeated by stronger reasons weighing in favour of interference.[46] Finally, one might claim that 'the family home is private' in order to declare an all-things-considered judgement that interference with events occurring within the home is unjustifiable.

As I will argue below, there is reason to suspect that the public/private distinction is not terribly helpful in thinking clearly about what prosecutors should do when faced with victims' requests to dismiss. That said, however, the distinction informs (either explicitly or implicitly) most of the literature on domestic-violence prosecution, and it does quite a lot of work in setting out the issues under consideration in this book. Thus, before critiquing (and ultimately rejecting) the distinction between public and private, it is worth investigating just what kind of work it might accomplish in answering our motivating question.

1. Domestic violence as contingently public?

The public/private divide is frequently invoked in arguments regarding the proper criminal justice response to domestic violence. The role played by this distinction varies considerably across a wide spectrum of arguments. At one end lies a descriptive account of the domestic sphere as private (in the sense that members' conduct is typically unobserved by outsiders, involves a small group of people, and is typically not subject to interference) which gives rise to a normative conclusion that domestic violence *should* be private (in the sense that the

My use of the term 'defeasible' below is intentionally vague as between these meanings, since the matter need not be resolved here.

[45] This account of the role of the public/private divide in practical reason is broadly inspired by Gavison's discussion regarding the descriptive/normative dimensions of these terms. Gavison (n 39 above) 8–9.

[46] While I employ the metaphor of weight or strength regarding reasons, I do not mean to imply that all reasons are commensurable. Raz, *Morality of Freedom* (n 43 above) 321–66.

criminal justice system's interference with the domestic sphere is presumptively or absolutely unjustifiable).[47]

This argument is invalid on its face, since it lacks a normative premise to justify the presumption of non-interference.[48] The suppressed premise required to salvage the logic of this argument would state as follows: 'the fact that conduct occurring in the domestic sphere is typically unobserved by outsiders, involves a small group of people, and/or is typically not (in fact) subject to interference generates reasons against the criminal justice system interfering with such conduct.' With this normative premise in place, the argument is logically valid, but unsound, since the suppressed premise is implausible. Indeed, the fact that such conduct typically is unobserved by outsiders, involves a small group of people, and/or is not (in fact) subject to interference may very well generate reasons in *favour* of interference. Still, before feminist legal reforms took hold in the 1970s, this view of domestic violence dominated the criminal justice response.[49] Violence in the home was viewed as a matter ill-suited to intervention by the criminal justice system, and this non-interventionist approach dictated prosecutorial policy (or rather 'non-prosecutorial' policy) until recent decades. A man's home was still his castle, and the right to rule one's roost was rarely challenged by police or prosecutors.[50]

At the other end of the spectrum is the claim that notwithstanding the descriptively private features of the domestic sphere, the criminal justice system's

---

[47] Gavison (n 39 above) 35, noting this leap from the descriptive to normative as a mistake in practical reasoning.

[48] This argument should be distinguished, however, from ones which claim that the criminal justice system should not interfere with domestic violence because domestic violence is not a wrongful act in the first place. There is no need for a veil of privacy to protect husbands from being interfered with when they hit their wives, because (so the argument goes) there is nothing wrong with husbands hitting their wives. Some forms of this argument claim that domestic violence is not wrong irrespective of the victim's consent (eg, the claim that it is a husband's proper role and duty to correct his wife and children through physical punishment). Other forms of this argument set limits on what counts as permissible (non-wrongful) violence, such as the oft-cited example of a 'rule of thumb' which permitted husbands to beat their wives with a switch no bigger than their thumbs. N Lemon, *Domestic Violence Law* (St Paul, MN: West, 2001) 1–11. (For discussion of whether this rule actually ever existed at common law, see H Kelly, 'Rule of thumb and the folklaw of the husband's stick' (1994) 44 J of Legal Education 341, 353.) Finally, another form of this argument claims that the victim's consent (where present) makes the violence not wrongful, as opposed to merely making it a private wrong. It is possible that this thinking might have grounded the decision in *R v Wilson* [1997] QB 47, but the court's arguments on this point are not clear. See n 52 below.

[49] On this account of domestic violence, see generally, R Siegel, 'The rule of love: Wife beating as prerogative and privacy' (1996) 105 Yale L J 2117, 2121–30.

[50] It would, however, be incorrect to claim that domestic violence was not challenged by law during this time, since laws prohibiting battery have always been generally applicable to cases of domestic violence (it is just that these laws have rarely been enforced). It would perhaps be less incorrect to claim that such violence was not challenged 'by police and prosecutors' at this time. However, some police officers did challenge domestic violence informally through 'summary justice' measures. C Hoyle, *Negotiating Domestic Violence: Police, criminal justice and victims* (Oxford: OUP, 1998) 140–1, citing S Choongh, *Policing as Social Discipline* (Oxford: Clarendon, 1997).

interference in domestic-violence cases *is* presumptively justifiable. As Gavison notes:

the 'privacy' of the family is often invoked to mask the exploitation and battering of family members. Such exploitation and violence should be matters of public concern, and the fact that they occur within the family should not be used to provide them with immunity.[51]

According to this argument then, the descriptively private features of the domestic sphere do not generate any reasons against interference. Rather, domestic violence is viewed as an essentially public matter in the sense that the criminal justice system should interfere when domestic violence occurs.

In between these two extremes, we find arguments that rest on an understanding of domestic violence as contingently public in nature. That is to say, the descriptively private features of the domestic sphere give rise to a presumption of privacy, but that presumption is defeated upon satisfaction of one or more contingencies. Typically, these contingencies come in three flavours: (1) if the victim does not consent to the violence;[52] (2) if the victim requests criminal justice intervention; and/or (3) if the level of violence inflicted (or risked) is high. The first contingency is the least controversial way to invoke the public/private distinction in domestic-violence cases: if the victim consented to the violence, then (so the argument goes) the matter remains private; but if the victim did not consent, then the matter is public.[53]

Occasionally, it is suggested that in order to secure a public character, an incident of domestic violence must satisfy multiple contingencies, including both the victim's non-consent to the violence and either the victim's request for criminal justice intervention or the infliction (or risk) of a high level of violence.[54] Whilst this approach has largely been rejected by most academic commentators, it has found one recent advocate in Linda Mills:

I believe that women should be entitled to their privacy to the extent that they want to maintain that privacy. If women ... want the police and/or courts to intervene, either

---

[51] Gavison (n 39 above) 24.

[52] This contingency envelops nearly all domestic-violence cases, but see, eg, *R v Wilson* [1997] QB 47, where the defendant successfully avoided conviction for GBH on grounds that his wife consented to his branding of her buttocks. The court ruled that 'activity between husband and wife, in the privacy of the matrimonial home, is not, in our judgment, a proper matter for criminal investigation, let alone criminal prosecution.' This case may be understood as a domestic-violence case involving wrongful conduct which nonetheless was deemed not to be a proper target for criminal justice intervention because domestic violence was understood as contingently public—ie, contingent on the victim's non-consent to the violence.

[53] Note the difference between this account and an account which claims that consented-to violence is not wrongful in the first place. See n 48 above.

[54] L Mills, *Insult to Injury: Rethinking our responses to intimate abuse* (Oxford: Princeton University Press, 2003) 5. See also L Sherman, *Policing Domestic Violence: Experiments and dilemmas* (New York: Free Press, 1992) 256–7, recommending 'victim-directed arrest'.

because they ask for it or because their situation poses great risk of harm, the state should respond with appropriate assistance... [55]

Despite Mills' recent attempt to resurrect the multiple contingency approach to understanding the public character of domestic violence, this view remains the minority view in the current literature.[56] Rather, on most modern accounts, domestic violence is deemed public wrongdoing simply in virtue of the fact that the victims have not consented to the violence, irrespective of whether a particular victim affirmatively requests intervention or is subjected to high levels of violence.

2. Domestic violence as defeasibly public?

Another way in which the public/private divide is commonly invoked in arguments regarding the proper criminal justice response to domestic violence is in the claim that the public character of domestic violence is defeasible. In other words, whilst domestic violence is held to be a public wrong (either essentially or contingently), it is claimed that this public character is capable of being defeated under certain circumstances. Not surprisingly, not just any circumstances will do the trick. For example, if friends or family members express their desire for the matter to be treated privately, their wishes will not defeat the public nature of the wrong. Rather, on this account, only the victim's freely chosen conduct can defeat the public nature of the wrong. If the victim freely requests that her domestic-violence case be dismissed, her request does defeat the public nature of the event (so the argument goes) and thus draws a veil of privacy around the incident.

This account makes good sense if we view domestic violence as a contingently public matter in the first place. Since (on that account) it is the victim's lack of free choice (non-consent) that is key to making domestic violence a matter of public concern in the first place, it seems correct to conclude that we should defer to the victim's free choice in determining whether and when that public character is defeated. On this account then, when faced with victims' requests to dismiss domestic-violence cases, prosecutors should abide by the victims' wishes.[57]

---

[55] Ibid 5.

[56] Linda Mills' work, for example, has been met with strong (often scathing) critique. A Acorn, 'Surviving the battered reader's syndrome, or: A critique of Linda G Mills' *Insult to Injury: Rethinking Our Responses to Intimate Abuse*' (2005) 13 UCLA Women's LJ 335; D Coker, 'Race, poverty, and the crime-centered response to domestic violence' (2004) 10 *Violence Against Women* 1331; W Dekeseredy, '(Review) *Insult to Injury: Rethinking our Responses to Intimate Abuse*, by Linda G Mills' (2004) 44 British J of Criminology 621; E Stark, 'Insults, injury, and injustice: Rethinking state intervention in domestic-violence cases' (2004) 10 *Violence Against Women* 1302.

[57] Implicit in this formulation is the questionable assumption that prosecutors are able to determine whether victims' requests reflect their freely chosen wishes to have their cases dismissed, or whether they are simply engaged in performative withdrawals. See Chapter 1, section E.

Thinking of domestic violence as a defeasible public wrong (ie, defeasible upon the victim's freely chosen request to dismiss) is helpful for keeping separate two issues: (1) whether the victim's request to dismiss defeats the public character of the event (which, on this account, it would); and (2) whether the victim's request to dismiss defeats the wrongful character of the event (which, on this account, it would not). These are distinct issues and should not be confused. There is, however, some evidence that these issues have been confused both in the academic literature and in law enforcement's understanding of the effect of victims' requests to dismiss. Anne Cretney and others, for example, have documented the thinking of police officers who equate the victim's failure to pursue criminal prosecution with 'giving permission' to the abuser.[58]

This confusion, which equates a victim's request to dismiss with her consenting to the violence, tends to obscure the important distinction between: (1) a matter that is none of the criminal law's business because it does not involve wrongdoing; and (2) a matter that is none of the criminal law's business because it involves *private* wrongdoing. If we accept that the criminal law's business is delimited in this way (ie, that some things are simply none of the law's business), then thinking of domestic violence as a defeasible public wrong is helpful in avoiding this confusion of thought.

The defeasible-public-wrong account of domestic violence has influenced many arguments advocating dismissal of domestic-violence cases upon the victim's request.[59] For example, this account clearly underpins Linda Mills' approach, according to which domestic violence gains its public character by satisfying at least two of three contingencies, and it loses its public character immediately upon the victim's request to dismiss. To continue treating domestic violence as a public matter in the face of the victim's request to dismiss, on Mill's account, is to indulge the prosecutor's unjustified 'impulse to play God'.[60]

A considerably more appealing version of the defeasible-public-wrong account of domestic violence has been advanced by Carolyn Hoyle and Andrew Sanders under the title of the 'victim empowerment' model of domestic-violence prosecution.[61] This model favours a pro-arrest police response to domestic violence, non-molestation conditions placed on the suspect's pre-charge release, and victim support provided through specially trained domestic violence officers who,

---

[58] A Cretney and others, 'Criminalizing assault: The failure of the offence against society model' (1994) 34 British J of Criminology 15, 19. Andrew Ashworth seems to draw a similar connection in a non-domestic violence context. Ashworth (n 38 above) 113.

[59] Eg, Mills (n 54 above); L Goodmark, 'Law is the answer? Do we know that for sure? Questioning the efficacy of legal interventions for battered women' (2004) 23 Saint Louis U Public L Rev 7; N Mordini, 'Mandatory state interventions for domestic abuse cases: An examination of the effects on victim safety and autonomy' (2004) 52 Drake L Rev 295; D Zlotnick, 'Empowering the battered woman: The use of criminal contempt sanctions to enforce civil protection orders' (1999) 56 Ohio State LJ 1153.

[60] Mills (n 54 above) 49.

[61] C Hoyle and A Sanders, 'Police response to domestic violence: From victim choice to victim empowerment?' (2000) 40 British J of Criminology 14.

ideally, can provide flexible intervention services to assist victims at various stages of exiting from violent relationships.[62] One appealing aspect of this model is the condition that the victim's request to dismiss is not immediately assumed to reflect her true wishes. Rather, there is recognition that victims often face manipulation by defendants, family members, and even law enforcement officials—all of whom may have an interest in the criminal prosecution being dismissed.[63]

This risk of manipulation suggests that any sustainable account of domestic violence as a defeasible public wrong should adopt a Feinbergian 'presumption of nonvoluntariness' in evaluating such requests.[64] On this view, the initial presumption in evaluating such requests should be grounded in the suspicion that victims have been coerced or otherwise placed under illicit pressure in making requests to dismiss. As Feinberg has explained, when we encounter a person who seems to be acting against his or her interests, yet we wish to give effect to her free choices, we should adopt an initial presumption of non-voluntariness. This presumption reflects a level of 'extra caution' in approaching the question of whether a person's conduct is freely chosen. Where the presumption applies, it reflects our expectation that, under the circumstances, the person's conduct is likely not voluntary. Adopting a sceptical stance toward such conduct fulfils 'our need to make sure' that the victim's conduct reflects her true choice.[65] This presumption, however, does not imply a burden of proof on the victim's part to prove that her request to dismiss is free from coercion;[66] rather it merely speaks to a requirement that the victim be provided a basic level of safety, time for reflection, and material resources which may support the likelihood that her request reflects her true wishes. Once those conditions are met (so the argument goes) the victim's request to dismiss defeats the public character of the event: the matter is no longer the law's business, and therefore the prosecutor should dismiss the case.

This, in essence, is the answer to the motivating question as recommended by Hoyle and Sander's victim empowerment model.[67] The thing that most distinguishes the victim empowerment model from other approaches to our question is the implicit view that the public character of domestic violence is defeasibly contingent on the victim's (empowered) choice:

the question of whether or not to prosecute would follow on from the victim's assessment of the direction she wants her life to go. The choice would be that of the victim.[68]

---

[62] Ibid 31.
[63] Ibid 17.
[64] Feinberg (n 42 above) 124.
[65] Ibid.
[66] Ibid 125.
[67] Hoyle and Sanders (n 61 above).
[68] Hoyle and Sanders (n 61 above) 32. For another version of the argument that some (non-serious) criminal offences may properly be understood as transitioning from public to private upon the victim's withdrawal, see RA Duff and SE Marshall, 'Communicative punishment and the role of the victim' (2004) 23 Criminal Justice Ethics 39, 45.

Such an approach is in sharp contrast with the view that the public character of otherwise criminal violence is *indefeasible*. Ashworth seems to endorse this indefeasibility view when he claims that 'in principle, the victim's personal desire not to have the suspected offender prosecuted should be subordinated to the public interest'.[69] Shazia Chaudhry and Jonathan Herring have similarly resisted an account of domestic violence as a defeasible public wrong, claiming that the state's human-rights obligations under international law ground an indefeasible duty to prosecute domestic violence 'even where the victim is stating that she does not want the "benefit" of a criminal prosecution'.[70]

3. Was that helpful?

In the preceding literature review regarding the prosecution of domestic violence, the private/public distinction appears to be somewhat helpful in understanding and critiquing the relevant arguments. Particularly once the issues of contingency and defeasibility are distinguished, it is possible to gain a better appreciation for the differences between the types of arguments offered in the literature, and the types of mistake encountered in the course of making these arguments. For example, a clear difference arises between Linda Mills' version of domestic violence and the version offered by Carolyn Hoyle and Andrew Sanders, despite the fact that all of these authors would broadly fall into the same 'anti' camp (ie, the anti-mandatory prosecution camp).[71] The concept of defeasibly public wrongdoing is helpful in observing the similarities between Mills on the one hand and Hoyle and Sanders on the other (all agree that domestic violence is a defeasible public wrong), whilst the concept of contingent public wrongdoing is helpful in observing their differences (only Mills conceives the public character of domestic violence as requiring the satisfaction of multiple contingencies). Further, the public/private divide proves helpful in avoiding the confusion of thought generated by conflating a victim's request to dismiss with a victim's consent to the violence. So, provisionally, the verdict is yes: the public/private distinction is a somewhat helpful conceptual tool in answering our motivating question.

But whilst the public/private divide undoubtedly pays off in terms of analytic neatness, it comes with a cost: in creating a category of 'private' which facilitates the protection of important interests from interference by others, it also creates a category of 'private' in which some people are left free to exploit and abuse others with impunity. It seems to me that what is really important to protect is not the

---

[69] Ashworth (n 38 above) 113. Ashworth makes this point in the context of gang violence, but takes a less certain view when it comes to domestic-violence cases. A Ashworth and M Redmayne, *The Criminal Process: An evaluative study* (3rd edn, New York: OUP, 2005) 200.

[70] S Choudhry and J Herring, 'Righting domestic violence' (2006) 20 Intl J of Law and the Family 95, 101.

[71] On the distinction between 'pros' and 'antis', see Chapter 1, section F.

'private' realm but rather the *value* of what is done within it. As Gavison observed, it is 'the substance of the activity rather than its public or private context, [which] determines its value'.[72] This point suggests that we would do equally as well, if not better, in protecting important interests from interference *and* removing impunity from those who engage in veiled exploitation and abuse, if we were to consider the values at stake *directly* rather than relying on generalizing approximations of value provided by the public/private divide. On the whole, it appears that the public/private dichotomy generates neat analytic categories at the expense of obscuring the very values that underlie the distinction. Often in conceptual analysis, the neatness we purchase is worth the price; but given the illegitimate use to which the public/private distinction has been put in the context of domestic violence, I believe that the price we pay for its use is simply too high.

C. Conclusion

This chapter has investigated two possible ways of answering the question motivating this book (what should public prosecutors do when victims withdraw their support for the prosecution of domestic-violence cases?). A legal formalist approach was considered first but rejected due to its inability to account for the type of discretion prosecutors necessarily exercise in virtue of their role and the normal lack of justification for legal directives which purport to mandate uniform prosecutorial response in such cases. A more promising set of answers to our motivating question was explored by relying on the public/private distinction. This distinction helped to clarify some disparate strands of the academic literature and to avoid potentially limiting confusions of thought regarding the nature of domestic-violence cases in which victims withdraw their support for the prosecution. However, in the end, it was determined that the cost of thinking in terms of the public/private dichotomy is too high. Out of concern that this conceptual tool does more to obscure domestic-violence cases than to illuminate them, it was rejected as a basis for further inquiry.[73]

In what follows, I will make a fresh start, attempting to avoid traps laid by the public/private distinction and instead focusing directly on identifying the values

---

[72] Gavison (n 39 above) 37. Gavison, however, rejects this argument because she believes it threatens to 'reduce the question [of criminalization] to a debate about the morality of the conduct'. It is unclear to me why Gavison makes this leap from a consideration of the public/private divide (and the values which inform this distinction) to questions of criminalization. Surely it is worth exploring the values which inform our conceptual distinctions—ie, self-consciously engaging in what Julie Dickson calls 'indirect evaluation'—without committing ourselves to any plan of action with regard to criminalization. J Dickson, *Evaluation and Legal Theory* (Oxford: Hart, 2001). In any event, the moral status of the conduct is only one part of a proper analysis of whether such conduct should be criminalized.

[73] There is, however, one sense of 'public' I would like to retain: public prosecutor. See Chapter 3, section A.2.

at stake in prosecuting domestic-violence cases and the reasons generated by such values. In the next three chapters (which together constitute the second of this three-part book), I will provide an account of prosecutorial action, value, and reason in analysing prosecutorial discretion generally. Finally, in Part III, I will revisit the question of domestic violence directly. In Chapter 8, I apply my analysis of prosecutorial discretion to our motivating question, while in Chapter 9 I consider the supposed rights and duties of domestic-violence victims in the context of domestic-violence prosecutions.

PART II
A FRESH START

3

Prosecutors: What They Are and What They Do

The next three chapters take a step back from our motivating question (what should public prosecutors do when victims withdraw their support for the prosecution of domestic-violence cases?) and consider the question of prosecutorial action, value, and reason more generally. This step back is justified, I believe, in light of the basic principle of practical reasoning. According to this principle, the answer to any question which takes the form 'what should rational beings do when . . . ?' is simply 'act rationally'.[1] The basic answer is a tautology (but a potentially illuminating one, as we shall see below). It is tautologous because the proposition that one should act rationally is equivalent to the proposition that one should do the right thing—or at least one of several right things that may be done consistently with practical reason, for it may be the case that there is no distinctively right action fully determined by reasons.[2] However, insofar as reasons exist to guide one's action, one should follow those reasons so far as they lead. That is simply to say, again, that as rational beings, we should act rationally.

If we grant that prosecutors are rational beings, then we can formulate a basic answer to our motivating question: when victims withdraw their support for the prosecution of domestic-violence cases, prosecutors should act rationally. In order to elaborate upon this basic answer, we must attend to the *reasons* that apply to prosecutors qua prosecutors. Attending to such reasons requires an account of the *values* that can be realized through prosecutorial action (for, as will be discussed below, such values normally generate reasons for action). Providing an account of values that can be realized through prosecutorial action requires a preliminary understanding of what constitutes prosecutorial action. This chapter attempts to provide such an understanding.

---

[1] My meaning here is consistent with the notion that acting rationally consists in realizing the normative significance of facts and responding appropriately. J Raz, *Engaging Reason* (New York: OUP, 1999) 70, but I will not further explore the concept of acting rationally, since doing so would take us too far afield from the issues of applied prosecutorial practical reasoning under consideration in this book.

[2] J Finnis, *Natural Law and Natural Rights* (Oxford: Clarendon, 1980) 284–6, discussing Aquinas' use of the concept *determinatio*.

This chapter outlines an account of prosecutors and prosecutorial action, providing a rough basis for understanding what we consider when we consider prosecutors and prosecution, by attempting to identify the rationally salient features of this role and practice.[3] The discussion in this chapter provides merely a brief, skeletal outline of what prosecutors are and what constitutes prosecutorial action. The aim here is to provide something more along the lines of a descriptive account of these concepts, rather than a full-blown normative account. I am conscious, however, of the fact that claims by theorists to be engaged in purely descriptive conceptual analysis have become somewhat passé in recent years, and I do not mean to revive this methodology here. Indeed, I agree with John Finnis that theory cannot proceed in an entirely value-free manner, since some 'judgment of significance and importance must be made if theory is to be more than a vast rubbish heap of miscellaneous facts'.[4] However, following Julie Dickson, I resist the implication Finnis draws from this observation. According to Dickson, Finnis takes the position that 'once the process of evaluating what is important about [a concept] has begun, there is, so to speak, no place to stop', and so the theorist must engage in full-blown normative evaluation of his subject in order to make sense of it.[5] In contrast, I think it is possible to provide a helpful, albeit incomplete, account of the salient ('significant', 'important') features of what prosecutors are and what they do, without providing a full-blown normative account of the prosecutorial role and prosecutorial actions. Such an account would accomplish what my first sentence above promises: it would provide 'a rough basis for understanding what we consider when we consider prosecutors and prosecution'.[6]

The account provided below attempts to explain and defend the following claims: (1) that prosecutors are people who act in the role of legal prosecutorial official on behalf of the state and (potentially) their communities; and (2) that prosecutorial actions are actions that prosecutors take qua prosecutors, consisting of both prosecutorial *pursuit* actions and prosecutorial *non-pursuit* actions.

A. What Prosecutors Are

1. Prosecutors are people

For a start, it is worth observing that whatever else they may be, prosecutors are people. This observation is important because it highlights the simple fact that

---

[3] In what follows, I will use the term 'prosecutor' to refer to public prosecutors, as private prosecutions are beyond the scope of my inquiry.

[4] Finnis (n 2 above) 17.

[5] J Dickson, *Evaluation and Legal Theory* (Oxford: Hart, 2001) 45. Dickson's characterization is based in part on her reading of Finnis' work and her personal observation of Finnis' presentations in law seminars at the University of Oxford. Ibid 45 fn 26.

[6] More directly normative accounts of the role of prosecutors and prosecutorial action will be possible once we have considered the values that can be realized through prosecutorial actions. See Chapters 4 and 5.

prosecutors are subject to morality: all of the moral reasons that apply to human beings generally apply to prosecutors too.[7] Since prosecutors are also legal officials, it is tempting to think that they are principally subject to law and to treat the question of whether and to what extent they are also subject to morality as a secondary matter. Framing the question in this way focuses our concern on how to limit the role of moral reasons in guiding prosecutorial action in favour of a system in which prosecutorial action is guided exclusively by legal reasons. This is a popular approach to thinking about prosecution, widely reflected in the academic literature regarding prosecutorial ethics and discretion. As noted earlier, this literature in general reflects an overriding concern to 'confine, structure and check' prosecutorial discretion with legal rules,[8] whilst some more extreme contributions evidence an almost pathological fear of any gap in the positive law which allows space for prosecutors to exercise the dreaded 'unfettered moral discretion'.[9] Ideally, or so it is claimed by those who endorse this approach, prosecutors should be guided entirely (or as far as possible) by legal reasons and not by moral reasons.

I agree with Raz in thinking that this way of framing the issue leads to confusion. Moral reasons apply to prosecutors simply in virtue of the fact that they are people, and indeed prosecutors would not be subject to legal reasons if they were not subject to moral reasons.[10] We can therefore avoid some confusion by recognizing that because they are people, prosecutors are first and foremost guided by moral reasons, not legal reasons. As Raz puts the point, we should not 'start with the law and ask what room it makes for morality'—but rather start with morality and ask what contribution the law makes to morality.[11]

Granted, however, prosecutors are not just any old people. They are people who stand in a certain role within legal systems. As such, when a person acts qua prosecutor she acts qua legal official. In adopting this role, she makes a promise to follow legal norms as far as they can take her whilst engaged in legal reasoning qua prosecutor.[12] So it is true of course that prosecutors are guided by legal

---

[7] J Raz, 'Incorporation by law' (2004) 10 Legal Theory 1, 2–7, making an analogous point with respect to judges.

[8] K Davis, *Discretionary Justice* (Baton Rouge: Louisiana State University, 1969). For a review of the body of literature generated by Davis' work, see R Levin, 'The administrative law legacy of Kenneth Culp Davis' (2005) 42 San Diego L Rev 315. Davis' call to confine, structure, and check discretion in the administrative arena has been put to extensive use in the field of prosecutorial ethics. E Luna, 'Principled enforcement of penal codes' (2005) 4 Buffalo Crim L Rev 515, 594; J Vorenberg, 'Decent restraint of prosecutorial power' (1981) 94 Harvard L Rev 1521; D Johnson, 'The organization of prosecution and the possibility of order' (1998) 32 Law and Society Rev 247, 297.

[9] L Griffin, 'The prudent prosecutor' (2001) 14 Georgetown J of Legal Ethics 259, 262, 307. See also, Chapter 2, section A.2 ('How far should law get us?').

[10] Raz (n 7 above) 7. This thought is echoed by Finnis: 'Law, fit to take a directive place in practical reasoning towards morally sound judgment, is for the sake of human persons'. J Finnis, 'Natural law theories' (2007) *Stanford Encylopedia of Philosophy* <http://plato.stanford.edu// law-theories/#HumPerNotLawCreButProPoi>, accessed 26 August 2008.

[11] Raz (n 7 above) 2.

[12] That is, whilst engaged in 'reasoning to establish the existing content of the law on a given issue, reasoning from the existing content of the law to the decision [she] should reach in a case…,

reasons when reasoning qua prosecutors; but none of this detracts from the primacy of moral reasoning, for it is due to moral reasons that prosecutors came to be bound to follow legal reasons in the first place. In other words, the reasons why a prosecutor is justified (*if* she is justified) in engaging in legal reasoning qua prosecutor, and the reasons why she is justified (*if* she is justified) in applying legal norms in so doing, are moral reasons—not least of which are the moral reasons generated by her promise to act qua prosecutor.[13]

The key to guiding prosecutorial discretion, therefore, is not to develop a system in which moral considerations play no role in guiding prosecutorial action—but rather to develop an account of how and when legal norms should exclude some of the moral considerations which otherwise would guide prosecutorial decision-making, and how such norms should organize the non-excluded moral considerations which necessarily do guide prosecutorial discretion.

2. Prosecutors are state (and perhaps community) representatives

The next important point to observe in outlining what prosecutors are, is that prosecutors are representatives of their states (and may also represent their communities as well). Let us take each step in turn. In acting qua prosecutor, one acts on behalf of the state. In England and the US, for example, prosecutors act in the name of the 'Queen' or the 'People of...', the 'State of...', or the 'City of...'.[14] This observation helps explain the sense in which prosecutorial action *is* state action. It is important to note the kind of claim being advanced here: it is a conceptual claim regarding the role of prosecutor and the nature of prosecutorial action. The claim is simply that prosecutors act on behalf of their state in the sense that they act as agents of the state.

Of course, the tenability of this claim assumes some threshold level of stability and political legitimacy enjoyed by the state, the criminal justice system of that state, and the office of prosecutor within that system. For example, in the last days of the Ceaușescu regime before the state of Romania fell, we can understand the Romanian prosecutors as having transitioned from acting in the role of 'prosecutors' to acting in the role of 'paper-shufflers': from acting as agents of the state to engaging merely in the pretence of such agency. Before the descent

and reasoning about the decision [she] should reach in a case, all things considered'. J Dickson, 'Interpretation and coherence in legal reasoning' (2005) *Stanford Encyclopedia of Philosophy* <http://plato.stanford.edu//reas-interpret/> accessed 26 August 2008.

[13] Under certain conditions, of course, prosecutors might *not* be justified in making such a promise: taking on the role of prosecutor might be an unjustifiable choice. A Smith, 'Can you be a good person and a good prosecutor?' (2001) 14 Georgetown J of Legal Ethics 355. See also, L Green, 'The duty to govern' (2007) 13 Legal Theory 167, for exploration of the foundations of state officials' obligations to act *qua* official, ie to govern.

[14] Regina is understood as guardian of the Commonwealth and therefore representative of the community. On the notion that public prosecutors act on behalf of states, see I Brownlie, *Principles of Public International Law* (5th edn, Oxford: OUP, 1988) 450–1.

into anarchy which preceded the execution of Ceauşescu and the total collapse of the communist state, when a Romanian prosecutor filed a piece of paper entitled 'indictment' with the proper clerks in the proper government office, the act counted as a prosecutorial action: specifically, the act of charging a defendant with a criminal offence. In so doing, the prosecutor acted on behalf of the state. As the state descended into anarchy, however, a prosecutor filing an identical piece of paper in the very same office would count as nothing but a bizarre parody of prosecutorial action. Prosecutors' actions counted less and less as prosecutorial actions and more and more as mere paper-shuffling as the week progressed, because there was less and less of a state for prosecutors to represent qua prosecutors. So the claim that prosecutors act on behalf of their states is conceptual in the following sense: prosecutors cannot exist without a state for them to represent, and if prosecutors do exist, then they act on behalf of (as agents of, as representatives of) their states.

Often, if a state enjoys a high degree of political legitimacy and is accepted as a legitimate authority by the members of the relevant community, then prosecutors can be understood (again, conceptually) to be acting on behalf of that community as well.[15] This form of the claim that prosecutors act on behalf of their communities, if they do so, is also a conceptual claim about the nature of prosecutorial action. Again, the tenability of this claim in any given context is contingent on the satisfaction of certain legitimacy conditions adhering in the relationship between the relevant state, its criminal justice system, and the community which it purports to represent. Typically, of course, these conditions are not met, due to what Antony Duff has characterized as the 'radical disparity between the actual character of our legal institutions and [an] account of the proper nature of law, of the criminal trial and of punishment'.[16]

The same point applies to prosecutions generally: insofar as a gap exists between the actual and ideal, prosecutors cannot properly be understood as representatives of their communities. I will not go into detail regarding the conditions that must adhere before it would be appropriate to conceptualize prosecutors as representatives of their communities; but suffice it to say that at a minimum, such legitimacy would entail a particular attitude by prosecutors in calling members of the community to account:

[an] attitude... [that] expresses a conception of them as fellow members of a normative community, ... not as mere objects of our anger or as enemies to be fought or disposed of, by whose values we are collectively both bound and protected. It is to address them, and call them to judgment, in terms of a set of values to which we claim that the addressees are or should be committed just as we are. It is to recognize the need both to explain to

---

[15] The sense of community I adopt here is based roughly on Duff's account, which he describes as a normative ideal grounded in a communitarian version of liberalism. See generally, RA Duff, *Punishment, Communication, and Community* (Oxford: OUP, 2001) ch 2.

[16] RA Duff, *Trials and Punishment* (Cambridge: Cambridge University Press, 1986) 11.

them why we are responding in this way, and to attend to their explanations and defences of what they did—in other words, to try to engage with them in a communicative enterprise of judgement and of normative truth-seeking.[17]

I will refer to this attitude and the conditions it would generate as political legitimacy conditions. When prosecutorial action is conducted in a context which meets a certain threshold of political legitimacy conditions, prosecutors can be understood (as a conceptual matter) to be acting as representatives of their communities. This is not to say, however, that all prosecutorial action in such circumstances will necessarily be in the best interests of the prosecutor's community. (We will return to this point below.)

To review then, claiming that a prosecutor acts on behalf of her state is importantly distinct from claiming that a prosecutor acts on behalf of her community. The former is a conceptual necessity if we are to make any sense of the role of prosecutor, whilst the latter may be conceptually true when certain conditions adhere, but these conditions are not necessary in order to make sense of the role of prosecutor. In other words, whilst prosecutors necessarily represent their state, they may very well fail to represent their community.

My reason for emphasizing that these two points are conceptual in nature is to avoid any ambiguity between these claims and similar ones that might be understood as full-blooded normative claims.[18] For example, nothing I have claimed about 'what prosecutors are' has been meant to express a normative claim that prosecutors *should* act on behalf of their states or communities. To clarify this distinction between conceptual and normative claims, consider the proposition that 'the woman who provides the egg and gives birth to the child should be the child's biological mother'. Stated in such terms, this claim is bizarre. Rather, a woman who both provides the egg and gives birth to the child simply *is* the child's biological mother. The point is a conceptual one; but the use of the word 'should' may be thought to introduce a confusing suggestion of normativity to the proposition. There's no *should* about it: the proposition expresses a conceptual claim about the woman's role and the meaning of her action: when the woman who provided the egg gives birth to the child, she acts qua the child's biological mother.

Normative and conceptual claims can of course be easily confused when we talk about people 'acting on behalf of' other people or groups of people, perhaps because 'acting on behalf of X' sounds a lot like 'acting *in the best interests* of X'. For this reason, it is tempting to interpret my claims regarding prosecutors acting 'on behalf of the state' or acting 'on behalf of their community' as normative ones: that prosecutors *should* act on behalf of (in the best interests of) the state and *should* act on behalf of (in the best interests of) their communities. And of course they should; but that's not my point here. Rather, when I write 'on behalf

---

[17] RA Duff and others, *The Trial on Trial, vol 3: Towards a Normative Theory of the Criminal Law* (Oxford: Hart, 2007) 138.

[18] My thanks to Andrew Ashworth for drawing this potential confusion to my attention.

of', I mean 'as agent or representative of', not 'in the best interests of'. It follows that irrespective of whether prosecutors act in the best interests of their states, they are still acting on behalf of the state in the conceptual (agency) sense whenever they act qua prosecutors; and irrespective of whether prosecutors act in the best interests of their communities, they are still acting on behalf of their communities in the conceptual (agency) sense whenever they act qua prosecutors and the threshold of political legitimacy conditions apply. For example, consider state prosecutors in the US who failed to charge white suspects for lynching African Americans, despite sufficient evidence to do so.[19] Assuming that the threshold political legitimacy conditions applied vis-à-vis the prosecutor and the white majority community, the prosecutors can be understood as having acted on behalf of the white majority community, in the sense that they acted as agents of that community when they failed to prosecute lynchings. This conceptual point remains true even though the prosecutor's actions were not in the best interests of that community.[20]

By acknowledging the force of the conceptual claim that prosecutors act on behalf of their communities (as agents) even when they fail in their normative task to act in the best interests of their communities, we can come to understand the way in which prosecutorial actions can have a detrimental effect on the character of a community: how, for example, prosecutorial action can in part constitute the white majority community above as more racist, *ceteris paribus*.[21] Prosecutorial action may, of course, also reconstitute the character of a community to make it *less* racist, *ceteris paribus*.[22] We will return to these points in the next section.

To recap, understanding the conceptual claim that prosecutors act on behalf of their states requires that we assume some minimal degree of existence of both the state and its criminal legal system. In unstable or transitional systems, it may not be entirely clear to what extent, if at all, prosecutors act on behalf of the state. Moreover, understanding the conceptual claim that prosecutors act on behalf of their communities requires that we *further* assume the existence of threshold

---

[19] SE Tolany and EM Beck, *A Festival of Violence: An analysis of Southern lynchings, 1882–1930* (Urbana: University of Illinois Press, 1995); J Madison, *A Lynching in the Heartland: Race and memory in America* (New York: Palgrave, 2001); IB Wells-Barnett, *On Lynchings* (Amhurst: Humanity Books, 2002).

[20] This point assumes an account of the relationship between interest and well-being that is roughly consistent with J Raz, *The Morality of Freedom* (Oxford: OUP, 1986) ch 12.

[21] On the ability of criminal trial procedures to reconstitute the character of a community, see S Clark, '"Who do you think you are?" The criminal trial and community character' in RA Duff and others (eds), *The Trial on Trial, vol 2: Judgment and Calling to Account* (Oxford: Hart, 2006).

[22] I take this point to be consistent with the thought motivating a series of interesting articles by Anthony Alfieri in which he writes of 'the transformative role of prosecutors' (A Alfieri, 'Color/identity/justice: Chicano Trials' (2005) 53 Duke LJ 1569, 1576); and the 'redemptive role for prosecutors' (A Alfieri, 'Retrying race' (2003) 101 Michigan L Rev 1141, 1144). These character-based considerations motivate Alfieri to advocate the adoption of race-consciousness in the exercise of prosecutorial discretion. A Alfieri, 'Prosecuting race' (1999) 48 Duke LJ 1157; A Alfieri, 'Prosecuting violence/reconstructing community' (2000) 52 Stanford L Rev 809.

political legitimacy conditions adhering vis-à-vis the prosecutors and the relevant community.[23] In many legal systems, where political legitimacy conditions are questionable, it may not be entirely clear to what extent, if at all, prosecutors act on behalf of their communities.[24] However, assuming that these minimal thresholds are met, we can then understand prosecutors' actions as constituting (in part) the community's actions.[25] Indeed, in a normatively ideal criminal justice system, there is no space between a prosecutor acting qua prosecutor and the community *itself* acting: in such systems, the prosecutor's actions are constitutive of the community's actions.[26]

B. What Prosecutors Do

Prosecutors engage in prosecutorial action.[27] Prosecutorial action, it will be assumed, begins with the charging decision: the point where investigation (a police action) transitions into a choice between accusing and not accusing a potential defendant of a criminal offence.[28] It is far less clear, and perhaps less important for the purpose of this book, to determine precisely when prosecutorial action ends. Suffice it to say that I will limit my considerations below to the trial stage, which ends either in conviction or acquittal/dismissal.[29]

---

[23] Prosecutors may of course act on behalf of (represent) only a portion of the community: those people with respect to whom the prosecutors adopt the attitude outlined in the quote above (at n 17). So, for example, in failing to prosecute lynchings, the prosecutors' actions (if habituated) can be understood to constitute the character of the white community as more racist; but there is no reason to think that the prosecutors' racist conduct thereby reconstitutes the character of the African American community as more racist.

[24] Given the radical disparity between the actual and the ideal in prosecutorial practices and criminal justice systems more generally noted by Duff (n 16 above), it is unlikely that any prosecutor acts on behalf of (represents) every member of her political community.

[25] I take this point to be consistent with J Raz, 'The problem of authority: Revisiting the service conception' (2006) 90 Minn L Rev 1003, 1041–4, when he notes that '[legitimate] authorities' actions are our actions'.

[26] RA Duff and others (n 21 above) 4. The actions of a community are, of course, constituted by more than simply the actions of its prosecutors—eg, even within the criminal justice system, the actions of witnesses, judges, juries, etc constitute (in part) the community's actions—and moreover, of course, communities act in a myriad of ways unrelated to the criminal justice system.

[27] Prosecutors also engage in prosecutorial belief formation, testing, maintenance, etc, but for the sake of simplicity here, we will refer to both prosecutorial action and belief as prosecutorial action, and will not address the special problems of belief formation, testing, maintenance, etc.

[28] Compare an account of prosecutorial action which includes investigations in D Richman and W Stuntz, 'Al Capone's revenge: An essay on the political economy of pretexual prosecution' (2005) 105 Columbia L Rev 583. My account is consistent with the 'traditional model ... [in which] prosecutors prosecute and investigators investigate'. D Richman and others, 'Panel discussion: The expanding prosecutorial role from trial counsel to investigator and administrator' (1999) 26 Fordham Urban LJ 679, 680–1. Thus, where police are granted authority to make charging decisions, such situations are best understood as police acting *qua* prosecutors.

[29] Thus the prosecutor's potential role in sentencing and appellate proceedings will not be considered.

1. Two kinds of prosecutorial action

Prosecutorial actions come in two flavours: pursuit and non-pursuit. Acts of prosecutorial *pursuit* are those which initiate criminal cases and move them towards conviction. Such actions include filing criminal charges and conducting trials, etc. Acts of prosecutorial *non-pursuit* prevent the initiation of criminal cases and impede conviction. Such actions include declining an opportunity to file criminal charges (ie, 'no-charging') and dismissing pending charges before or during trial. Some prosecutorial actions, such as engaging in plea negotiations, display a mix of pursuit and non-pursuit qualities.

Two benefits flow from distinguishing these types of prosecutorial action. First, the distinction highlights the fact that prosecutors do more than simply prosecute: sometimes they choose *not* to prosecute. Either way, prosecutors act qua prosecutors, whether they prosecute or not. This point is often obscured in discussions of prosecutorial action because, in common usage, the term 'prosecution' is associated with only the pursuit form of prosecutorial action: 'the action of pursuing; a literal pursuit, chase, or hunting'.[30] By distinguishing prosecutorial actions of pursuit (eg, charging) from prosecutorial actions of non-pursuit (eg, dismissing), we avoid the limiting confusion that prosecutors act qua prosecutors only when they are in their 'attack dog' mode. To the contrary, prosecutors act qua prosecutors equally so whether on the attack, abeyance, or outright retreat.

The second benefit to be gained from characterizing prosecutorial actions in terms of pursuit and non-pursuit is to limit the universe of actions which are properly understood as prosecutorial actions. Actions that lack the character of being either pursuit or non-pursuit actions are not prosecutorial actions, for they do not involve the prosecutor acting qua prosecutor. Rather, they involve people who happen to be employed as prosecutors acting in another role—eg, in their personal capacity, or in a professional capacity that is only contingently associated with and is conceptually distinct from their prosecutorial role. For example, in the course of a typical day, prosecutors frequently engage in actions that are not prosecutorial actions. Some obvious examples occur in every workplace and include things such as taking toilet breaks and telling jokes to colleagues. Clearly, when prosecutors perform these acts, they do not act qua prosecutors but rather act in their personal capacity. Less obvious examples include prosecutors speaking at press conferences, developing public information campaigns, organizing papers within case files, scheduling hearing times on the court's docket, and interviewing alleged victims and witnesses. The first two involve prosecutors acting in a professional capacity, but in a role that is distinct from their prosecutorial role. We might refer to the role fulfilled by the prosecutor in undertaking these actions as that of a 'public information minister', 'public education liaison', etc;

---

[30] Oxford English Dictionary Online (1989) 'pursuit' <http://dictionary.oed.com> accessed 7 April 2007.

but it would be a mistake to think of a prosecutor speaking at a press conference or developing public information campaigns as acting qua prosecutor in so doing. People employed as prosecutors may engage in such actions, but when they do so they are not engaged in *prosecutorial action*.

The examples of organizing papers within case files and scheduling hearing times on the court's docket point to the sense in which prosecutors occasionally act in an administrative capacity. These actions are the type that many office workers find themselves busy with throughout the work day, and yet in performing these actions, prosecutors are not acting in their principal professional roles. Recognition of this role-distinction is the reason why newly hired attorneys often grumble when made to spend all day in front of the photocopier: the oft heard complaint, 'I thought I was hired as a lawyer, not a secretary!' reflects this role-distinction in practice.

The more difficult example is that of interviewing alleged victims and witnesses. When such interviews are conducted in order to decide whether to bring charges against an alleged offender, they have an investigative character. In investigative interviews, prosecutors are properly understood to be acting in a pre-accusatory (pre-prosecutorial) context, wherein the issue of pursuit or non-pursuit has not yet ripened. In this context, prosecutors are best understood to be acting not qua prosecutors, but rather to be acting in a distinct but related role of investigator.[31] However, when such interviews are conducted in order to decide whether to continue existing charges against an alleged offender, to revisit a previous decision not to charge a defendant, or to prepare a victim or witness for trial testimony, they are properly included within the scope of prosecutorial action because they directly affect decisions of pursuit/non-pursuit.

2. Prosecutorial action and character

In order to explain the connection suggested above between prosecutorial action and the character of a state (and community), I will note some basic assumptions regarding the concept of character which inform this work and explore the relationship between character and prosecutorial action. First, I assume that it makes sense to understand actions as capable of possessing character; which is to say that I believe we can usefully employ the notion of 'the character of an action'. Thus, for example, lying is not merely *evidence* of a dishonest character trait; a lie can itself be understood to possess the character of being dishonest. The character of an action is constituted by the thoughts, attitudes, and motivations that dispose the agent to engage in actions of that particular character. Disposition to engage in actions of a particular character consist of 'dispositions to think in certain ways, to notice certain things, to see certain considerations as reasons for action, and to see (or not to see) certain actions as options.'[32]

---

[31] Richman and others (n 28 above) 680–1.
[32] RA Duff, 'Choice, character, and criminal liability' (1993) 12 Law and Philosophy 345, 366.

Closely related to this point is my second assumption: actions are constitutive of character traits. This claim is, however, distinct from my first insofar as it enables us to make sense of the way in which honest, generous, courageous, etc actions *relate* to honest, generous, courageous, etc character traits: namely, such actions *constitute* the corresponding character traits (ie, the relationship between the action and the character trait is constitutive). These first two assumptions reflect my rejection of Hume's claim that actions serve merely as evidence (signs) of character.[33] On my account, actions are constitutive of character traits and, moreover, a character trait cannot be said to exist without being constituted through action.[34]

There is some debate in the literature regarding whether a character trait can be said to exist absent actions which possess the corresponding character: so, for example, whether it can be said that someone is courageous on the basis of his thoughts, attitudes, and motivations, even if he never acts in a courageous manner (perhaps, for example, because he is never presented with an opportunity to act courageously). I do not wish to enter this thicket here; but suffice it to say that I shall endorse a view advocated by Antony Duff:

> The point about someone who has not yet faced a situation that calls for courage is *not* that we do not yet know whether he is courageous: rather, *there is as yet no fact of the matter to be known*... Rather, the conduct is itself an essential aspect of the character-trait... The action completes a picture that is incomplete without it.[35]

My third assumption is that it makes sense to understand groups of people, such as states and communities, as capable of possessing character traits: we can usefully employ the notions of 'the character of state' and 'the character of a community'.[36] It might be thought that this assumption is implausible because character is constituted not *only* through actions, but *also* through

---

[33] D Hume, *A Treatise on Human Nature* (4th edn, London: Penguin, 1985) 478. Claire Finkelstein seems to endorse an even more extreme separation between action and character when she claims that we can 'evaluate the person's action in isolation from facts about him that might explain why he behaved as he did'. C Finkelstein, 'Excuses and dispositions in criminal law' (2002) 6 Buffalo Crim L Rev 317, 326. While it is true that Jonathan Herring and I have previously endorsed the view that actions can be evaluated as prima facie wrongs in isolation from facts that might explain why the action was performed (see, MM Dempsey and J Herring, 'Why sexual penetration requires justification' (2007) 27 OJLS 467), Finkelstein seems to go even further and suggest that a more robust evaluation of action is possible without taking account of such facts; and it is this point I reject.

[34] I make no claim to the originality of my account and acknowledge my indebtedness to Duff (n 32 above).

[35] Duff (n 32 above) 372 (emphasis added).

[36] D Hume, 'Of national characters' in E Miller (ed), *Essays: Moral, political and literary* (Rev edn, Indianapolis: Liberty, 1985). Clearly my account of character, and thus national character, differs from Hume's, and it is not clear to me how he understands the notion of 'the character of a nation' whilst denying that character is constituted through action. Perhaps he uses the phrase rhetorically or endorses the view that nations have the sorts of moral dispositions required to constitute character traits. Nonetheless, my account of group character does bear some resemblance to Hume's insofar as we both agree that individual members of a group need not possess the character

thoughts, attitudes, and motivations—and since neither states nor communities have thoughts, attitudes, or motivations, then we might question whether states and communities have characters in the same way that people have characters.[37]

A number of responses to this concern are available. First, I could claim that when I write of 'the character of a state' and 'the character of a community', I am merely using the term 'character' in a rhetorical sense.[38] Second, I could deny any relationship between thoughts, attitudes, and motivations on the one hand, and character on the other. Third, I could claim that the state and community do indeed have thoughts, attitudes, and motivations. The first response strikes me as unsatisfying and the latter two as implausible. Instead, I will admit that character is constituted not *only* through actions but *also* through thoughts, attitudes, and motivations; and I will further admit that states and communities do not have thoughts, attitudes, or motivations.

But if both of these points are conceded, how can I make sense of the notion that states and communities have characters? The answer, I believe, lies in the relationship between all of these concepts. Thoughts, attitudes, and motivations give rise to dispositions to engage in actions: actions which possess a given character.[39] Admittedly, only individuals can have thoughts, attitudes, and motivations in the relevant sense, and thus only individuals can have dispositions to act in the relevant sense. However, where these dispositions exist, the corresponding actions can be performed by an agent in her individual capacity and/or by an agent in her capacity as representative of a group (state, community, etc). When the agent acts as a representative of a group, her actions thereby constitute the character of the group. For example, performing generous actions qua individual constitutes the character of the individual as a generous person; whilst performing generous actions qua representative of a group constitutes the character of that group as generous.[40]

The claim that character is constituted by action, when framed this way, does not deny the relevance of thoughts, attitudes, and motivations to constituting character; but neither does it suppose that thoughts, attitudes, and motivations

---

trait attributable to the group (or at least not to the same extent), and that geographical boundaries do not determine the character of a people.

[37] My thanks to Victor Tadros for bringing this issue to my attention.

[38] Compare my (limited) use of the term 'inequality' in a rhetorical sense at Chapter 7, section E.2.

[39] For example, courageous thoughts, attitudes, and motivations give rise to dispositions to engage in courageous actions.

[40] I suspect these are not mutually exclusive categories, so that engaging in actions qua representative of a group not only constitutes the character of that group but also constitutes the character of the individual so acting. So, for example, the fact that the actions of Nazi soldiers (qua Nazi soldiers) constituted the character of Nazi Germany as cruel, anti-semetic, etc does not preclude the possibility (indeed, I would think the likelihood) that such actions also constituted the character of those soldiers qua individuals as cruel, anti-semetic, etc. Thus, the notion of 'simply doing ✦ one's job' cannot entirely prevent the moral stain that comes with such actions.

are *directly* relevant to constituting characters. Rather, it is possible (and I think more plausible) to suppose that actions constitute characters directly, whilst thoughts, attitudes, and motivations play an indirect role, constituting the character of the actions through the mediating role of dispositions.

One final assumption I will make regarding character and action is that in order to constitute a character trait, the relevant actions must be *habituated*.[41] One comes to possess the character traits of honesty, generosity, and courageousness only through habitually engaging in honest, generous, and courageous actions. Non-habituated acts of honesty, generosity, or courageousness do not an honest, generous, or courageous character make.[42] Moreover, importantly, habituation does not suggest a mindless repetition but instead an engaged and active exercise of practical reason toward the cultivation of character.[43]

Bearing all of this in mind then, I can now draw the following conclusions regarding prosecutorial action and character. Habituated prosecutorial actions constitute the character of the prosecutor's state, and if political legitimacy conditions adhere, they can also constitute the character of the prosecutor's community. This is not to say that the character of a state or community is constituted *in full* by prosecutorial actions, for clearly other agents' actions constitute the character of the state or community in part as well. Rather, my point here is simply that one thing prosecutors do is to constitute, through their habituated actions, the character of the groups they represent. It is hoped that the preceding discussion has made it a bit more clear precisely what this claim entails (and does not entail).

C. Conclusion

This chapter has briefly unpacked the role of prosecutor and the nature of prosecutorial action. I will return to these issues in more detail in subsequent chapters, but it is hoped that this skeletal outline has provided a sufficiently clear account of what I mean to take under consideration when I purport to consider the issue of prosecution. In sum, I have offered an account of prosecutorial action as, simply put, what prosecutors do qua prosecutors. When a prosecutor acts qua prosecutor, she acts as a representative of the state.[44] This point is important because it means that when a prosecutor acts qua prosecutor, the state

---

[41] N Sherman, *The Fabric of Character: Aristotle's theory of virtue* (Oxford: OUP, 1989) 176–83.

[42] In the next chapter, I will identify a value which corresponds to the constitution of valuable character traits (constitutive value). In identifying constitutive value, I do not mean to deny the value of acting honestly, generously, or courageously (or the disvalue of acting dishonestly, selfishly, cowardly) even where such actions are non-habituated (and thereby non-constitutive of character).

[43] Sherman (n 41 above) 176–83.

[44] 'State' here refers to the relevant unit of government represented by the prosecutor.

itself engages in that action.[45] In other words, prosecutors are state actors, and prosecutorial action is (one kind of) state action.[46]

With this broad outline as a starting point, the next two chapters turn to the issues of prosecutorial value and practical reason. These issues are of central importance to my inquiry, given two key assumptions which underpin what follows. First, I shall assume that when prosecutors engage in prosecutorial actions (of either the pursuit or non-pursuit variety), they should do so in accordance with practical reason. That is simply to say that prosecutors should reason about whether to pursue or not to pursue a given prosecution, and they should act (so far as reason will take them) in accordance with what reason would have them do.

In order to engage in practical reasoning when engaged in prosecutorial action, prosecutors must recognize and seek to act in accordance with the reasons that apply to them. But how is one to identify the reasons that apply to prosecutors? This question leads us to the second assumption which underpins my approach in what follows. I shall assume the truth of what I will call the 'normal correspondence thesis': in the normal course of things, the fact that A's engaging in action (X) can realize value (V) provides a reason for A to engage in X. In other words, values normally correspond to reasons, and conversely, reasons normally track values.[47] I will explore this thesis in more detail in Chapter 5, but it will suffice for now to note that if this thesis is true, then it follows that an attempt to identify the reasons that apply to prosecutors should begin by identifying the values that can be secured through prosecutorial action.

---

[45] This point assumes a minimal degree of legitimacy enjoyed by the criminal justice system in the relevant state. In unstable and/or transitional states, it may not be entirely clear to what extent, if at all, prosecutors act on behalf of the state. See discussion at text surrounding nn 14–26 above.

[46] *Massey* (1927) RIAA iv 155, cited in Brownlie (n 14 above) 450–1.

[47] This account is broadly consistent with J Gardner and T Macklem, 'Reasons' in J Coleman and S Shapiro (eds), *The Oxford Handbook of Jurisprudence and Philosophy of Law* (Oxford: OUP, 2002). It is also consistent with the general correspondence between reason and value assumed in Joseph Raz's early work. J Raz, *Practical Reason and Norms* (2nd edn, New York: OUP, 1999) 24–5. In later work, Raz leaves open the question of whether all values provide reasons for action. J Raz, *Engaging Reason* (New York: OUP, 1999) 252. On my account, normally, they do; but as discussed below, one way in which roles can affect practical reasons is by disrupting the normal correspondence between reason and value. See Chapter 5, Section B.

4

Prosecutorial Action and Value

This chapter identifies some of the values that can be realized through prosecutorial pursuit and non-pursuit actions. Prosecutorial actions can, of course, realize a myriad of values, and this chapter aims to identify some such values and organize our discussion of them so that we may understand more clearly the relationship between these values and the reasons they generate (or fail to generate) for prosecutors. I begin by identifying various ways in which prosecutorial actions might relate to value.[1] After drawing a preliminary distinction between *consequential* relationships to value and *intrinsic* relationships to value, I conclude that prosecutorial action is capable of relating to value in either or both ways. Stated somewhat differently, prosecutorial actions can have consequential value, intrinsic value, or both.[2]

Briefly, my account of prosecution and value proceeds as follows. The consequential value of prosecutorial action is the value such action has in virtue of its actual or expected consequences; whilst the intrinsic value of prosecutorial action is the value such action has that is *not* the value of its actual or expected consequences. Within the category of intrinsic value, I distinguish four types of value: telic, expressive, retributive, and constitutive. The telic value of prosecutorial action is the value such action has insofar as it attempts to secure valuable consequences, even when those consequences are neither expected nor actually realized (eg, the value of near-futile attempts). The expressive value of prosecutorial action is understood herein as the value such action has insofar as it denounces wrongdoing or exonerates the blameless. The retributive value of prosecutorial action is the value such action has insofar as it imposes suffering upon wrongdoers commensurate to their wrongdoing. Finally, the constitutive value of prosecutorial action is the value such actions have insofar as they constitute valuable character traits in the prosecutor's state and/or community. This account of prosecutorial value,

---

[1] I mean to include both positive and negative aspects of value, so prosecutorial action may realize (positive) value or (negative) value. Generally in what follows, I use the term 'value' to cover both the positive and negative. Where relevant, I will specify negative value by using the term 'disvalue'.

[2] I suppose that some prosecutorial actions might also be devoid of value (ie, fail to realize either positive-value or disvalue), but such instances would be exceptional and I will not consider them here.

it is hoped, will lay the groundwork for an account of prosecutorial practical reasoning in the next chapter.

A. Prosecution and Consequential Value

The consequential value of prosecutorial action is the value that such action has in virtue of its actual or expected consequences. In other words, the relationship between the prosecutorial action and the value realized is a consequential relationship.[3] Often this type of value is referred to as 'instrumental value' rather than consequential value, but I decline to adopt this usage here because I think it generates some confusion. For example, Joseph Raz, whose account of value I otherwise endorse, uses the term 'instrumentally valuable' to refer both to something that 'derives its value from the value of its consequences' and something 'that derives [its value] from the fact that it makes certain consequences more likely'.[4] It is not clear to me what Raz means in the first formulation. He could mean that something is instrumentally valuable insofar as it derives its value from its *actual* consequences, or (more broadly) from its *actual or expected* consequences. I take him to endorse the latter meaning (and it is this formulation I adopt in describing that which is consequentially valuable). But a formulation of instrumental value that incorporates *expected* value is significantly different than a formulation stated in the second quote from Raz, where he claims that something is intrinsically valuable insofar as it derives its value from the fact that it makes certain consequences *more likely*.[5] Surely an action may be *expected* to realize a given consequence without actually making that consequence *more likely*, and conversely, an action may make a given consequence more likely without that consequence being expected. To avoid this confusion, I will decline to adopt Raz's concept of instrumental value and will limit my account here to consequential value, which shall be understood as the value an action has in virtue of its actual or expected consequences.[6]

Prosecutorial actions can, of course, have consequential value; for example, they might result in the conviction and subsequent punishment of the guilty,[7] reduction in crime,[8] reduced fear of crime, etc. Indeed, the most widely cited

---

[3] Christine Korsgaard refers to this relationship as an extrinsic relationship. C Korsgaard, 'Two distinctions in goodness' (1983) 92 *Philosophical Rev* 169, 170.

[4] J Raz, *The Morality of Freedom* (Oxford: OUP, 1986) 177, 200.

[5] Ibid.

[6] My reasons for rejecting the confusion generated by Raz's use of the term 'instrumental value' will (hopefully) become more apparent in the discussion of telic value below. See section B.1, below.

[7] The punishment envisioned here is the kind meted out by a sentencing judge subsequent to conviction, not the punishment often experienced as part of the experience of being prosecuted itself.

[8] Eg, P Robinson and J Darley, 'Does criminal law deter? A behavioural science investigation' (2004) 24 OJLS 173; P Keenan, 'The new deterrence: Crime and policy in the age of globalization' (2006) 91 Iowa L Rev 505.

account of the purpose of prosecutorial action adopts an exclusive focus on consequential value: the aim of prosecutorial action, it is claimed, is that the guilty shall not escape conviction, nor shall the innocent suffer conviction.[9] And certainly, the belief that prosecutions have consequential value features prominently in the development (or at least marketing) of aggressive prosecutorial policies.[10]

Moral theories that identify right and wrong actions exclusively on the basis of consequential value are consequentialist moral theories, or consequentialism for short. By consequentialism I mean to refer to the proposition, which claims that 'the only reasons for or against the performance of any action are [generated by] the [value of the] consequences that its performance or non-performance will or may have'.[11] I take this proposition to be roughly equivalent to the claim that the only values which generate reasons for or against the performance of an action are those values which are consequentially related to the action in question. In other words, consequentialists reject either the claim that intrinsic (non-consequential) values exist, or the claim that intrinsic values generate reasons for action, or both. The first claim is incoherent; but the second is merely implausible.

The first claim is incoherent because any theory of value, even one which informs a consequentialist moral theory, must give an account of intrinsic value: the value something has that is *not* the value of its consequences. For, in order to understand why something is valuable in virtue of its consequences, we have to give an account of why that thing's consequences are valuable. If we limit our account of value exclusively to consequential values, then the only account we can offer is that the thing's consequences are valuable in virtue of their consequences. And so on, and so on. We can never reference out to a source of intrinsic value to explain why some consequences are valuable. By limiting one's account of value to consequential value (and thus denying the existence of intrinsic value), one cannot give a coherent account of *why* consequences are valuable, and thus cannot give a coherent account of value.

---

[9] *Berger v US* (1935) 294 US 78, 88.

[10] A Little, 'Balancing accountability and victim autonomy at the International Criminal Court' (2007) 38 Georgetown J of Intl L 363, 364, claiming that 'aggressive prosecution policies can provide some measure of deterrence' in domestic-violence cases. Notably, however, the author provides no empirical evidence to back up this claim, citing only one study relating to the deterrent effects of arrest (not prosecution) in domestic-violence cases. Indeed, there appears to be very little in the way of empirical support for the proposition that prosecution itself has any deterrent effect whatsoever on crime generally. The only study I have located directly on this topic concerns domestic-violence prosecution and demonstrates that any deterrent effect seems to arise as a consequence of the victim's degree of control over prosecutorial decisions, rather than the prosecution itself. D Ford and MJ Regoli, 'The preventive impact of policies for prosecuting wife batterers' in E Buzawa and C Buzawa (eds), *Domestic Violence: The criminal justice response* (Thousand Oaks: Sage, 1996). Empirical studies regarding the effect of the criminal law generally provide reason to question whether any purported deterrent effect in fact exists. Robinson and Darley (n 8 above).

[11] Raz (n 4 above) 268.

Even if one acknowledges the existence of intrinsic value, however, one might still make the second consequentialist move by denying the possibility that intrinsic values generate reasons for action and claiming instead that only consequential values generate action reasons. If this claim is true, then consequential value would be the only type of value that matters in evaluating prosecutorial action. All of the reasons that apply to prosecutors would be grounded in consequential values, so whilst intrinsic values may exist, they would not matter in any determination of how prosecutors should act.

But *is* consequential value the only type of value that matters in evaluating prosecutorial action? Surely not. Consider the following example. Donald is charged with a crime. Being charged makes Donald wish to avoid being convicted. In order to avoid being convicted, Donald kills all of the witnesses against him. Donald is acquitted due to lack of evidence. This turn of events emboldens both Donald and other people to commit more offences than they otherwise would have done and, furthermore, to kill the witnesses against them if and when they are charged in those offences. Assume that if Donald had never been charged with the primary offence, he would not have murdered all of those witnesses, he and others would have committed fewer further offences, and the witnesses to any further offences which were committed would not have been murdered. In such a case, the consequential disvalue of prosecuting Donald is clear: it caused an overall increase in both primary crime and witness-murder. Meanwhile, most if not all of the consequential values sought by the prosecution were not realized: Donald was not convicted, he was not punished for his crime, neither he nor others were deterred from further offending, the fear of crime was not reduced, etc. It is of course still possible that some consequential value was realized through prosecuting Donald: perhaps charging Donald with the primary offence caused his primary victim (and/or that victim's family, friends, community, etc) to experience a sense of satisfaction; but even so, we might easily conclude that any value found in their satisfaction is (all consequential values considered) vastly outweighed by the prosecution's consequential disvalue.

If all of this were true, then those who endorse consequentialism would likely conclude that prosecuting Donald was unjustifiable. For this reason, I want to suggest that consequentialist moral theories are not intuitively appealing in evaluating most prosecutorial actions. To illustrate this claim, I will continue considering the prosecution of Donald. The intuitive appeal of relying exclusively on consequentialism in this case depends on the primary offence at issue. If the primary offence Donald was charged with was dropping chewing gum on the pavement, we would likely agree that (given the disastrous consequences of the prosecution) it would have been better not to prosecute Donald in the first place. At first glance, it appears that one can reach this conclusion based solely on consequential moral reasoning, and so the appeal of consequential theories remains untouched. But what if the primary offence Donald was charged with was murder? Would Donald's prosecution still seem unjustifiable? If we believe that actions are valuable only in virtue of their consequences, then we should conclude that the prosecution of Donald for murder is still unjustifiable, since the prosecutorial action (charging) had consequential disvalue (ie, many more murders) which far outweigh the action's consequential value (ie, satisfaction for victim's family, etc).[12] If we resist this conclusion—if we think Donald's prosecution for murder may be justifiable despite its murderous consequences—then we are resisting the intuitive appeal of using exclusively consequentialist moral reasoning in evaluating prosecutorial action.

If the history of organized-crime prosecution is any indication, we often find consequential moral reasoning inadequate when it comes to evaluating the prosecution of serious crimes such as murder. It sometimes seems that prosecutions of organized-crime figures cause more bloodshed than they prevent; yet we often conclude that such prosecutions are justified despite their apparent consequential disvalue. Some folks might find such prosecutions justifiable because they believe the prosecutions are consequentially valuable on the whole or in the long run. Perhaps they believe that organized-crime figures would be even further emboldened to commit murders and other serious crimes if these prosecutions were not undertaken: so, on the whole (so the thought goes), such prosecutions realize more consequential value than disvalue. Or perhaps they believe that the increased bloodshed caused by such prosecutions is the short-term cost we must pay in order to realize the full consequential value of such prosecutions in the long run.

Of course those hopeful folks might be right—maybe things would be much worse if we stopped such prosecutions—or maybe in the long run such prosecutions will make things better than they otherwise would be. This is simply to acknowledge the possibility that apparently consequentially disvaluable prosecutions might actually be consequentially valuable on the whole or in the long run—and thus such prosecutions may be justifiable based solely consequential moral reasoning.

But of course the hopeful folks might be wrong, and if they are, then we have to consider whether actually consequentially disvaluable prosecutions may nonetheless be justifiable. Many less hopeful folks (me included) would conclude that some such prosecutions can be justifiable despite their actual consequential

---

[12] You might think I'm stacking the decks here by ignoring some of the consequential value from Donald's prosecution. Perhaps the consequential value of charging Donald was not merely that the victim's family received satisfaction but further that the community as a whole was made to feel reassured in the knowledge that a suspected murderer was being held to account for his crime. But we can easily imagine that this additional consequential value does not tip the scales of consequential value in favour of prosecution. If, for example, every time a suspected murderer was charged with murder, he or she murdered all of the witnesses in the case and moreover increased the rate of primary murders, any reassurance that members of the wider community might feel as a consequence of the first prosecutions would eventually be diminished as they came to realize the disastrous consequences of such prosecutions. Eventually they would come to feel dread upon learning of further prosecutions (which, *ex hypothesi*, will lead more and more murders). So, in extreme enough circumstances, we can hypothesize a state of affairs in which prosecutions are consequentially disvaluable.

disvalue. Part of the reason one might be tempted to think this way is that we believe prosecutions can have value that is *not* the value of their consequences: such prosecutions can have *intrinsic* value. Moreover, we think that the intrinsic value of such prosecutions (in the right situations) can be weighty enough to out-weigh a prosecution's conceded consequential disvalue.

B. Prosecution and Intrinsic Value

If I am right in thinking that prosecutions can have intrinsic value, then it becomes important to understand what I mean by this claim. It is one thing to provide a general definition of intrinsic value as 'the value that action has which is *not* the value of its actual or expected consequences'; but this is not a terribly illuminating account of intrinsic value. It treats the word 'intrinsic' as mere placeholder for the concept 'non-consequential'. If my claim regarding the intrinsic value of prosecutorial action is to be properly understood, the concept of intrinsic value must be unpacked a bit more. I undertake that project in this section, by providing an account of four distinct types of intrinsic value: telic, expressive, retributive, and constitutive values.

Preliminarily, however, it is important to note (so as to avoid) the temptation to mistake intrinsic value for ultimate value. This mistake is common in accounts of intrinsic value which claim that intrinsic value is the value something has 'per se' or 'in itself'.[13] This mistake is demonstrated, for example, in Robert George's claim that something is 'intrinsically valuable if it provides an ultimate... rea-son for action'.[14] It is of course conceivable that someone might endorse such a proposition, and if so, then I would understand them to be using the label 'intrin-sic value' to refer to ultimate value. There is no *mistake*, exactly, in substituting this usage for the sake of simplicity, when the distinction bears no rational sig-nificance, or when one is attempting to engage with literature that adopts such terminology. But George's conflation of intrinsic value and ultimate value does strike me as a mistake, not least because is gives rise to a misinterpretation of Raz's account of intrinsic value.[15] *Pace* George, I take Raz's account of intrinsic

---

[13] Not all such accounts make the mistake I am about to discuss, however. For example, although Christine Korsgaard claims that intrinsic goodness (value) is the value a thing has 'in itself', she is careful to explain that this claim simply means that the value of the thing does not come from another (extrinsic) source. I take Korsgaard's reference to extrinsic goodness to be roughly equivalent to my use of consequential value and our use of intrinsic value to be roughly similar. Korsgaard (n 3 above) 170.

[14] R George, *Making Men Moral* (Oxford: Clarendon, 1993) 178.

[15] Specifically, George cites Raz in support of his claim captured in the quotation above. George's misreading of Raz, if indeed it is one, seems to have been influenced by Donald Regan's critique of *The Morality of Freedom*. D Regan, 'Authority and value: Reflections on Raz's *The Morality of Freedom*' (1989) 62 Southern Cal L Rev 995.

value (which I endorse) to draw a sharp distinction between intrinsic value and ultimate value:

> Something is intrinsically good or valuable if it is valuable independently of the value of its actual or probable consequences... But not everything which is intrinsically valuable is also of ultimate value.[16]

Rather, for Raz, something is of ultimate value only if it is both intrinsically valuable *and* if its 'value need not be explained or be justified by reference to ([its] contribution to) other values'.[17]

With this confusion avoided, I can now give an account of some different types of intrinsic value that can, in principle, be realized through prosecutorial action. Two points bear noting before I proceed. First, none of the intrinsic values I discuss below should be understood as ultimate values; rather, each is conditional in some sense, and these conditions require explanation. Second, the list of intrinsic values I discuss below is not exhaustive: additional kinds of intrinsic values may be realized through prosecutorial action. However, I will limit my concern to these four types of intrinsic value because I believe they are best suited to explaining the kinds of reasons that apply to prosecutors both generally and in the particular case of domestic-violence prosecutions.

1. Telic value

Irrespective of whether a prosecutorial action actually achieves or is expected to achieve a valuable consequence, it may nonetheless count as an *attempt* to secure valuable consequences. Such an attempt (even if it fails) has intrinsic value: it has a value that is not the value of its actual or expected consequences.[18] The relationship between prosecutorial action and value in the case of attempts is what I will call a telic relationship: the prosecutorial action *aims* at achieving a consequential value, without necessarily achieving it or even expecting that it will be achieved.[19] Correspondingly, I will refer to the type of intrinsic value realized in such attempts as *telic value*.

---

[16] Raz (n 4 above) 200, 177, respectively.

[17] Raz (n 4 above) 200.

[18] If the attempt succeeds, then it has both intrinsic (telic) value (qua attempt) and consequential value.

[19] Conversely, an action which achieves a valuable consequence bears a consequential relationship to that value, irrespective of whether the actor aimed at achieving the valuable consequence. Gardner illustrates this point with the example of phoning his mother on her birthday, by relating the action of dialling his mother's phone number to the value of talking to his mother on her birthday. Dialling his mother's phone number may be consequentially valuable, if he actually succeeds in talking to his mother, or if talking to his mother is an expected consequence of his action. He can realize this consequential value through his action, however, even if his action does not amount to an attempt to talk to his mother (eg, if he accidentally dials her number whilst trying to order a pizza). On my account, dialling his mother's phone number in an *attempt* to talk to his mother is intrinsically valuable, even if he never actually succeeds in talking to her and even if it is not expected that he will talk to her (eg, if she is out and her mobile gets spotty reception). His

It is important to note the precise meaning of the term 'telic' as I use it. Often, telic is meant to refer to the relationship between an action and its actual or expected consequences,[20] or what I have referred to as a consequential relationship between action and value. A telic relationship, as I use that term here, refers to the relationship between an action and its aimed-for but not necessarily achieved or even expected consequences.

In order for an action to bear a telic relationship to value, it must be *possible* for that action to achieve valuable consequences, and this possibility must be recognized by the actor.[21] This insight can be broken down into three propositions. First, for an act to have telic value, it must amount to an attempt to achieve a given consequence. If an actor believes that a given consequence is wholly unachievable from her action, then her action cannot conceivably amount to an attempt to achieve that consequence.[22] Second, for an act to have telic value, it actually must be possible for the attempt to succeed. Gardner offers an example of an attempt doomed to fail in which he, a non-swimmer, stands on a cliff top, watching a man drown in a stormy sea below.[23] Assuming Gardner's attempt to save the man cannot possibly succeed, his attempt cannot have telic value. This is not to say, however, that he cannot attempt to save the man. So long as he believes there is some possibility of success (even if he is wrong), then he can still try to save the drowning man (even if his trying is in fact doomed to fail). In such case, his act may have expressive value, but it will not have telic value.[24] Third, for an act to have telic value, the attempted consequences must be valuable. There is no telic value in trying to do wrong;[25] rather, the telic value of the attempt is parasitic to the value of the aimed-for consequences.

Prosecutorial action has telic value when it aims to achieve a valuable consequence, and it is at least possible that the prosecutorial action might contribute to

attempt is intrinsically valuable, because while it is valuable, its value is not the value of its actual or expected consequences. If his mother complains that he did not ring her on her birthday, he can point to his attempt to ring her in justifying his conduct: eg, 'I tried to ring you all day, but I couldn't reach you!' The only reason it makes sense to point to his attempts in his defence is because these attempts have value which is not the value of their consequences. J Gardner, 'The wrongdoing that gets results' (2004) 18 *Philosophical Perspectives* 53, 54–5.

[20] My use of 'telic' is similar to the sense in which Christine Korsgaard uses the term 'teleological' in C Korsgaard, 'Teleological ethics' in E Craig (ed), *Routledge Encyclopedia of Philosophy* (London: Routledge, 1998) <http://www.rep.routledge.com//> accessed 14 November 2008.

[21] However, this is not to say that the actor must expect the consequence. One who recognizes X as a possible, albeit wildly unlikely, consequence of one's action does not *expect* X to follow as a consequence of the action.

[22] 'Someone who recognizes that his trying will not contribute to his succeeding cannot conceivably try.' Gardner (n 19 above) 57.

[23] Ibid.

[24] As Gardner notes, futile attempts might still have expressive value, such as the value of 'express[ing] undying love for the drowning man in an act of futile self-sacrifice'. Gardner (n 19 above) 57.

[25] Attempting to do wrong has telic disvalue. Moreover, if you attempt to do wrong and succeed in doing wrong, then your action has both telic disvalue (qua an attempt to do wrong) and consequential disvalue (qua an action with wrongful consequences).

securing those consequences. For example, assuming that it is valuable to convict criminal wrongdoers, the action of charging a defendant with an offence has telic value if: (1) it is done in an attempt to secure the defendant's conviction; (2) the defendant is in fact a criminal wrongdoer; and (3) it is at least possible that charging him will contribute to his conviction. If all of these conditions apply, then the act of charging has telic value, even if the defendant is not in fact convicted and it is not expected that he will be convicted. So, for example, even if a federal US prosecution brought in response to a racist lynching did not result in conviction and was not expected to result in conviction, it would nonetheless bear telic value as an attempt to secure a conviction.[26]

2. Expressive value

Expressive value is perhaps the most obvious places to look for intrinsic value in prosecutorial action, as the expressive function of the criminal justice system has generated a wide literature, and underlying these accounts is the assumption that prosecutorial action can and often does have expressive value.[27] Two points of clarification should be noted at the outset. First, what I label 'expressive value' is roughly equivalent to what Raz discusses in the context of 'symbolic reasons' (what I assume he would call 'symbolic value' if he were to phrase the point in terms of value rather than reason).[28] Second, although my choice to use the term 'expressive' conflicts with Duff's use of the term 'communicative', our understandings of these terms are largely (but perhaps not entirely) consistent. As Duff has correctly noted, '[e]xpression requires only one who expresses', whereas communication implies a 'reciprocal and rational engagement' between one who expresses and one who responds.[29] I interpret his point to mean that communication requires both an action by the initial expressive agent and an action by the responding agent; without both actions, there is no communication.

On my account then, communication is best understood as a consequential value of prosecutorial action. A prosecutorial action (say, charging) is the initial action, whilst the response (say, the defendant's plea) is a consequence of that prosecutorial action. Duff, however, seems to imply that communication can exist simply in virtue of an expression which *aims* to engage the respondent as an active participant in communication. As he puts it, 'communication requires

---

[26] Note that the telic value identified here is distinct from the other kinds of intrinsic value (eg, expressive, constitutive value) that may be realized by such prosecutions.

[27] Eg, J Feinberg, 'The expressive function of punishment' in J Feinberg, *Doing and Deserving: Essays in the theory of responsibility* (Princeton: Princeton University Press, 1970) 95–118; J Hampton, 'The moral education theory of punishment' (1984) 13 *Philosophy and Public Affairs* 208; J Hampton, 'Punishment, feminism, and political identity: A case study in the expressive meaning of the law' (1998) 11 Canadian Journal of Law and Jurisprudence 23.

[28] J Raz, *The Authority of Law* (Oxford: OUP, 1979) 255–6.

[29] RA Duff, *Punishment, Communication and Community* (Oxford: OUP, 2001) 79.

someone to or with whom we *try* to communicate'.[30] I find this conceptualization of communication perplexing. If we *try* to do something, it must be conceptually possible for us to fail in doing that thing.[31] If we *try* to communicate with someone and fail, then we have not communicated. So whilst I agree that communication requires someone to or with whom we try to communicate, I would add the further condition that communication requires that our attempt to communicate succeed. If we succeed in communicating, the value of communication strikes me as consequentially related to prosecutorial action, whereas if we fail, the value of communication strikes me as bearing a telic relationship to prosecutorial action. Either way, I do not conceive of communication as an intrinsic value of prosecutorial action. This point, of course, is not intended to deny the significant value of communication in the criminal justice process; it is merely to clarify my understanding of how best to provide an account of this concept.

Returning to expressive value directly then, it is evident that prosecutorial action serves an expressive function. For example, charging (a form of prosecutorial pursuit action) serves the expressive function of denunciation. 'Denunciation' is preferred here over the term 'condemnation' insofar as denunciation connotes an accusatorial stance, preliminary in nature and open to revision; whereas condemnation connotes finality more appropriate to the expressive meaning of conviction. As such, denunciation is, I believe, the more appropriate concept for capturing the nature of prosecutorial pursuit actions such as charging. As Duff has noted, a 'criminal indictment... is an institutional analogue of a moral accusation'.[32]

The expressive value of prosecutorial pursuit action lies in its denunciation of wrongdoing and wrongdoers.[33] Charging a defendant with murder, for example, denounces murder as wrong and denounces the defendant as a wrongdoer. If murder *is* wrong, then denouncing it *as* wrong is expressively valuable. Even if the charging has no consequential value, it may still have intrinsic value in virtue of its expressive function of denunciation. Even if murders do not decrease, even if no one ever comes to recognize the wrongness of murder, even if fear of being murdered continues unabated, the intrinsic expressive value of denouncing murder as wrong subsists. If the defendant *is* a wrongdoer, then denouncing him *as* a wrongdoer is also intrinsically valuable. Even if he does not change his ways, even if no one else recognizes that he is a wrongdoer, even if he does not suffer as a result of being denounced, the intrinsic expressive value of denouncing him as a wrongdoer subsists. On the flipside, if we assume (as I do) that exonerating

---

[30] Ibid.

[31] J Gardner, 'Law's aim in law's empire' in S Hershovitz (ed), *Exploring Law's Empire* (Oxford: OUP, 2006) 216.

[32] RA Duff, *Trials and Punishment* (Cambridge: Cambridge University Press, 1986) 116.

[33] This point assumes that it is intrinsically valuable to denounce wrongdoing and wrongdoers. Such intrinsic value is, of course, conditional on the charged offence being an instance of moral wrongdoing and the defendant being a culpable wrongdoer.

the innocent is intrinsically valuable, then prosecutorial non-pursuit actions possess intrinsic expressive value in cases where the conduct that could have been charged is in fact not wrongful[34] and/or where the potential defendant is not a culpable wrongdoer.[35]

But how much value does expression have? How are we to understand this value? One promising line of thought is that the value of denouncing wrongdoing and wrongdoers is a close cousin of the moral value of truth-telling. Telling the truth has value that is not the value of its consequences. But depending on the circumstances, telling the truth may not have a great deal of intrinsic value. It all depends on what one is telling the truth about. For example, when I am visited by a friend who comes to meet my new baby, and she declares, 'Wow, you still look as pregnant as the day you gave birth!', she might be speaking the truth—but it's a cruel truth; and the intrinsic value of her truth-telling is easily outweighed by the disvalue of her cruelty—which is simply to say that some truths are not valuable enough to bother telling, all things considered.

But when it comes to crime, telling the truth (through denunciation of wrongdoing) arguably has more significant intrinsic value. Of course, as with truth-telling, it all depends on the nature of wrongdoing and wrongdoers that we denounce. The more wrongful the wrongdoing and wrongdoers, the more intrinsic value there is in denouncing them. Return for a moment to the prosecution of Donald, which had the disastrous consequence of causing many more primary crimes to be committed and gave rise to a multitude of attendant witness-murders. I hypothesized two different primary offences Donald might have committed: dropping chewing gum on the pavement or murder. Assuming that both offences are wrongful, it is intrinsically valuable to denounce both. But assuming that murder is *more* wrongful than dropping chewing gum, it is *more* intrinsically valuable to denounce Donald in the murder prosecution—which is simply to acknowledge the fact that the intrinsic value of denouncing wrongdoing does not serve to justify every prosecution of wrongful conduct. Sometimes it is best to let relatively less wrongful conduct go un-denounced rather than to invite disvaluable consequences. But if Donald's primary offence was murder, then we must decide whether the intrinsic value of denunciation outweighs the consequential disvalue of the prosecution. Even in the case of murder, the suggestion seems implausible. Whilst it is good to denounce wrongdoing, is it not better

---

[34] Consider a jurisdiction in which homosexual sex is criminalized. Assuming (as I do) that this conduct is *not* morally wrongful, then prosecutorial non-pursuit actions which decline to charge people with this offence, despite the legal availability of the charge, is expressively valuable for that reason alone.

[35] This situation could arise either when the potential defendant is factually innocent in the sense that 'they got the wrong guy', or where the potential defendant committed the elements of the criminal offence, but was not morally culpable in so doing (eg, self-defence cases). With these conditions met, prosecutorial non-pursuit actions in such cases (eg, declining to file charges against such potential defendants) are therefore expressively valuable.

to prevent further such wrongdoing? If we have to choose between the two, we might reasonably find that the truth would be better left unsaid.[36]

Before leaving the topic of expressive value, it is important to note the ways in which telic values are both similar to and distinct from expressive values in prosecutions. Telic and expressive values are similar insofar as both are intrinsic values (ie, they have a value that is not the value of their consequences).[37] They are importantly distinct, however, insofar as either can be realized independently in any given prosecution. For example, a criminal prosecution may be expressively valuable insofar as it denounces a wrongful murder, irrespective of whether it has any telic value as an attempt to convict the murderer.[38] From this we can conclude that a prosecution which amounts to an entirely futile attempt need not lack intrinsic value, since it could have expressive value even though it lacks telic value.[39]

On the flipside, a criminal prosecution may have telic value but lack expressive value. For example, consider again the murder case against Donald, but this time, imagine that the prosecutor opted not to charge Donald and that this decision was made in an attempt to prevent the extra murders that would flow as a consequence from such prosecution. Assuming that it is valuable to prevent murders and that 'no-charging' Donald would at least possibly prevent murders, then 'no-charging' Donald has telic value: it counts as an *attempt* to achieve valuable consequences. However, 'no-charging' a murderer is not expressively valuable, since it fails to denounce wrongdoing. In this case, the prosecutorial action of 'no-charging' has telic value but lacks expressive value.

3. Retributive value

Prosecutorial action has retributive value insofar as it brings suffering upon wrongdoers commensurate to their wrongdoing.[40] Take the Michael Jackson trial

---

[36] This point assumes that expressive value is unlikely on its own to outweigh significant consequential disvalue.

[37] This is not to deny that both telically and expressively valuable actions may be consequentially valuable as well. Most obviously, telically valuable actions are consequentially valuable when they achieve their aimed-for valuable consequences (plus they may be consequentially valuable in virtue of their contribution to the achievement of other valuable consequences that were not aimed for). Also, expressively valuable actions may be consequentially valuable—as when prosecutorial action that denounces wrongdoing has the consequence of convincing wrongdoers to mend their ways.

[38] I suspect this kind of thinking might drive some prosecutors to bring exceptionally weak cases against people whom they believe (on some level) to be innocent, simply for the sake of expressively condemning horrific crimes. I do not mean to suggest that such a prosecution would be justified, all things considered, but merely that it would have some expressive value as a condemnation of a horrific wrong.

[39] Although again, as above, I am doubtful as to whether the expressive value standing alone would carry the day.

[40] For discussions of retribution as a guiding principle in sentencing and as a general theory of criminal law, see respectively, A von Hirsch, *Past or Future Crimes: Deservedness and dangerousness*

for example, and grant the twin assumptions that Jackson did the things that he was alleged to have done, and that he did so without justification or excuse (that he was, in other words, 'factually guilty').[41] Of course, in the end he was acquitted. The question therefore arises: given the acquittal, what, if any, value was there in the prosecutors pursuing this case?[42]

Aside from the possible telic and expressive values (and indeed, perhaps consequential values) that might have been realized, we must consider a separate category of intrinsic value that was almost definitely served in the Jackson case: the retributive value found in suffering by wrongdoers. Whether this value was realized through the prosecutorial action in this case is contingent upon a number of factors. First, in order for any retributive value to have been realized through Jackson's prosecution, we would have to assume that he was factually guilty and moreover that he was morally culpable for his conduct (for, if these conditions were not satisfied, then no retributive value can have been realized through his prosecution) Next, we would have to assume that Jackson suffered what Malcolm Feeley has called 'the process as punishment'.[43] Now, for those who followed the events surrounding the prosecution, there can be little doubt that if anyone has ever suffered the process as punishment, Michael Jackson surely did.[44] Finally, the retributive value, if any, in his suffering extends only so far as it is commensurate to his wrongdoing, by which I mean suffering up to the point that is deserved and no further. If we assume that there is value in wrongdoers suffering commensurate to their wrongdoing, and if the conditions listed above are satisfied, then Jackson's suffering, which arose as a consequence of the prosecution, had retributive value.[45]

But clearly there is something problematic about the conclusion that using the process as punishment can have value, even when the person being punished is *ex hypothesi* guilty and deserving of punishment. Why is that? There are at least two possible answers to explain the discomfort this conclusion provokes. First, we might be wrong to think there is any value to be realized here. Perhaps those who

in the sentencing of criminals (Manchester: Manchester University Press, 1986); and M Moore, *Placing Blame: A theory of criminal law* (Oxford: Clarendon, 1997).

[41] W Laufer, 'The rhetoric of innocence' (1995) 70 Washington L Rev 329, fn 4. I do not mean to imply that Jackson was factually guilty or impugn the jury's verdict of acquittal in his case. I am simply using Jackson's case as the basis for a hypothetical discussion which seeks to illustrate the nature of retributive value.

[42] Commentary following the acquittal questioned whether the prosecution was 'a complete waste' of prosecutorial resources. 'Editorial' *Daily News* (New York: 14 June 2005).

[43] MM Feeley, *The Process is the Punishment* (New York: Russell Sage, 1979).

[44] JM Broder and N Madigan, 'Michael Jackson cleared after 14-week child molesting trial' (New York Times, online version, posted 14 June 2005) <http://www.nytimes.com/2005/06/14/national/14jackson.html> accessed 3 November 2008, noting that '[o]ver the course of the trial...Mr. Jackson appeared more pale and gaunt with each passing week and was briefly hospitalized several times'.

[45] Again, I am merely assuming Jackson's factual guilt and culpability to illustrate the nature of retributive value. I do not mean to suggest anything regarding the truth of these matters.

endorse the idea of retributive value are simply mistaken: perhaps there really is not any value in wrongdoers suffering commensurate to their wrongdoing. There is, however, a second and (I believe) more plausible explanation for our discomfort: whilst there *is* a value to be realized here (ie, retributive value is genuine value), this value does not generate reasons for prosecutors and thus, this value cannot contribute to the justification of prosecutorial pursuit action. This possibility will be examined further in the next chapter.

4. Constitutive value

A fourth type of intrinsic value that can be realized through prosecutorial action is what I shall call constitutive value. In order to understand the nature of this value, it is necessary first to observe that actions constitute character traits in the actor.[46] The relationship between the actions that constitute a character trait and the character trait itself is not a consequential relationship; it is not as if our actions are merely contingently, consequentially related to our characters. Rather, our actions are constitutive of our characters: ie, the relationship between action and character is constitutive.

Second, some character traits can be valuable: for example, traits such as those typically understood as virtues, including generosity, courage, honesty, etc. When our actions realize valuable character traits, the actions bear constitutive value. Moreover, the value of these character traits is not (only) the value of their consequences. Of course, generosity, courage, honesty, etc may very well have valuable consequences: generosity may have the valuable consequence that a worthy charity is funded; courage may have the valuable consequence of saving a life; honesty may have the valuable consequence of causing someone to disbelieve a harmful lie, etc. But my point here is simply that the consequential value of these character traits is not their only value: they also bear intrinsic value. Indeed, even if these character traits are consequentially *dis*valuable, they still retain intrinsic value.[47] For example, assume that generosity is an intrinsically valuable character trait. If this is so, then *even if* your generosity has bad consequences, it still has intrinsic value.[48] For example, if you routinely donate 15 per cent of your

---

[46] This point will be qualified below in discussing the two further requirements that the actions be habituated and that habituated actions are only character-constituting if they are actions for which we are consequentially responsible.

[47] Conversely, an intrinsically disvaluable (or value-neutral) character trait might have valuable consequences. Imagine that a lazy person wins the lottery. If she were not so pathetically lazy, she would take the money and spend it on fabulous holidays. Instead, because she is so lazy, she never spends any of her winnings and dies a wealthy woman. Her philanthropic children use her lottery winnings to fund research that cures a horribly painful and deadly disease. If our lottery winner had not been so lazy, the disease would never have been cured: thus an intrinsically disvaluable (or perhaps intrinsically value-neutral) character trait (laziness) had valuable consequences (facilitating a cure for the disease).

[48] We would of course wish to know about the consequences in evaluating whether one's conduct is justifiable, all things considered.

earnings[49] to a charity which assists refugee children from war-torn areas, then you are a generous person.[50] But imagine that the charity uses your money to pay the salaries of aid workers who sexually abuse the refugee children. In such case, the consequences of your generous actions are disvaluable, but the consequential disvalue of your generosity does not impugn the intrinsic value of your being generous. You are still a generous person, and that character trait is intrinsically valuable, even if your generosity has bad consequences.[51]

But what does all this have to do with the intrinsic value of prosecution? Prosecutorial actions (like all actions) can constitute character. If prosecutors have a settled tendency to act in a given way in respect of some issue of character, their actions will thereby constitute the corresponding character trait. If prosecutors routinely plea-bargain with white defendants and refuse to do so with non-white defendants, or if they routinely require third-party corroborating testimony before proceeding with the prosecution of rape cases, then certain character traits (racism and sexism respectively) are thereby constituted through those habituated prosecutorial actions.[52]

The insight that habituated prosecutorial actions can constitute such disvaluable character traits is neither surprising nor terribly original: it is a common complaint that prosecutors are sexist and racist (or at least have been sexist and racist historically, or perhaps continue to be sexist and racist in certain places). My point here is that such complaints point to perceived flaws in the prosecuting authorities' characters and are based upon evaluations of the prosecutors' habituated actions.

The observation that prosecutorial actions can constitute character traits is important, however, because prosecutorial actions can constitute (in part) the character of the state and the community. Accepting that communities have characters requires acknowledgement of the fact that, just like individual people,

---

[49] I'm assuming that 15 per cent marks the precise amount that causes you to forgo unnecessary luxuries but does not impose undue hardship upon you or those financially dependent upon you, so that your charitable donations hit the virtuous median between the vicious extremes of stinginess and spendthriftness.

[50] More precisely, you are a generous person with respect to charitable financial giving. You might be a miser or spendthrift when it comes to other matters. You might refuse to take the time to comfort a depressed co-worker, which would make you miserly with your time. You might repeatedly lend household items to neighbours who never return them, which would make you a spendthrift with your personal possessions.

[51] The situation I have in mind here is distinct from Michael Slote's claim regarding 'admirable immoralities'. M Slote, *Goods and Virtues* (Oxford: Clarendon, 1983) ch 4. Slote's argument was directed toward establishing the existence of character traits that themselves have a tendency to cause us to act immorally. In my hypothetical, there is no reason to think that the intrinsically valuable character trait (generosity) has such a tendency. Like Marcia Baron, I think Slote's attempt to defend the existence of admirable immoralities fails because the admirable (valuable) character traits can be conceptually prised from their disvaluable consequences. M Baron, 'On admirable immorality' [1986] *Ethics* 558.

[52] For more of the concept of sexism and how it relates to the broader category of patriarchy, see Chapter 7, section D.2.

communities can be more or less generous, courageous, loyal, trustworthy, arrogant, aggressive, industrious, rude, cooperative, affectionate, etc.

One kind of character trait that is of particular interest in the context of prosecution is the kind that is constituted in an individual or community in virtue of his/her or its response to certain types of wrongdoing. Some individuals and communities respond to some types of wrongdoing appropriately: eg, they denounce and condemn the wrongdoing.[53] Of course, some individuals and communities fail to respond to some types of wrongdoing appropriately. If such inappropriate responses to wrongdoing continue, and the individual or community *habitually* fails (unjustifiably and inexcusably) to denounce and condemn the wrongdoing, then these habituated responses constitute in the individual and society a disvaluable character trait which corresponds to the type of wrongdoing at issue. If, for example, an individual is often faced with colleagues making racist slurs and she habitually fails (unjustifiably and inexcusably) to denounce and condemn such wrongful, racist conduct, her habituated failure constitutes in her a more racist character *ceteris paribus*. Similarly, if a community habitually fails (unjustifiably and inexcusably) to denounce and condemn those who commit racist hate crimes, the community's habituated failure constitutes in that community a more racist character *ceteris paribus*.

It is important to remember that for every such disvaluable character trait that might be constituted in an individual or community, the opposite trait may also be constituted. Habitually denouncing and condemning wrongful actions constitutes in the community a valuable character trait in opposition to the wrongdoing at issue. So for example, habitually denouncing and condemning racism constitutes in the community a valuable character trait of being in opposition to racism (what we might call 'non-racist' or 'anti-racist').

Character traits constituted by habitual opposition to wrongdoing are intrinsically valuable: they have a value that is not the value of their consequences. Of course, such character traits may *also* have a value that is the value of their consequences. For example, the fact that a society develops a progressively less racist character would probably reduce the amount of racist violence in that society. But then again it might not. A small but active gang of violent racists may react to the reconstitution of the society's character as it becomes progressively less racist by committing a huge amount of racist violence. I will refer to this kind of consequence as a 'backlash effect'. Consider the claim that the 'backlash effect' explains why the incidence of rape has increased despite more aggressive prosecution of rape offences. Such an argument would claim that some men are reacting to the anti-patriarchal reconstitution of modern society by punishing women through the perpetration of more rapes than would have been perpetrated if society had simply

---

[53] Denunciation and condemnation are merely examples and are not meant to exhaust the list of appropriate responses to wrongdoing.

remained more patriarchal.[54] Women are being punished (so the argument goes), as a consequence of our communities' increasingly feminist character. Irrespective of whether this theory bears empirical merit, it points to an important fact that the contingent consequences of a society's character shifts are varied and uncertain; some may be valuable, others may not. My point here is simply that regardless of the consequences, it is intrinsically valuable that a community constitute in itself character traits grounded in opposition to wrongdoing.

Prosecutorial actions can constitute (in part) the character of the community in one of two ways: in virtue of the prosecutor's role as representative of her community, and in virtue of the community's collective responsibility for the prosecutor's conduct.

(a) Constituting the character of a community (part one): Prosecutors as community representatives

Prosecutorial actions can constitute (in part) the character of a community insofar as prosecutors function as representatives of their community. This point follows on from the conceptual account of prosecutors and prosecutorial action offered in Chapter 3.[55] I argued there that prosecutors act on behalf of (as representatives of) the state and (potentially at least) their communities. As a conceptual matter, prosecutorial action *is* state action, and if certain threshold political legitimacy conditions are met, then prosecutorial action is (again, as a conceptual matter) the community's action as well. When these conditions are satisfied, there is no conceptual space between the prosecutor acting and the community acting. It follows that in such circumstances, habituated prosecutorial action constitutes (at least in part) the character of the state and (more importantly for our purposes) the community.

I cushioned this point somewhat by claiming that it is true only 'in part', because of course prosecutors are not the only people whose actions can constitute the character of a community. Most obviously, actions by other state actors (eg, police officers, judges, politicians) and community leaders who function as representatives of the community (eg, some religious leaders) can also constitute the character of the community. But it does not end there: the character of a community can also be constituted through the collective responsibility of its members.

(b) Constituting the character of a community (part two): Collective responsibility

In addition to being constituted by the habituated actions of its representatives, the character of a community can also be constituted through actions for which

---

[54] For examination of the relationship between rape rates and the rise of gender equality more generally, see K Martin, L Vieraitis and S Britto, 'Gender equality and women's absolute status: A test of the feminist models of rape' (2006) 12 *Violence Against Women* 321; D Russell, *The Politics of Rape* (New York: Stein and Day, 1975).

[55] See Chapter 3, sections A and B.

members of the community are collectively responsible. But what does it mean to be collectively responsible? First consider what it means to be responsible, full stop. It is helpful to distinguish two senses of responsibility: basic and consequential.[56] To be responsible in a basic sense is to be able to respond to the reasons that apply to you (to be 'response-able'). To be responsible in a consequential sense means that the consequences of your actions are properly visited upon you; eg, if you commit a wrongful action, it is proper for you to be condemned, whereas if you commit a praiseworthy action, it is proper for you to be praised. To be consequentially responsible implies that one is basically responsible. You cannot properly be subject to condemnation or praise for your actions unless you were able to respond to the reasons that applied to you in performing those actions. In the context of wrongdoing, furthermore, to be consequentially responsible for your wrongful action is to act without justification or excuse. When I mention responsibility hereafter, I will be referring to consequential responsibility.

Responsibility is grounded in the way in which people respond to the reasons that apply to them. In that sense, responsibility is always an individual matter and not a collective matter (and thus the notion of collective responsibility is somewhat of a moral fiction). At first glance, the notion of collective responsibility might be thought to contradict this thought—it may be thought to suggest that those who are *collectively responsible* for an action are *responsible collectively* for that action. But responsibility is never a collective matter in that sense. You have your reasons, and I have mine—and every member of a collective group of people has his or her own reasons that apply to him or her.[57]

Usually, the notion of collective responsibility is invoked in the context of collective responsibility for wrongdoing. For example, some of the most illuminating work regarding collective responsibility has taken as its focus the question of the German people's collective responsibility for Nazi war crimes.[58] Whilst communities can be understood as collectively responsible for good things too,[59] our concern here is with collective responsibility for wrongdoing. In the context of wrongdoing, collective responsibility is grounded in responsibility for failing to conform to reasons generated by another's wrongdoing. So, for example, if the German people were collectively responsible for Nazi war crimes, it is not because

---

[56] This distinction is based on J Gardner, 'The mark of responsibility' (2003) 23 OJLS 157.

[57] This point is not meant to deny the many ways in which our reasons for action are grounded in the interests and welfare of other people and our relationships with other people.

[58] HD Lewis, 'Collective responsibility' (1948) 24 *Philosophy* 3; K Jaspers, *The Question of German Guilt* (New York: Ashton, 1961); H Arendt, 'Collective responsibility' in J Bernhauer (ed), *Amor Mundi: Explorations in the faith and thought of Hannah Arendt* (Boston: Lancaster, 1987).

[59] Just as wrongful action normally generates reason to denounce and condemn the wrong and wrongdoer (as discussed below), so too does valuable action normally generate reason to praise the action and commend the actor. Complying with these reasons makes us (in a sense) collectively responsible for the commendable action: when we praise a hero, a bit of his moral light shines on us. This idea may explain why sports fans rightly take pride in their teams' triumphs: they are (in a collective sense) responsible for the triumph in virtue of their support for the teams.

they *literally* committed the crimes themselves,[60] but rather because they were responsible for failing to conform to the reasons generated by the Nazi's wrong-doing.[61] If a particular German citizen should have denounced and condemned these wrongs but failed to do so (without excuse or justification), then she was consequentially responsible for her failure. It is this responsibility—her respon-sibility for failing to denounce and condemn Nazi war crimes—that makes her collectively responsible for those crimes.

Collective responsibility can be both retrospective and prospective. For exam-ple, I can be collectively responsible for another's wrong that was committed in the past in virtue of my (unjustified and unexcused) failure to condemn that per-son's wrongdoing. I will call this type of responsibility retrospective collective responsibility. Equally, I can be collectively responsible for another's wrongdoing committed in the future because in the past, I failed to conform to the reasons I had to prevent similar kinds of wrongdoing. I will call this type of responsibility prospective collective responsibility.

First consider an example of retrospective collective responsibility. Let's say my friend says to me, 'I'm sick and tired of waiting for children to cross the street while I'm driving—they take so darn long to get across the road! So, yesterday I intentionally ran over a particularly slow kid with my car and killed him. That'll teach those brats to dilly-dally.' Assuming that my friend was responsible for her conduct,[62] her wrongdoing generates a reason for me (at least) to condemn what she has done. My response probably should go something like this: 'Oh my, you murdered an innocent child—that's horrible!' Of course, there might be rea-sons why I properly might fail to offer such a response: I might not be basically responsible;[63] I might be justified in not condemning her wrongdoing;[64] or I might be excused in not condemning her wrongdoing.[65] But if none of these con-ditions apply, and if I fail to condemn her wrongdoing, then I am responsible for my failure—and to that extent, I am collectively responsible, in a retrospective

---

[60] Of course, some of the German people did literally commit the crimes themselves; but those cases speak to instances of individual responsibility for the atrocities. Thus a single German person may be both individually and collectively responsible for Nazi war crimes insofar as he literally committed the crimes himself and failed to denounce and condemn other Nazis for committing such crimes.

[61] I shall assume that Nazi war crimes were the kind of wrong that generated reasons for the German people to denounce and condemn the wrongdoing. Indeed, as 'crimes against humanity' I believe it is uncontroversial that they were the kind of wrong that generated reason for everyone (not just Germans) to denounce and condemn them. MM Dempsey, 'Sharing reasons for crimi-nalization? No thanks . . . already got 'em!' in P Robinson, K Ferzan, and S Garvey (eds), *Criminal Law Conversations* (OUP, forthcoming).

[62] Assuming, in other words, that she was consequentially responsible for her conduct, meaning she was basically responsible and she was neither justified nor excused in running over the child.

[63] Eg, she may be confessing to me whilst I lie in a coma.

[64] Eg, I may have decided to report her to the police and do not want to risk tipping her off to my plan by responding harshly to her confession.

[65] Eg, it turns out the child was mine, and I am so overwrought with grief that I can barely speak.

sense, for her wrongdoing. My collective responsibility for my friend's wrongdoing stems from my own wrongful failure to respond appropriately to the reasons that applied to me vis-à-vis her wrongdoing. In this sense then, we can see again that collective responsibility is somewhat of a moral fiction:[66] I did not kill the child, but in wrongly failing to condemn it, I bear some (collective) responsibility for my friend's wrongdoing.

Collective responsibility also applies in a prospective sense. My failure to conform to reasons that applied to me yesterday can make me collectively responsible for another's wrongdoing today. Slightly altering the above hypothetical, imagine that my friend tells me that on her way to work tomorrow, she will kill any child who walks too slowly (in her opinion) across the street. Upon hearing of her plans, I have reason to stop her from killing children: to talk her out of it, to report her to the police or psychiatric services, to hide her car keys, to warn parents of slow-walking children to avoid her path, etc. Suppose that I do none of these things, and I have no justification or excuse for my failure. If my friend follows through with her plan and kills a child, I am collectively responsible for that child's death, in a prospective sense.

But what then does it mean to say that a *community* is collectively responsible for wrongdoing? I cannot purport to answer this question fully here, but I will simply note that collective responsibility need not lie with *all* of the members of that community. In any community, for example, some members will likely lack basic responsibility (eg, young children, the comatose, etc) and thus will not be collectively responsible in virtue of the fact that they lack the capacity for consequential responsibility, which sets a precondition for collective responsibility. Their lack of basic responsibility means they cannot be consequentially responsible for their failure; and since collective responsibility arises from one's consequential responsibility relative to the reasons generated by the primary wrong, those who lack basic responsibility cannot be collectively responsible. This is why, even if the German people were, as a community, collectively responsible for Nazi war crimes, it would not follow that German babies or the German comatose were collectively responsible for these crimes. In other words, collective responsibility can be imputed to a community without implying that every member of that community bears collective responsibility.

Additionally, other members of the community who *are* basically responsible may nonetheless lack consequential responsibility because they are justified or excused for their failure to respond to the reasons generated by the primary wrong at issue. Again, justification and excuse block one's consequential responsibility,

---

[66] This moral fiction is similar to the concept of command responsibility, except that command responsibility only operates in a prospective sense. For example, when a military commander is held responsible under the doctrine of command responsibility for the rapes committed by his troops on civilians, the claim is not that the commander actually engaged in rape—but rather that he had reason to know that his troops were liable to engage in such conduct and failed to respond to such reasons.

thus barring one's collective responsibility, which is a necessary precondition for collective responsibility. So even if the German people, as a community, were collectively responsible for Nazi war crimes, we might still conclude that some (basically responsible) members of this community were not collectively responsible for Nazi atrocities. For example, consider a German who secretly worked with the Allied forces to defeat the Nazis. In order to maintain his undercover operations, he declined publicly to denounce and condemn Nazi crimes, and indeed even participated in Nazi parades, signalling 'Heil Hitler', and so on. Assuming that his actions were justified in virtue of the need to maintain his cover, he is not consequentially responsible for his failure to denounce and condemn the Nazi crimes, and thus he is not collectively responsible for those crimes. In a similar vein, Germans who were extremely mentally or physically ill during the relevant time, or who were placed under extreme enough coercive threats, etc, would not properly be deemed collectively responsible for their failure to denounce and condemn the Nazi crimes because their consequential responsibility would be blocked by operation of an excuse. As in the cases above, even if the German people were, as a community, collectively responsible for Nazi war crimes, it would not follow that German undercover operatives or those labouring under mental or physical illness or extreme duress were collectively responsible for these crimes. Again, collective responsibility can be imputed to a community without implying that every member of that community bears collective responsibility.

A parallel observation can be made with respect to the *character traits* of a community: a community can be said to have a character without implying that every member of that community shares that trait. For example, even if a community is racist, it does not follow that every member of the community is racist. Indeed, the claim that a community is racist is perfectly consistent with the notion that individual members (even White members) do not share that trait in their own individual characters.

So what does all of this mean for the constitutive value of prosecutorial action? First, it means that prosecutorial actions may have constitutive value insofar as: (1) prosecutors function as representatives of their communities (ie, when the political legitimacy conditions are fulfilled); and (2) in so doing, prosecutors engage in habituated actions that are directed toward the cultivation of a valuable character trait. In such circumstances, those prosecutorial actions which contribute to constituting the valuable character trait will bear constitutive value. Second, it means that prosecutorial action may have constitutive value even if prosecutors do *not* function as representatives of their communities (ie, even if the political legitimacy conditions are not fulfilled), provided that: (1) prosecutors engage in habituated actions that are directed toward the cultivation of a valuable character trait; and (2) the community is collectively responsible for these prosecutorial actions (eg, the community praises, supports, commends such actions).

Conversely, prosecutorial actions may have constitutive *disvalue* in one of two ways. First, prosecutorial actions may have constitutive disvalue insofar as: (1)

prosecutors function as representatives of their communities; and (2) in so doing, prosecutors engage in habituated actions that are directed toward the cultivation of a disvaluable character trait. Second, prosecutorial actions may have constitutive disvalue even if prosecutors do *not* function as representatives of their communities, when: (1) prosecutors engage in habituated actions that are directed toward the cultivation of a disvaluable character trait; and (2) the community is collectively responsible for those prosecutorial actions (eg, the community fails to denounce and condemn such actions).

C. Conclusion

The point of this chapter has been to examine the kinds of value that can be realized through prosecutorial action. Whilst some kinds of value are quite commonly cited in the criminal academic literature (for example, it is common to find discussions of consequential values such as deterrence,[67] and intrinsic values of the retributive[68] and expressive[69] varieties), it is far less common to come across accounts that reflect a concern with telic value,[70] and with few exceptions, constitutive value seems to be all but ignored in the criminal academic literature.[71] As such, this chapter provided some necessary clarification for understanding the values of prosecutorial actions and, it is hoped, laid the groundwork for providing an account of prosecutorial practical reasoning in the next chapter.

In Part III of this book (specifically in Chapter 8), I will return to some of this issues explored in this chapter and apply these insights to the particular case of prosecuting domestic violence. In particular, I will emphasize the relevance of constitutive value in the effective prosecution of domestic violence, arguing that domestic-violence prosecutors have the opportunity to reconstitute the character of their communities as less patriarchal (more feminist) *ceteris paribus*.

---

[67] See Robinson and Darley (n 8 above); Keenan (n 8 above).

[68] See Moore (n 40 above).

[69] See Feinberg (n 27 above); Hampton (1984) (n 27 above); Hampton (1998) (n 27 above).

[70] But see Duff's acknowledgement that 'sometimes what matters will be the attempt to achieve [penitential communication], even if we are sure that the attempt is doomed to fail'. RA Duff, 'Penal communications: Recent work in the philosophy of punishment' (1996) 20 Crime and Justice 1. I take his point to be illustrating a concern with telic rather than consequential value.

[71] To my knowledge, two possible exceptions to this point may exist. The first is found in the work of Anthony Alfieri, who touches on themes consistent with my account of constitutive value, whilst not conceptualizing the point in such terms. A Alfieri, 'Prosecuting race' (1999) 48 Duke L J 1157; A Alfieri, 'Prosecuting violence/Reconstructing community' (2000) 52 Stanford L Rev 809; A Alfieri, 'Retrying race' (2003) 101 Michigan L Rev 1141; A Alfieri, 'Color/Identity/Justice: Chicano trials' (2005) 53 Duke L J 1569. The second is authored by Sherman Clark, whose account of criminal procedural rules emphasizes their character-constituting function. S Clark, '"Who do you think you are?" The criminal trial and community character' in RA Duff and others (eds), *The Trial on Trial, vol 2: Judgment and calling to account* (Oxford: Hart, 2006).

5

Reasons for Prosecutors

This chapter builds upon the account of prosecutorial action and value offered in the two preceding chapters and makes further claims regarding the kinds of reasons that apply to prosecutorial action. In other words, this chapter provides a general account of prosecutorial practical reasoning. Before I seek to identify the reasons that apply to prosecutors, however, I will address a logically prior question: *why does it matter what reasons apply to prosecutors?* The answer to this question lies in prosecutors' need to justify their actions. Generally, if the reasons that apply to a given agent weigh in favour of her performing a given action, then that is at least a good start to justifying her action.[1] If this is so, then any inquiry regarding the justification of prosecutorial actions should seek to identify the reasons that apply to prosecutors qua prosecutors. But why embark on an inquiry regarding the justification of prosecutorial action in the first place? Are prosecutorial actions even in need of justification? I will not address this issue in detail here, but suffice it to say I believe they are: both prosecutorial pursuit actions and prosecutorial non-pursuit actions are in need of justification.[2]

It is, of course, a common observation that the criminal justice system is in need of justification, but this concern is typically articulated in terms of the need to justify state punishment.[3] This same concern for justification, however, can be appropriately directed toward prosecutorial action as well. First consider

---

[1] J Gardner, 'Justification and reasons' in A Simester and ATH Smith (eds), *Harm and Culpability* (Oxford: Clarendon, 1996). The claim that the balance of reasons is merely a good start down the road to justification is meant to imply that more is required (specifically, the agent must act for the reasons that render her action justifiable). In what follows, however, I will not consider this additional wrinkle in the theory of justification I presuppose.

[2] I will not discuss whether prosecutorial actions are best understood as mere prima facie wrongs (capable of being cancelled) or whether they constitute pro tanto wrongs (capable of being outweighed, but still to be regretted). See Chapter 2 at text to n 44. My intuition suggests that, at very least, prosecutorial *pursuit* actions are pro tanto wrongs, so that even when justified, prosecutorial pursuit actions may be understood to leave a 'moral residue'. For similar observations regarding the penal sanction, see D Husak, 'Why Criminal Law? A Question of Content' (2008) 2 Criminal Law and Philosophy 99.

[3] '[A]ll punishment is mischief: all punishment in itself is evil... [I]t ought only to be admitted in as far as it promises to exclude some greater evil.' J Bentham, *An Introduction to the Principles of Morals and Legislation* (New York: Prometheus Books, 1781, reprint 1988) 170. See also, N Lacey, *State Punishment: Political Principles and Community Values* (London: International Library of Philosophy, Routledge, 1988).

prosecutorial pursuit actions, such as charging a defendant with a criminal offence and subjecting him to trial: typically these actions involve the infliction of a great deal of suffering such as public humiliation, fear of further sanction through conviction and punishment, the time and expense of mounting a defence, interference with his valuable life plans, etc.[4] This infliction of suffering and interference with the defendant's personal autonomy calls for justification.

More contentiously perhaps, I shall assume that many instances of prosecutorial *non-pursuit* action *also* call for justification. Take an easy example for starters: you are attacked one night by a gang of thugs, who beat you severely and steal your wallet. You report the matter to the police, your assailants are identified and arrested, and the police approach the prosecutor to make a charging decision. The prosecutor, to your surprise, declines to file charges against the suspects. My claim here is that this prosecutorial non-pursuit action calls for justification: the refusal to charge is at least prima facie wrong, and the prosecutor's non-pursuit action will only be justified if she acted for undefeated reasons against charging the suspects.[5] It is possible of course that not *all* prosecutorial non-pursuit actions call for justification. For example, if the police arrest a suspect for murder and submit the case for charging, but evidence arises in the interim establishing an iron-clad alibi for the suspect, then the prosecutor's decision to no-charge the case would not be properly deemed even prima facie wrongful and thus would not call for justification. But in cases where prosecutors have sufficient evidence to proceed to trial against a culpable suspect who has engaged in criminal wrongdoing, the decision to no-charge the case (or to discontinue a pending case in such circumstances) does call for justification.[6]

In light of the need prosecutorial action has for justification, and the relationship between justification and reasons, it is therefore necessary to identify the reasons that apply to prosecutors. This chapter attempts to identify those reasons in an effort to articulate the considerations that might justify prosecutorial actions. The argument presented below proceeds in five steps. First, I introduce

---

[4] On the suffering caused by prosecution, see M M Feeley, *The Process is Punishment* (New York: Russell Sage, 1979).

[5] I am conceptualizing the 'call for justification' here as a need for the prosecutor to act for undefeated reasons when committing a prima facie or pro tanto wrong. There is of course another way to conceptualize a call for justification—as the communication of reasons by the prosecutor to some person who has standing to call her to account. I have avoided this latter conceptualization of justification in order to avoid (to the extent possible) the debate regarding relational responsibility. RA Duff, 'Who is responsible? For what? To whom?' (2005) 2 Ohio State Journal of Criminal Law 441; J Gardner, 'The mark of responsibility' (2003) 23 OJLS 157; RA Duff, 'Criminal responsibility: municipal and international' (draft), presented at the Oxford Jurisprudence Discussion Group (4 May 2006) <http://www.law.ox.ac.uk/cell.shtml> accessed 27 August 2008.

[6] For discussion of some reasons that may justify non-pursuit action, see W LaFave, 'The prosecutor's discretion in the United States' (1970) 18 American Journal of Comparative Law 532, 533–5. On the issue of having 'sufficient evidence to proceed to trial', see CPS, Code for Crown Prosecutors (2004) 5–7; A Ashworth and Redmayne, *The Criminal Process: An evaluative study* (3rd edn, New York: OUP, 2005) 178–84; J Baldwin, 'Understanding judge ordered and directed acquittals in the Crown Court' [1997] Crim LR 536, 541–2.

the normal correspondence thesis, which I take to be the key to understanding the kinds of reasons that apply to prosecutors, and I compare its meaning to the slogans 'the good precedes the right' and 'the right precedes the good'. Second, I identify two limitations to the normal correspondence thesis, one grounded in physical impossibility and (more tentatively) one grounded in logical impossibility. Third, I consider the relationship between wrongdoing and reasons as it relates to criminal prosecutions. Fourth, I discuss the distinction between (1) reasons to do something yourself and (2) reasons to help someone else do something. This distinction will illuminate the importance of having public criminal prosecutors and will go some way toward defending the criminal justice system against abolitionist critiques of the kind offered by Nils Christie.[7] Thus, as the double entendre captured in the title of this chapter suggests, I hope to present an account *both* of the reasons that apply to prosecutors, *and* the reasons why the role of public prosecutor is a valuable one. Finally, I consider the impact that authoritative directives (such as justified laws and policies) have on prosecutors' rational horizons.

A. The Good and the Right

Normally, reason tracks value, which is to say that if a person *can* realize a value through her action, then normally she will have a reason to act so as to realize that value. I will refer to this proposition as the normal correspondence thesis.[8] This proposition may be thought to evoke the slogan 'the good precedes the right'; but any similarities should not be overemphasized. In particular, one should not be led to think that the normal correspondence thesis is grounded in consequentialist moral theory.[9] Consequentialist moral theories, such as utilitarianism, are often thought to prioritize the good over the right, by defining right action in terms of the maximization of consequential value. So, for a utilitarian, a right action is generally thought to be that which has the consequence of maximizing utility.[10] The account of the relationship between value and reason captured in the normal correspondence thesis differs from such a consequentialist moral theory in at least three respects. First, it does not posit a single unit of value (eg, utility) but instead is consistent with the assumption that a plurality of values

---

[7] N Christie, 'Conflicts as property' (1977) 17 British J of Criminology 1.

[8] The normal correspondence thesis is largely based on the account of the relationship between reason and value discussed in J Gardner and T Macklem, 'Reasons' in J Coleman and S Shapiro (eds), *Oxford Handbook of Jurisprudence and Philosophy of Law* (Oxford: OUP, 2002), although some points of distinction will be noted below.

[9] S Scheffler (ed), *Consequentialism and its Critics* (Oxford: OUP, 1988); J Raz, 'Consequentialism: An introduction' in J Raz, *The Morality of Freedom* (Oxford: Clarendon, 1986); P Petit, 'Consequentialism' in P Singer (ed), *A Companion to Ethics* (Oxford: Blackwell, 2000).

[10] See ibid; JS Mill, *Utilitarianism* (Indianapolis: Hackett, 1861, reprint 1979); J Smart and B Williams, *Utilitarianism: For and against* (Cambridge: Cambridge University Press, 1973).

exists, many of which may be incommensurable.[11] Second, it does not conceive of value as something that ought to be, or necessarily can be, maximized. Third, as should be clear from the previous chapter, the account of value assumed herein does not focus solely on consequential values but recognizes the rational salience of intrinsic values as well.

Further, the proposition that the good precedes the right is incomplete insofar as it fails to account for the role that reasons play in determining what counts as justifiable (right) action. On my account, values (the good) do not determine the right; rather *reasons* determine the right (ie, they determine, more or less, what counts as justifiable action). If one acts for undefeated guiding reasons, then one's conduct is justified (right).[12] This claim remains true even if the justified (right) action fails to realize the greatest value from amongst the various options available to the agent. Indeed, it is often the case that right action will not realize the greatest value in any given situation. Four situations illustrate this point:

1. Right (justified) action will not realize the greatest value when the action in question is one of many right actions available to the agent, some of which realize greater value than others, and the agent justifiably chooses from amongst them an action that realizes a lesser amount of value as compared to some or all of the other options.

2. Right (justified) action will not realize the greatest value when the values at stake are incommensurable, thereby limiting the extent to which we can make sense of the claim that any one of them realizes the 'greatest' value.[13]

3. Right (justified) action may not realize the greatest value when the reasons an agent has to realize some significant values are excluded from the agent's rational horizons by second-order reasons.[14]

---

[11] Raz (n 9 above) 321–66; R Chang (ed), *Incommensurability, Incomparability, and Practical Reason* (London: Harvard University Press, 1997). As I understand it, the slogan 'the good precedes the right' means something along the following lines: the realization of value (the good) provides the basis for determining (precedes) what counts as justifiable action (the right). The phrasing of this slogan in terms of 'the right' rather than say 'a right option', suggests that only one course of action is justified vis-à-vis any given agent's options at any given time. If that is what it means, then I disagree. In what follows, I shall assume that numerous justified (right) actions may exist on an agent's rational horizons at any given time. For example, I may be justified in continuing to write this chapter, and I may also be justified in taking my children for a walk on this beautiful sunny day. Each activity realizes incommensurable values, and so *ceteris paribus* each activity may count as a justifiable or right action.

[12] Gardner (n 1 above).

[13] Such was the case in my example in n 11 above, where I chose between the two justified activities of continuing to write this chapter versus taking my children for a walk. Each activity was capable of realizing incommensurable values: those realizable through academic pursuits versus those realizable through parent–child interaction.

[14] Promises provide a wealth of such examples. Just after I promise Amy that I will help her move into a new house next Tuesday, Beth asks me to help her move into her new house on that same day. Beth has few friends in the area and a bad back, whereas Amy is perfectly able-bodied and has plenty of friends who could help her in my stead. I will realize the greatest value through my actions if I cancel my plans with Amy and help Beth; yet, in virtue of my promise to Amy, I

4. Right (justified) action may not realize the greatest value where when some of the values at stake fail to generate first-order reasons for the agent.[15]

A final way in which the normal correspondence thesis is distinct from the slogan 'the good precedes the right' is that the thesis allows for the existence of reasons grounded in something *other* than value. The normal correspondence thesis is therefore consistent with the existence of axiological (value-grounded) as well as deontological (duty-grounded) bases for reasons.[16] The normal correspondence thesis, in other words, is not meant to deny that reasons can *also* be generated by things such as promises, relationships, attitudes, and legitimate authorities.[17] My point here is simple and two-fold: (1) that duties generate first-order (inclusionary) moral reasons for action even if those actions do not realize value; and (2) that duties generate second-order (exclusionary) reasons independently of whether such exclusions facilitate the realization of value.

Whilst I have been at pains in this section to distance my account from those that prioritize the good over the right, it is equally important to distinguish my account from those that claim to prioritize the right over the good, but I will do so only briefly. Rawls is perhaps the most famous exponent of the priority of the right over the good.[18] If all he meant by this slogan was to reject consequentialist moral theories such as utilitarianism (and that seemed to be his major target in making this point), then I am in agreement with him, consistent with what has been stated above. Yet if the priority of the right over the good is taken as a methodological prescription for how we should go about thinking about justifiable (right) action, then I must dissent, for I believe it is helpful first to think in terms of value (the good) that might be realized by one's actions, and then to determine how these diverse values might populate our rational horizons with first-order reasons. Once the array of value-based first-order reasons has been established, it then becomes helpful to think in terms of reasons generated by things like promises, relationships, attitudes, and legitimate authorities. As described above, these can add to, organize, and exclude the first-order reasons that populate our rational horizons. Only at this point, with all considerations

am bound to help her. Such is the rational power of promises. By promising to help Amy, I exclude from my rational horizons the first-order reasons I have to help Beth. So, despite the fact that helping Beth would realize the greatest value, my only justified choice in this scenario is to keep my promise to Amy (assuming, of course, that Amy doesn't release me from my promise).

[15] As discussed below, such limitations arise in at least two kinds of situation: physical and logical impossibility.

[16] R Audi, *The Good in the Right* (Oxford: Princeton University Press, 2004) 152–3. I do not take a position here on whether doing one's duty has intrinsic value. It is common to claim that there is no intrinsic value in acting from duty, but see B Herman, 'On the value of acting from the motive of duty' (1981) 90 *Philosophical Review* 359; M Baron, 'On the alleged repugnance of acting from duty' (1984) 81 *Journal of Philosophy* 197.

[17] This is not meant to be a closed list but merely to illustrate some ways in which reasons can be grounded in something other than the realization of value.

[18] J Rawls, *A Theory of Justice* (revised edn, Cambridge: Belknap, 1999) 392–6.

taken into account, is it helpful to arrive at conclusions regarding what counts as justifiable (right) action. So, in this weak methodological sense, the account herein does prioritize the good over the right; but I hope it is now somewhat more clear what is meant by this claim.

B. The Normal Correspondence Thesis

To review, the normal correspondence thesis states that normally reason tracks value, which is to say that if a person *can* realize a value through her action, then normally she will have a reason to act so as to realize that value. It follows from this thesis that if I can save life, I have a reason to save a life. Note, however, that it does *not* follow from this thesis that I *should* save that life, all things considered. The normal correspondence thesis only does reason-generating work: it does not address ultimate questions of all-things-considered justification.[19] If the normal correspondence thesis is true, however, then considering its implications in combination with the previous chapter's account of value will illuminate a great deal about the first-order reasons that apply to prosecutors.[20]

It might be thought that the normal correspondence thesis is based upon a rather promiscuous account of reasons; that it mingles value and reason together with insufficient discrimination. Admittedly, there is very little space between a theory of value and a theory of reason according to this thesis. All values generate reasons, at least for someone.[21] However, there is cause to suspect that the normal correspondence thesis fails to operate in some situations, so that 'relative to some agents and for some actions, some values do not correspond to reasons'.[22] In this sense, the normal correspondence thesis does allow for some degree of discrimination between a theory of value and a theory of reason.

Exceptions to the normal correspondence thesis might arise in cases of either physical or logical impossibility.[23] The exception of physical impossibility features in my formulation of the normal correspondence thesis as stated above, insofar as the formulation requires that a person *can* realize a value through her action. Sometimes, of course, we *cannot* realize a value through our actions: it is physically

---

[19] Indeed, my arguments do not even speak of whether the weight of value-based reasons for action corresponds to the weight of the values which generated them; so, it might be the case that heavy-weight value generates a 90-lb weakling of a reason. I take no position on this matter.

[20] Of course, insofar as the previous chapter offered an incomplete account of the values that can be realized by prosecutorial action, the account of prosecutorial practical reasoning offered herein is similarly incomplete.

[21] Value-bearing facts always have rational salience, for someone at least, and if a value-bearing fact lacks rational salience, the disruption 'is always relative to particular people and particular actions by those people'. Gardner and Macklem (n 8 above) 456.

[22] Ibid 457. This explains why I have called it the *normal correspondence thesis*: it only applies under normal circumstances.

[23] Ibid.

impossible to do so. Take Gardner's example of a non-swimmer standing on a cliff top, watching a man drown below in a stormy sea.[24] For Gardner, this hypothetical illustrates a case of physical impossibility: saving the drowning man would have value, but the non-swimmer cannot realize this value through his action. If he dives into the stormy sea, Gardner supposes, both men will surely drown. Thus, since the non-swimmer's actions cannot realize the value of saving the drowning man's life, the non-swimmer has no reason to save him.[25] Because saving the drowning man is neither an actual nor expected consequence of the non-swimmer's actions, the non-swimmer has no consequential-value-grounded reason to save him. Moreover, because (*ex hypothesi*) the attempt cannot possibly succeed, the non-swimmer has no telic-value grounded reason to try to save the man's life either. The physical impossibility of realizing a value through one's action blocks the generation of consequentially and telically grounded reasons for that agent. Thus, the non-swimmer has no consequentially or telically based reasons to save the drowning man.

1. Logical impossibility exceptions and the role of the prosecutor

A second (possible) exception to the normal correspondence thesis arises in the case of logical impossibility. This exception does not feature in my formulation of the normal correspondence thesis, not least because I am not entirely convinced that it is an actual exception to the thesis. Gardner and Macklem believe that it is, and illustrate the logical impossibility exception with the example of F, who has irritated his friend through a series of overdone attempts to please the friend.[26] After the friend expresses his frustration with F's continued attempts to please him, F 'promises not to try to please' his friend any further. Gardner and Macklem continue:

Of course, if he keeps this promise, part of the value of his doing so will be that it pleases his friend. Yet if F acts in order to please his friend, if that value is operative in his reasoning, he will break his promise. It follows that the value of pleasing his friend gives F no reason to keep his promise, despite the fact that this value is part of the value of keeping the promise. F has every other reason to keep his promise, but not this one.[27]

I remain sceptical as to whether logical-impossibility exceptions form genuine exceptions to the normal correspondence thesis, but in what follows, I will assume that such exceptions do exist.

[24] J Gardner, 'The wrongdoing that gets results' (2004) 18 *Philosophical Perspectives* 53, 55–7; see also discussion in Chapter 4, text surrounding n 23.

[25] I shall assume that the non-swimmer has no expressive reasons to make a futile attempt to save the drowning man. A futile attempt to save the man may have expressive value in, say, 'express[ing] undying love for the drowning man in an act of futile-self-sacrifice'. Gardner (n 24 above) 57. Thus, there may very well be expressively grounded reasons to try to save the man, despite the lack of consequentially and telically grounded reasons.

[26] Gardner and Macklem (n 8 above).

[27] Ibid 455.

What implications follow from this assumption with respect to criminal prosecutorial action? Do logical-impossibility exceptions sometimes disrupt the normal correspondence thesis with respect to the relationship between the values that can be realized through prosecutorial action and the reasons that prosecutors have? In other words, can the moral position of prosecutors be analogized to the moral position of F, for whom a value failed to generate a reason? Addressing this question will require some attention to the proper formulation of the normative role of prosecutor.

Very little philosophical work has been done on the proper formulation of the normative role of prosecutor. As Jonathan Rogers has recently observed, '[t]heorists have paid insufficient theoretical attention to the structure of the prosecutorial decision-making process'.[28] I would add to this that even less attention has been paid to the substance of the prosecutorial decision-making process. What is missing is a body of philosophical literature that articulates and explains the normative principles that inform the role of the prosecutor and thus affect the reasons prosecutors have qua prosecutors. To the extent that such principles are articulated, for example in professional codes of ethics, they appear in the form of slogans such as 'the role of the prosecutor is to seek justice, not merely to convict'.[29] Slightly more detailed accounts are available in the academic literature regarding professional ethics, but this literature does not provide significant insight into the nature of the prosecutor's role.[30]

It is not my intention to fill this gap in the literature here but simply to direct our attention to one kind of substantive normative principle which might be thought to shape the role of prosecutor and thus affect the reasons prosecutors have qua prosecutors. This specific normative principle I have in mind is grounded in the prosecutor's bureaucratic role within the criminal process. The criminal process,

---

[28] J Rogers, 'Restructuring the exercise of prosecutorial discretion in England' (2006) 26 OJLS 775, 802.

[29] United States Model Code of Professional Responsibility EC 7–13.

[30] Instead, this literature is mostly focused on offering specific prescriptions for prosecutorial action in response to 'ethical chestnuts', such as whether prosecutors should proceed when they do not believe the defendant is guilty, whether prosecutors should engage in plea and/or sentence bargaining, and how prosecutors should negotiate the line between engaged advocacy and excessive zeal. See generally A Sanders and R Young, 'The ethics of prosecution lawyers' (2004) 7 Legal Ethics 190; M Blake and A Ashworth, 'Some ethical issues in prosecuting and defending criminal cases' [1998] Crim LR 16; K Crispin, 'Prosecutorial ethics' in S Parker and C Stamford (eds), *Legal Ethics and Legal Practice: Contemporary issues* (Oxford: Clarendon, 1995); D Nicolson and J Webb, *Professional Legal Ethics: Critical interrogations* (Oxford: OUP, 1999) 227–30. Interesting additions to this literature in the US context include M Cassidy, 'Character and context: What virtue theory can teach us about a prosecutor's ethical duty to "seek justice"' (2006) 82 Notre Dame LR 635; F Zacharias, 'Specificity in professional responsibility codes: Theory, practice, and the paradigm of prosecutorial ethics' (1993) 69 Notre Dame LR 223; and S Fisher, 'In search of the virtuous prosecutor: A conceptual framework' (1988) 15 American J Crim Law 197. Notably, in the most philosophically sophisticated account of legal ethics I have discovered, the topic of criminal prosecution goes virtually unmentioned. D Luban, *Lawyers and Justice: An ethical study* (Princeton: Princeton University Press, 1988) 61–2 (briefly noting prosecutors' duty to disclose exculpatory evidence), 170–1 (reciting the ABA Code 7–13 dictate that prosecutor's 'duty is to seek justice, not merely to convict').

as with any bureaucratic system, is based on the principle of the division of labour. Certain actors within any bureaucracy are charged with the responsibility of realizing certain ends, and the same holds true within the criminal justice system. In most common-law jurisdictions, this division of labour is roughly drawn along the following lines: police investigate alleged offences; prosecutors accuse alleged offenders and either seek to establish their guilt or exonerate them; judges rule on legal matters arising in the course of investigation and prosecution and pass sentence; and members of the post-conviction bureaucracy (eg, jailors, probation officers, etc) carry out the criminal punishment as determined by the judge.

With this understanding of the role of prosecutor in the context of a bureaucratic system as background, I will turn directly to the question of whether logical impossibilities generated by the role of prosecutor create exceptions to the normal correspondence thesis. It strikes me as possible that this is so, for it seems that some roles do have such an effect on the relationship between value and reason. That is to say that sometimes, in virtue of our acting in a certain role, it is logically impossible for our actions to realize certain values: in order to realize those values, we would have to (if we could) step outside our role in acting, or step into a new role.

Consider the role of International Red Cross (IRC) humanitarian-aid workers. The role of the IRC aid worker is to provide medical (or other) assistance whilst not taking sides in hostilities; remaining neutral is central to the IRC's role in hostile contexts.[31] The point here is not simply that IRC workers *should not* take sides; it is that qua IRC workers they cannot realize the value of taking sides. In order for one who is employed as an IRC worker to realize the value of taking sides, she would have to step outside of her IRC role and act qua an individual, not qua an IRC worker.[32] Another way of making this point is to say that this particular role-based constraint of the IRC worker is more than simply a rule that the IRC happens to have adopted because it is believed, on the whole, that it enables IRC aid workers to realize greater value through their work. Rather, the constraint is a conceptual component of the IRC's role within conflicts. If this account of the role of the IRC worker is correct, then any values that may be realized by taking sides in international hostilities simply do not generate action reasons for IRC workers.

If we apply the above considerations to prosecutorial action and the value of retribution, we can conclude that in virtue of their role qua prosecutors, it is logically impossible for prosecutors to realize the value of retribution. If the conceptual nature of the role of prosecutor excludes them from inflicting punishment within the criminal justice system, then retributive value fails to generate reasons for prosecutors. If there is an impermeable conceptual barrier between 'prosecutor' and 'punisher', then the prosecutor's role generates a logical impossibility exception to

---

[31] J Pictet, 'Fundamental principles' International Red Cross <http://www.icrc.org> accessed 26 August 2008.

[32] This is not to say that the IRC worker would have to step outside her role in order to take sides or engage in hostilities but merely that *in order to realize the value of* taking sides or engaging in hostilities, she would have to step outside her role.

the normal correspondence thesis. In other words, prosecutors have no retribution-grounded reasons qua prosecutors to cause wrongdoers to suffer.

Assuming that this conceptual account of the prosecutor's role is accurate, the claim which follows is far more significant than the mere assertion that prosecutors *should not* realize retributive value; rather, the claim is that they *cannot* do so qua prosecutors. In order to realize the value of retribution, one who is employed as a prosecutor must step outside her role,[33] just as the IRC aid worker would have to step outside her role in order to realize the value of taking sides or engaging in hostilities. None of this is to suggest, however, that it is *physically impossible* for prosecutors to engage in conduct that brings suffering upon a wrongdoer. Indeed, a great deal of prosecutorial pursuit action does just that.[34] The point here is that when prosecutors bring suffering upon a wrongdoer, this suffering has no retributive value. Retributive value is a kind of value that prosecutors are logically (conceptually) unable to realize in virtue of their role. Thus, retributive value thus does not generate reasons for prosecutorial action.

If the logical impossibility exception holds and the account of the role of prosecutor above is correct, then it follows that one of the values identified in Chapter 4 (retributive value) fails to satisfy the normal correspondence thesis relative to prosecutorial action. In other words, retributive value fails to generate reasons for prosecutors. So, whilst there *is* value in wrongdoers suffering commensurate with their wrongdoing on account to their being prosecuted, this value generates no reason for prosecutors to pursue this value.[35]

2. Revisiting the role of prosecutor: How contingent is it?

Perhaps, however, I am wrong in thinking that the role of prosecutor generates a logical impossibility exception to the normal correspondence thesis relative to retributive value.[36] In other words, maybe I have misjudged the conceptual nature of the role of prosecutor: maybe there is no role-related conceptual divide between 'prosecutors' and 'punishers'. Indeed, maybe it is a mistake to think that the role of prosecutor has much of a normatively substantive conceptual nature whatsoever. Perhaps the only thing that can be said about the conceptual nature of the role of prosecutor is something like this: the role of prosecutor entails making charging decisions and trying cases; but beyond that, the role may develop in any number

---

[33] This is not to say that the prosecutor would have to step outside her role in order to engage in retributive action (ie, action that brings suffering upon a wrongdoer commensurate with his wrongdoing) but merely to say that *in order to realize the value of retribution (retributive value)*, she would have to step outside her role as prosecutor.

[34] Feeley (n 4 above).

[35] Some prosecutors take solace following an acquittal in having made the defendant suffer the burden of prosecution. It follows from the above that there is no proper source of solace to be found for prosecutors in causing such suffering, even if it is deserved.

[36] I thank John Gardner for pushing me on this point, despite my refusal to budge.

of ways based on local contingencies; some of these developments may include the possibility that prosecutors will function as punishers, and some will not.

If this account of the role of prosecutor is correct, then we should conclude that our understanding of the distinction between 'prosecutor' and 'punisher' is a mere contingency, subject to change, and is therefore not conceptually fundamental to the role of prosecutor. If this were true, we might just as easily reconceive the role of prosecutor so as to adopt an understanding of prosecutor that draws no distinction between 'prosecutor' and 'punisher'. On this account of the role of prosecutor, filing criminal charges against defendants and trying cases could be specifically designed to serve a punishment function: these actions would be *intended* to impose suffering upon defendants, rather than merely imposing suffering as a regrettable side effect. Under this revised account of the prosecutor's role, there would be no reason to make the process any less punitive: indeed, there would be reason to make it even *more* arduous, humiliating, costly, time-consuming, etc.

This account of the role of the prosecutor strikes me not only as unpalatable, but also as wildly implausible. The question of whether a prosecutor can also be a punisher does not strike me as a question to be answered as a matter of contingency: rather, it strikes me as a conceptual matter. Thus, any state that purports to have prosecutors who, qua prosecutors, are empowered to inflict punishment must be operating with a fundamentally different concept of prosecutor than the one we use. I would have to conclude that this state is simply calling this role 'prosecutor', when really what they have is a system of punishment without prosecution.

C. Wrongs and Reasons

Up to this point, I have assumed that the normal correspondence thesis presents an uncontroversial account of how prosecutors get many of their first-order reasons. I have noted some hesitancy regarding whether retributive value generates reasons for prosecutors; but as to all other values identified in Chapter 4, it has been assumed that these values *do* generate reasons for prosecutors. I will now pause for a moment to consider the possibility that the reader will resist the move dictated by the normal correspondence thesis. Do the consequential, telic, expressive, and constitutive values articulated in Chapter 4 generate reasons for prosecutors?

To review, my claim is that there are values (of many different kinds) that can be realized through prosecutors acting in response to criminal wrongdoing, and these values generate reasons for prosecutors to act in response to criminal wrongdoing. I might rephrase these points more simply as follows: *criminal wrongdoing generates reasons for prosecutorial action*. This proposition may strike some as counter-intuitive, for typically it is believed that wrongs generate reasons, principally or exclusively, for the *victims* of the wrongdoing. To the extent that others have reason to hold wrongdoers accountable at all (so the counterclaim goes), those reasons are parasitic upon the victims' reasons.

In the context of criminal law, the most extreme version of this counterclaim was advanced by Nils Christie.[37] On Christie's account, criminal wrongdoing generates reasons for the victim to hold the wrongdoer accountable, but it does not generate reasons for anyone else to hold the wrongdoer accountable. This view led Christie to conclude that wrongdoing generates a property interest in the victim, and thus attempts to hold wrongdoers accountable through the criminal law are best understood as 'stealing the victim's conflict'.[38]

In resisting the abolitionist implications of Christie's account, it is sometimes argued that everyone has a reason to hold criminal wrongdoers accountable because such wrongdoing wrongs everyone. The more attractive version of this argument interprets the phrase 'wrongdoing wrongs everyone' as a conceptual claim: ie, to wrong one is to wrong all. More commonly, this phrase is interpreted as a contingent claim: ie, when wrongdoing actually does wrong everyone, then it generates reasons for everyone to hold the wrongdoer accountable. In either event, wrongs (can or necessarily do) generate reasons for everyone to hold wrongdoers accountable in virtue of the fact that what was done (contingently or necessarily) wronged everyone. As applied to criminal law, this view concludes that a wrongdoer should be held to account by the criminal justice system only under certain conditions:

if and because [their wrongs] 'threaten the social order'; or if and because they cause 'social volatility'; or because such attackers must be punished in order to incapacitate them from further such attacks or in order to deter potential attackers; or because the attacker takes an unfair advantage over all law-abiding citizens (he accepts the benefits of their law-abiding self-restraint, whilst avoiding the burden on self-restraint himself).[39]

Marshall and Duff present a compelling argument against this version of how wrongdoing generates reasons to hold wrongdoers to account. They begin by claiming that a wrongdoer should be held accountable not because he has wronged everyone but rather because of the wrong he does to the individual victim.[40] Illustrating their point with the example of rape, Marshall and Duff observe:

We do not criminalize rape, and punish rapists, because rape causes social volatility; or because the rapist takes unfair advantage over his law-abiding fellow citizens... [41]

This point is surely correct; but the claim that follows is more questionable. The real reason why we criminalize rape and punish rapists, according to Marshall

---

[37] Christie (n 7 above).
[38] Conflicts have been 'taken away from the directly involved parties... [and become] other people's property'. Christie (n 7 above) 5.
[39] S Marshall and RA Duff, 'Sharing wrongs' (1998) 11 Canadian J of Law and Jurisprudence 7, 12.
[40] Ibid.
[41] Ibid 12.

and Duff, is 'because of the nature of the wrong that the rapist does to his victims'.[42] For Marshall and Duff, these final words ('to his victims') appear crucial. On their account, the reason we criminalize rape (or any other wrong that may properly be criminalized) is because we *share* the wrong done to the victim. The authors employ the example of rape once more to illustrate their account of sharing wrongs:

Consider how a group of women might respond to a sexual attack on one of them... They may see it as a collective, not merely an individual wrong (as an attack on them), insofar as they associate and identify themselves with the individual victim. For they define themselves as a group, in terms of certain shared identity, shared values, mutual concern—and shared dangers which threaten them: an attack on a member of the group is thus an attack on the group—on their shared values and their common good. The wrong does not cease to be 'her' wrong: but it is also 'our' wrong insofar as we identify ourselves with her... A group can in this way 'share' the wrongs done to its individual members.[43]

Marshall's and Duff's view is appealing, but it fails to distinguish clearly between conceptual and contingent interpretations of the claim that 'wrongdoing wrongs everyone'.[44] At first the authors appear to adopt a contingent interpretation when stating, '[t]he wrong does not cease to be "her" wrong: but it is also "our" wrong insofar as we identify ourselves with her'.[45] In other words, the wrong is one principally done to her, but (as a contingent matter) the wrong might also qualify as one done to us *if* we 'identify ourselves with her'.[46] We are provided with a list of the various ways in which people might identify themselves with the victim and thereby share her wrong: by having a 'certain shared identity, shared values, [and/or] mutual concern'.[47] It is safe to assume that there are many other ways in which a group might identify itself with a particular victim. Marshall and Duff imply as much when they make the leap from a 'group of women' sharing the wrong of rape suffered by one woman to the larger 'community' sharing the wrong of that rape. Thus, we should assume that the list provided does not exhaust the grounds upon which a wrong may be shared, since even an idealized community would not necessarily share an identity, values, or concern with a particular victim of a wrong which, nonetheless, we would think it appropriate to prohibit under the criminal law.

Consider the example of a radical individualist, Izzy, who so despises the idea of being part of any political community that she chooses to leave her home in Homeville and live on a deserted island. She rejects any shared identity with any

---

[42] Ibid.

[43] Ibid 19–20.

[44] What follows is based on MM Dempsey, 'Sharing reasons for criminalization? No thanks...already got 'em!' in P Robinson, K Ferzan, and S Garvey (eds), *Criminal Law Conversations* (forthcoming).

[45] Marshall and Duff (n 39 above) 19.

[46] Ibid.

[47] Ibid.

community, does not share any community's values, and has no concern for any community or its people. She is truly a lone wolf. Imagine further that Izzy is kidnapped and forcibly taken to Polityville, where she is raped. Presumably, the community of Polityville would share the wrong done to Izzy under Marshall and Duff's account, but not in virtue of any shared identity, values, or concern with Izzy.[48] Rather, the basis for sharing the wrong would presumably be found in the mere fact that Izzy was within the geographic borders of Polityville at the time she was raped. This empirical contingency would then provide a basis upon which the community of Polityville may properly share Izzy's wrong and prosecute her rape as a criminal offence under its laws and in its criminal justice system.

It is difficult, however, to see why such an empirical contingency should be thought to have such normative implications. Why should Izzy's mere physical location generate reasons to hold her wrongdoers accountable which otherwise would not exist? On the flipside of this question, one may ask whether there are any coherent limits to the contingencies capable of doing this normative 'wrong-sharing' work. Imagine a group of people who choose to live on the island of Separatonia, apart from the rest of the world, and who reject the identity, values, and concerns of the 'global community'. One day, half of the Separatonians set about systematically torturing and exterminating the other half through murder, rape, enslavement, etc. Throughout it all, the victims never doubt their commitment to rejecting the identity, values, and concerns of the global community. They never once seek help from outside the island, nor do they wish help to be provided. They would sooner be tortured and die than accept help from outside. On Marshall and Duff's account, on what basis, if any, would outsiders share the wrongs done to these victims?

Duff has suggested a possible answer to this problem: in such cases, the wrongs done to the victims on the island of Separatonia may be shared by outsiders simply in virtue of our shared humanity.[49] The severity of the wrongdoing at issue is the key to Duff's move: the case of the Separatonians is saliently different, Duff might claim, because the wrongdoing at issue constitutes 'crimes against humanity'.

To say that a crime is a 'crime against humanity' could…be to say that it is a kind of wrong that properly concerns humanity as such—ie, every human being in virtue simply of their shared humanity.[50]

---

[48] Unless, of course, Marshall and Duff would allow for the sharing of wrongs against the victim's wishes—in which case, their account would start to look very much like a case of 'stealing' wrongs. See Christie (n 7 above).

[49] RA Duff, 'Criminal responsibility: Municipal and international' (draft), presented at the Oxford Jurisprudence Discussion Group (4 May 2006) <http://www.law.ox.ac.uk/cell.shtml> accessed 27 August 2008. Note, however, that the cited paper was a draft of a work in progress, and thus I do not purport to have a clear understanding of Duff's final views on this matter.

[50] Ibid 22.

Thus, in cases of systematic torture and extermination, for example, Duff concedes that such wrongdoing generates reason for everyone to hold the wrongdoers to account, because the wrongdoing wrongs everyone qua human beings. This concession, of course, raises the question of why certain cases of wrongdoing should be thought to generate reasons for everyone and other cases of wrongdoing should not.

Later in their account of how wrongs generate reasons, Marshall and Duff seem to adopt an interpretation of the claim 'wrongdoing wrongs everyone' which suggests that this is a conceptual claim. They state: 'the attack on this individual victim is itself also an attack on us'.[51] If this statement is intended as a conceptual claim about wrongdoing, then we need no longer search for a relevant connection between the victim and community (in their shared identity, value, concern, geographic location, or any other contingency) in order to understand why a wrong to a specific person rightly concerns us all; rather we can simply acknowledge that a wrong to an individual is (conceptually) a wrong to everyone. If one concedes this point, it follows that responsibility does not require any particular standing beyond our status as human beings. It is not, therefore, an essential (basic) feature of responsibility that we are called to account by some *particular* person or group of persons.[52]

Once this point is recognized, we may ask: what, if anything, is to be gained by calling an account of responsibility 'relational' if it does not claim that the response in question is owed to some rational beings and not to others? I believe there *is* still a benefit in characterizing responsibility as relational, insofar as such talk highlights the issue of *who* is calling the wrongdoer to account. If we fail to attend to this issue, then we risk obscuring an important distinction between: (1) reasons everyone has to call a wrongdoer to account to everyone (simply in virtue of our shared humanity); and (2) reasons everyone has to help a victim call the wrongdoer to account to herself. We will consider the importance of this distinction below.

D. Reasons to Do It Yourself and Reasons to Help Someone Else Do It

Criminal wrongdoing generates at least two types of reasons for people in at least two different roles. This combination produces four sorts of reasons:

1. reasons for the community to hold the wrongdoer to account to everyone (collectively);

---

[51] Marshall and Duff (n 39 above) 20.

[52] Pace RA Duff, 'Who is responsible? For What? To Whom?' (2005) (n 5 above). Pace Gardner, however, it may still be the case that responsibility is basically relational. J Gardner, 'The mark of responsibility' (2003) 23 OJLS 157. My point here is simply that responsibility, even if basically relational, does not necessarily require any particular *standing* beyond one's status as a human being.

2. reasons for the victim to hold the wrongdoer to account to the victim;

3. reasons for the community to help the victim hold the wrongdoer to account to the victim;

4. reasons for the victim to help everyone (collectively) hold the wrongdoer to account to everyone.

If we were to divide up these reasons along the lines typically drawn between criminal law and tort, we might conclude as follows: the sorts of reasons reflected in (1) serve to justify criminal prosecutions;[53] the sorts of reasons reflected in (2) serve to justify tort claims; the sorts of reasons reflected in (3) call for the creation, maintenance, and funding of a well-functioning tort system;[54] and the sorts of reasons reflected in (4) call for victims to cooperate with criminal prosecutions. Reasons of the sort reflected in (3) and (4) are best understood as reasons to help others in the completion of valuable projects. As Gardner and Macklem have noted, '[e]verybody's personal engagement with valuable activities is in principle everybody's business'.[55] If this is so (and I shall assume it is), and if we assume that it is valuable for a victim to be provided the opportunity to hold her wrongdoer to account directly to herself, then this value generates reasons for her community to create, maintain, and fund a well-functioning tort system. Assuming it is valuable that the community be able to hold a wrongdoer to account directly to everyone (collectively), then this value generates reasons for the victim to cooperate in that process (ie, not to request dismissal of criminal charges, to testify if called to do so, etc).

Acting on the first two types of reasons denounces the wrongdoing; acting on the second two types of reasons assists another in pursuing a valuable project. A community that acts on reasons of the sort reflected in (1) denounces the wrongdoing at issue on behalf of everyone: the expressive function of the conduct is attributable to the collectivity. A victim who acts on reasons of the sort reflected in (2) denounces the wrongdoing on her own behalf: the expressive function of her conduct is not attributable to anyone else. A community that acts on reasons of the sort reflected in (3) expresses its solidarity with one of its members. It displays its community character of kindness, support, fellow-feeling, etc by helping the victim in her valuable project of holding the wrongdoer to account. Finally, a victim who acts on reasons of the sort reflected in (4) expresses her identification with her community. She displays her individual character of good citizenship,

---

[53] These sorts of reasons have resulted in prosecutions proceeding in the name of the local polity (eg, the State, Regina, etc)—but more recently with the creation of the International Criminal Court, we now see prosecutions proceeding in the name of 'the international community' (ie, everyone).

[54] These sorts of reasons have resulted in the development of private-law causes of action, courts of tort/contract/equity, legal assistance funding for civil claims, etc.

[55] Gardner and Macklem (n 8 above) 458.

self-sacrifice for the greater good, etc by helping the community in its valuable project of holding the wrongdoer to account.

This analysis has at least one important implication. It is only when the community calls the wrongdoer to account directly to the community that the community expresses its *own* denunciation of the wrongdoing. For this reason, it remains important that criminal prosecutions proceed in the name of the community (or, proximately, in the name of the State, Regina, etc); for it is only in prosecuting in the name of the community that the community directly denounces the wrongdoing.[56] Further, this consideration goes some way toward explaining why expanding the victim's role in the criminal justice system (and some forms of restorative justice) may threaten the expressive and constitutive function of criminal law.[57] If, for example, victims are permitted to join prosecutions as co-prosecuting parties to the litigation, or if victims are given a decisive vote in whether and what charges are brought and whether such charges should proceed, then the prosecution will serve the reasons outlined in (1) less and less, and will thereby diminish the opportunity such reasons provide for the community to denounce wrongdoing directly in its own name.

If we reconceive the criminal process as one in which the community merely helps victims to hold wrongdoers accountable, then we risk losing the procedural context in which the community calls wrongdoers to account directly to the community. In other words, we lose a procedural context in which the principal expressive function is to express the *community's* direct denunciation of the wrongdoing. This loss would be an important one—a loss that cannot be salvaged by the community's other expressive outlets (eg, criminal legislation, sentencing).[58]

If the preceding arguments hold, then the normal correspondence thesis does indeed generate reasons for prosecutors, not simply in the sense of 'identifying those reasons that apply to prosecutors', but in the sense of 'establishing reasons why we should have prosecutors'. Some of the values at stake when wrongdoing is

---

[56] I believe a similar thought motivates A Harel, 'Why only the state may inflict criminal sanctions: The case against privately inflicted sanctions' (2008) 14 Legal Theory 113.

[57] For more on the potential inadequacies of the use of restorative justice in domestic-violence cases, see J Stubbs, 'Beyond apology?: Domestic violence and critical questions for restorative justice' (2007) 7 Criminology and Criminal Justice 169.

[58] Prosecution, of course, is not the only method by which a community can expressively denounce wrongdoing: this can also be accomplished through public information campaigns targeting specific kinds of wrongdoing, as well as through other aspects of the criminal justice system such as judicial actions of conviction and/or sentencing. But prosecutorial actions speak to the disvalue of some wrongs in an importantly different way than do these other methods, because prosecutorial actions *denounce* rather than *condemn*. Prosecutorial actions (pursuit actions, anyway) denounce, whereas these other actions condemn. Denunciation kicks off a moral dialogue; condemnation ends it. With respect to some wrongs, grounded in what Kahan has called 'sticky norms', it is crucial to engage in a moral dialogue of denunciation when confronted with the wrong, rather than merely offering blanket condemnation. Kahan, 'Gentle nudges vs. Hard shoves: Solving the sticky norms problem' (2000) 67 Univ Chicago L Rev 607. See also, Chapter 10, section A ('Why Prosecution?').

at issue generate reasons for the community as a collectivity to hold wrongdoers accountable: to denounce the wrongdoing and wrongdoer *in the name of the community*, rather than merely helping the victim do so in her own name. It follows that the kinds of values identified in Chapter 4 do generate first-order reasons for prosecutors and that when prosecutors act on these reasons as representatives their communities, the communities are properly understood as denouncing the wrongdoing and wrongdoers directly.

E. The Impact of Justified Authoritative Directives and Principles on Prosecutorial Reasons

Given the arguments above, it will be taken as established that the kinds of values identified in Chapter 4 do generate first-order reasons for prosecutors. Thus, prosecutors' rational horizons are in large part populated by the kinds of reasons generated by these values. But, of course, prosecutors' rational horizons are also structured by second-order reasons grounded in justified authoritative directives and principles such as justified laws and policies which bind their exercise of discretion.[59] Particular jurisdictional laws and policies that apply to the prosecutor, if justified, legitimately exclude first-order reasons that otherwise would guide prosecutorial action.

For example, consider the rational affect that a justified policy directive might have on a prosecutor's decision whether to act on the basis of a particular victim's wishes. Start by identifying the kind of value at stake, which we might suppose is a consequential value we might call victim satisfaction. This kind of value is grounded in things such as the relief, enhanced sense of safety, etc, that a victim might feel as a consequence of a particular kind of prosecutorial action. Since there is nothing necessarily inconsistent between the role of prosecutor and the prosecutor acting in furtherance of such values, there is basis to suppose that this value generates first-order reasons for the prosecutor. However, depending on the laws and policies of a particular jurisdiction, these reasons may be excluded from the prosecutor's rational horizons. The question comes down to whether the particular laws and policies are justified, and I will address this question by reference to Raz's normal justification thesis.[60]

Depending on the context, a particular jurisdiction might be justified in directing its prosecutors not to act pursuant to the victims' wishes. Consider a

---

[59] On the distinction between first- and second-order reasons, see J Raz, *Practical Reason and Norms* (2nd edn, New York: OUP, 1999) 39–40, 178–99. See also, Chapter 2 (n 30 above). To review, second-order reasons are either positive (reasons to act upon one's first-order reasons) or negative (reasons not to act upon one's first-order reasons). Raz refers to negative first-order reasons as exclusionary reasons.

[60] J Raz, *Ethics in the Public Domain* (Oxford: OUP, 1994) 214. See also, Chapter 2 (n 31 above).

jurisdiction where the prosecutors habitually defer to the victim's wishes in every case, so that the office of prosecutor has become little more than an instrument for vengeful victims. Whenever a prosecution is desired by the victim, the prosecutors engage in pursuit actions. Conversely, whenever a victim requests that a case be discontinued, the prosecutors engage in non-pursuit actions. No weight is accorded in the prosecutors' reasoning to the other values that might be realized through prosecutorial action and the reasons these values might generate. In such a jurisdiction, it may be justifiable to enact a law which excludes reasons generated by the victims' wishes from prosecutors' rational horizons. Such laws or policies may provide a service to the prosecutors in this jurisdiction, who otherwise are too weak-willed to comply with the reasons that apply to them when faced with what they incorrectly judge to be the overwhelming weight of reasons generated by victims' wishes.[61] By requiring them to exclude such reasons from their rational horizons, the law or policy may enable the prosecutors better to comply with the reasons that actually apply to them. If so, the law or policy is justified, and the reasons are thereby excluded.

F. Conclusion

The purpose of this chapter was to provide a general account of prosecutorial practical reasoning. It did so somewhat indirectly, by clarifying the normal correspondence thesis and considering a series of potential objections and limitations to this account of how reasons for prosecutors are normally generated. This indirect approach is, I believe, necessary in light of the fact that if the normal correspondence thesis is true, it is very difficult to say much of anything of a precise nature regarding the reasons that guide prosecutorial action. Indeed, if the thesis is true, then reasons for prosecutors are potentially as numerous as the values that prosecutorial actions can realize. Given the broad array of different values identified in Chapter 4 (not to mention the myriad of values I have not considered) it is tempting to respond to the question of 'what reasons guide prosecutorial action?' by simply saying, 'all of 'em'. Such a response, of course, would not be terribly illuminating in thinking about the justification of prosecutorial action, and so I have attempted in this chapter both to narrow and to focus the implications that follow from the normal correspondence thesis.

In the next part of this book, I will narrow my focus considerably more, by turning my attention directly to domestic violence. At this point, it may be helpful to return to the motivating question introduced in Chapter 1: what should public prosecutors do when victims withdraw their support for the prosecution of domestic-violence cases? The basic answer, as explained and elaborated upon in this part of the book, is simply 'prosecutors should act rationally: they should

---

[61] As such, the policy directive may be justified under Raz's normal justification thesis.

act in accordance with practical reason'. I have also attempted to provide a better understanding of the implications that follow from this basic answer.

However, it is possible to identify a more fully elaborated answer to the motivating question, and this more elaborate answer will be developed and defended in Part III of this book. In sum, my answer is that very often public prosecutors should continue domestic-violence prosecutions despite the victims' requests to dismiss. In defending this answer, I will examine the reasons weighing in favour and against so-called 'victimless' prosecutions. In particular, I will emphasize what will be characterized as feminist reasons for such prosecutions, and I will argue that *ceteris paribus* domestic-violence prosecutors should act for such reasons. In other words, all other things being equal, domestic-violence prosecutors should act qua feminist prosecutors, and very often this will mean pursuing 'victimless' prosecutions.

PART III

CONSIDERING DOMESTIC VIOLENCE

6

What Counts as Domestic Violence?[1]

This chapter analyses the conceptual structure of domestic violence and critiques various influential accounts of domestic violence presently operating in the criminal justice system, legal and sociological academia, and domestic-violence advocacy communities. First, I present a preliminary analysis of domestic violence which distinguishes its three key elements: violence, domesticity, and patriarchy. Second, I develop an explanatory model of domestic violence based upon these elements. Third, I examine and critique four principal accounts of domestic violence, each of which reflects the conflicting ways in which the concept of domestic violence is used in the language and methodology of the criminal justice system, academia, and advocacy communities. Finally, I endorse a distinction between domestic violence in its strong sense (where domestic violence tends to sustain or perpetuate patriarchy[2]) and domestic violence in its weak sense (where it does not).

A. Setting the Stage

Two sets of lively, extensive, and often heated debates regarding domestic violence have been aired in the academic literature in recent decades. The first has been conducted in the sociological literature for nearly three decades and addresses the issue of gender prevalence in domestic violence.[3] The second has been conducted in the legal literature for nearly two decades and addresses the question of how the criminal legal system should respond in domestic-violence cases when the victim does not want the suspected offender to be arrested and/or later requests that charges be dismissed.[4]

---

[1] This chapter is a slightly amended version of MM Dempsey, 'What counts as domestic violence? A conceptual analysis' (2006) 12 William and Mary J of Women and the Law 301.

[2] I provide a detailed account of patriarchy in Chapter 7.

[3] The phrase 'gender prevalence' used herein refers to the rate at which males commit domestic violence against females as compared to the rate at which females commit domestic violence against males. The debate regarding gender prevalence in domestic violence was sparked by the early work of Susan Steinmetz, who claimed to document the allegedly widespread phenomenon of 'husband battering'. S Steinmetz, 'The battered husband syndrome' (1977) 2(3–4) *Victimology* 499.

[4] See, eg, J Zorza, 'The criminal law of misdemeanor violence (1970–1990)' (1992) 83 J of Crim L and Criminology 46; Editors, 'New state and federal responses to domestic violence' (1993) 106 Harvard L Rev 1528.

Oddly, the sociological debate has had little significant influence on the legal debate.[5] One possible reason for this lack of academic cross-fertilization may be the fact that the sociological debate has largely centred on the issue of research methodology.[6] In the sociological context, the question of what counts as domestic violence has been understood principally as a methodological question of how domestic violence ought to be measured. Perhaps it is because many legal academics are reluctant to engage with questions grounded in sociological research methodologies that the legal academic literature has failed to employ insights developed in the sociological literature to examine the underlying conceptual question of what counts as domestic violence. Whatever the reason, this failure is regrettable, and the analysis which follows in this chapter is one step towards its rectification.

This chapter does not aim to settle the existing legal or sociological debates regarding domestic violence. Rather, its aim is simply to set forth a clearly developed conceptual analysis of domestic violence, one that will bring clarity to the broader argument set forth in this book.[7] Developing a detailed understanding of domestic violence represents a crucial step in my argument because, as Gardner has noted, not all crimes are 'covered by a single moral map'.[8] In keeping with this observation, I believe that domestic-violence offences call for a conceptual analysis that illustrates its distinctions from other types of wrongdoing. In this sense, what follows can be understood as an exercise in the moral cartography of domestic violence: it provides a moral map that can (in part) inform and guide the exercise of prosecutorial discretion in such cases.[9]

[5] While the sociological debate has been noted in a law review article by Linda Kelly, the author fails to take seriously the conceptual and evaluative issues which underlie this conflict and, instead, simply assumes that family-violence researchers have accurately captured the 'empirical reality' of domestic violence. L Kelly, 'Disabusing the definition of domestic abuse: How women batter men and the role of the feminist state' (2003) 30 Florida State University L Rev 791. For discussion of family violence researchers, see section D.2 below.

[6] Eg, H Johnson, 'Rethinking survey research on violence against women' in RE Dobash and R Dobash (eds), *Rethinking Violence Against Women* (Thousand Oaks: Sage, 1998); RE Dobash and R Dobash, 'The context-specific approach' in R Finkelhor, R Gelles, and G Hotaling (eds), *The Dark Side of Families: Current family violence research* (Beverley Hills: Sage, 1983); D Saunders, 'Wife abuse, husband abuse, or mutual combat? A feminist perspective on the empirical findings' in K Yllo and M Bograd (eds), *Feminist Perspectives on Wife Abuse* (Newbury Park: Sage, 1988); M Straus and others, 'The revised conflict tactics scales (CTS2): Development and preliminary psychometric data' (1996) 17 *J of Family Issues* 283; K Yllo, 'Political and methodological debates in wife abuse research' in K Yllo and M Bograd (eds), *Feminist Perspectives on Wife Abuse* (Newbury Park: Sage, 1988); DR Loseke, RJ Gelles, and MM Cavanaugh, *Current Controversies on Family Violence* (Thousand Oaks: Sage, 2005).

[7] This chapter, therefore, aims not merely to track linguistic usage or to stipulate a meaning of domestic violence, but rather to explain what is important about domestic violence and to establish an evaluative test for the concept. B Bix, 'Conceptual questions and jurisprudence' (1995) 1 Legal Theory 465.

[8] J Gardner, 'Crime: In proportion and perspective' in A Ashworth and M Wasik (eds), *Proportion and Perspective in Fundamentals of Sentencing Theory: Essays in honour of Andrew von Hirsch* (Oxford: Clarendon, 1998) 48.

[9] Note, however, that I do not express an opinion here on the question of whether the special part of the criminal law should seek to set domestic-violence offences apart, for example, by

This chapter proceeds in three steps. The first section unpacks three conceptual elements that constitute domestic violence: violence, domesticity, and patriarchy. The second section employs these three conceptual elements to develop an explanatory model of domestic violence. The final section uses this explanatory model to clarify and critique three influential accounts of domestic violence (the violence account, domestic account, and patriarchy account) and to explain and defend a fourth account of domestic violence (Michael Johnson's account).

B. Three Elements of Domestic Violence

Domestic violence is best understood in terms of three distinct elements: violence, domesticity, and patriarchy. In this section, I examine each of these elements.

1. Violence

There are two senses of violence from which I wish to distance my account, both of which can be categorized as legitimist accounts of violence. Such accounts 'incorporate a strong notion of illegitimacy into the very meaning of violence' and typically go so far as to conclude that all violence is normatively illegitimate.[10]

(a) Traditional legitimist accounts

The first sense of violence is reflected in what I will refer to as the 'traditional legitimist accounts' of violence. There are two aspects of such accounts worth noting at this point: (1) they conceive of all violence as illegitimate by definition; and (2) they adopt a narrow conception of what counts as violence, typically restricting their focus to the direct, physical use of force. Traditional legitimist accounts are prevalent in the philosophical literature, where they typically come in one of three flavours: political legitimist accounts, legal legitimist accounts, and moral legitimist accounts. Stanage, for example, bases his account of violence on its political illegitimacy, claiming that violence is best understood in the context of a political civil order and that violent acts are by definition 'dis-ordered and un-civil'.[11] In contrast, Hook conceptualizes violence on the basis of its legal or moral illegitimacy, defining violence as 'the illegal or immoral use of force'.[12] The normative framework

specifically enacting an offence of 'domestic violence' or the like. For arguments in favour of such an offence, see V Tadros, 'The distinctiveness of domestic violence: A freedom based account' (2005) 65 Louisiana L Rev 989.

[10] CAJ Coady, 'The idea of violence' (1986) 3 *Journal of Applied Philosophy* 3.

[11] S Stanage, 'Violatives: Modes and themes of violence' in S Stanage (ed), *Reason and Violence: Philosophical investigations* (Oxford: Basil Blackwell, 1974) 226.

[12] S Hook, 'Ideologies of violence' in S Hook (ed), *Revolution, Reform and Social Justice* (Oxford: Basil Blackwell, 1976) 225.

upon which one bases a claim of illegitimacy, however, is not always made explicit in traditional legitimist accounts of violence. For example, Girvetz offers a traditional legitimist account of violence when he defines violence as 'illegitimate and unsanctioned acts', but he fails to answer the question: illegitimate and unsanctioned as to *what system of norms*?[13]

I reject legitimist accounts of violence for reasons explained in section B.1(c) below. However, I will still make use of the concept of illegitimacy to further my analysis, by dividing categories of action into the legitimate and illegitimate. For the sake of clarity and consistency with terminology in other chapters of this book, however, I will substitute the terms 'justified' and 'unjustified' for the terms 'legitimate' and 'illegitimate'. Since I am invoking the concept of justifiability, I must answer the question that Girvetz did not, and clearly specify the normative system referenced by my claims. The normative system I wish to invoke is that of morality rather than legality, political legitimacy, or some other notion of normative justification. In other words, when I claim that an act is justified or unjustified below, I mean that it is *morally* justified or unjustified.[14] At this point, I do not attempt to develop or defend any particular set of moral norms that might further explicate such claims. Rather, this chapter is concerned only to develop a model within which competing accounts of domestic violence can be better understood.

(b) Structuralist accounts

Next I wish to distance my account of domestic violence from a second sense of violence: what I shall call structuralist accounts. There are two things worth noting about such accounts at this point: (1) they conceive of all violence as unjustified by definition (ie, they are examples of legitimist accounts of violence); and (2) they adopt a broad view of what counts as violence, including both the direct, physical use of force (which is referred to as 'personal violence') and the existence of structural inequalities (which is referred to as 'structural violence').[15] The concept of structural violence is the key to understanding structuralist accounts. Structural violence, according to these accounts, includes all social structures that sustain or perpetuate 'unequal power and...unequal life chances', and such structures are deemed, by definition, to constitute violence.[16]

---

[13] H Givertz, 'An anatomy of violence' in S Stanage (ed), *Reason and Violence: Philosophical investigations* (Oxford: Basil Blackwell, 1974) 185.

[14] My discussion here may suggest too strict a division between normative systems such as law, politics, and morality. I do not mean to suggest that these systems can properly be understood as conceptually unrelated, but merely want to point out that it would be helpful if accounts of violence that claim that violence is illegitimate would clarify their normative framework for making such a claim.

[15] J Galtung, 'Violence, peace and peace research' (1969) 6 *Journal of Peace Research* 167.

[16] Galtung (n 15 above) 171; Coady (n 10 above) 4.

Structuralist accounts of violence inform a great deal of modern political discourse.[17] Notable amongst structuralist accounts is Galtung's foundational work on peace and violence, wherein he claimed that all unjust social conditions (such as poverty) are best understood as forms of violence.[18] The point of characterizing structural inequalities as violence is to launch a normative attack against such inequalities—ie, to claim that they are by definition normatively illegitimate. The logic goes something like this: all violence is bad, all structural inequality is violence; therefore, all structural inequality is bad. The first premise is borrowed from traditional legitimist accounts of violence, the second premise marks the structuralist accounts' unique contribution to the analysis of violence, and the conclusion reflects the political awakening that advocates of structuralist accounts hope will result from their argument. I reject structuralist accounts of violence for reasons explained in section B.1(c) below. I will, however, use the concept of structural inequality to further my analysis of patriarchy in Chapter 7.

(c) Critique of legitimist accounts

I reject the first premise of legitimist accounts of violence (ie, that all violence is normatively illegitimate) because this premise strikes me as conflating normative and empirical accounts of violence. This conflation creates two problems. The first problem crops up when legitimists identify what counts as violence as an empirical matter based upon their normative understanding of violence. According to their normative understanding of violence, all violence is unjustified. If this understanding sets the benchmark for what counts as violence as an empirical matter, one will be unable to identify as violent any actions which *are* justified. Such an approach should be rejected because it obscures important ways in which the concept of violence actually functions in the English language. For example, shooting and killing someone is typically understood as a violent act, whilst the question of its justifiability is treated as a distinct issue. Under normal usage, it is possible to make sense of the claim that a person who shoots and kills an attacker in self-defence has committed a *violent but justified* act. If, however, one begins with the normative assessment of the act and allows that to control the empirical assessment, then one cannot understand the act of shooting and killing in self-defence as an act of violence.[19] Due to the legitimist accounts' inability to conceptualize such acts as violent, I believe they are unhelpful in understanding the concept of violence and the ways that the concept is used in the criminal justice system.

The second problem mirrors the first and crops up when legitimists attempt to identify what counts as violence as a normative matter based on their

---

[17]   Eg, P Farmer, 'On suffering and structural violence: A view from below' (1996) 125 *Daedalus* 261; V Gallagher, *The True Cost of Low Prices: The violence of globalization* (Maryknoll: Orbis, 2006).

[18]   Galtung (n 15 above).

[19]   Eg, Galtung claims that people killed by an earthquake do not die a violent death. Galtung (n 15 above) 168–9.

understanding of violence as an empirical matter, without stopping along the way to conduct an independent normative evaluation of the act in question. This approach leads to a tremendous amount of question-begging in legitimist accounts of violence.[20] Since legitimist accounts view all violence as unjustified by definitional fiat, once they have identified an act of violence as an empirical matter, they jump to the conclusion that the act is unjustified, thereby ignoring the fundamental normative question of whether a certain act which may be properly identified as violent on an empirical assessment should or should not be considered unjustified on a normative assessment.

Finally, I reject the second premise of the structuralist accounts of violence (ie, that all structural inequalities are violence). While I believe that structuralist accounts provide a compelling tool in progressive political discourse—a means of challenging preconceived notions regarding the legitimacy of social conditions, and of motivating society to awaken to and perhaps remedy existing injustices—I believe that little is gained from conflating the concepts of structural inequality and violence. Rather, I believe that violence and structural inequality are best understood as distinct (albeit often related) concepts. Moreover, in terms of reflecting common usage and facilitating the joining of issue with policymakers, I believe that structuralist accounts of violence are unsatisfying insofar as they fail to reflect the way the concept of violence is used within the criminal justice system.

(d) A proposed non-legitimist, narrow account of violence

I propose that violence can best be understood under a non-legitimist, narrow account. This account of violence does two things: (1) it creates conceptual space in which to understand violence as either morally justified or unjustified; and (2) it adopts a narrow view of what counts as violence, focusing on the direct, physical use of force. First, my account of violence includes both legitimate violence and illegitimate violence. Specifically, under my account, violence is merely a pro tanto wrong, the doing of which can be morally justified, all things considered.[21] In this sense, my account is consistent with Coady's view that 'the resort to violence even when morally justifiable should commonly be regarded as a matter for regret'.[22] Second, my account of violence rejects the notion of structural violence and instead conceives of violence narrowly, as the direct, physical use of force. My use of the word 'direct' is meant to imply a rejection of accounts of negative responsibility such as the one offered by John Harris, whereby the failure to

---

[20] Some of this question begging is illustrated in the CTS methodology of family violence researchers, discussed below at text surrounding nn 70–80.

[21] On the distinction between prima facie and pro tanto wrongdoing, see Chapter 2, n 44.

[22] Coady (n 10 above) 17.

prevent violence is understood as doing violence.[23] My use of the word 'physical' is meant to reinforce my rejection of the notion of structural violence, wherein violence is understood in terms of states of affairs rather than actions. Note, however, that my use of the word 'physical' is not meant to suggest any requirement that violent acts result in injury or damage (such as bruising, etc). In other words, on my account, violent acts are no less violent for their failure to cause injury or damage.[24] Finally, my use of the word 'force' refers to the exertion of energy or strength upon an object.[25] In this sense, a storm can be said to be violent; but as my topic is the criminal law, I will focus on the ways in which people are violent.

Before moving on, I wish to draw a distinction between what I mean by 'violence' and what I mean by 'abuse'. This distinction will be drawn further and clarified below in section C, but for now it may clarify matters to mention that my use of the concept 'abuse' serves as an umbrella category that includes both *violent abuse* and *non-violent abuse*. Further, some forms of violence can be understood as members of a completely distinct category from that of abuse (ie, there exists a category of non-abusive violence).[26]

2. Domesticity

What makes violence into domestic violence? One tempting but not terribly illuminating approach to answering this question is what I refer to as the 'recipe approach': simply take the concept of violence, add domesticity, and mix. I believe this approach is both incomplete and conceptually inadequate; but I will not address those issues in this section.[27] Rather, in this section, I will clarify what I mean by 'domesticity' and begin to unpack the reasons why domesticity is relevant to understanding domestic violence.

Domesticity is simply 'the quality or state of being domestic' or possessing a 'domestic character'.[28] But what does it mean for violence to possess a domestic character? I address this question below by examining two common ways of characterizing the difference between domestic violence and what we might call 'generic violence'.

---

[23] J Harris, *Violence and Responsibility* (London: Routledge, 1980) 24–47. The ascription of responsibility for omissions (or 'negative actions') is beyond the scope of this book. Suffice it to say that I will be concerned primarily with violent acts rather than omissions.

[24] This is where my account departs from Coady (n 10 above) 15.

[25] 'Force, n1' Oxford English Dictionary Online <http://dictionary.oed.com///00087777> accessed 27 August 2008.

[26] Eg, violent self-defence.

[27] The incompleteness of this approach will be illuminated in my discussion of the final element of domestic violence (patriarchy) in section B.3 below. The conceptual inadequacy of the recipe approach will be addressed in section C, where I build an explanatory model of domestic violence which examines the various relationships that exist between elements of domestic violence, rather than simply mixing all of the elements together.

[28] 'Domesticity, a' Oxford English Dictionary Online <http://dictionary.oed.com///50068492> accessed 27 August 2008.

(a) Location

One way to differentiate domestic violence from generic violence is to focus on the location in which the violence occurs. While no statutory provisions or government policies in the US or England define domestic violence by reference to its physical location, the relevance of location to understanding domestic violence is reflected in government reports and academic literature, which often characterize domestic violence as 'violence in the home'.[29]

Why might the location of the violence be relevant to understanding what counts as domestic violence? One possible answer to this question points to the location of the home as a 'private' sphere, where people's conduct is protected from external scrutiny. Under this account, generic violence is conceptualized as 'public' violence, and domestic violence is conceptualized as 'private' violence.[30] Paradigms of generic violence include violent acts which occurs in 'public' locations (such as pubs or streets), whereas paradigms of domestic violence include violent acts which occur in 'private' spaces (such as the home). Historically, the public/private dichotomy was used as a basis upon which to prevent criminal prosecution of domestic violence, even when victims actively sought assistance from the criminal justice system.[31] More recently, however, with increasing criminal justice intervention into domestic violence (particularly in cases where the victim requests assistance) the historical conception of domestic violence as a 'private' matter has been eroded.[32]

Another possible reason why location might be relevant to understanding what counts as domestic violence points to the symbolic significance of the home as a place of comfort, safety, and protection. As Gardner and Shute have noted with regard to rape, '[o]ften the special symbolism of a particular act or class of acts is tied to the particular symbolism of acts which are regarded as their moral opposites'.[33] When violence occurs within the home, a moral opposition

---

[29] Eg, HMCPSI, *Violence in the Home* (2004); R Gelles, *The Violent Home* (Newbury Park: Sage 1974); N L Clark, 'Crime begins at home: Let's stop punishing victims and perpetuating violence' (1987) 28 William and Mary L Rev 263; T Faragher, *Private Violence and Public Policy* (London: Routledge, 1985).

[30] See discussion and critique of the public/private dichotomy at Chapter 2, section B. For further critique, see S Boyd, *Challenging the Public/Private Divide: Feminism, Law and Public Policy* (Buffalo: University of Toronto Press, 1997); N Lacey, 'Theory into practice? Pornography and the public/private dichotomy' in A Bottomley and J Conaghan (eds), *Feminist Theory and Legal Strategy* (Oxford: Blackwell, 1993); J Landes (ed), *Feminism, the Public and the Private* (Oxford: OUP, 1998); CA MacKinnon, *Toward a Feminist Theory of the State* (Cambridge: Harvard University Press, 1989) 168; K O'Donovan, *Sexual Divisions in Law* (London: Weidenfeld and Nicolson, 1985); M Thornton (ed), *Public and Private: Feminist legal debates* (Melbourne: OUP, 1995).

[31] S Edwards, *Policing 'Domestic' Violence: Women, the law and the state* (London: Sage, 1986) 49–51.

[32] C Hoyle, *Negotiating Domestic Violence: Police, criminal justice and victims* (Oxford: OUP, 1998).

[33] S Shute and J Gardner, 'The wrongness of rape' in J Horder (ed), *Oxford Essays in Jurisprudence* (Oxford: OUP, 2000) 210, examining the particular significance of sexual penetration in understanding the wrongness of rape.

between 'home as danger' and 'home as protection' is established. Thus, to the extent that home-based violence is the symbolic antithesis of safety and security in the home, location becomes important to understanding the concept of domestic violence.

(b) Relationship of parties

Another potentially fruitful way to differentiate domestic violence from generic violence is to focus on the nature of the relationship between the parties. In paradigmatic cases of generic violence, the parties typically have no significant pre-existing relationship, whereas in domestic violence, the parties necessarily stand in a domestic relationship to one another: a relationship characterized by intimacy, familial ties, or a shared household.[34]

Focusing on the nature of the relationship between the parties is the most common way of differentiating domestic violence from generic violence in US and English law.[35] The relevant types of relationships have been defined in a number of ways, more or less broadly. The most common way of defining a domestic relationship in US codes is in terms of a 'family or household member', which typically includes relationships between spouses, parents and children, siblings, and current or former intimate partners—and less frequently includes extended familial relations (eg, up to fourth-degree consanguity),[36] platonic room-mates,[37] and the relationship between elderly or disabled persons and their caregivers.[38]

In England, there is no codified definition of domestic violence, but various formulations have been developed which identify the relevant relationship in terms of 'a close or family relationship',[39] 'adults who are or have been intimate partners or family members',[40] or 'an intimate or family type relationship'.[41] The criminal offence of causing or allowing the death of a child or vulnerable adult specifically targets domestic relationships, defining this concept in terms of those who are 'members of the same household'.[42] Finally, the criminal offence of breach of non-molestation order potentially applies to any

---

[34] 'Domestic, a' Oxford English Dictionary Online <http://dictionary.oed.com///50068482> accessed 27 August 2008.

[35] N Lemon, *Domestic Violence Law* (2nd edn, St Paul: West, 2005), discussing US criminal and civil law; R Bird, *Domestic Violence: Law and practice* (5th edn, Bristol: Jordan, 2006), discussing English civil law.

[36] Alaska's Definition of Domestic Violence AK ST 18.66.990(4)(E).

[37] New Jersey's Definition of Domestic Violence NJSA 2C:25–19.

[38] Illinois Domestic Violence Act of 1986 750 ILCS 60/103(6).

[39] CPS, Policy for Prosecuting Cases of Domestic Violence (2005).

[40] Home Office, 'Domestic Violence' <http://www.homeoffice.gov.uk/victims/crime/violence> accessed 4 May 2008.

[41] Women's Aid (Britain's largest anti-domestic-violence advocacy organization), 'About Domestic Violence' <http://www.womensaid.org.uk> accessed 27 August 2008.

[42] Domestic Violence Crime and Victims Act 2004 s 5.

'associated persons', a category that includes a broad array of relationships including:

spouses and former spouses, civil partners and former civil partners, cohabitants and former cohabitants, those who have agreed to marry each other or to enter a civil partnership, those who live or have lived in the same household otherwise than merely by reason of being the other party's employee, tenant, lodger or boarder, parties to the same family proceedings, those who are parents of or have parental responsibility for a child, relatives and parties connected through adoption.[43]

Why might the relationship between the parties be relevant to understanding what counts as domestic violence? Again, two answers present themselves, each of which tracks the discussion above regarding the relevance of the location of the violence. First, domestic relationships carry strong connotations of privacy that transcend the physical location of the parties at any given moment. Second, the special symbolism of physical affection within many domestic relations, and its contrast with physical violence in such relationships, may explain the particular relevance of the relationship in conceptualizing domestic violence.[44] Insofar as a loving touch, hug, or kiss is understood to represent the ideal expression of physical affection between romantic partners or parents and children, this may explain why, when replaced by a slap or punch, such violence is considered particularly problematic.

3. Patriarchy

What, if any, role does patriarchy play in understanding domestic violence? In this section, I briefly explain the concept of patriarchy and unpack some of its key features.[45] In subsequent sections, I employ the concept of patriarchy to delineate two types of domestic violence and to highlight the differences between competing accounts of domestic violence.

My account of patriarchy will be explained in more detail in the next chapter, but suffice it for now to say that patriarchy is a wrongful structural inequality. Structural inequalities are functions of social structures, the 'sets of rules and principles that govern activities in the different domains of social life'.[46] When social structures sustain or perpetuate the uneven distribution of social power, they can be understood as structural inequalities. Structural inequalities inform our practical understanding regarding the way the world works, by providing a context for recognizing which people generally hold power in relation to which

---

[43] H Reece, 'The end of domestic violence' (2006) 69 MLR 770, 771 (critiquing this expansion in 'associated persons'), discussing Family Law Act 1996 s 62(3), as amended by Domestic Violence Crime and Victims Act 2004, part one.

[44] Shute and Gardner (n 33 above).

[45] I explain my account of patriarchy in more detail in Chapter 7.

[46] T Schatzki, 'Structuralism in social science' (1998) Routledge Encylopedia of Philosophy Online <http://www.rep.routledge.com//R036?ssid=467079195&n=2#> accessed 13 April 2007.

other people. Like acts of violence, acts that tend to sustain or perpetuate structural inequalities constitute pro tanto wrongs, but they have the potential (at least
analytically) to be rendered justifiable all things considered.[47] That said, what
follows is based in part on the assumption that patriarchy is usually unjustifiable,
all things considered.[48]

Patriarchy can be understood as closely related to the concepts of power and
control. Power is the ability or entitlement to exercise control over another person,
and in any given relationship, the more powerful person may use his or her power
as an instrument of control over the less powerful person. Power, in the sense I
employ herein, is an inherently social concept. As Hannah Arendt has observed:

> Power is never the property on an individual; it belongs to a group...When we say of
> somebody that he is 'in power' we actually refer to his being empowered by a certain
> number of people...*potestas in populo*, without a people or group there is no power...[49]

I agree with Arendt's account of power as deriving from one's social group.[50] Thus,
I believe that it makes sense to conceptualize patriarchy in terms of the social
group of gender. This comment is not intended to essentialize or reduce diverse
peoples' experiences of patriarchy or gender.[51] Rather, it is merely intended to
reflect the view that there is something useful to be gained from working with
concepts based on social groups such as 'women' and 'men', and in recognizing
that social power is often granted or denied on the basis of one's gender.[52]

C. An Explanatory Model of Domestic Violence

In this section, I present an explanatory model of domestic violence using the
three elements examined above. This model presents a philosophical analysis

---

[47] See Chapter 2, n 44. The realm of justifiable structural inequality is arguably quite limited:
eg, adult–child inequality. JS Mill, 'On the Subjection of Women' in R Wolheim (ed), *Three Essays:
On Liberty; Representative Government; The Subjection of Women* (Oxford: OUP, 1975). Note,
however, that some commentators claim that even this inequality is unjustifiable. S Firestone, *The
Dialectic of Sex* (New York: Morrow, 1970); C Parton, 'Women, gender oppression and child abuse'
in VACS Group (ed), *Taking Child Abuse Seriously: Contemporary issues in child abuse theory and
practice* (London: Unwin Hyman, 1990). I will not, however, explore the adult–child structural
inequality or parent–child domestic violence further.

[48] S Walby, *Theorizing Patriarchy* (Oxford: Blackwell, 1990).

[49] H Arendt, *On Violence* (London: Allen Lane, 1970) 44, as cited in Stanage (n 11 above)
225–6.

[50] Power inequalities can exist between people removed from their social groups (eg, between
two inhabitants of an otherwise deserted island), but one's sense of entitlement to such power (in
the sense that I use the concept here) is ultimately grounded in an understanding of the relative
power relations between social groups. This point is well illustrated in Robinson Crusoe's sense of
entitlement to power upon encountering Friday, a sense grounded in Crusoe's previous experience
of racist structural inequalities.

[51] See discussion at Chapter 7, section A ('On Being Feminist').

[52] CA MacKinnon, *Feminism Unmodified* (Cambridge: Harvard University Press, 1987) 170,
defining men [and women] as 'the status of masculinity [and femininity] that is accorded to [peo-
ple] on the basis of their biology but is not itself biological'.

of domestic violence along with several of its key related concepts, and provides a framework within which to explain and critique leading accounts of domestic violence. The model described in Figure 1 consists of four spheres. Three intersecting spheres represent the elements discussed in section B above: violence, domesticity, and patriarchy. Each of these three spheres represents an array of acts, any of which can be characterized respectively as 'a violent act', 'an act taking place in a domestic context', and 'an act which tends to sustain or perpetuate patriarchy'. The fourth sphere cuts across all three of these intersecting elements and delineates acts that are all-things-considered unjustified from acts that are all-things-considered justified. This fourth sphere is called the 'sphere of moral justification'. Unjustified acts fall within this sphere, whilst justified acts fall outside this sphere. The outline of this sphere is presented as a broken line, which is meant to represent the contested nature of the moral judgements attributed to many of the concepts that fall at the sphere's edges and penumbra.

The intersections of the various spheres create space for 13 distinct conceptual categories that represent concepts of, or related to, domestic violence. Each of these categories is discussed below in a list which corresponds to the numbers located within each conceptual space. The list provides brief accounts of different forms of domestic violence and their key related concepts, as well as examples of the actions represented by each concept in the model.[53] Where appropriate, the labels I will apply to various concepts hereinafter are also noted.

This model serves two purposes: (1) it enables me to explain (in section D) the nature of the disagreements that exist in the literature regarding the correct use of the concept 'domestic violence'; and (2) it presents a philosophical analysis of domestic violence and some key related concepts, which, I contend, reflects the correct use of these concepts. However, while my model provides space for 13 concepts, I do not mean to imply that every conceptual category should be understood as corresponding to an existing usage or social phenomena. Some numbers may simply reflect empty categories: conceptual place-holders that assist in making distinctions but do not accurately account for current social realities. Ultimately, this model is meant to provide a framework for explaining and critiquing rival accounts of domestic violence. My hope is that with the assistance of a clear conceptual model, we can better understand and critique the leading accounts of domestic violence and better appreciate the assumptions and values that underlie current debates regarding the prosecution of such cases.

The 13 conceptual categories represented in the explanatory model are as follows:

[53] Many of the examples provided below evidence a feminist point of view, the point of view through which I am approaching the concept of patriarchy. Given the intersectionality of patriarchal structural inequality with other forms of structural inequality, such as racism and heterosexism, other examples may be generated by adopting a different point of view. See Chapter 7, section A for discussion of intersectionality and relevance of point of view in appreciating patriarchy.

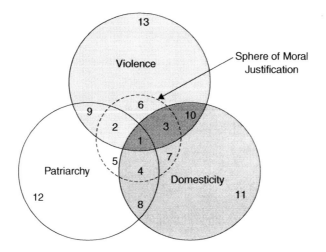

Figure 1. Explanatory model of domestic violence

1. Violent act occurring in a domestic context, which tends to sustain or perpetuate patriarchy and is, all things considered, unjustified. I will refer to
   this concept as 'domestic violence in its strong sense'. The classic paradigm of
   domestic violence in its strong sense is 'wife battering'.

2. Violent act occurring in a non-domestic context, which tends to sustain or
   perpetuate patriarchy, and is, all things considered, unjustified. The paradigm
   of this violence is stranger rape.

3. Violent act occurring in a domestic context, which does not tend to sustain
   or perpetuate patriarchy but is, all things considered, unjustified. I will refer
   to this concept as 'domestic violence in its weak sense'. Examples include the
   actions of a woman who slaps her male partner on the cheek to convey offence
   and the actions of a victim of domestic violence in its strong sense who engages
   in unjustified violent retaliation against his or her abuser.

4. Non-violent act occurring in a domestic context, which tends to sustain or
   perpetuate patriarchy and is, all things considered, unjustified. I will refer to
   this concept as 'domestic abuse'. Examples of domestic abuse include refusal
   to allow the abused person contact with friends or family, demands to know
   the abused person's location and companions at all times, refusal to allow the
   abused person to work outside the home or have access to money, etc.

5. Non-violent act occurring in non-domestic context, which tends to sustain
   or perpetuate patriarchy and is, all things considered, unjustified. Examples
   include the telling of a sexist joke in the workplace and other forms of non-
   physical sexual harassment.

6. Violent act occurring in a non-domestic context, which does not tend to sustain or perpetuate patriarchy but is, all things considered, unjustified. I will refer to this concept as 'generic violence'. A paradigm of generic violence is a pub brawl.

7. Non-violent act occurring in a domestic context, which does not tend to sustain or perpetuate patriarchy but is, all things considered, unjustified. I will refer to this concept as 'domestic conflict'. Examples include situations in which people lose their temper with their domestic partners or family members because they are annoyed, in a bad mood, tired, etc.[54]

8. Non-violent act occurring in a domestic context, which tends to sustain or perpetuate patriarchy but is, all things considered, justified. This kind of conduct likely reflects an empty conceptual category.[55]

9. Violent act occurring in a non-domestic context, which tends to sustain or perpetuate patriarchy but is, all things considered, justified. Again, this kind of violence likely reflects an empty conceptual category.

10. Violent act occurring in a domestic context, which does not tend to sustain or perpetuate patriarchy and is, all things considered, justified. The classic paradigm of this kind of violence is the case of a battered wife who shoots her abusive husband in self-defence, and further examples include play fighting between intimate partners (eg, pillow fighting), horseplay between siblings, etc.

11. Non-violent act occurring in a domestic context, which does not tend to sustain or perpetuate patriarchy and is, all things considered, justified. Examples include hugging one's partner, playing a game with one's child, helping one's sibling clean the house, etc.

12. Non-violent act occurring in a non-domestic context, which tends to sustain or perpetuate patriarchy but is, all things considered, justified. As with categories 8 and 9 above, this kind of conduct likely reflects an empty conceptual category.

13. Violent act occurring in a non-domestic context, which does not tend to sustain or perpetuate patriarchy and is, all things considered, justified. One example is the stabbing of a stranger-attacker in self-defence, and further examples include violent acts inherent to sporting games.

Several of the categories above (8, 9, and 12) may reflect empty conceptual categories, which is to say that tokens of the kinds of conduct described therein may not actually exist in the world. By constructing these conceptual placeholders, I have allowed for the possibility that conduct which tends to sustain or

---

[54] Compare this category to language used in the introduction to the Conflicts Tactic Scale, discussed below at text to n 73.

[55] Whether any instance of conduct can be appropriately included in this category depends inter alia on whether an instance of conduct which tends to sustain or perpetuate patriarchy can be justified.

perpetuate patriarchy can be justified. However, by suggesting that these conceptual categories may in fact be empty, I have committed myself to the view that it is highly unlikely (albeit not conceptually impossible) to identify an actual instance of such conduct as justified.

D. Four Accounts of Domestic Violence

There are four principal accounts of domestic violence currently operating in the criminal justice system, academic literature, and advocacy communities. This section explains the usage of the concept of domestic violence under each account and describes the nature of the conflicts and similarities between competing accounts. In addition to providing a brief overview of each account's approach to domestic violence, I will use the model developed in section C to explain what counts as domestic violence under each account and which concepts are most closely related to domestic violence under each account. It bears stating up front that these accounts overlap considerably, and common usage often jumps back and forth between them depending upon the context of a given discussion. That said, I believe there are significant differences between these accounts, and in order to understand the literature and policy debates regarding the prosecution of domestic violence, it is necessary to appreciate the nuances of these distinctions.

1. Violence account

The violence account is the dominant understanding of domestic violence in the criminal justice system. As its name suggests, this account highlights the importance of the violence element in understanding domestic violence. Consistent with this outlook, this account is often invoked to justify a strict, formalistic law-enforcement response to domestic violence, along the lines represented by the slogan 'domestic violence is a crime' and the call to 'take domestic violence seriously'. Patriarchy is not deemed a necessary element for understanding domestic violence under the violence account. Rather, domestic violence tends to be viewed solely in terms of violence and domesticity. In particular, this account emphasizes the relevance of physical harm caused by violence occurring in a domestic context. For example, law-enforcement officers are encouraged to think of themselves as engaged in 'homicide-prevention' and to view every case of domestic violence as a potential homicide.[56]

Paradigms of domestic violence in this account include domestic homicide, attempted homicide, and acts of violence that cause permanent disability

---

[56] Eg, Michigan refers to its domestic violence police specialists as its 'Homicide Prevention Task Force'. MCAD Violence, 'Governor initiates domestic violence homicide prevention task force' <http://www.mcadsv.org//cc02_01.html> accessed 4 May 2007.

or scarring physical injury. Violence (understood in terms of its physical con-sequences) is the element which, if altered in nature or severity, controls the centrality of the paradigm cases. Thus, a push or slap which does not result in any physical injury is not considered a central case of domestic violence under this account. The only exception to this generalization is when the push or slap is committed in a context that ranks high on a 'lethality assessment index': a measurement tool that aims to predict the risk that a domestic-violence offender will kill his victim.[57] Absent a high threat of lethality, a simple push or slap that causes no injury will be highly marginalized, to the point that it is unlikely to be conceptualized as a 'real' case of domestic violence.

In terms of the concepts charted on my explanatory model in section C, the violence account understands domestic violence as encompassing both [1] and [3]. However, this account is ultimately unsatisfying because it does not make any distinction between domestic violence in its strong sense [1] and its weak sense [3].[58] The concept most closely related to domestic violence on this account is generic violence [6], which serves as the standard by which domestic violence and all institutional responses to domestic violence are to be measured. In other words, 'taking domestic violence seriously' under the violence account amounts to treating domestic violence similarly to generic violence.[59]

The violence account marks an important historical turn in the treatment of domestic violence by the criminal justice system. However, this account has been rightly criticized by feminist advocates for its failure to consider patriar-chy in conceptualizing domestic violence. The bulk of these criticisms have been expressed in debates regarding dual arrests.[60] Complaints that strict, formalistic crime-control policies have resulted in high numbers of domestic-violence vic-tims being arrested are often, in essence, complaints against the violence account, which fails to appreciate the role of patriarchy in understanding what counts as domestic violence.[61]

---

[57] N Websdale, 'Lethality assessment tools: A critical analysis' VAWnet <http://new.vawnet. org/category/Main_Doc.php?docid=387> accessed 3 November 2008.

[58] This failure to distinguish between the strong and weak senses of domestic violence results from the violence account's elision of patriarchy in conceptualizing domestic violence.

[59] Ironically, empirical research suggests that treating domestic violence similarly to generic violence results in extremely high dismissal rates in domestic-violence cases, since prosecutions are unlikely to proceed absent victim support even in generic violence cases. A Cretney and oth-ers, 'Criminalizing assault: The failure of the offence against society model' (1994) 15 British J of Criminology 34. Thus it is not clear what the violence account's call to 'take domestic violence seriously' means given its unsatisfying conceptualization of domestic violence as closely related to generic violence.

[60] Dual arrest occurs when both victim and batterer are arrested in cases where batterers subject the victims to domestic violence in its strong sense [1], and victims commit domestic violence in its weak sense [3], or more problematically, merely defend themselves against the batterers' attacks [10].

[61] D Coker, 'Crime control and feminist law reform in domestic violence law: A critical review' (2001) 4 Buffalo Crim L Rev 801. Ironically, some who criticize law enforcement for arresting and prosecuting victims who engage in retaliatory violence [3] are the same folks who praise the police

2. Domestic account

The domestic account is the most influential account of domestic violence in the social-science academic literature and is the dominant approach to empirical research in the US.[62] The research performed by its adherents has produced the world's most widely cited statistics regarding the prevalence of domestic violence.[63] There are two important aspects to understanding the domestic account: its theoretical approach to answering the question of what counts as domestic violence, and its methodological approach to measuring domestic violence for the purpose of empirical research. I will address each of these aspects respectively below.

Theoretically, the domestic account emphasizes the role of the domestic context as the crucial element in understanding what counts as domestic violence.[64] Like the violence account, the domestic account is ultimately unsatisfying because patriarchy becomes relatively superfluous in understanding what counts as domestic violence. As Faith Elliott has noted, this account takes 'the family rather than gender inequality as its [primary] unit of analysis'.[65] It views patriarchy as merely 'one factor among many, and minimizes the importance of men's power in structuring family relationships'.[66]

The central case of domestic violence under the domestic account involves parties who stand in a close, familial domestic relationship to one another. Cases of domestic violence under this account are considered to be more or less central depending upon the nature of the domestic relationship at issue. Paradigms include spousal assault[67] and child abuse, whilst cases involving cousins or platonic room-mates, for example, are highly marginalized—to the

---

for 'tak[ing] domestic violence seriously' by enacting mandatory arrest laws grounded in a violence account. M Wanless, 'Mandatory arrest: A step toward eradicating domestic violence: But is it enough?' [1996] U of Illinois L Rev 533, 559.

[62] Key works reflecting this account include: R Gelles, *Intimate Violence in Families* (3rd edn, Thousand Oaks: Sage, 1997); R Gelles and M Straus, *Intimate Violence* (New York: Simon & Schuster, 1988); R Gelles, *The Violent Home* (Newbury Park: Sage, 1974); M Straus, R Gelles, and S Steinmetz, *Behind Closed Doors: Violence in the American family* (Garden City, NY: Bantam, 1980); M Straus, 'The conflict tactics (CT) scales' (1979) 40 *Journal of Marriage and the Family* 75; M Straus and R Gelles, 'Societal change and change in family violence from 1975 to 1985 as revealed in two national surveys' in M Straus and R Gelles (eds), *Physical Violence in American Families* (New Brunswick, NJ: Transaction, 1990); M Straus and others, 'The revised conflict tactics scales (CTS2): Development and preliminary psychometric data' (1996) 17 *Journal of Family Issues* 283.

[63] See citations, ibid.

[64] For this reason, proponents of the domestic account often refer to domestic violence as 'intimate violence', 'family violence', or 'violence in the home', thereby emphasizing the importance of the domestic context in understanding domestic violence. See L Mills, 'Intimate violence as intimate: The journey and a path' (2003) 9 Cardozo Women's L J 461.

[65] FR Elliot, *Gender, Family & Society* (London: MacMillan, 1996).

[66] Ibid 177.

[67] The term 'spousal assault' is used intentionally here (rather than 'wife assault') in order to clarify that the domestic account regards wife assault and husband assault equally as paradigmatic of domestic violence. Steinmetz (n 3 above) 5.

point that such cases are unlikely to be understood as 'real' cases of domestic violence.[68] Unlike the violence account, however, central paradigms of domestic violence remain central under the domestic account irrespective of the degree of resulting physical harm or lethality risk. So, for example, the leading adherents to the domestic account have argued that paradigms of domestic violence range 'from spanking to murder' and that each should be understood as equally central.[69]

Methodologically, adherents to the domestic account often employ an empirical research tool called the Conflict Tactics Scale (CTS).[70] The CTS is a questionnaire developed by family violence researcher Murray Straus and his colleagues at the University of New Hampshire during the 1970s. With slight revision, the CTS remains one of the most widely used quantitative empirical-research methods for measuring the overall prevalence and gender prevalence[71] of domestic violence.[72] The CTS is a 'tick-the-box' type survey in which domestic violence is understood as arising out of symmetrical interpersonal conflicts, which the parties dysfunctionally attempt to resolve through the use of violence. This context of symmetry is well reflected in the introduction to the CTS:

No matter how well a couple gets along, there are times when they disagree, get annoyed with the other person, or just have spats or fights because they're in a bad mood or tired or for some other reason. They also use many different ways of trying to settle their differences. I'm going to read some things that you and your (spouse/partner) might do when you have an argument. I would like you to tell me how many times...in the past 12 months...[read item].[73]

The CTS goes on to ask questions that capture data regarding physical acts committed by the respondents, without asking questions that might provide relevant data upon which to evaluate the normative legitimacy of the acts. For example, the CTS fails to gather data that might facilitate distinctions between unprovoked assaults and self-defence[74] or distinctions between attacks and play-fighting.[75] As such, the CTS's 'tick-the-box' approach excludes information that

---

[68] Gelles and Straus (1988) (n 62 above) 59–67.

[69] Ibid 54.

[70] Straus (1979) (n 62 above); Straus and others (1996) (n 62 above).

[71] 'Gender prevalence' refers to the rate at which males commit domestic violence against females as compared to the rate at which females commit domestic violence against males. See n 3 above.

[72] Johnson (n 6 above) 27.

[73] Straus (1979) (n 62 above); Straus and others (1996) (n 62 above).

[74] W Dekeseredy and M Schwartz, 'Measuring the Extent of Woman Abuse in Intimate Heterosexual Relationships: A Critique of the Conflict Tactics Scales' (1998) National Resource Center on Domestic Violence <http://new.vawnet.org/Assoc_Files_VAWnet/AR_ctscrit.pdf> accessed 3 November 2008.

[75] D Currie, 'Violent men or violent women: Whose definition counts?' in RK Bergan (ed), *Issues in Intimate Violence* (Thousand Oaks: Sage, 1998), reporting on research which included in-depth interviews as a follow-up to administration of the CTS survey and, through the interviews,

might facilitate relevant normative distinctions in deciding whether an act counts as domestic violence.

Employing my explanatory model from section C once more, the domestic account understands domestic violence (theoretically) as including both [1] and [3].[76] The concepts most closely related to domestic violence are domestic abuse [4] and domestic conflict [7].[77] Methodologically, the CTS fails to differentiate between [1], [3], and [10] in operationalizing its concept of domestic violence. In other words, the CTS lumps together justified violence committed in a domestic context (eg, self-defence, play-fighting) [10] with both types of unjustified violence in a domestic context ([1] and [3]) and then counts them all equally as domestic violence.

The domestic account's methodological conflation of justified and unjustified acts under the heading of 'domestic violence' is both linguistically confusing and conceptually problematic. It is linguistically confusing because the domestic account's operationalization of the term 'domestic violence' conflicts with common usage. Under common usage, the term 'domestic violence' includes only unjustified acts and does not include justified ones. For example, when a battered woman shoots and kills her abusive husband in self-defence (and her actions are justified, all things considered), she is not typically characterized as having committed 'domestic violence', nor is the deceased abuser typically characterized as a 'victim of domestic violence'.[78] Indeed, proponents of the domestic account adopt this usage as well, which makes their methodological operationalization of domestic violence all the more confusing and unsatisfying.

Moreover, the domestic account's methodological conflation is conceptually problematic because it suggests a fundamental inconsistency between theory and method within the domestic account. Theoretically, the domestic account adopts a non-legitimist account of domestic violence, consistent with the usage described above, wherein one can make sense of the notion that an action is both violent and justified. However, the CTS fails to operationalize this theoretical distinction between unjustified acts of violence in a domestic setting (ie, domestic violence) and justified acts of violence in a domestic setting (ie, not domestic violence, but something else, eg, self-defence). The CTS's failure to operationalize this distinction means that adherents to the domestic account measure a much wider phenomenon in their empirical research than the phenomenon which they

discovering that some playful acts, such as tossing a stuffed teddy bear during a play fight, were counted as 'serious violence' under the CTS scales.

[76] As with the violence account, patriarchy does not play a necessary role in conceptualizing domestic violence in the domestic account, and thus there is no clear distinction drawn between domestic violence in its strong [1] and weak [3] senses.

[77] Again, since patriarchy is the only thing distinguishing [4] and [7], the distinction between these conceptual categories is not strongly drawn in the domestic account.

[78] These linguistic conventions reflect the correct use of the concept domestic violence, as reflected in my analysis set out in section C, wherein domestic violence in its strong sense [1] and weak sense [3] are unjustified all things considered.

deem problematic in their theoretical account.[79] Straus, father of the domestic account and creator of the CTS, has acknowledged this failure while dismissing critics with the claim that his approach is justified:

The criticism that the CTS does not take into account the context and meaning of acts is analogous to criticizing a reading test for failing to account for the reasons a child reads poorly...[80]

This passage illustrates the extent to which Straus has fundamentally misapprehended the nature of the critique levelled at his CTS methodology. Rather, the proper analogy for the critique faced by the CTS is found in a reading test that operationalizes the concept 'reading' in such an overly broad manner as to include acts such as reciting the letters of each word in its concept of 'reading' and which, moreover, fails to distinguish reading-as-pronunciation (eg, the sense in which I can still manage to 'read' French) and reading-as-comprehension (eg, the sense in which I can no longer read French because I have forgotten the meaning of the words). A reading test which fails to make these distinctions is a test open to criticism for failing to operationalize the concept of reading in a way that corresponds to a proper theoretical account of the concept. The CTS, I contend, is open to similar criticism, and thus Straus' response to the criticisms levelled against the CTS misses its mark.

3. Patriarchy account

The patriarchy account is the standard conceptualization of domestic violence within anti-domestic-violence advocacy communities, and it informs a great deal of empirical research on domestic violence, particularly in England.[81] Unlike the

[79] This inconsistency has formed the target for a wide body of literature critical of the CTS methodology: R Berk, 'Mutual combat and other family violence myths' in D Finkelhor and others (eds), *The Dark Side of Families: Current family violence research* (Beverley Hills: Sage, 1983); P Mahoney, L Williams, and C West, 'Violence against women by intimate relationship partners' in C Renzetti, J Edelson, and RK Bergan (eds), *Sourcebook on Violence Against Women* (Thousand Oaks: Sage, 2001); G Margolin, 'The multiple forms of aggressiveness between marital partners: How do we identify them?' (1987) 13 *Journal of Marital and Family Therapy* 77; K Yllo, 'Using a feminist approach in quantitative research' in R Finkelhor, R Gelles, and G Hotaling (eds), *The Dark Side of Families: Current family violence research* (Beverley Hills: Sage, 1983); K Yllo, 'Through a feminist lens: Gender, power and violence' in R Gelles and D Loseke (eds), *Current Controversies on Family Violence* (Thousand Oaks: Sage, 1993). Occasionally, books of collected essays include contributions reflecting both domestic accounts and critiques of the domestic account. Eg, RK Bergan, *Issues in Intimate Violence* (Thousand Oaks: Sage, 1998); DR Loseke, RJ Gelles, and MM Cavanaugh, *Current Controversies on Family Violence* (Thousand Oaks: Sage, 2005).

[80] Straus (1996) (n 62 above) 285.

[81] The leading proponents of the patriarchy account in empirical research are the Manchester-based Rebecca and Russell Dobash. Key works reflecting this account include RE Dobash and R Dobash, *Violence Against Wives: A case against the patriarchy* (New York: Free Press, 1979); RE Dobash and R Dobash, 'Community response to violence against wives: Charivari, abstract justice and patriarchy' (1981) 28(5) *Social Problems* 563; RE Dobash and R Dobash, 'The nature and antecedents of violent events' (1984) 24 *British J of Criminology* 269; RE Dobash and R Dobash,

violence account and domestic account, the patriarchy account (as its name suggests) does take patriarchy into consideration in conceptualizing domestic violence. However, under this account, patriarchy is a *necessary* element in determining what counts as domestic violence. In other words, violent acts occurring in a domestic context are *only* considered domestic violence if they also sustain or perpetuate patriarchy. This account is therefore unsatisfying due to its failure to recognize any distinction between domestic violence in its strong and weak senses.

Patriarchy account-based research in the US has produced the most influential depiction of the dynamics of domestic violence: the power and control wheel.[82] According to this account, patriarchal forms of power and control constitute the core of domestic violence; domestic abuse forms a pinwheel spreading out from this core, and acts of domestic violence are presented as existing at the outer edges of the wheel. The purpose of depicting domestic violence in this way is: (1) to emphasize the central role of patriarchy in understanding what counts as domestic violence; (2) to establish conceptual connections between different types of domestic abuse; and (3) to suggest that domestic abuse may be as much (if not more) of a problem than acts of physical violence.[83]

In terms of the concepts charted on my explanatory model in section C above, the only sense of domestic violence recognized under the patriarchy account is domestic violence in its strong sense [1]. Domestic violence in its weak sense [3] is not understood as domestic violence.[84] The concepts most closely related to domestic violence are those unjustified acts that sustain or perpetuate patriarchy, even where the acts do not involve violence [4, 5] and even when they do not occur in domestic contexts [2, 5]. Given its primary focus on patriarchy, this account perceives very close resemblances between domestic violence [1] and stranger rape [2].[85] These

---

'The response of the British and American Women's Movements to violence against women' in J Hanmer and M Maynard (eds), *Women, Violence and Social Control* (London: MacMillan, 1987); RE Dobash and R Dobash, *Women, Violence and Social Change* (London: Routledge, 1992); RE Dobash and R Dobash, *Rethinking Violence Against Women* (Thousand Oaks: Sage, 1998); RE Dobash and R Dobash, 'Separate and intersecting realities: A comparison of men's and women's accounts of violence against women' (1998) 4 *Violence Against Women* 382; RE Dobash and R Dobash, 'Women's violence to men in intimate relationships: Working on a puzzle' (2004) 44 British J of Criminology 324. Research based on a patriarchy account of domestic violence has also been widely conducted in the US. Yllo (n 79 above); K Yllo and M Bograd, *Feminist Perspectives on Wife Abuse* (Thousand Oaks: Sage, 1988); S Das Gupta, 'Just like men? A critical view of violence by women' in M Shepard and E Pence (eds), *Coordinating Community Responses to Domestic Violence* (Thousand Oaks: Sage, 1999).

[82] E Pence and M Paymar, *Power and Control: Tactics of men who batter* (Duluth: DAIP, 1993). See Fig 2.

[83] Ibid.

[84] The failure of the patriarchy account to recognize domestic violence in its weak sense conflicts with my account and has drawn criticism from proponents of the domestic account (who do not draw any distinction between domestic violence in its strong and weak senses). M Straus, 'The controversy over domestic violence by women' in XB Arriaga and S Oskamp (eds), *Violence in Intimate Relationships* (Thousand Oaks: Sage, 1999) 21.

[85] This resemblance is exemplified in feminist advocacy organizations that target domestic violence alongside non-domestic sexual assault. Coalitions organized around these two concepts are

Figure 2. Power and Control Wheel, Duluth Domestic Abuse Intervention Project, used with permission.

resemblances are grounded in the belief that both domestic violence and stranger rape tend to sustain and perpetuate men's patriarchal control over women.[86]

Proponents of this account have been criticized for discounting the relevance of other forms of structural inequality, such as racism, heterosexism, and economic inequality.[87] Furthermore, they have been criticized for viewing the heterosexual family as a site of oppression for women. Such criticisms come in

particularly prevalent in the US, which has no fewer than 18 joint domestic violence and sexual assault coalitions at the state and federal levels. 'Domestic Violence Resources' Feminist Majority Foundation <http://www.feminist.org/911/crisis.html> accessed 4 May 2007.

[86] Eg, D Russell, *Rape in Marriage* (2nd edn, Bloomington: Indiana University Press, 1990) 191–4.

[87] Elliott (n 65 above) 182. For a detailed discussion of this critique and possible responses, see Chapter 7, section A.

two flavours: an external critique and an internal critique. The external critique is politically conservative and based on the joint claims that patriarchy is legitimate and thus the heterosexual family as traditionally constructed under patriarchy is not problematic.[88] The internal critique is politically progressive and based on the joint claims that the family often serves as 'a site of resistance and solidarity against racism for women of color' and therefore 'does not hold a central place in accounting for women's subordination'.[89]

4. Johnson's account

In the mid-1990s, an American sociologist, Michael Johnson, attempted to transcend the debates between proponents of the domestic account of domestic violence and the patriarchy account of domestic violence by developing a radically new approach to operationalizing the concept of domestic violence in empirical research. His primary innovation was to divide domestic violence into two distinct concepts: (1) patriarchal terrorism ('intimate terrorism'); and (2) common couple violence ('situational couple violence').[90]

The key to Johnson's analytic approach lies in a methodological critique of the selection bias affecting the empirical research conducted by proponents of both the domestic account and the patriarchy account. Research subjects chosen by those advancing a patriarchy account of domestic violence are typically drawn from women's shelters/refuges, police reports, and court cases.[91] The bias inherent in such sampling techniques has given rise to criticism levied by proponents of the domestic account, who in turn claim that their own random sampling techniques are free from such bias.[92] However, as Johnson explains, the domestic account's samples are equally biased, because proponents of the domestic account

---

[88] See sources cited in J Bartowski, 'Debating Patriarchy: Discursive disputes over spousal authority among evangelical family commentators' (1997) 36 *Journal for the Scientific Study of Religion* 393.

[89] Walby (n 48 above) 14 citing b hooks, *Feminist Theory: From margin to center* (Cambridge: South End Press, 1984).

[90] M Johnson, 'Patriarchal terrorism and common couple violence: Two forms of violence against women' (1995) 57 *Journal of Marriage and the Family* 283. Johnson subsequently changed the names of his key concepts to 'intimate terrorism' and 'situational couple violence' so as not to 'beg the question of the connections with patriarchy that are so clear in heterosexual relationships (but not so clear in same-sex relationships in which there is an intimate terrorist) ... and [to avoid] the risk of trivialization [inherent in the term] *common* couple violence'. E-mail from Michael Johnson, Pennsylvania State University, to Michelle Madden Dempsey, Oxford University (13 September 2004) (on file with author).

[91] Eg, E Stanko, 'Unmasking what should be seen: A study of the prevalence of domestic violence in the London Borough of Hackney' in E Edna and K Laster (eds), *Domestic Violence: Global responses* (Bicester: AB Academic Publishers, 2000).

[92] M Straus, 'Injury and frequency of assault and the "representative sample fallacy" in measuring wife beating and child abuse' in R Gelles and M Straus (eds), *Physical Violence in American Families* (New Brunswick: Transaction, 1990), as cited in M Johnson, 'Conflict and control: Images of symmetry and asymmetry in domestic violence' in A Booth, A Crouter, and M Clements (eds), *Couples in Conflict* (Hillsdale, NJ: Lawrence Erlbaum, 2001) 96.

'do not in fact interview random samples' but instead 'interview those who do not refuse to be interviewed'.[93] With refusal rates of up to 40 per cent, the domestic account's sampling technique systematically excludes large populations amongst whom dynamics of power and control may be most pronounced.[94]

Based on these bilateral sampling errors, and the further observation that the different sampling techniques target 'virtually non-overlapping populations', Johnson hypothesized that each type of research actually measures a different type of domestic violence.[95] The first type of domestic violence Johnson identified, 'intimate terrorism', is measured by research grounded in a patriarchy account of domestic violence. Common characteristics of intimate terrorism include the following:

• It is overwhelmingly committed by men against women.

• It appears to be motivated by men's desire to achieve (patriarchal) power and control over their intimate partners.

• There is usually a clear distinction between victim and non-victim, in part because persistent violence and abuse are likely (over time) to suppress the victim's efforts to fight back.

• The violence tends to escalate over time.[96]

The second type of violence, what Johnson labels 'situational couple violence', is measured by domestic account-based research, and its common characteristics include the following:

• It is committed by both men and women in roughly equal numbers.

• It appears to be motivated by a desire 'to get one's own way in a particular conflict situation, within a relationship in which there is not a general pattern of power and control'.

• The distinction between victim and non-victim often breaks down since the violence is more likely to be mutual and reciprocal between the parties.

• The violence tends to be intermittent and de-escalate over time.[97]

Subsequent to drawing this principal distinction, Johnson identified an additional type of violence that may take place in a domestic context: 'violent resistance', in which victims of intimate terrorism use physical violence against their batterers (eg, when battered women kill their abusive husbands).[98]

In terms of the concepts charted on my explanatory model in section C above, Johnson's intimate terrorism corresponds to domestic violence in its strong sense [1], while Johnson's situational couple violence and violent resistance (when illegitimate all things considered) correspond conceptually to domestic violence

[93] Johnson (n 92 above).
[94] Ibid.   [95] Ibid 97.
[96] Ibid 97, 101.   [97] Ibid 97–8.   [98] Ibid 101.

in its weak sense [3]. Finally, legitimate violent resistance corresponds conceptually to the legitimate use of violence in a domestic context [10].

I believe that Johnson's account draws a number of appropriate and necessary distinctions in conceptualizing domestic violence. In theory, his account is consistent with my analysis of domestic violence, insofar as his distinction between intimate terrorism and situational couple violence resembles my distinction between domestic violence in its strong [1] and weak [3] senses. Thus, my theoretical account of domestic violence is largely consistent with Johnson's key distinctions. Yet my theoretical account goes further than Johnson's, insofar as it examines the underlying conceptual elements which inform these distinctions: violence, domesticity, and patriarchy. Additionally, my account analyses the conceptual resemblances between domestic violence and key related concepts such as stranger rape [2], domestic abuse [4], sexual harassment [5], generic violence [6], domestic conflict [7], domestic self-defense [10], etc.

E. Conclusion

The purpose of this chapter has been to analyse the concept of domestic violence in order to provide a full account of why these actions are wrongful and, thus, may inform the proper exercise of prosecutorial discretion. I believe that this account was required in order to move forward with my argument regarding the reasons that guide prosecutorial discretion in domestic-violence cases; for, as noted in my introductory chapter, I believe that very little of interest can be said about the proper function of the criminal justice system or the exercise of prosecutorial discretion generally without having a detailed appreciation of the particular wrongful conduct at issue.[99] It is hoped, therefore, that this chapter provided at least a good start toward understanding the wrongful conduct at issue when we consider domestic-violence prosecutions.

The key analytic distinction drawn in this chapter has been between domestic violence in its strong sense and domestic violence in its weak sense. (This distinction will prove significant in Chapter 8, where I consider what kinds of reasons might guide prosecutorial discretion in domestic-violence cases.) Throughout this book, I resist the temptation to adopt a 'recipe approach' to understanding domestic violence, whereby domestic violence is simply understood as a mixture of violence and domesticity. Instead, I have presented a more complex philosophical analysis of domestic violence, which, briefly stated, goes like this:

• Domestic violence and its related concepts consist of complex intersections of three elements: violence, domesticity, and patriarchy.

---

[99] See Chapter 1, text to nn 16–17.

- Domestic violence has two senses. In its strong sense, domestic violence reflects the intersection of violence, domesticity, and patriarchy; in its weak sense, domestic violence reflects the intersection of only violence and domesticity.

- In order for the concept of domestic violence to be correctly applied, the act in question must be unjustified all things considered.

In addition, I examined several principal accounts of domestic violence in the legal and sociological literature and provided critiques of these accounts. My critiques were grounded in the explanatory model of domestic violence set forth in Figure 1. I concluded that the violence account of domestic violence and the domestic account of domestic violence are both unsatisfactory because they fail to recognize the relevance of patriarchy in conceptualizing domestic violence, and therefore conflate domestic violence in its strong and weak senses. I concluded that the patriarchy account is also unsatisfactory because it fails to recognize that the concept of domestic violence can be correctly applied even where the act in question does not tend to sustain or perpetuate patriarchy, and thereby obscures the existence of domestic violence in its weak sense. In contrast to the first three accounts of domestic violence, I concluded that Michael Johnson's account is largely satisfactory. Moreover, I explained how my analysis of domestic violence improves upon Johnson's account, by illuminating the conceptual elements that inform the distinctions and resemblances between domestic violence and its related concepts.

Given the tremendous amount of work done by the concept of patriarchy in my account of domestic violence, it is now incumbent upon me to provide a more detailed account of this concept as well. For, if the account of domestic violence set forth herein is plausible, it follows that in order to understand the wrong of domestic violence, one must also understand patriarchy. And so, in the next chapter, I present a detailed account of the wrong of patriarchy.

7

Patriarchy

This chapter offers an account of patriarchy. It should be noted at the outset that I do not claim to present a complete philosophical analysis of patriarchy, nor do I attempt to account for every sense in which the term is properly used. Rather, I use the term patriarchy more as a placeholder, to represent the nature of the particular kind of wrong against which feminism is concerned to act. Moreover, I use the notions of 'being patriarchal' and 'being feminist' to capture particular kinds of character traits which stand in opposition to one another. By providing an account of what being patriarchal means, I hope to illuminate by contrast what it means to be feminist, and thus to clarify my claim that *ceteris paribus* domestic-violence prosecutors should be feminists.

A. On Being Feminist

My approach in this chapter (and indeed, throughout the book) is clearly grounded in the assumption that categories of identity are important subjects of inquiry and can serve a useful explanatory role in law and philosophy, particularly as these disciplines are concerned with issues of social justice. I will take this point as given and will not seek to defend its plausibility here. However, as my approach is also grounded in the assumption that the identity categories of 'men' and 'women' are useful in this regard, I will begin by discussing some concerns that might arise in light of this assumption.

The critique I have in mind here is that of 'gender essentialism', which Angela Harris has defined as 'the notion that a unitary, "essential" women's experience can be isolated and described independently of race, class, sexual orientation, and other realities of experience'.[1] The anti-essentialist critique has been articulated from two distinct methodological approaches, which I will label 'progressive rationalism' and 'postmodernism' respectively. The former is consistent with the methodology of feminist practical reasoning adopted in this book, whilst the latter takes rationality as antithetical to feminism.[2] Not surprisingly, given my

---

[1] A Harris, 'Race and essentialism in feminist legal theory' (1990) 42 Stanford L Rev 581, 585.
[2] Chapter 1, section C.

discussion in Chapter 1, I consider versions of the anti-essentialist critique which are grounded in a progressive rationalist methodology to be more persuasive than their postmodernist counterparts.

One form of the progressive-rationalist anti-essentialist critique criticizes feminist accounts of patriarchy for drawing analogies between patriarchy and other forms of oppression, especially racism.[3] Such an analogy, it is claimed, 'obscures the dissimilar access to power white and nonwhite women experience, as well as the power white women have over nonwhite women and men'.[4] While this obscuring effect is indeed problematic, it seems that is not so much the mere drawing of the analogy which is of concern to anti-essentialists; rather, it is instead the drawing of this analogy naïvely.[5] The account of patriarchy I offer in this book occasionally relies on this problematic analogy, insofar as I claim that both racism and patriarchy are forms of structural inequality. Thus, I am guilty of drawing the analogy which is presumptively forbidden by this first type of anti-essentialist critique. For that reason, and because I agree that there is good reason to be wary of accounts which draw upon this analogy, it is worth acknowledging upfront the 'dangers and limitations' inherent in my account.[6]

A key danger risked by drawing an analogy between patriarchy and other forms of structural inequality is that doing so tends to privilege the attributes, needs, and interests of white, straight, able-bodied, upper-class women. 'To privilege' in this sense means roughly to treat the attributes, needs, and interests of such women as definitive of the attributes, needs, and interests of women as a whole, thereby overestimating the explanatory power of white, straight, able-bodied, upper-class women's experiences and perspectives. A crucial limitation risked by drawing an analogy between patriarchy and other forms of structural inequality is that doing so tends to silence the voices of women who do not share the experiences and perspectives of white, straight, able-bodied, upper-class women. This danger and limitation combine to form a compelling anti-essentialist critique against much feminist scholarship:

The result of [a] tendency toward gender essentialism, I argue, is not only that some voices are silenced in order to privilege others (for this is an inevitable result of categorization, which is necessary both for human communication and political movement), but that the voices that are silenced turn out to be the same voices silenced by the mainstream legal voice... among them, the voices of black women.[7]

---

[3] Examples of this analogy are most prominent in the work of feminist abolitionists. For a historical comparison of the patriarchy–slavery analogy in the US and UK feminist abolitionist movements, see C Midgely, *Sisterhood and Slavery: Transatlantic antislavery and women's rights* (British Abolitionism and Feminism in Transatlantic and Imperial Perspective, Proceedings of the Third Annual Gilder Lehrman Center International Conference at Yale University, 25–8 October 2001). The analogy has persisted in other contexts, however, eg, S de Beauvoir and HM Parshley (trans), *The Second Sex* (New York: Alfred Knoff, 1953).

[4] LM Alcoff, 'Racism' in A Jaggar and IM Young (eds), *A Companion to Feminist Philosophy* (Oxford: Blackwell, 2000) 475.

[5] Ibid.	[6] Ibid.	[7] Harris (n 1 above) 585.

Importantly, as suggested in the quotation from Harris above, the progressive rationalist anti-essentialist critique does not deny the usefulness of employing categories of identity. As Harris explains, feminism need not deny the existence of categories such as men and women, nor refuse to think in terms of generalizations regarding women's experience. Indeed, it would be impossible to conceive of the concept of feminism if we did not employ categories such as men, women, and patriarchy. Without such categories, '[w]e are reduced to individuals'[8] and robbed of the ability to 'explicitly [address] how women fare as a group'.[9] Rather, Harris simply urges feminists to 'make our categories explicitly tentative, relational, and unstable', rather than assuming that privileged women's perspectives define women's experiences generally.[10]

Postmodern forms of the anti-essentialist critique reject the very 'idea that particular characteristics can be identified with women over time and across cultures'.[11] This point is importantly different from the progressive-rationalist version of anti-essentialism, which merely claims that accounts of patriarchy can (and typically do) generate obfuscation insofar as they wrongly posit white, straight, able-bodied, economically privileged women's attitudes, needs, and interests as representative of all women's attitudes, needs, and interests. It is one thing to say that the way we have categorized is unhelpful or indeed detrimental to social justice; it is quite another to reject the project of categorization altogether. While the progressive-rationalist argument does the former, the postmodern argument does the latter.

The postmodern anti-essentialism argument rests on 'the view that there is no such thing as "women" because there are always other aspects to women's identities and bases other than sex for their oppressions'.[12] In this sense, the postmodern argument can be understood as grounded on the claim that there are no essential human universals, and it is this claim which I resist. As MacKinnon has correctly noted:

The postmodern attack ... proves a bit too much. Inconveniently, the fact of death is a universal—approaching 100%. Whatever it means, however it is related-to culturally and spiritually, whatever happens after it, it happens. Much to the embarrassment of the [postmodern] anti-essentialists, who prefer flights of fancy to gritty realities, life and death is even basically a binary distinction—and not a very nuanced one either, especially from the dead side of the line ... So the idea that there is nothing essential, in the sense that there are no human universals, is dogma. Ask most anyone who is going to be shot at dawn.[13]

---

[8] CA MacKinnon, 'Points against postmodernism' (2000) 75 Chicago-Kent L Rev 687, 698.

[9] L Alexander, 'What we do and why we do it' (1993) 45 Stanford L Rev 1885, 1890.

[10] Harris (n 1 above) 586.

[11] MacKinnon (n 8 above) 697, citing T Higgins, 'Anti-essentialism, relativism, and human rights' (1996) 19 Harvard Women's LJ 89, 91 fn 14.

[12] MacKinnon (n 8 above) 695.

[13] Ibid 698–9.

In rejecting the postmodern argument, I assume the truth of what Martha Nussbaum has characterized as 'Aristotelian essentialism': 'the view that human life has certain central defining features'.[14] This type of essentialism, I believe, is crucial to any coherent project of social justice. As Nussbaum has noted, 'without such an account, we do not have an adequate basis for an account of social justice ...'[15] While I am in sympathy with Nussbaum's account of Aristotelian essentialism and its implicit rejection of postmodern anti-essentialism, I do not deny that the progressive rationalist version of the anti-essentialist critique calls for a response from anyone who, like me, posits an analogy between patriarchy and other forms of structural inequality. How then can an account of patriarchy best avoid the dangers and limitations generated by depending upon this analogy? How can my account of patriarchy avoid running afoul of the progressive rationalist's version of the anti-essentialist critique?

One possible resource for addressing these concerns may be found in the notion of intersectionality. In a series of articles in the late 1980s and early 1990s, Kimberle Crenshaw and other critical-race legal theorists introduced to the US legal academy the notion of intersectionality in discourse regarding categories of identity.[16] As characterized by Nancy Levit, methodologies which embrace intersectionality endorse the joint claims that 'subordinated individuals might not fit neatly in a single identity group' and 'minority group members' interests splinter on various issues'.[17]

The claim that subordinated individuals might not fit neatly in a single identity group is ecumenical enough to be embraced by any plausible account of categories of identity. It would be terrifically odd and nonsensical for someone to posit an account of identity which denied such a proposition. Indeed, it would be bizarre to claim that any individuals (much less just 'subordinated' ones) fit neatly into a

[14] M Nussbaum, 'Human functioning and social justice: In defense of aristotelian essentialism' (1992) 20 *Political Theory* 202, 205.

[15] Ibid 205. This point is echoed by MacKinnon's refusal to abandon this type of essentialism in favour of postmodernism's denial of social reality: 'we cannot have this postmodernism and still have a meaningful practice of women's human rights.' Note MacKinnon's limited rejection of 'this' postmodernism, which is intended to delineate between a particularly problematic brand of US feminist postmodernism and much Continental postmodernism, which is not a subject of criticism. MacKinnon (n 8 above) 694.

[16] K Crenshaw, 'Demarginalizing the intersection of race and sex: A black feminist critique of antidiscrimination doctrine, feminist theory, and antiracist politics' [1989] U of Chicago Legal Forum 139; K Crenshaw, 'Mapping the margins: Intersectionality, identity politics, and violence against women of color' (1991) 43 Stanford L Rev 1241. The first legal academic literature to pick up on this notion includes R Delgado and J Stefancic, 'Why do we tell the same stories? Law reform, critical librarianship, and the triple helix dilemma' (1989) 42 Stanford L Rev 207; M Matsuda, 'Pragmatism modified and the false consciousness problem' (1990) 63 Southern California L Rev 1763. Whilst interest in the notion of intersectionality began as a trickle, it quickly exploded into a cottage industry of legal academic production, featuring in an average 102 law review articles per year throughout the last decade. Westlaw search string: intersectionality & DA(1988–2006), database JLR (14 April 2007). The notion of intersectionality has received comparatively little attention in the UK legal academy.

[17] N Levit, 'Theorizing the connections among systems of subordination' (2002) 71 U of Missouri Kansas-City L Rev 227, 228.

single identity group. Thus, the power of intersectional methodological does not rest simply in flagging up this obvious truth. Rather, the more important contribution made by the intersectionality method is to suggest a more productive way to conceptualize multiple identities.

Prior to the rise of intersectionality, the dominant approach to thinking about multiple identities was the 'additive approach'. According to this approach, the proper way to understand the disadvantage experienced by a black woman, for example, was to conceive of her disadvantage on the basis of gender as something that was simply added to her disadvantage on the basis of race. This approach was adopted by courts in adjudicating discrimination claims and often resulted in the following type of injustice: Plaintiff X, a black woman, claims to have been discriminated against on grounds of race and sex by operation of an employment policy, and she grounds her claim in a theory of disparate impact. In order to determine whether she has been impermissibly discriminated against under an additive approach to identity, the court first examines the impact of the employment policy on black people generally (men and women) and finds no evidence to support her claim. Second, the court examines the impact of the employment policy on women generally (black and white) and again finds no evidence to support her claim. The plaintiff's response, that the court has misconstrued the nature of her claim by separating her racial identity from her gender identity and that, instead, she has been discriminated against as a black woman, falls on deaf ears under this approach.[18]

Intersectionality offers an improvement on how we conceptualize identity insofar as it instructs us to realize that identities are not additive but are instead indivisible and intersecting. Thus, while we can understand someone's identity as a woman, we cannot understand what being a woman means for her without taking into account her other intersecting identities. In other words, 'what it means to be a woman'[19] and 'women's attributes, needs and interests'[20] (two key terms that will inform my account of patriarchy below) are grounded in more than gender identity: they are shaped by all of the intersecting identities that constitute a human being.

However, intersectionality theorists' second claim as articulated by Levit above (ie, that individuals who are disadvantaged by structural inequality have interests that 'splinter on various issues') is somewhat less productive of clear thinking. First, this claim is somewhat vague. If it simply means that such individuals realize values in different ways, have different comprehensive goals, or require different

---

[18] Recognizing the injustice generated by the additive approach to conceptualizing identity, courts have begun to recognize a degree of intersectionality in adjudicating discrimination claims, but have limited such claims to the 'just pick two' rule, according to which claims for intersectional discrimination are recognized where the plaintiff alleges that she has been discriminated against as a black woman, for example, but not as a black lesbian woman. Levit (n 17 above) 229.

[19] T Macklem, *Beyond Comparison: Sex and discrimination* (Cambridge: Cambridge University Press, 2003) 33–9.

[20] D Réaume, 'Comparing theories of sex discrimination: The role of comparison' (2005) 25 OJLS 547, 549.

resources for living successful lives, then the claim strikes me as obviously true. If the claim means that such individuals have different interests in the sense that they perceive themselves to have wants and desires which are inconsistent with other such individuals' wants and desires, then again the claim strikes me as not at all surprising and quite likely to be true. Finally though, if the claim means that such individuals have different interests in the sense that 'it is in the interest of a white woman to sustain and perpetuate racism' or 'it is in the interest of a straight woman to sustain and perpetuate heterosexism', etc, then I take the claim to be grounded upon an inadequate account of what human interests entail.

This final formulation of the claim, and the inadequate account of human interests it arguably assumes, has been challenged by the emergence of a growing legal academic literature coined 'post-intersectionality'.[21] This approach recognizes that wrongful structural inequalities have a tendency to reinforce one another.[22] Thus, on this account, it is decidedly *not* in the interest of a white woman to sustain and perpetuate racism, nor is it in the interest of a straight woman to sustain and perpetuate heterosexism, since the sustenance and perpetuation of one wrongful structural inequality has the tendency to sustain and reinforce others. Post-intersectionality recognizes that 'it is difficult, perhaps impossible, to eliminate one form of subordination without attacking the entire edifice of interlocking oppressions'.[23] For this reason, as Trina Grillo has noted, structural inequalities such as patriarchy, racism, and heterosexism 'cannot be dismantled separately because they mutually reinforce each other. Racism uses sexism as its enforcer. Homophobia enforces sexism by making people pay a heavy price for departing from socialized gender roles.'[24]

A closely related point is the notion that wrongful structural inequalities 'are themselves intersectional', and therefore social forms such as patriarchy, racism, heterosexism, etc, are best understood as 'interrelated, rather than conflicting, phenomena'.[25] This notion has been claimed as an original contribution by post-intersectionality theorists, but even it does not represent a break from inter-sectionality theory, it is certainly an important methodological point and one

---

[21] P Kwan, 'Jeffrey Dahmer and the Cosynthesis of Categories' (1997) 48 Hastings LJ 1257.

[22] Levit (n 17 above) 230–1.

[23] N Ehrenreich, 'Subordination and symbiosis: Mechanisms of mutual support between sub-ordinating systems' (2002) 71 U of Missouri Kansas-City L Rev 251, 255, cited in Levit (n 17 above) 236.

[24] T Grillo, 'Anti-essentialism and intersectionality: Tools to dismantle the master's house' (1995) 10 Berkeley Women's LJ 16. This point is not entirely original to post-intersectionality. For several decades, it has been recognized and written about by lesbian feminists who recognized that patriarchy and heterosexism are mutually reinforcing structural inequalities. Ironically, these accounts were published in the years immediately preceding the US legal academy's interest in intersectionality. See eg S Pharr, *Homophobia: A weapon of sexism* (Inverness, CA: Chardon Press, 1988); A Rich, 'Compulsory heterosexuality and lesbian existence' (1980) 15 *Journal of Women's History* 11.

[25] Levit (n 17 above) 231, citing DL Hutchinson, 'Identity crisis: "Intersectionality", "multidi-mensionality", and the development of an adequate theory of subordination' (2001) 6 Michigan J of Race and Law 285, 290.

that is rightly emphasized in the new literature.[26] As Levit correctly observes, this move is helpful insofar as it takes intersectional methodology as traditionally applied to the individual and moves it to the systemic level.[27]

If wrongful structural inequalities are best understood as intersecting with one another, however, then what sense can we make of an argument that characterizes itself as concerned principally with a *particular* structural inequality such as racism, patriarchy, etc? Shouldn't anyone who endorses the insights of post-intersectionality eschew any characterization of their work as 'anti-racist', 'feminist', etc, and simply characterize it as 'anti-structural inequality-ist'? Well, yes and no. Endorsing post-intersectionality analysis commits one to the proposition that anti-racist, feminist, or other particularist types of arguments cannot be adequately conceived or deployed without an appreciation of the intersecting nature of all wrongful structural inequalities. However, this commitment does not prevent one from self-consciously adopting a particular point of view in constructing and deploying arguments against wrongful structural inequalities. Thus, we may conceive of a feminist point of view which is particularly concerned to recognize and respond to the reasons generated by the wrongful structural inequality of patriarchy—and we may conceive of an anti-racist point of view which is particularly concerned to recognize and respond to the reasons generated by the wrongful structural inequality of racism (and so on).

Adopting a particularist point of view is, therefore, not inconsistent with the insights of post-intersectionality theory: it is merely to assume that at least some of the salient features of situations involving wrongful structural inequality are best understood by reference to particular kinds of structural inequalities such as racism, patriarchy, etc. The point of view I adopt in what follows is an explicitly *feminist* point of view; one which assumes that at least some of the salient features of women's condition are best understood by reference to patriarchy. This point of view does not deny that a variety of other considerations, including other intersecting structural inequalities, are also relevant to a fully illuminated account of women's condition. Rather, it merely shines one particular light on this issue, so as to illuminate an admittedly partial yet nonetheless salient aspect of women's condition.

B. Three Senses of Patriarchy

As Carole Pateman has noted, the meaning of patriarchy 'is a vexed question' that has generated 'wide-ranging debate among feminists'.[28] In its most basic and

---

[26] The claim of originality has been disputed by P Malavet, 'Outsider citizenships and multidimensional borders: The power and danger of not belonging' (2005) 52 Cleveland State L Rev 321; DL Hutchinson, 'New complexity theories: From theoretical innovation to doctrinal reform' (2002) 71 U of Missouri Kansas-City L Rev 431.
[27] Levit (n 17 above) 231.
[28] C Pateman, *The Sexual Contract* (Stanford: Stanford University Press, 1988) 19.

unilluminating sense, patriarchy can be understood as a form of political power; but this account does little to explain the nature of the power at issue, consider whether its exercise is morally problematic, or explain why this situation might be a matter of particular concern to feminists. While I do not claim to present a complete philosophical analysis of every sense in which the concept of patriarchy may properly be used, I will attempt to develop a sense of patriarchy which addresses the three issues noted above. Before unpacking this notion, it will be necessary to distinguish three related senses of patriarchy.

In one sense, patriarchy can be understood as a form of political authority held by governments. It is this first sense which Robert Filmer defended in his *Patriarcha*[29] and which John Locke took as his foil in his *First Treatise of Government*.[30] Filmer, who was concerned to defend the divine right of kings, traced political governmental authority to the natural right of fathers to rule their offspring, ultimately tracing all political power back to the Biblical first father, Adam.[31] One of Locke's criticisms of Filmer was that even if parenthood grounded authority over one's children, such authority would necessarily be shared between the father and mother. In this way, Locke brought the supposed exclusive political authority of kings (patriarchy in the first sense) into question. As Carole Pateman has correctly observed, however, Locke's alternate account of political authority (social contract theory) did not reject patriarchy so much as merely debunk Filmer's version of it; for on Locke's account, men had the power to bind their wives and children in the social contract.[32]

Locke's alternative account of political authority brings into view the second sense of patriarchy: a more diffuse understanding of patriarchy as the power that men hold over women within the family. As Pateman persuasively argues, the civil freedom made possible by the Lockean social contract ultimately depends on this second sense of patriarchy.[33] In a third sense, patriarchy can be understood even more diffusely, as a collection of social forms which constitute a structural inequality, whereby men hold systematic social power in society more generally.[34] It is this final sense of patriarchy to which we turn now and which forms the basis of this chapter.[35]

---

[29] R Filmer, *Patriarcha: Or, the natural power of kings* (London: Chiswell, 1680).

[30] J Locke, *Two Treatises on Government* (London, 1821; reprint Cambridge: CUP, 1991).

[31] Filmer (n 29 above) 71.

[32] Pateman (n 28 above).

[33] Ibid. This form of patriarchy as governance is also the sense which informs Markus Dubber's use of the concept in his critique of the police power. MD Dubber, '"The power to govern men and things": Patriarchal origins of the police power in American law' (2004) 52 Buffalo L Rev 1277.

[34] Pateman (n 28 above), see especially chs 7 and 8.

[35] It should be noted that the analysis of patriarchy offered in this chapter is not an attempt to provide a historically specific account of the economic, material, or legal practices which establish and maintain men's systematic social power over women. Rather, it is merely an attempt to provide a philosophical account of this social reality. Compare, E Stark, *Coercive Control: How men entrap women in personal life* (New York: OUP, 2007) 172–4.

C. Patriarchal Character and Social Forms

One's actions may possess a patriarchal or non-patriarchal (ie, feminist) character. To understand this claim, it is first necessary to note that patriarchy (in the
third sense identified above) is best understood as constituted by numerous social
forms. The language of social forms was developed by Joseph Raz to account for
forms of behaviour, arrangements, complex activities, ways of life, etc, which are
widely practised in a society.[36] The existence of a particular social form makes
certain types of action possible within that society. Raz's birdwatching example
is illustrative:

Activities which do not appear to acquire their character from social forms in fact do so.
Bird watching seems to be what any sighted person in the vicinity of birds can do. And
so he can, except that that would not make him into a bird watcher. He can be that only
in a society where this, or at least some other animal tracking activities, are recognized as
leisure activities, and which furthermore shares certain attitudes to natural life generally.
The point is that engaging in the same activities will play a different role, have a different
significance in the life of the individual depending on social practices and attitudes to
such activities.[37]

In Raz's theory of human well-being, social forms serve as the grounding of
comprehensive goals, success in which is a central element of one's well-being.[38]
Whilst Raz's account of social forms focuses upon their positive aspects, showing
how they support the realization of *valuable* goals and contribute to the living
of *successful* lives, there is no reason to think that social forms have any necessary tendency to be valuable as opposed to disvaluable, to ground valuable goals
as opposed to disvaluable ones, or to contribute to the living of successful lives
as opposed to unsuccessful ones. Undoubtedly, many social forms do present
opportunities for people to adopt valuable comprehensive goals in life, and this
in turn contributes to their living successful lives. For example, the existence of
social forms such as friendship, family, and birdwatching present opportunities
for people to adopt valuable comprehensive goals such as having friends, families,
and being a birdwatcher—all of which may be crucial to the success of their lives.
All the same, however, the existence of other, disvaluable social forms such as
criminal underworlds, organized paedophilia, and white supremacism present
opportunities for people to adopt disvaluable comprehensive goals such as being
mob hitmen, members of child pornography rings, or neo-Nazis, each of which
contributes to their living unsuccessful lives.[39]

---

[36] J Raz, *The Morality of Freedom* (Oxford: OUP, 1986) 307.
[37] Ibid 311.
[38] Ibid 307.
[39] Raz concedes as much when he stipulates that the relationship between well-being and social
forms depends on the assumption that the social forms at issue are morally sound, thus implying
that morally unsound social forms can exist. Ibid 319.

Just as the action of watching a bird can acquire its character from the social form of birdwatching, the same is true of patriarchal actions in their relation to the numerous social forms which constitute patriarchy. For example, it might seem that any individual male could engage in patriarchal action by dominating a female, say by enslaving her to serve him. And so perhaps a man could do so. But that fact alone would not make his actions patriarchal, for his actions can only be properly understood as patriarchal in character if they are performed in the context of a society in which patriarchal social forms exist. As Raz states, 'the same activities will...have a different significance depending on social practices and attitudes' in the society in which they take place.[40] This is so because social forms consist of conventions which assign 'symbolic meaning to certain modes of behaviour'.[41] It is for this reason that I have adopted Raz's phrase 'social forms' as opposed to 'social practices', which suggests a rather antiseptic concern 'exclusively with behaviour, and attitudes to behaviour', in contrast to the complex web of symbolic meanings generated through the 'shared beliefs, folklore, high culture, collectively shared metaphors and imagination, and so on' embedded within social forms.[42]

No social form is easily explained or described to one who has not participated in that form or at very least experienced life within a society that supports it. Typically, direct experience is required to fully appreciate the meanings and symbols generated by the social form. This is so because such meaning and symbols are 'dense', in the sense that they consist in 'more than individuals, even those with experiences in [the social form], can explicitly describe'.[43] For this reason, an adequate understanding of patriarchy, a dense social form, can only be obtained through living within a patriarchal society. Of course, even when people participate in a given social form, there remains the possibility these participants will fail to grasp its central features. Consider the case of people participating in the social form of friendship for selfish ends: they believe that the central feature of having friends is to get ahead in the world, to appear important, and to have someone to help you move house or drop you to the airport when you go on holiday. Such people fail to appreciate the central features of the social form of friendship, despite their participation in this form, and they thus fail to understand fully the nature of friendship, despite having friends.

Moreover, when people live in a society that does not support certain social forms, they will necessarily fail to understand fully the nature of those social forms, since they are denied the opportunity to participate in them. For example, I have thus far lived my life in societies that do not support the social form of bulubulu, a Fijian customary tribal practice of apology and reconciliation following breaches of social norms involving conduct that ranges from theft and

---

[40] Ibid.   [41] Ibid 350.
[42] Ibid 311.   [43] Ibid 312.

elopement to battery and rape.[44] As I have not experienced living within a society that supports this social form, I cannot but fail to have a full appreciation of both its symbols and meanings, and the character of the actions that its existence as a social form makes possible.

Even when a full appreciation of a social form is lacking, something approaching an adequate understanding can nonetheless be obtained. However, mere description of the social form is inadequate to this task.[45] Rather, as Raz has noted, some level of understanding of the social form can be indirectly obtained through media such as fiction, drama, and narrative storytelling.[46] It is not surprising therefore that the methodology of narrative storytelling as consciousness-raising has featured prominently in the feminist movement and critical-race theory literature, as these methods may provide the best means to share knowledge of the social forms of patriarchy and racism, thereby exposing and clarifying the types of wrongs that these movements are concerned to denounce.[47]

With this background in mind, the stage is now set to unpack (to the extent possible) three hallmarks of the social forms which constitute patriarchy. Before proceeding, however, I offer a general disclaimer: my account offers what I hope to be a plausible understanding of patriarchy as it currently exists in dominant cultures of modern US and UK societies. Since social forms are not static, talk of 'patriarchy as it currently exists' is somewhat artificial. Perhaps, however, if my account is general and malleable enough, it will allow me to account for some key characteristics of patriarchy as it is developing and being experienced, principally in both the US and UK, but with some relevance also to its manifestation in other societies and communities as well (eg, either in non-dominant communities within the US or UK, or in societies and communities currently existing outside of these nations or existing at different times). Success in this ambition, however, is doubtful, and as such the account offered below makes no claim to universality.

D. Patriarchy as a Wrong

Patriarchy systematically limits women's access to options that are critical to the success of their lives. It will be assumed that to limit a person's access to options

---

[44] SE Merry, *Human Rights and Gender Violence: Translating international law into local justice* (London: University of Chicago Press, 2005) 113–33.

[45] Raz (n 36 above) 312.

[46] Ibid.

[47] CA MacKinnon, *Toward a Feminist Theory of the State* (Cambridge: Harvard University Press, 1989) 83–105; K Bartlett, 'Feminist legal methods' (1990) 103 Harvard L Rev 829, 863–7; A Johnson, 'Defending the use of narrative and giving content to the voice of color: Rejecting the imposition of process theory in legal scholarship' (1994) 79 Iowa L Rev 803. Understanding patriarchy and racism as dense social forms explains why even fictionalized accounts can make valuable contributions to understanding these phenomena, contrary to the argument advanced in D Farber and S Sherry, *Beyond All Reason: The radical assault on truth in American law* (Oxford: OUP, 1997).

that are critical to the success of his or her life is a wrong. As women are people, patriarchy is therefore wrong.[48] The limitations which constitute patriarchy typically arise in one or more of three forms: sex discrimination, sexism, and misogyny. This section will provide an explanation of sex discrimination, sexism, and misogyny, understood here as elements of patriarchy.

1. Sex discrimination

'The wrong of sex discrimination', Timothy Macklem has correctly observed, 'has to do with the inability to pursue a successful life.'[49] Typically, sex discrimination has to do with the inability of women to pursue successful lives, but as discussed below, it can also deny men valuable options. At the outset it is crucial to note that sex discrimination does not entail any intentional denial of valuable opportunities to women. Rather, actions that are sexually discriminatory rest on a mistake: they consist in 'treating a woman in ways that would be proper if she was as [the discriminator] takes her to be, but are improper given the person she is'.[50] Macklem has described this phenomenon as grounded in a misunderstanding of 'what it is to be a woman', but a more helpful formulation is offered by Denise Réaume, who observes that sex discrimination is better understood as grounded in a 'misconception of women's attributes, needs, or interests'.[51]

Sex discrimination, thus conceived, thrives in societies that embrace 'widespread promulgation of a false or irrelevant conception'[52] of women's attributes, needs, or interests. For example, sex discrimination typically thrives in societies that hold the widespread mistaken belief that all women find ultimate fulfilment within the domestic sphere (in the role of wife and mother). On the basis of this mistaken belief, these societies tend to support the expectation that women should perform the majority of domestic functions such as child-rearing, housecleaning, food preparation, etc. In light of the belief that these tasks provide women with all of the valuable options in life they could possibly want, such societies give little or no thought to ways in which men might share in the performance of these activities. Moreover, as women are thought to be totally fulfilled within the home, few if any valuable options are created for women to work outside the home in these societies. Material support such as reliable and affordable childcare and flexible working schedules are thought unnecessary since women are believed to be capable of realizing all of their valuable options by staying at home to raise their children.[53] Thus, a clear line develops between what is deemed

---

[48] The next section (Patriarchy as Structural Inequality) will address the systematic nature of this wrong.

[49] Macklem (n 19 above) 188.

[50] Ibid 151.

[51] Réaume (n 20 above) 549.

[52] Macklem (n 19 above) 154.

[53] Ibid 21–2, discussing the constraints of women's domestic social role.

'women's work' and what is deemed 'men's work', and deviations from this model are neither encouraged nor supported.

Importantly, this account of sex discrimination is grounded in the claim that wrongful discrimination is not a matter of comparison: the wrongness of sex discrimination is not grounded in the violation of any principle of equality.[54] Rather, the moral significance of sex discrimination—indeed, 'the moral significance of any misconception about human beings—is a product of its tendency to frustrate its subjects' capacity to lead successful lives'.[55] This understanding of wrongful discrimination is consistent with the account of discrimination and equality offered by Elisa Holmes.[56] As Holmes has noted, people concerned with opposing unjust discrimination typically assume that some relationship exists between anti-discrimination rights and equality, but 'the precise nature of this assumed relationship is often left ambiguous or at least inexplicit'.[57] Often when anti-discrimination norms fail to achieve their proponents' aims, the failure is explained in terms of a deficiency in those particular anti-discrimination norms, which aim merely at 'formal equality' rather than the preferred 'substantive equality'.[58] Formal equality is understood as the principle of treating like cases alike, and this conception of equality is deemed inadequate because it cannot account for the moral quality of differences grounded in historical oppression.[59] Substantive equality, in contrast, is perceived as the better option insofar as it explicitly recognizes and attempts to redress historical subordination.[60] Neither notion of equality, however, explains what makes wrongful discrimination wrong, for the answer is simply not to be found in notions of equality. As Raz correctly observes:

We only have reason to care about inequalities in the distribution of goods and ills, that is of what is of value or disvalue for independent reasons. There is no reason to care about

---

[54] Thus the title of Macklem's book: *Beyond Comparison*, ibid.

[55] Ibid 147.

[56] E Holmes, 'Anti-discrimination rights without equality' (2005) 68 MLR 175. This similarity is perhaps not surprising given the influence that Joseph Raz has had on the work of both Macklem and Holmes, although oddly neither mention the apparent influence of Raz's work on equality. Raz (n 36 above) 217–44. For further discussion of Raz's account of equality, see section B. For a similar account of equality, see P Westen, 'The empty idea of equality' (1982) 95 Harvard L Rev 537.

[57] Holmes (n 56 above) 175.

[58] Eg, CA MacKinnon, *Sex Equality* (New York: University Casebook Series, Foundation Press, 2001) 3–43; S Fredman, *Discrimination Law* (Oxford: Clarendon, 2002). The distinction between formal and substantive equality has been adopted by the Canadian Supreme Court in *Andrews v Law Society (British Columbia)* 1989 Carswell BC 16.

[59] Aristotle typically gets the blame for coming up with this inadequate conception of 'formal equality' (S Broadie and C Rowe (trans), *Aristotle's Nichomachean Ethics* (Oxford: OUP, 2002)). However, as Gardner has demonstrated, this attribution is a myth based upon a popular misreading of Aristotelian ethics. J Gardner, 'The virtue of justice and the character of law' [2001] Current Legal Problems 1, 9–12.

[60] CA MacKinnon, *Are Women Human? And other international dialogues* (London: Harvard University Press, 2006) 7; CA MacKinnon, 'Reflections on sex equality under law' (1991) 100 Yale LJ 1281.

inequalities in the distribution of grains of sand, unless there is some other reason to wish to have or to avoid sand.[61]

Sex discrimination is harmful not only to women, but to men as well. In principle, sex discrimination can be grounded in misconceptions of both women's and men's sexual attributes, needs, and interests. Failures to recognize the ways in which women and men are similar and the ways in which we are different, insofar as these similarities and differences are relevant to the options we require to live valuable lives, ground sex discrimination. When these misconceptions result in actions that deny human beings what they are entitled to, those actions constitute sex discrimination. Viewed through this lens, we can see that sex discrimination comes in at least two flavours. The first is grounded in misconceptions that result in the denial of valuable options to women in particular. Such misconceptions result in men being accorded goods which ought to have been accorded to both sexes. When this occurs, men obtain the goods they deserve, but women do not. 'In this situation, only women are denied what they deserve, and it is accordingly the task of feminism to condemn and seek to remedy this situation.'[62]

The second flavour of sex discrimination is grounded in misconceptions which result in the denial of valuable options to both sexes. As Macklem observes:

[T]o the extent that the truth of sexual identity reveals that sexual difference is real and relevant but other than we have taken it to be, the prevailing misconception of the character of sexual difference will have ensured that neither sex has received the goods it is capable of enjoying... [since] goods whose allocation is based on a false understanding of the people to whom they are directed offer opportunities that those people cannot use and purport to satisfy needs that they do not have. At best they are empty in the hands of those to whom they are assigned; at worst they impose upon those people a futile task, that of attempting to live up to the misconception of themselves that would make possession of those goods valuable. In this situation, neither sex is offered the goods that it deserves, and it is accordingly the task of feminism to expose the false character of our present conception of sexual identity and to give effect to the true meaning of sexual difference.[63]

Macklem, I believe, accurately identifies the nature of sex discrimination; yet his account suggests (wrongly, I believe) that sex discrimination is the sole explanation of women's disadvantage in society.[64] He claims, for example, that 'any allegation as to the particular character of the disadvantage that women now experience must be read as an allegation as to the particular character of what

---

[61] Raz (n 36 above) 235. References to equality in the context of wrongful discrimination are often best understood as referring to equality in a rhetorical sense. Ibid 227–9. For further discussion and application of equality in its rhetorical sense, see section E.

[62] Macklem (n 19 above) 116.

[63] Ibid 116–17.

[64] In supplement to Macklem's account, I think women's disadvantage in society is best explained in a three-fold manner, by reference to sex discrimination, sexism, and misogyny.

it means to be a woman.'[65] Thus, for Macklem, there is no form of disadvantage women experience which is *not* grounded in a misconception of what it means to be a woman. It follows then that, for Macklem, 'in order even to contemplate the question of sexual disadvantage...we must agree on the content of what it means to be a woman'.[66] This is a tall order, and one which Macklem himself shies away from in his book.[67] The fact that he fails to provide any account of this content belies his claim that 'there is nothing obscure or inaccessible about what it means to be a woman: it is the stuff of everyday living'.[68] Rather, as the concerns discussed in section A above reflect, we should not be too quick to think that there are easy answers to be had to the question of what it means to be a woman or, in Réaume's terms, what women's attributes, needs, or interests might be.[69]

2. Sexism

One uncontested component of what it means to be a woman is this: to be a woman is to be human.[70] Thus, there is no room for any misconception or misunderstanding when it comes to the fact that women's attributes, needs, or interests are, at very least, consistent with the basic attributes, needs, and interests of human beings. When Macklem claims that all of 'the disadvantage that women now experience is in fact the product of a failure to understand what it means to be a woman', he implicitly ignores the fact that some of the disadvantage women currently experience result from a denial of the basic ingredients of a successful life required by all human beings.[71] Contrary to Macklem's claims, it is not the case that 'the disadvantage that women now experience in our society can only be the product of our misconception of what it means to be a woman'.[72] Rather, some of that disadvantage is the product of recognizing precisely what women are...and just not caring. Macklem is right, however, to note that this type of wrongful conduct (which he does not label) is not the same thing as sex discrimination. Instead, we should understand it as a distinct aspect of patriarchy, one which I will label 'sexism'. In what follows, I will understand sexism as the failure to provide women what we need to live valuable lives, when that failure is grounded in a *failure to value women*, as opposed to being grounded in a misconception of what it means to be a woman.

In a long footnote, Macklem attends to this type of disadvantage as it is particularly experienced by women in certain societies, and he rightly declines to label

---

[65] Macklem (n 19 above) 154.
[66] Ibid.
[67] Ibid 39.
[68] Ibid 38.
[69] Réaume (n 20 above) 549.
[70] The title of MacKinnon's recent collection of essays notwithstanding, there appears to be no serious debate on this point. MacKinnon (2006) (n 60 above).
[71] Macklem (n 19 above) 154.
[72] Ibid 155.

it as sex discrimination.[73] The particular manifestation of sexism that captures Macklem's attention is a phenomenon first identified by Amartya Sen in his article 'More than one hundred million women are missing'[74] and noted by Martha Nussbaum in her book *Sex and Social Justice*.[75] Macklem comments:

> As I read Nussbaum, in certain societies that are poor and sexually discriminatory, women die earlier than they do in poor and non-discriminatory societies, because customs and politics describe women as unfit to engage in activities that would make them respected, valued, and so worthy of nourishment and medical treatment...Yet it is not clear to me that the wrong Nussbaum describes is one of sex discrimination...[because] the wrong Nussbaum describes is a wrong to any person, however understood...It does not take an accurate perception of women's capacities, and the respect that would give rise to, to know that women, as human beings, are entitled to food, shelter, and medical treatment.[76]

My point here is two-fold. First, Macklem is right to resist Nussbaum's characterization of this disadvantage as sex discrimination. It is not. Rather, it is a distinct type of disadvantage, which I have labelled sexism. Moreover, this type of disadvantage is surely relevant to understanding the character of the disadvantage that women suffer; since being denied adequate food, shelter, and medical treatment constitutes a denial of valuable options for living a successful life. Therefore, second, Macklem is wrong to claim that 'any allegation as to the particular character of the disadvantage that women experience must be read as an allegation as to the particular character of what it means to be a woman'.[77] Instead, at least some of that disadvantage may be read as an allegation that, despite a perfectly clear understanding of what it means to be a woman, women are nonetheless being denied valuable options for living successful lives based on the failure to value women. With this added dimension of patriarchy in focus we can conclude that 'in order...to contemplate the question of sexual disadvantage...we must [either] agree on the content of what it means to be a woman',[78] or if we are already in agreement on that matter, then we must understand the disadvantage as arising out of the failure to value women.

Macklem's failure to recognize what I have labelled sexism as a distinct form of disadvantage suffered by women appears to arise from his willingness to leap from having 'an accurate perception of women's capacities' to having 'the respect that [perception] would give rise to'. Macklem seems to assume that respect for women as human beings will necessarily follow from having an accurate perception of women as human beings. To know that women are human is, for Macklem, to respect them (ie, to value them) as human. Yet, if this were so, the wrong done to the missing women identified by Sen would be inexplicable. It could only be

---

[73] Macklem (n 19 above) 151, fn 26.

[74] A Sen, 'More than one hundred million women are missing' (20 December 1990) *New York Review of Books*.

[75] M Nussbaum, *Sex and Social Justice* (Oxford: OUP, 1999) 32.

[76] Macklem (n 19 above) 151, fn 26.   [77] Ibid 154.   [78] Ibid.

understood as a bizarre coincidence rather than a systematic disadvantage based on sex. To avoid this confusing limitation of thought, we must recognize that in some cases where women experience disadvantage, people know perfectly well what women are and what women need; but they simply do not respect (value) women qua women to a sufficient degree to provide for women's needs.

The foregoing explains the differences between sex discrimination and sexism, but these two aspects of patriarchy share similarities as well. Like sex discrimination, for example, sexism does not necessarily entail the intentional denial of valuable opportunities to women. One who engages in the type of sexist conduct identified by Sen need not, for example, think 'Since we're facing a drought this year, I will intentionally deprive women of food and water so that I can keep enough reserves for the men. I realize this will result in the death of many more women than men, but so be it. I do not value women, so that consequence is not a concern to me.' Of course, such conduct, based on such reasoning, would count as sexist; but my point here is that sexism can be manifest in unintentional ways as well. For example, sexism can be just as easily grounded in the kind of callous lack of regard for women that is manifest in a food and water distribution plan that prioritizes the provision of reserves to members of the military, when the military consists exclusively of men. The intention in such an instance would be to ensure that the military are provided with adequate reserves of food and water. Whilst the result would be to deprive women of adequate food and water, this deprivation would not be intentional. Rather, it would simply result as a natural consequence of a system that fails to value women. Such a system could easily be conceived and executed without anyone in charge ever conceiving of the possibility, much less intending, that it will lead to the disproportionate deaths of women. Indeed, they might not even realize the consequences of their sexism until they were burying the (mostly female) bodies.

In the type of disadvantage that I have labelled sexism, there is no misconception about the fact that women are human, or that humans deserve access to basic universal goods: there is simply a denial of goods to humans who are women. There is no attempt to rationalize this denial of goods, for example, on grounds that women are a type of human who do not require such goods. Such rationalizations would constitute sex discrimination, not sexism. However, sexism differs in at least one important respect from the third and final component of patriarchy (misogyny) in the following way: whilst sexism consists in denying to women that which is good, misogyny consists in securing to women that which is evil.

3. Misogyny

Misogyny shall be understood as the malicious securing of disvalue (evil) for women. In its lexical sense, misogyny is simply the hatred or dislike of women.[79]

---

[79] 'Misogyny' Oxford English Dictionary Online <http://dictionary.oed.com///> accessed 4 May 2007.

As the term is employed here, misogyny entails a practical attitude of seeking disvalue for women that is manifest through what we will refer to as misogynist action. Importantly, misogyny does not consist merely in misapprehending women's attributes, needs or interests; nor does it consist simply in failing to value women. Rather, misogyny entails maliciously choosing evil for women because they are women. Examples of misogynist action are replete in the writings of Andrea Dworkin, who documented a myriad of sexualized forms of misogyny found in violent pornography.[80] One of the clearest examples of misogyny in this genre is found in the phenomenon of snuff films: pornography in which women are literally murdered on film for the purpose of sexually exciting the viewer.[81]

Other examples of misogynist action can found in the actions of some serial killers who actively seek out women to kill because they hate women.[82] The recent explosion of serial killings targeting women in the Ciudad Juárez region of Mexico, and the failure of local law-enforcement authorities to respond effectively to these murders, provide an apt illustration of the distinctions between sex discrimination, sexism, and misogyny. Since 1993, more than 400 women have been abducted and murdered in this Mexico–US border region. The forensic evidence indicates that many of the women were subjected to days of sexual torture before being killed, usually by strangulation or beating.[83] The response (or lack thereof) from the local law-enforcement authorities has captured the attention of international human-rights organizations such as Amnesty International, which has accused the officials of the 'systemic failure to prevent and punish many of the crimes against women in Ciudad Juárez'.[84]

Assuming that the serial killer(s) who are targeting women in Ciudad Juarez are doing so because the victims are women, we may understand the killers as visiting upon women a specific type of disadvantage: namely, torture followed

---

[80] See generally A Dworkin, *Woman Hating* (New York: Plume, 1974); A Dworkin, *Letters from a War Zone* (Chicago: Lawrence Hill Books, 1993).

[81] B LaBelle, 'Snuff: The ultimate in woman-hating' in L Lederer (ed), *Take Back the Night* (New York: William Morrow, 1980). I offer no defence of any claims regarding the prevalence of misogyny as compared to other aspects of patriarchy, although I suspect that the prevalence of each aspect ranks roughly in the order I have presented them here: sex discrimination as most common, sexism as somewhat less common, and misogyny as relatively uncommon. For a contrary argument to the effect that misogyny is a common phenomenon, see A Jukes, *Why Men Hate Women* (London: Free Association Books, 1993).

[82] J Bindel, 'Terror on our streets' *Guardian* (London: 13 December 2006) <http://www.guardian.co.uk/suffolkmurders/story/0,,1970938,00.html> accessed 29 August 2008; A Hill and others, 'Sexual sadism and sadistic personality disorder in sexual homicide' (2006) 8 *J of Personal Disorders* 671; T Gratzer and J Bradford, 'Offender and offense characteristics of sexual sadists: A comparative study' (1995) 40 *J of Forensic Science* 450.

[83] D Weissman, 'The political economy of violence: Toward an understanding of the gender-based murders of Ciudad Juárez' (1995) 30 North Carolina J of Intl L and Commercial Regulation 795; Amnesty International, 'Mexico: Killings and abductions of women in Ciudad Juarez and the city of Chihuahua—The struggle for justice goes on' (20 February 2006) (AI Index: AMR 41/012/2006) <http://www.amnestyusa.org/document.php?id=ENGAMR410122006> accessed 29 August 2008.

[84] Amnesty International (n 83 above).

by death.[85] If we assume that the killers are not confused about what kinds of people these women are (for example, the killers are not labouring under the misapprehension that their victims are the kind of people who can survive being tortured, strangled, and left in the desert), then we may safely conclude that the killings are not instances of mere sex discrimination. Moreover, if we assume that the killers are not out to kill indiscriminately and simply happen to come upon women when they are out looking for victims, thus victimizing women simply because they cannot be bothered to seek out greater variety in their victims, then we may safely conclude that the killings are not instances of mere sexism. Rather, it appears more likely that the killers are targeting women to torture and kill specifically for the purpose of visiting upon women pain and death. They appear to be motivated by a hatred of women which is consistent both with the recognition of women's humanity and with some understanding of the value of human life, combined with an intentional choice to act against that value by affirmatively seeking evil for women. In other words, it appears likely that the killers are engaged in acts of misogyny.

Compare the killer(s)' actions to the actions of the local law-enforcement officials who have persistently failed to respond effectively to the ongoing slaughter. Assuming the officials recognize that the women victims are bound by the natural laws of mortality which bind all human being (eg, they do not expect these victims to miraculously rise from the dead), then we may safely conclude that their systemic failure to prevent and punish these crimes is not simply a case of sex discrimination. Assuming as well that the officials' systematic failure is not based on their own hatred of women and a concomitant desire to see the murders continue so as to visit evil upon the victims qua women, then we can conclude that their failure is not misogynistic in nature. Rather, what seems more likely is that the officials have failed to respond effectively to these murders due to sexism: the failure to value the lives and welfare of the women victims. The value of the victims' lives apparently has been dismissed by the officials—not recognized to have the same value it otherwise would if the victims had been male. It is for this reason that the officials' failure to act has been taken up as a cause by organizations concerned to advance the human rights of women: this failure constitutes an instance of sexism that disadvantages women qua women.

E. Patriarchy as a Structural Inequality

Patriarchy is a structural inequality.[86] This section hopes to explain what is meant by this claim, but I should confess at the outset that structural inequality is a bit

---

[85] The knock-on effect of the killings, of course, is also to reduce dramatically the quality of life for those women still living in Ciudad Juarez, due to the fear of being victimized, and the disadvantage suffered by those women who have left the region in order to avoid victimization.

[86] More specifically, patriarchy is a structural inequality consisting of numerous reinforcing social forms which bear hallmarks of sex discrimination, sexism, and/or misogyny.

like Hart's elephant: I can recognize it when I see it, but I cannot define it.[87] As Iris Marion Young similarly noted, the concept of structure itself 'is notoriously difficult to pin down';[88] and one might reasonably expect that adding the notion of inequality to the mix only serves to add further slipperiness (and indeed it does).[89] Still, despite these difficulties, the term remains a commonly used (albeit rarely explained) concept in recent discussions of social injustice in legal academic literature.[90] Since I take my account of patriarchy to fall within the ambit of that which is targeted by this literature, I will adopt the term 'structural inequality' and will attempt to provide an account of this concept that goes some way toward clarifying both the sense in which I use the term and its relationship to patriarchy.

1. Patriarchy as structural

In its most basic and unilluminating sense, structural inequality is a function of social structures, or 'sets of rules and principles that govern activities in the different domains of social life'.[91] Social structures which tend to sustain or perpetuate the unequal distribution of social power can be understood as structural inequalities. One important function served by the concept of structural inequality is that it informs our understanding of how individuals' lives can be shaped, at least in part, by social structures that result in those persons being denied an adequate range of valuable options for leading successful lives. These denials cannot be properly understood merely as the product of individual choices or simply as discrete events in which valuable options have been denied but rather are best understood as systematic in nature.

As a form of structural inequality, patriarchy is neither episodic nor discrete, but is in its nature systematic. As Marilyn Frye has observed, the systematic nature of patriarchal structural inequality denies valuable options to women much as the intertwined wires of a birdcage deny flight:

The cage makes the bird entirely unfree to fly. If one studies the causes of this imprisonment by looking at one wire at a time, however, it appears puzzling. How does a wire only a couple of centimetres wide prevent a bird's flight? One wire at a time, we can neither describe nor explain the inhibition of the bird's flight. Only a large number of wires

---

[87] HLA Hart, *The Concept of Law* (2nd edn, Oxford: OUP, 1994) 14.

[88] IM Young, *Inclusion and Democracy* (Oxford: OUP, 2002) 92, 98.

[89] Inequality here functions in its rhetorical sense. Raz (n 36 above) 227–9.

[90] More than 64 law review articles published since 1988 employ the term 'structural inequality' in the context of discussing racism, patriarchy, and homophobia. Westlaw search string: "Structural Inequality" /P (racis! patriarch! sexis! homophob!), databases JLR, UK-JLR (search conducted 5 January 2009).

[91] T Schatzki, 'Structuralism in social science' (1998) Routledge Encyclopedia of Philosophy Online <http://www.rep.routledge.com//R036?ssid=467079195&n=2#> accessed 13 April 2008.

arranged in a specific way and connected to one another to enclose the bird and reinforce one another's rigidity can explain why the bird is unable to fly freely.[92]

Iris Marion Young shares this conception of structural inequality and adopts Frye's simile of the birdcage to illustrate the nature of structural inequality, which she describes as follows:

[Structural inequality] contains many strands of difficulty or difference from others that, taken one by one, can appear to be the result of decision, preferences, or accidents, [but] when considered together . . . and when compared with the life story of others, they reveal a net of systematic denials in the range and adequacy of life options.[93]

In a similar vein, Ruth Gavison has correctly noted the implications of the systematic nature of structural inequality in the context of domestic violence:

When women are battered at home, it is not because each particular victim has triggered an unfortunate 'individual' tragedy . . . Social structures are involved, social structures which are not simply 'natural'. They are person-made, and they benefit males.[94]

Social structures consist of social forms in the sense that they consist of 'forms of behaviour which are in fact widely practised in . . . society' and which shape the significance and meaning of actions by assigning 'symbolic meaning to certain modes of behaviour' through complex webs of 'shared beliefs, folklore, high culture, collectively shared metaphors and imagination, and so on'.[95] Social structures are, however, somewhat less susceptible to variation through the initiative of individuals or small groups than are common social forms. Raz offers the example of an 'ordinary conventional marriage' as an example of a 'widely shared social form' that is susceptible to a significant degree of variation through the initiative of individual couples:[96]

Many marriages, perhaps all, are not that conventional. They are based on a shared perception of a social form while deviating from it in some respects. They are deviations on a common theme, and they can typically be that because the social form itself recognizes the existence of variations . . . A couple may evolve an 'open' marriage even though this form is unknown to their society. But an open marriage is a relation combining elements of a conventional marriage and of a sexual pursuit which is kept free of emotional involvement. It is a combination of elements of two socially recognizable forms.[97]

Social structures, in contrast, are best understood as consisting of social forms which are mutually reinforcing and thus not nearly as susceptible to variation and/or combination with otherwise inconsistent social forms. The term

---

[92] Young (n 88 above) 92–3, discussing M Frye, *The Politics of Reality* (Trumansberg, NY: Crossing Press, 1983).

[93] Young (n 88 above) 93.

[94] R Gavison, 'Feminism and the public/private distinction' (1992) 45 Stanford L Rev 1, 20.

[95] Raz (n 36 above) 310, 311, 350.

[96] Raz (n 36 above) 309.

[97] Ibid.

'structure' itself is suggestive of a more or less stable physical form, and whilst 'structure' is principally used in a metaphorical sense when referring to structural inequalities,[98] its physical connotation is nonetheless illuminating insofar as it suggests a certain degree of immutability and inflexibility to structural inequalities.[99] Due to these qualities, the initiative of individuals or small groups will not be as likely to succeed in carving out deviations from the structural inequality as such efforts might be when directed against discrete social forms. Whilst Raz is correct to note that some social forms 'recognize the existence of variations', part of what makes structural inequalities relative stable over time is the extent to which they resists such variations.[100]

As such, we should not expect structural inequalities such as patriarchy or racism, for example, to be subject to substantial deviation or outright avoidance in the way we might expect to see deviation from or avoidance of other social forms. Consider marriage once again: one substantial deviation on this social form is exemplified in the practice of couples living together as partners without the legal or religious sanction of marriage. In a very real sense, many of these couples are participating in a social form which is a variation on marriage: they understand themselves and are understood by others to be partners in the same sense spouses are understood as partners. We might expect them to explain their choice not to marry formally in terms such as 'we consider ourselves married, so why do we need a piece of paper to prove it?' Equally, however, some other couples are participating in a social form which positions itself in opposition to marriage: the very point of refusing the legal and religious trappings of marriage is thereby to avoid participating in this social form. We might expect this group of couples to explain their choice not to marry in terms such as 'Marriage leads to divorce. We're happy as we are, so why invite trouble by getting married?' From this we can see that marriage is a highly malleable and indeed altogether avoidable social form. Individual couples can, of their own initiative, shape their lives in such a way as to participate in a variation on marriage, or even choose to remain together as partners despite rejecting marriage altogether. The same is not true, however, with respect to structural inequalities. Short of escaping from society to a deserted island, we cannot escape the structural inequalities that shape our lives and give meaning and significance to many of our actions. Structural inequalities cannot simply be wished away, and the actions of individuals and/or small groups cannot realize substantial deviation from or avoidance of structural inequalities. Thus, for example, whilst an individual man and woman living together in a

---

[98] Iris Marion Young, however, has emphasized the literal relevance of physical structures in understanding the nature of some structural inequalities, drawing upon the example of inadequate housing as a physical structure which in part constitutes the structural inequality of poverty in urban ghettos. Young (n 88 above) 96–7.

[99] IM Young, *On Female Body Experience: 'Throwing like a girl' and other essays* (New York: OUP, 2005) 20.

[100] Raz (n 36 above) 309.

patriarchal society can certainly attempt to deviate from patriarchy in their lives, and indeed may seek altogether to avoid participating in patriarchy, this structural inequality will remain a resilient and abiding force shaping the meanings and symbols of the social context in which they live. For this reason, those who claim to be able to live free from the influence of structural inequalities such as patriarchy or racism (eg, by claiming to be colour-blind, etc) are by and large kidding themselves.

This claim is not meant to suggest that structural inequality is entirely immune to variation through individual or small group initiative. It is merely to claim that such variation is likely to be frustrated at this level due to the relative immutability and inflexibility of structural inequality, and thus if any variations are to be realized, they are likely to be achieved at the societal level. Furthermore, ultimate destruction of a structural inequality is a project that requires transformation at the societal level. Individuals and small groups simply cannot think their way out of structural inequalities whilst simultaneously continuing to participate in the societies which sustain and perpetuate those structural inequalities. It is, however, impossible to be precise as to the degree of deviation in a structural inequality achievable through individual and small group initiative. As Raz has noted with respect to social forms, '[i]t is no more possible to delimit in advance the range of deviations... than it is to delimit the possible relations between the literal and the metaphorical use of an expression'.[101]

So, we may concede that some variation on structural inequality is possible. We might acknowledge that there are relatively more or less patriarchal arrangements in marriages, for example. In some traditional marriages, the significance and meaning of behaviours which constitute the marriage relationship are often grounded in patriarchal 'shared beliefs, folklore, high culture, collectively shared metaphors and imagination, and so on',[102] whilst, in more progressive marriages, couples may consciously reject these patriarchal trappings. Consider the example set by families in which the mother is the 'breadwinner' while the father is the primary caregiver to the children.[103] Even where both parties sincerely endeavour

---

[101] Ibid.

[102] Raz (n 36 above) 311.

[103] As reported by stay-at-home-dad, Bill Dow, the trappings of patriarchy are not so easily avoided:

> When you are at the playground with 10 other mothers, it's easy to feel like a fish out of water. It doesn't matter how progressive you feel yourself to be... or how much you love being with your kids, you're still a man in concentric worlds of women and children. You stand out and you stand outside the circle, listening to conversations you can't participate in. You know you're hurting your career prospects. You know that many men look down on your choice, or at least wonder if your choice means you can't hold down a real job.

This account is reported on the progressive father's blog, Daddy Dialectic. <http://daddy-dialectic.blogspot.com/2006/04/dad-vs-mr-mom.html> accessed 29 August 2008. For similar accounts of the economic and socio-political constraints to changing gender based structural inequalities, see D Canary and TM Emmers-Sommer, *Sex and Gender Differences in Personal Relationships* (New York: Guildford Press, 1998) 156–61.

to create a non-patriarchal relationship, the social structure of patriarchy proves resistant. In order for non-patriarchal relationships to be fully realized, the parties would have to live within a society that adequately supported alternatives to patriarchy: a society in which sexism does not restrict women's pay in the workforce and devalue men for taking on female roles, and where people are able to perceive their authentic attributes, needs, and interests unaffected by the misconceptions of sex discrimination, so as to shape their comprehensive goals in a way that contributes to their living valuable lives.

2. Patriarchy as inequality

Briefly, we will revisit the issue of equality to explain what is meant by the claim that patriarchy is a structural inequality. Phrasing the matter in this way suggests that structural inequality is concerned with principles of equality. But some principles of equality, such as Ronald Dworkin's famous 'principle of equal concern and respect' are not, strictly speaking, concerned with equality.[104] They are not, as Raz puts it, 'strictly egalitarian'.[105] Instead, they are concerned with what we might call, again following Raz, 'rhetorical' egalitarianism.[106] The reference to inequality in the phrase 'structural inequality' is concerned with this type of principle of equality: rhetorical egalitarianism.

All principles of entitlement to a good generate claims of rhetorical egalitarianism in the sense that all those who have equal qualification under the particular principle have an equal right to the good. This sense of equality does not, however, entail strict egalitarianism. It does not, for example, entail that each person who qualifies should be provided the same amount of the good. For example, consider the principle of a human right to drinkable water.[107] This principle can be formulated as a principle of equality in the following way: 'all persons are equally entitled to drinkable water'. Yet nothing in this formulation suggests a strict egalitarian meaning behind the principle. As between a small child and a full-grown adult, for example, we may distribute unequal amounts of potable water without violating the principle that all persons are equally entitled to drinkable water. This point illustrates that the term 'equal' in the formulation of this principle serves a rhetorical function. Its purpose is not to serve equality as a value in itself but 'to promote the cause of those who qualify under independently valid principles' such as 'all persons are entitled to adequate amounts of potable drinking water'.[108]

---

[104] R Dworkin, *Taking Rights Seriously* (London: Duckworth, 1978) 180–3, 272–8.
[105] Raz (n 36 above) 228.
[106] Ibid.
[107] J Sanlon, A Cassar, and N Nemes, 'Water as a human right?' (IUCN Environmental Law and Policy Paper No 51, UNDP 2004).
[108] Raz (n 36 above) 228.

Rhetorical egalitarian claims borrow from the language of equality in order 'to gain from the good name that "equality" has in our culture'.[109] In most cases, as in Dworkin's principle of equal concern and respect, these claims 'amount to little more than an assertion that all human beings are moral subjects'.[110] As Raz has noted, borrowing from the language of equality can make such principles more attractive, persuasive, and effective in realizing the independently valid principles which they advance under the cover of equality; and if so, 'so much the better'.[111] We may, however, pay a price in terms of intellectual confusion when we borrow from the language of equality to articulate principles that are egalitarian in merely a rhetorical sense.

It is for this reason that I was tempted to avoid the confusing phrase 'structural inequality' in articulating the nature of patriarchy. There is no denying, however, that the social form of patriarchy has been and is widely understood from a feminist perspective as a problem of equality, if only in its rhetorical sense.[112] It would therefore be all but impossible, or at least terrifically awkward, to engage with the literature regarding patriarchy and feminism without resort to the language of equality. Sometimes this borrowing of egalitarian language has generated confusions of thought in feminist literature, but more often it is employed in a harmless, not terribly confusing rhetorical sense which facilitates recognition of feminists' concerns to a wide audience.

F. Conclusion

The term 'patriarchy' as understood in this book is used in a particular sense: not as a form of state governance as it is commonly understood in traditional political theory but rather as a wrongful structural inequality, as it is commonly understood in feminist theory. The notion that certain actions can possess a patriarchal character was explained in this chapter, in terms which understand patriarchy as consisting of Razian social forms. Where patriarchy exists in a society, actions can be understood as patriarchal in character or non-patriarchal (feminist) in character. It follows from this point, along with points regarding the constitution of character made in Chapters 3 and 4,[113] that engaging in habituated actions of a patriarchal or non-patriarchal (feminist) character may constitute in the agent a patriarchal or non-patriarchal (feminist) character.

---

[109] Ibid.
[110] Ibid.
[111] Ibid.
[112] No fewer than 4.927 law review articles published in the US and UK currently in print borrow from the language of equality in the context of discussing patriarchy and/or feminism. Westlaw search string: (patriarch! feminis!) /s (equal! inequal!), databases JLR, UK-JLR (search conducted 5 January 2009).
[113] See Chapter 3, section B.2 and Chapter 4, section B.4.

In addition to these points, this chapter has explained and defended the notion of patriarchy as a wrongful structural inequality. The wrongness of patriarchy was analysed in terms of three aspects: sex discrimination, sexism, and misogyny. In sum then, this chapter has presented a detailed account of patriarchy, which better illuminates the conceptual analysis of domestic violence offered in Chapter 6. It is hoped that Chapters 6 and 7, taken as a whole, provide an adequate understanding of the wrongful conduct at issue when we consider domestic-violence prosecutions. In the next chapter, I will consider the sense in which habituated prosecutorial actions can constitute a patriarchal or non-patriarchal (feminist) character in the state and/or community, and the relevance of this point to determining the reasons that guide domestic-violence prosecutorial action.

8

Domestic-violence Prosecution: Justification and Effectiveness

This chapter attempts to tie together the analyses and arguments set forth in Part II of the book with the account of domestic violence and patriarchy set forth thus far in Part III. My approach to this task will be to return to the motivating question set out in Chapter 1: what should public prosecutors do when victims withdraw their support for the prosecution of domestic-violence cases? The chapter addresses two ways in which one might respond this question: the first speaks to the issue of justification, whilst the second speaks to the issue of effectiveness.

In terms of structure, this chapter is broken into two main sections which correspond to each of these two ways of answering the motivating question. The first section addresses the issue of justification by tracking the ideas developed in Part II of the book: providing an account of what domestic-violence prosecutors are and what they do; identifying the kinds of values that domestic-violence prosecutorial actions can realize; and examining which of these values provide domestic-violence prosecutors with reasons which may render their actions justifiable. By justifiable, I simply mean *permissible* all things considered.[1] If it is correct to suppose that justified action is merely permissible, then there may exist conceptual space between what makes domestic-violence prosecutorial actions *permissible* (justifiable) and what might make such actions *effective*. Prosecutorial actions in domestic-violence cases, in other words, may be fully justified without being particularly *effective* qua domestic-violence prosecutorial actions.[2]

---

[1] In other words, I reject what Marcia Baron has called the 'positive rightness thesis'. M Baron, 'Justifications and excuses' (2005) 2 Ohio State J of Crim L 387, 396. Contra P Robinson, *Criminal Law Defences* (St Paul: West, 1984) 70, 83. For discussion of the ambiguity of accounts of justification that merely claim that justified action is not wrongful (without further specifying whether the action is merely permissible or commendable) such as the account of justification offered in G Fletcher, *Rethinking Criminal Law* (Boston: Little Brown, 1978)), see J Dressler, 'New thoughts about the concept of justification in the criminal law: A critique of Fletcher's thinking and rethinking' (1984) 32 UCLA L Rev 61, 69–77.

[2] Conversely, prosecutorial actions might be effective without being justified, but we will consider that possibility in section B.

A. Justifying Domestic-violence Prosecutorial Actions

This section examines what might justify prosecutorial action in domestic-violence cases in which victims request dismissal of the charges.[3] If the arguments and analyses set out in part two of this book are plausible, the question of justification calls for a three-step answer. First, I will examine what domestic-violence prosecutors are and what they do; second, I will identify (some of) the values that might be realized through domestic-violence prosecutorial action; and third, I will consider the reasons that apply to prosecutorial action.

1. Domestic-violence prosecutors: What they are and what they do

Following from the ideas outlined in Chapter 3, domestic-violence prosecutors are people who act as representatives of their states and, if certain political legitimacy conditions exist, as representatives of their communities. These points do not require further development here. What may require further development, however, is the very notion of a 'domestic-violence prosecutor'. This phrasing may be thought to suggest that only designated domestic-violence prosecutors are at issue. For example, if a particular prosecutors' office does not have a specialized Domestic Violence Unit or does not assign prosecutors to dedicated domestic-violence caseloads, then the notion of domestic-violence prosecutor may be thought not to materialize. I do not, however, mean to imply anything of the sort. Rather, the notion of a domestic-violence prosecutor is simply intended to identify a person who acts qua prosecutor relative to a domestic-violence case (irrespective of whether she is regularly assigned to prosecute such cases). So, for example, although I served in the traffic division in my first months of prosecuting, I would occasionally file petitions to revoke defendants' probation in their traffic cases on grounds that the defendants were alleged to have committed domestic-violence offences. Indeed, some of my first 'victimless' prosecutions of domestic violence were filed in the traffic court, within the context of revoking defendants' probations and having them re-sentenced for their previous drink-driving convictions.[4]

---

[3] For the sake of simplicity, I will not attend to the distinction between justifiable and justified action. Roughly, I take the distinction to go something like this: in engaging in action which is prima facie wrongful, if one acts consistently with one's undefeated guiding reasons, then one's actions are *justifiable*; whereas if one acts *for* one's undefeated guiding reasons (ie, if those reasons are also one's explanatory reasons for acting), then one's action is *justified*. On the distinction between guiding and explanatory resons, see J Gardner, 'Justification and reasons' in A Simester and A Smith (eds), *Harm and Culpability* (Oxford: Clarendon, 1996), reprinted in J Gardner, *Offences and Defences* (OUP, 2007) 91–120.

[4] I developed this practice in response to existing policies regarding the prosecution of domestic-violence cases at the time, which led to high rates of dismissal in cases of victim withdrawal. While the domestic-violence prosecutors at the time did not generally pursue the primary

The prosecutors assigned to dedicated management of domestic-violence offences in my office at this time typically chose not to take pursuit action in cases where the victims did not cooperate with the investigation, and thus such cases were uniformly no-charged or dismissed upon the victims' requests to do so. Some of the suspects in these no-charged cases and some of the defendants in the dismissed cases were on probation for traffic offences such as driving under the influence of alcohol at the time of the alleged domestic-violence offences. Rather than allowing the domestic-violence offences to go unpursued, I would use the domestic-violence offence as a basis for revoking the suspects' probation in their traffic cases.[5] In this sense, although I was officially designated as a traffic prosecutor during these months, I also functioned as a domestic-violence prosecutor.

Domestic-violence prosecutors engage in both prosecutorial pursuit and non-pursuit actions in domestic-violence cases. This distinction may be thought too blunt, since some prosecutorial action is difficult to characterize as either pursuit or non-pursuit action.[6] For example, where specialized prosecution units do exist, prosecutors are called upon to engage in sorting actions: making decisions (and acting upon decisions) regarding what kinds of cases are at issue. Does a particular case count as a case of domestic violence for the purpose of assigning the case to a particular courtroom or prosecutorial division? When a suspect throws a chair at the wall during an argument with his wife at the pub, is the case a case of domestic violence? Or is it a property offence? Or is it an offence against public order?

In being called upon to make these decisions, we can understand the prosecutor as engaged in domestic-violence prosecutorial pursuit actions in those cases in which the offence is identified and treated as domestic violence, whilst the prosecutor can be understood as engaged in domestic-violence prosecutorial non-pursuit actions in those cases in which the offence is identified and treated as something other than domestic violence. The decision to categorize a case as domestic violence is akin in some important respects to the paradigmatic prosecutorial pursuit actions of charging and trying a case; and the decision to categorize a case as something other than domestic violence is akin in some important respects to the paradigmatic non-pursuit actions of no-charging

---

domestic-violence charges in such cases, they were content to allow me to use the underlying facts of the domestic-violence offences to serve as the basis for revoking defendants' probations in unrelated traffic cases. Typically, the revocation of probation resulted in the defendants receiving far harsher penalties than they would have received had they been convicted on the original domestic-violence charge, since the presiding traffic judge was particularly aggressive in re-sentencing defendants who had failed to comply with the conditions of their probation in drink-driving cases.

[5] It was routinely a condition of probation that defendants refrain from committing any other criminal offence during the time of probation. Thus, proof that a defendant on probation for a traffic offence had committed domestic violence was sufficient grounds for revoking the defendant's probation and causing him to be resentenced in the underlying traffic case.

[6] For more on this point, see section B.4 below.

and dismissing charges. Thus, in some instances it makes sense to characterize a domestic-violence prosecutor's conduct vis-à-vis a case as prosecutorial non-pursuit action, despite the fact that the suspect in that case is charged with a criminal offence, tried, and convicted. From the perspective of determining whether the prosecutor is engaged in domestic-violence prosecutorial pursuit or non-pursuit action, the treatment of the case is one of non-pursuit, since the case is not pursued qua a case of domestic violence.

This point raises a wrinkle in the earlier, simplified distinction between pursuit and non-pursuit action. Generally, that distinction reflects the difference between prosecuting a case (eg, charging, trying, etc) and letting it go unprosecuted (eg, no-charging, dismissing pending charges, etc). But once the complexity of domestic violence is added to the picture, we can understand prosecutorial pursuit actions to include actions that cast a net around those cases identified as domestic violence, and we can understand prosecutorial non-pursuit actions to include declining the opportunity to cast such a net. Thus, the fact that a case is met with domestic-violence prosecutorial non-pursuit action does not necessarily imply that the underlying case will not meet with another type of prosecutorial pursuit action. For example, our pub-chair-throwing suspect may not be pursued as a domestic-violence offender, but he may be pursued as a property or public-disorder offender.

Domestic-violence prosecutorial actions, of either the pursuit or non-pursuit variety, can reconstitute in part the character of the state (and community). This notion was developed somewhat in Chapter 3, but two points bear noting as we revisit the issue in the context of domestic-violence prosecutions. First, the key character traits at issue in the context of domestic-violence prosecution are the traits of being patriarchal on the one hand and being non-patriarchal (feminist) on the other.[7] Second, if my earlier arguments regarding the potential for prosecutorial action to reconstitute in part the character of the state (and community) are sound, then it follows that domestic-violence prosecutorial actions are capable of constituting the character of the state (and community) as more or less patriarchal, *ceteris paribus*.

This point requires further elaboration in order to connect it to one of the central claims of this book: domestic-violence prosecutors should be feminists, *ceteris paribus*. In order to make sense of this claim, I must explain what it means for domestic-violence prosecutors to be feminists, and why it matters that they are feminists. If my earlier claim that 'actions constitute character' is true, and if prosecutors can act on behalf of their states (and perhaps their communities), then why should it matter whether we think of domestic-violence prosecutors themselves as feminists? Shouldn't we be concerned only with whether their actions taken on behalf of the state (and community) are feminist?

The answer to these questions is found in my earlier dual concession that character is constituted *not only* through actions but *also* through thoughts, attitudes,

---

[7] See Chapter 7.

and motivations; and that states (and communities) do not have thoughts, attitudes, or motivations.[8] Upon conceding these points, I continued to defend the notion that states (and communities) have characters, and my defence was based on the relationship that exists between: (1) thought, attitude, and motivation; (2) action; and (3) character. Thoughts, attitudes, and motivations, I claimed, give rise to dispositions to engage in actions—actions which possess a given character. So for example, feminist thoughts, attitudes, and motivations give rise to dispositions to engage in feminist actions. Since only individuals can have thoughts, attitudes, and motivations in the relevant sense, only individuals can have dispositions to act in the relevant sense. That is why it matters that domestic-violence prosecutors are feminists: without the thoughts, attitudes, and motivations that give rise to dispositions to engage in feminist actions, the prosecutors are not able to engage in habituated feminist actions on behalf of the state (and community)—and if they are not able to engage in habituated feminist actions on behalf of the state (and community), then their actions cannot (re)constitute the character of the state (and community). However, when a domestic-violence prosecutor *does* have a feminist disposition, the corresponding feminist actions *can* be performed in her capacity as representative of the state (and community), thus reconstituting its character.

My version of the claim that character is constituted by action therefore does not deny the relevance of thoughts, attitudes, and motivations of individual agents; but neither does it suppose that thoughts, attitudes, and motivations are *directly* relevant to constituting characters. In other words, the fact that domestic-violence prosecutors have feminist thoughts, attitudes, and motivations does not itself affect the character of the state (and community). Indeed, even if these prosecutors act in accordance with the dispositions grounded by their feminist thoughts, attitudes, and motivations, these actions do not necessarily affect the character of the state (and community). Rather, in order to affect (reconstitute) the character of the state (and community), domestic-violence prosecutors must act *qua state (and community) representatives* in accordance with the dispositions grounded by their feminist thoughts, attitudes, and motivations.[9] They must both *have* such dispositions and *act* upon them in their prosecutorial role. In other words, the domestic-violence prosecutors must both *be* feminists *and* engage in habituated feminist actions qua prosecutors.

2. Domestic-violence prosecutorial action and value

As with all prosecutorial actions, domestic-violence prosecutorial actions can have either consequential or intrinsic value. While the discussion below does not purport to identify every value that might be realized by domestic-violence

---

[8] Chapter 3, section B.2.
[9] Moreover, such actions must be habituated; but I will not revisit this point here.

prosecutorial actions, it does attempt to identify some of the salient values that have been noted in the academic literature regarding domestic-violence prosecutions which may be relevant to justifying prosecutorial actions in such cases.

(a) Consequential values

Prosecutorial actions in domestic-violence cases can, of course, have consequential value, such as the punishment of batterers, the increased safety of particular victims, or the prevention of domestic violence more generally. Louise Ellison recently highlighted the relevance of consequential values in prosecutorial action, in the context of defending 'victimless prosecutions' of domestic violence. Whilst Ellison relies on a concept of consequential value in which 'all of the various interests and goals of the criminal justice system' are valued only insofar as they serve 'to maximize freedom',[10] not all accounts of the consequential value in domestic-violence prosecutorial action are similarly reductivist. For example, Mary Asmus, and others have identified a plurality of consequential values that may be realized by domestic-violence prosecutions, such as increasing the number of assailants who enter batterers' treatment programmes and increasing the percentage of victims who believe that the criminal justice system is helpful in ending the abuse.[11]

These accounts emphasize the consequential value(s) of prosecutorial *pursuit* actions, but importantly, domestic-violence prosecutorial *non-pursuit* actions may also have valuable consequences. In some cases non-pursuit actions may have consequential value insofar as they exonerate non-culpable actors: for example, when a prosecutor declines to charge a domestic-violence victim for killing her abuser in self-defence, or dismisses pending charges that had been unjustly filed against a victim pursuant to an overly aggressive mandatory arrest and charge policy.[12]

Interestingly, domestic-violence prosecutorial non-pursuit actions can also realize consequential value even when they lead to the non-prosecution of culpable domestic-violence offenders. David Ford has convincingly demonstrated that such non-pursuit actions can have valuable consequences in terms of enhancing victim safety and access to power resources in the abusive domestic relationships:

[10] L Ellison, 'Prosecuting domestic violence without victim participation' (2002) MLR 834, 852, citing A Sanders and R Young, 'From suspect to trial' in M Macguire, R Morgan, and R Reiner (eds), *Oxford Handbook of Criminology* (Oxford: OUP, 2002).

[11] M Asmus and others, 'Prosecuting domestic abuse cases in Duluth: Developing effective prosecution strategies from understanding the dynamics of abusive relationships' (1991) 15 Hamline L Rev 115, 150.

[12] For discussion of the problem of domestic-violence victims being unjustly prosecuted under unduly aggressive prosecution policies, see S Miller, *Victims as Offenders: The paradox of women's violence in relationships* (London: Rutgers University Press, 2005); D Coker, 'Crime control and feminist law reform in domestic violence law: A critical review' (2001) 4 Buffalo Crim L Rev 801, 831; E Sack, 'Battered women and the state: The struggle for the future of domestic violence policy' [2004] Wisconsin L Rev 1657, 1680.

Victims can be empowered by controlling prosecution as a resource for managing conjugal violence...Particularly if she wants to stop further violence, deterrence may operate when she can demonstrate the credibility of a threat [of prosecution]. Ultimately,
however, she must be able to withdraw the threat if she secures a favourable settlement.
In other words, the effective use of prosecution as a power resource is premised on the
victim's ability both to demonstrate a significant threat and to control activities relevant
to the threat, including its withdrawal.[13]

On Ford's account, the dismissal of pending criminal charges against
batterers—ie, domestic-violence prosecutorial non-pursuit action—is crucial to
realizing the consequential values of victim safety and empowerment. In a similar vein, Hoyle and Sanders have noted that non-pursuit actions such as declining
to charge following the arrest of a domestic batterer can also realize consequential
values in terms of victim safety and empowerment.[14] Indeed, on their account,
the disvalue which often accompanies prosecutorial pursuit actions in domestic-
violence cases means that prosecutorial non-pursuit actions are often the best way
to maximize consequential values.

(b) Intrinsic values

Prosecutorial actions can realize a myriad of intrinsic values, but in what follows
we will focus on just three: telic, expressive, and constitutive.[15] Telic value, as
discussed in Chapter 4, is value that an action has in virtue of its aimed-for but
not necessarily achieved or even expected consequences. In order for an action to
bear a telic relationship to value, it must be *possible* for that action to achieve valuable consequences, *and* this possibility must be *recognized* by the actor.

What is the relevance of this condition to understanding the value of prosecutorial action taken in response to a domestic-violence victim's request to dismiss
charges? The first level of relevance pertains to the question of prosecutors' beliefs
regarding the likelihood of success in prosecuting such cases. In cases where consequential value would be realized by convicting the defendant, it follows that
a corresponding telic value may be realized as well (even if the conviction is not
achieved), provided that prosecutorial pursuit action is undertaken as an *attempt*
to convict (ie, an attempt to secure that valuable consequence).

The realization of telic value can be blocked by the 'working rules' of the criminal justice system, which as Hoyle demonstrates, often lead domestic-violence

---

[13] D Ford, 'Prosecution as a victim resource: A note on empowering women in violent conjugal
relationships' (1991) 25 Law and Society Rev 313, 318–19.
[14] C Hoyle and A Sanders, 'Police response to domestic violence: From victim choice to victim
empowerment?' (2000) 40 British J of Criminology 14, 32.
[15] Notably then, retributive value will not be mentioned. This omission is justified in virtue of
the discussion in Chapter 5, which explained why retributive value may be thought not to generate reasons for prosecutors. Even if that discussion fails to convince, it remains the case that the
second-order reasons guiding prosecutorial discretion in the US and England (ie, the way the role
is conceived in these jurisdictions) would at very least exclude reasons grounded in retributive value
from prosecutors' rational horizons.

prosecutors to believe that a victim's withdrawal means that the case will necessarily fail to result in conviction.[16] If the prosecutor engages in pursuit action whilst believing that conviction is wholly unachievable from her actions, then her action cannot conceivably amount to an attempt to achieve conviction, and thus no telic value relative to conviction can be realized. This point speaks to the importance of prosecutors' attitudes towards the possibility of achieving valuable consequences through their actions: if prosecutors believe that valuable consequences are wholly unachievable through their actions, then they cannot realize any telic value through their actions; if, on the other hand, prosecutors believe that valuable consequences *are* possibly achievable through their actions, then they may be able to realize telic value through their actions (provided the next two conditions are met).

Next, it must be noted that even if the domestic-violence prosecutor believes the conviction (or other valuable consequence) is possible in a case where the victim withdraws support, that consequence must *actually* be possible in order for the prosecutors' actions to realize telic value. So, futile attempts to prosecute domestic-violence cases with no witnesses whatsoever, for example, will lack telic value relative to the consequential value of conviction.[17] And finally, as noted in Chapter 4, for a domestic-violence prosecutor's action to have telic value, the aimed-for consequences of her action must themselves be valuable. So, for example, if a conviction would *not* be valuable in the circumstances (eg, if the defendant is innocent or otherwise non-culpable), then the prosecutor's actions will also lack telic value relative to that consequence.

Expressive value is perhaps the most widely recognized intrinsic value discussed in the literature regarding the criminal justice response to domestic-violence cases. Victor Tadros has recently commented on this kind of value in connection with domestic-violence prosecutions, noting that criminal prosecutions have 'unique power to mark a public recognition of the wrongful nature of a particular kind of conduct and to stigmatize those who perpetrate that conduct'.[18] In a similar vein, advocates of pro-prosecution and mandatory prosecution policies in domestic-violence cases often cite the expressive value of such prosecutorial action, claiming that it 'sends a strong symbolic message that the community will not tolerate domestic violence'.[19]

---

[16] C Hoyle, *Negotiating Domestic Violence: Police, criminal justice and victims* (Oxford: OUP, 1998) 179–80.

[17] Of course, such actions might realize telic value relative to some other valuable consequence that *is* achievable.

[18] V Tadros, 'The distinctiveness of domestic violence: A freedom based account' (2005) 65 Louisiana L Rev 989, 1011.

[19] D Epstein, ME Bell, and LA Goodman, 'Transforming aggressive prosecution policies: Prioritizing victims' long-term safety in the prosecution of domestic-violence cases' (2003) 11 American U J of Gender, Social Policy and the Law 465, 466. See also L Ellison, 'Responding to victim withdrawal in domestic-violence prosecutions' [2003] Crim L Rev 760, 769, observing that prosecutorial pursuit actions against domestic batterers 'may serve a useful symbolic purpose,

Hoyle and Sanders also recognize the expressive value that can be realized through domestic-violence prosecutions which 'send a symbolic message that domestic violence is a crime, is wrong, and should be punished'.[20] This acknowledgement is followed up, however, by the observation that such messages are 'not usually very effective in [consequential] terms'.[21] This point is well taken: it is of course true that symbolic messages often are not consequentially valuable. Yet this comment regarding the lack of consequential value may risk under-emphasizing the relevance of intrinsic expressive value. An action that sends a message symbolizing the wrongfulness of wrongdoing, the criminality of crime, or the punitive deservedness of that which is deserving of punishment is prima facie intrinsically valuable, irrespective of its consequences. Even if no valuable consequences result from sending such a message, the intrinsic value of the message remains intact. It is therefore perhaps not entirely fair to criticize sending such a message on the grounds that they are not usually very effective in consequential terms, because the point (or at least one valuable point) of sending the message does not depend at all upon its consequences.[22]

Prosecutorial actions can also realize constitutive value: the value of constituting valuable character traits. As noted above, the two key character traits at issue in the discussion of domestic-violence prosecution are the disvaluable trait of being patriarchal and the corresponding valuable trait of being feminist (non-patriarchal). Being feminist is a character trait acquired through the performance of habituated action consistent with practical wisdom in response to the reasons generated by the wrong of patriarchy.[23] We can unpack this point further by observing that habituated actions which possess the character of being sexually discriminatory, sexist, and/or misogynist either constitute or strengthen a patriarchal character trait, whilst habituated actions that oppose sexual discrimination, sexism, and/or misogyny either constitute or strengthen a feminist character trait. Since patriarchy is wrongful, patriarchal actions generate reasons to denounce such actions.[24] If one habituates the denunciation of patriarchy, one

---

sending a clear message to perpetrators that violence between intimate partners in private is taken as seriously as violence between strangers in public'.

[20] Hoyle and Sanders (n 14 above) 32.

[21] Ibid. Hoyle and Sanders use the term 'instrumental' to refer to what I have classified as 'consequential' herein, thus I have replaced the word 'instrumental' with 'consequential' in brackets for ease of reading.

[22] It has been suggested to me that the expressive disvalue of actions performed by other players in the criminal justice system (eg, judges) might be thought to negate the expressive value of the prosecutor's actions; however, I believe this suggestion reflects a misunderstanding of my point. For example, consider a case where a prosecution results in a wrongdoer's conviction; yet later in the bureaucratic chain, the judge gives the defendant a very light sentence and tells him that his conduct was entirely understandable. On my account, the judge's actions do not negate the intrinsic value of the prosecutor's actions; rather, the judge's actions are merely a disvaluable consequence of the prosecutor's actions.

[23] On the wrong of patriarchy, see Chapter 7.

[24] Patriarchal actions also generate reasons to oppose patriarchy in other ways (eg, condemn it), but given the focus on prosecutorial action here and my earlier comments regarding the relevant distinctions between denunciation and condemnation, I will focus on denunciation here.

thereby (re)constitutes one's own character as less patriarchal (ie, more feminist) *ceteris paribus*. Moreover, if prosecutors act on such reasons in their capacity as state representatives (and community representatives), they thereby (re)constitute the character of their states (and communities) as more feminist (less patriarchal) *ceteris paribus*. We will consider further the relevance of constitutive value below in the context of prosecutions when the victims request dismissal.

3. Reasons for domestic-violence prosecutors

Assuming that my arguments in Chapter 5 regarding the normal correspondence thesis hold, then all of the values identified above generate first-order reasons for domestic-violence prosecutors.[25] But which of these reasons are relevant to justifying prosecutorial action in such cases? Our first task here must be to determine the balance of first-order reasons that apply to prosecutors in acting qua prosecutors. Second, we must identify any second-order exclusionary reasons that might apply to prosecutors, for example in virtue of justified authoritative directives or principles. If any such exclusionary reasons apply to prosecutors, they may direct the prosecutors not to act for some first-order reasons, and thereby affect the prosecutors' rational horizons in a way which alters what counts as justifiable prosecutorial action.[26]

First I will address prosecutors' first-order reasons. My claim here is that domestic-violence prosecutors have first-order reasons generated by consequential, telic, expressive, and constitutive values; and these values may be realized either through prosecutorial pursuit or non-pursuit actions. For example, with respect to consequential values, domestic-violence prosecutorial pursuit actions may enhance victim safety or increase a victim's sense of empowerment; or, as discussed above, such pursuit actions may have quite the opposite effect. Depending on whether these actions realize consequential value or disvalue, a corresponding first-order reason is generated for prosecutors either to prosecute or not to prosecute.

Intrinsic values are, of course, less susceptible to contingencies than are consequential values. For example, an attempt to enhance victim safety or increase a victim's sense of empowerment through prosecutorial action will have telic value, even if the attempt fails. Thus it can be said with more confidence that prosecutorial actions in domestic-violence cases which realize intrinsic values will generate reasons for prosecutors. Indeed, with respect to telic value, this point

---

[25] On the distinction between first- and second-order reasons, see J Raz, *Practical Reason and Norms* (2nd edn, New York: OUP, 1999) especially 39–40. Notably, I have omitted discussion of retributive values here based on the plausible suspicion considered in Chapter 5 that such values might not generate reasons for prosecutors. The remaining values (consequential, telic, expressive, and constitutive), however, will be understood to generate first-order reasons for domestic-violence prosecutors.

[26] On the rational function of exclusionary reasons, see ibid 35–48, 178–99 and postscript.

can be made with complete confidence, provided that it is possible for the prosecutor to achieve the aimed-for consequence, the consequence is valuable, and the prosecutor treats the possibility of achieving this value as her aim when acting. With respect to expressive and constitutive values, however, there is one exception to note: in order for a domestic-violence prosecutor to have a reason to prosecute which is grounded in either the expressive value of denouncing patriarchy or in the constitutive value of reconstituting her state (and community) as less patriarchal, the prosecutor must *accurately identify* those cases of domestic violence which *actually do* tend to sustain and perpetuate patriarchy. This point will be discussed further below in the section entitled 'The value of disaggregating two kinds of domestic violence', but the point here is simply that in order for such disaggregation to realize intrinsic value and thereby generate reasons for prosecutors, the prosecutors must get the line-drawing exercise right.

The balance of first-order reasons that apply to domestic-violence prosecutors will likely differ in each case. In some cases, pursuit actions will make the victims safer; in some cases, it may lead to their deaths. In some cases, the expressive value of denouncing patriarchy through prosecutorial pursuit actions will be minimal, other times it will be tremendous. Indeed, denunciation may even have consequential value insofar as it generates what Cass Sunstein has called a 'norm cascade' or 'norm bandwagon', through which general societal normative shifts in society are realized.[27] Given these variations, it would be impossible to catalogue all of the first-order reasons that apply to domestic-violence prosecutors. Particularly given my adoption of the normal correspondence thesis, the range of reasons at stake may be almost identical to the range of values that can be realized by domestic-violence prosecutorial action.[28]

In determining the balance of a prosecutor's first-order reasons, we should be careful not to assume that first-order reasons grounded in the realization of particular kinds of value necessarily trump first-order reasons grounded in other kinds of value. For example, we may suppose that reasons grounded in the realization of a particular kind of value, say the intrinsic value of denouncing patriarchy, are quite weighty reasons. We may even be tempted to think that such reasons will always outweigh countervailing reasons in first-order balancing. Following from these thoughts, we may be tempted to conclude that as a matter of first-order reasoning, prosecutors are always justified in acting for reasons grounded in that value. No matter what the consequences (so the argument goes), prosecutorial actions which denounce patriarchy will always be justified simply in virtue of

[27] C Sunstein, 'Social norms and social roles' (1996) 96 Columbia L Rev 903, 909. If an isolated one-off expressive denunciation of patriarchy—such as a particularly stirring and well-publicized closing argument at trial—causes others in a society to adopt non-patriarchal norms, then this one-off denunciation can be understood as having the consequential value of lessening or eliminating the wrong of patriarchy insofar as it causes (consequentially) the widespread habituated opposition of patriarchy by others.

[28] The notable (possible) exception being retributive value, which may not generate a reason for prosecutors. See discussion in Chapter 5.

their expressive value. This line of thought is mistaken, however, for the balance of first-order reasons in any prosecution cannot be predetermined simply by reference to the kinds of value to be realized through the proposed action. Reasons grounded in some kinds of value do not necessarily defeat reasons grounded in other kinds of value. This point holds for each of the different kinds of value we have considered: reasons grounded in consequential values do not necessarily trump reasons grounded in telic, expressive, or constitutive values; reasons grounded in telic values do not necessarily trump reasons grounded in consequential, expressive, or constitutive values; reasons grounded in expressive values do not necessarily trump reasons grounded in consequential, telic, or constitutive values; and (despite my interest in and focus upon this final kind of value) reasons grounded in constitutive values do not necessarily trump reasons grounded in consequential, telic, or expressive values.

Once the balance of first-order reasons has been determined, we must consider whether any second-order reasons apply to structure the prosecutors' rational horizons. Second-order reasons come in two flavours: positive and negative. Positive second-order reasons are reasons to act for particular first-order reasons. Negative second-order reasons are reasons not to act for particular first-order reasons. In Raz's terminology, positive second-order reasons are referred to as self-reflexive reasons, while negative second-order reasons are referred to as exclusionary reasons.[29] Both kinds of second-order reasons can be generated by the principles and justified authoritative directives that apply to domestic-violence prosecutors.

First consider positive second-order reasons. Assume, for example, that principles endorsed by the therapeutic jurisprudence movement are justified as they relate to domestic-violence prosecutors. A central principle of the therapeutic jurisprudence movement states that prosecutors should act so as to enhance the psychological and/or physical well-being of the victim.[30] If applicable, this principle generates self-reflexive reasons for domestic-violence prosecutors. As we have already established, the fact that a given prosecutorial action can realize the value of enhancing the victim's well-being generates a first-order reason for domestic-violence prosecutors to do so. But prosecutors can do as this reason would have them do irrespective of their motivation for so doing. A prosecutor might, for example, enhance a victim's well-being without trying to do so. However, if we assume that the principle of therapeutic jurisprudence applies to domestic-violence prosecutorial actions, then this principle generates a positive second-order reason for the prosecutors to act *for* the first-order reasons the prosecutors already have. In other words, the fact of victims' well-being generates both a reason to enhance their well-being, *and a reason to do so for the reason that doing so enhances their well-being.* Where such principles validly apply, it follows

---

[29] Raz (n 25 above).

[30] CC Hartley, 'A therapeutic jurisprudence approach to the trial process in domestic violence felony trials' (2003) 9 *Violence Against Women* 410.

that domestic-violence prosecutors who fail to act *for* the rights kinds of reasons may be justifiably criticized for being insufficiently motivated by the right kinds of reason.

In contrast, negative second-order reasons (ie, exclusionary reasons) shape prosecutors' rational horizons by providing them with reasons *not* to act for certain reasons. For example, consider a jurisdiction in which victims' requests to dismiss domestic-violence prosecutions are treated as absolute reasons to end the prosecutions.[31] The prevailing motto in such a prosecutors' office might be articulated as, 'If the victims don't care, why should we?' No weight is accorded in prosecutors' reasoning to any other reasons that might weigh in favour of prosecutorial pursuit action in these cases. Thus, not surprisingly, when prosecutors dismiss such cases, they often fail to conform to what their first-order reasons would have them do. Under such extreme circumstances, it would likely be justifiable to enact an authoritative directive which excludes reasons generated by victims' requests to dismiss from the prosecutors' rational horizons.[32] Indeed, it was just such a scenario I confronted when I first began prosecuting domestic-violence cases and it was for this reason that I adopted a mandatory prosecution policy at the outset of my tenure in the domestic-violence prosecution unit.[33] By adopting an authoritative directive which excluded consideration of victims' requests in deciding whether to dismiss prosecutions, I created a situation in which such decisions had to be made on the basis of other reasons which previously had been ignored. In such situations, authoritative directives can provide a service to the prosecutors in the jurisdiction, who are otherwise unable or unwilling to recognize and to act upon the range of reasons that apply to them.[34] By requiring prosecutors to exclude certain kinds of reasons from their rational horizons, justified authoritative directives enable prosecutors better to conform with the first-order guiding reasons that apply to them.[35] It follows in such instances that domestic-violence prosecutors may be justified in their actions even if they exclude from their considerations some of the first-order reasons that apply to them.

B. Effective Domestic-violence Prosecutorial Actions

Our motivating question (what should public prosecutors do when victims withdraw their support for the prosecution of domestic-violence cases?) can be

---

[31] On absolute reasons, see Raz (n 25 above) 27.

[32] This point applies Raz's normal justification thesis. J Raz, *Ethics in the Public Domain* (Oxford: OUP, 1994) 214.

[33] See Chapter 1, Section A.

[34] For this reason, Raz's account of authority is called the 'service conception' of authority. J Raz, 'The problem of authority: Revisiting the service conception' (2006) 90 University of Minnesota L Rev 1003.

[35] Raz (n 32 above) 214.

answered in a way which does more than merely identify the range of permissible (justified) actions: it can also be answered in a way which draws attention to what, in particular, makes domestic-violence prosecutions *effective*. This section addresses this second response to our motivating question and attempts to identify what counts as effective domestic-violence prosecutorial action. In sum, my claim is that effective prosecution of domestic violence is best understood as prosecutorial action that realizes certain kinds of values, specifically, values that are directly relevant to the project of ending domestic violence.

Above, we noted that conceptual space may exist between what makes domestic-violence prosecutorial actions *justified* and what makes them *effective*, so that a given course of action may be fully justified without being particularly effective qua domestic-violence prosecutorial action.[36] The converse of this claim also holds: a given course of action may be effective qua domestic-violence prosecutorial action without being justified. As such, it would be a mistake to think that effective domestic-violence prosecutorial action is always necessarily justified domestic-violence prosecutorial action.

1. What does effective prosecution of domestic violence mean?

Effectiveness is often used as the standard by which we evaluate criminal justice interventions into domestic violence.[37] However, effectiveness has not been clearly defined in the literature regarding domestic-violence prosecutions. One might easily agree that such prosecutions *should* be effective *ceteris paribus*— but what precisely does this mean? Effective in what way? Effective at achieving what? Effective toward what end? One thing is evident: effective prosecution of domestic violence means different things to different people—and often these meanings result in people talking past one another.

In connection with restorative justice, Barbara Hudson helpfully explains that such alternatives to the traditional criminal justice response can be 'effective' in the sense of 'reducing the likelihood of reoffending' and 'occasioning strong censure [of]...the behaviour of which the case is an example...'.[38] Whilst Hudson's account provides an informative baseline for considering the meaning of effectiveness, it is incomplete in one important way, which hopefully will be made clear below.

---

[36] Text to n 2 above.

[37] R Lewis, 'Making justice work: Effective legal interventions for domestic violence' (2004) 44 British J of Criminology 204; D Epstein, 'Effective intervention in domestic-violence cases: Rethinking the roles of prosecutors, judges, and the court system' (1999) 11 Yale J of Law and Feminism 3; J Garner, 'Evaluating the effectiveness of mandatory arrest for domestic violence in Virginia' (1997) 3 William and Mary J of Women and the Law 223; Asmus and others (n 11 above).

[38] B Hudson, 'Restorative justice and gendered violence: Diversion or effective justice?' (2002) 42 British J of Criminology 616, 626.

On my account, effective prosecution of domestic violence is best understood as prosecutorial action that realizes certain kinds of values—specifically, values that are relevant to the project of ending domestic violence. As discussed above, domestic-violence prosecutorial actions can realize values through either pursuit or non-pursuit actions; and these values can be either consequentially or intrinsically related to the prosecutorial actions. This section explains which of these values are best understood as relevant to the project of ending domestic violence. The explanation proceeds in two steps: first, we will examine the concept of ending domestic violence, and second, we will consider which values are directly relevant to this project. Before proceeding any further, however, it bears noting that no single action, prosecutorial or otherwise, is likely on its own to realize values that will entirely eliminate domestic violence. So the phrase 'ending domestic violence' should not be read as 'completely ending domestic violence in one fell swoop'. Instead, individual domestic-violence prosecutorial actions can be judged as more or less effective insofar as they realize values which contribute to this project.

2. 'Ending domestic violence'

What is meant by the phrase 'ending domestic violence'? In order to answer this question, we must return to the conceptual elements of domestic violence set out in Chapter 6. It is tempting to assume that all instances of domestic violence share a common set of conceptual elements and that one can therefore provide a unified account of this phenomenon. For example, as we noted in Chapter 6, some researchers offer a unified account of domestic violence which assumes that all such conduct consists of only two conceptual elements: violence and domesticity.[39] The specifics of the first account are hotly contested by a second group of researchers, but even this second group adopts a unified account of domestic violence, which is distinct from the first only insofar as acts of domestic violence are deemed necessarily to include an additional element: patriarchal power and control.[40] Thus, according to this second account, an act does not count as domestic violence unless it also tends to sustain or perpetuate patriarchy. As explained in Chapter 6, both of these accounts of domestic violence are inadequate. Rather, domestic violence is best understood in terms of a disaggregated account which differentiates domestic violence in its strong sense from domestic violence in its weak sense.

To review, domestic violence in its strong sense consists of violence that occurs in a domestic context and tends to sustain or perpetuate patriarchy; domestic violence in its weak sense consists of violence that occurs in a domestic context

---

[39] Chapter 6, section D.2.
[40] Chapter 6, section D.3.

but does not tend to sustain or perpetuate patriarchy.[41] It may be tempting to see resemblances between domestic violence in its weak sense and the unified account of domestic violence offered by the first group of researchers discussed above. However, my account is importantly different in the following respect: according to the first group of researchers there is no need to differentiate between instances of domestic violence that tend to sustain or perpetuate patriarchy and those that do not, whereas on my account, instances of domestic violence that tend to sustain or perpetuate patriarchy are importantly distinct and moreover constitute the central case of domestic violence (ie, domestic violence in its strong sense).

Whilst domestic violence in its strong sense maps well onto the account of domestic violence offered by the second group of researchers discussed above, that account is also significantly different from the disaggregated account I have endorsed. According to the account adopted by the second group of researchers, there is no need to recognize violence that occurs in a domestic context as domestic violence simply in virtue of those factors alone; rather, such violence only counts as domestic violence when it tends to sustain or perpetuate patriarchy. On their account, there is only one sense of domestic violence—what I refer to as domestic violence in its strong sense—and nothing else counts as domestic violence. In contrast, while my account recognizes that violence which occurs in a domestic context and tends to sustain or perpetuate patriarchy is the central case of domestic violence (ie, domestic violence in its strong sense), it also recognizes that an act of violence which occurs in a domestic context and does *not* tend to sustain or perpetuate patriarchy still counts as domestic violence (albeit in its weak sense).

With the distinction between domestic violence in its strong and weak senses in mind, we now can address the meaning of 'ending domestic violence'. Two important implications for the meaning of this phrase arise from the distinction between domestic violence in its strong and weak senses. First, 'ending domestic violence' means either ending domestic violence in its weak sense, ending domestic violence in its strong sense, or both. Second, whilst we can end domestic violence in its weak sense only by eliminating violence that occurs in a domestic context, we can end domestic violence in its strong sense either by eliminating violence that occurs in a domestic context *or* by eliminating the tendency of such violence to sustain or perpetuate patriarchy.

This second implication requires further explanation. When violence in a domestic context no longer has a tendency to sustain or perpetuate patriarchy, then we will have succeeded in ending domestic violence in its strong sense. As noted above, however, it is unlikely that such a change will occur in one fell swoop. Rather, the project of ending domestic violence in its strong sense (by eliminating the tendency of such violence to sustain or perpetuate patriarchy) is a project that likely requires numerous contributions. Each contribution to this

---

[41] Chapter 6, passim.

project is properly deemed effective insofar as it lessens the tendency of such violence to sustain or perpetuate patriarchy.

One way to lessen the tendency of domestic violence in its strong sense to sustain or perpetuate patriarchy is to lessen patriarchy in society more generally. In order to understand why this is so, we must recall that patriarchy is a structural inequality. As a structural inequality, patriarchy is both systematic and systemic: it is systematic insofar as it consists of mutually reinforcing social forms which function as a system; moreover, it is societally systemic insofar as the perpetuation and elimination of patriarchy are sensitive to societal systems more generally. Due to the relative immutability and inflexibility of patriarchal structural inequality, the project of eliminating domestic violence requires transformation at the societal level.

The upshot of recognizing patriarchy as a structural inequality is that the patriarchal character of individual relationships cannot subsist without those relationships being situated within broader patriarchal social structures. Patriarchy is, by its nature, a social structure—and thus any particular instance of patriarchy (such as an instance of domestic violence in its strong sense) takes its meaning from that social context. If patriarchy were entirely eliminated from society then patriarchy would not exist in domestic relationships, and thus domestic violence in its strong sense would not exist—even if domestic violence in its weak sense continued unabated. Moreover, if patriarchy were lessened in society generally, then *ceteris paribus* patriarchy would be lessened in domestic relationships as well, thereby directly contributing to the project of ending domestic violence in its strong sense.[42]

3. Values that are directly relevant to the project of ending domestic violence

A myriad of values can be realized through domestic-violence prosecutorial actions, but not all of them will be directly relevant to the project of ending domestic violence. In other words, as noted above, not all valuable domestic-violence prosecutorial actions, nor even all justifiable domestic-violence prosecutorial actions, are necessarily *effective* domestic-violence prosecutorial actions.[43] So, *which values* ground the effectiveness of domestic-violence prosecutions? Before we can answer the question we must first resolve the preliminary matter of determining which kind of domestic violence is at issue.

(a) *Domestic violence in its weak sense*

If one is asking which values are relevant to the project of ending domestic violence in its weak sense, then the answer is 'those values which contribute to the project

---

[42] On the important qualifier adopted here (*ceteris paribus*), see Chapter 10, section C.

[43] Conversely, the possibility exists that not all effective domestic-violence prosecutorial actions will be justifiable.

of eliminating violence occurring within a domestic context'. Contributions to this project can be realized by route of two distinct states of affairs: eliminating or lessening violence in the context of domestic relationships, or by eliminating or lessening domestic relationships which involve violence. In other words, you can remove the violence from the domestic or you can remove the domestic from the violence.

In order to determine whether either state of affairs counts as a value which contributes to the project of ending domestic violence, and whether such value generates reasons for domestic-violence prosecutors that might ground a claim of prosecutorial effectiveness, we must examine three questions: (1) can domestic-violence prosecutorial actions realize that state of affairs; (2) is that state of affairs intrinsically valuable;[44] and (3) does that state of affairs affect the nature of the wrongdoing at issue?

First, we might focus on eliminating or lessening the violence in domestic relationships. It is difficult to see how prosecutorial action might be intrinsically related to this state of affairs, and so we shall focus on eliminating or lessening the violence in domestic relationships as a possible consequence of prosecutorial action. Prosecutorial action can achieve this consequence in any number of ways, either through the deterrent effects which are commonly thought to follow as a consequence from prosecutorial pursuit actions, or the kind of violence-reducing effects Ford documented which sometimes follow as a consequence of prosecutorial non-pursuit actions.[45] In light of these consequences, which can (at least in principle) follow as a consequence of prosecutorial action in domestic-violence cases, our answer to the first question set out above is yes. Next, we must ask whether a state of affairs in which violence in domestic relationships is eliminated or lessened is intrinsically valuable. Again, our answer is yes, based on the following logic: the violence at issue is unjustified (ie, acts of domestic violence in its weak sense are instances of all-things-considered wrongdoing);[46] eliminating or lessening all-things-considered wrongdoing is intrinsically valuable;[47] therefore, eliminating or lessening the violence in domestic relationships is intrinsically valuable. Finally, we must ask whether eliminating or lessening the violence in domestic relationships affects the nature of the wrongdoing at issue (in other words, does it contribute to the project of ending domestic violence in its weak sense?). Again, the answer is yes, since eliminating or lessening the violence in domestic relationships directly affects one of the conceptual elements (violence) of domestic violence in its weak sense.[48] In other words, by removing the violence

---

[44] See Chapter 4, pp 61–2, defending the claim that any coherent moral theory must account for intrinsic value.

[45] Ford (n 13 above).

[46] See Chapter 6, section C.

[47] I take this point as not requiring a separate defence.

[48] Of course, this consequence also contributes to the project of ending domestic violence in its strong sense, but we will consider that further below.

from the domestic, we affect the nature of the wrongdoing at issue—transforming it from domestic violence in its weak sense into something else and thereby eliminating domestic violence.[49]

Thus, we can state with some confidence that we have identified the first kind of domestic-violence prosecutorial action which can properly be deemed effective: prosecutorial action which realizes the value of eliminating or lessening violence in domestic relationships. This point should, of course, come as no surprise, since much of the domestic-violence academic literature is grounded on the assumption that eliminating or lessening the violence is the key determinant in the effectiveness of prosecutorial actions.[50]

Second, we might focus on eliminating or lessening the number of domestic relationships in which violence occurs, since we might think that one way of ending *domestic* violence is to take all of the domestic relationships in which violence occurs and transform those relationships into non-domestic relationships. Voilà... (so the argument goes) the result would be the end of domestic violence. Let us accept for sake of evaluating this argument that it is possible to transform domestic relationships into non-domestic relationships simply by terminating the relationship through, for example, divorce and non-contact between the parties to the relationship.[51] Again, it is difficult to see how prosecutorial action might be intrinsically related to these states of affairs, and so we shall focus on eliminating or lessening the number of domestic relationships in which violence occurs as a possible consequence of prosecutorial action. In response to the first question posed above, we can answer in the affirmative by observing that prosecutorial action can achieve this consequence in any number of ways: prosecutorial pursuit actions might have the consequence of driving a wedge between a couple which ultimately leads to the severing of domestic ties;[52] or prosecutorial non-pursuit actions might have the bargained-for or enforced consequence that a couple separates and discontinues their relationship in exchange for dismissal. So, in

---

[49] Of course, we may not have succeeded in eliminating the wrongdoing from such relationships altogether. Indeed, non-violent domestic *abuse* may continue unabated even after the domestic violence has ceased—but nonetheless, the nature of the wrong qua an instance of domestic violence will have been eliminated.

[50] Most of this literature, however, has focused on the violence-deterrent effect of arrest rather than prosecution, eg J Schmidt and L Sherman, 'Does arrest deter domestic violence?' in E Buzawa and C Buzawa (eds), *Do Arrests and Restraining Orders Work?* (Thousand Oaks: Sage, 1996) 54–82; L Sherman and others, 'The variable effects of arrest on criminal careers: The Milwaukee domestic violence experiment' (1992) 83 J of Crim L and Criminology 137.

[51] Notably, it is no longer possible to give legal effect to this transformation. Compare previous legislation which defined domestic relationships in terms of *current* spouses/cohabitants only (Domestic Proceedings and Matrimonial Causes Act 1976; Matrimonial Homes Act 1983), with more recent legislation which defines domestic relationships in terms of both current *and former* spouses and cohabitants. Family Law Act 1996, ss 35–8.

[52] The use of no-contact orders to enforce separations motivate Jeannie Suk's criticism of what she characterizes as 'a form of state-imposed de facto divorce'. J Suk, 'Criminal law comes home' (2006) 116 Yale L J 2. See also C Hanna, 'Because breaking up is hard to do' (2006) 92 Yale L J Pocket Part <http://www.thepocketpart.org/2006/10/12/hanna.html> accessed 1 September 2008.

principle at least, prosecutorial actions can be consequentially related to a state of affairs in which the number of domestic relationships in which violence occurs is eliminated or lessened.

But does it follow that such prosecutorial actions count as the *effective* prosecution of domestic violence? Have we identified a second kind of value that is relevant to the project of ending domestic violence? The answer to this question depends on whether transforming violent domestic relationships into violent non-domestic relationships is an intrinsically valuable state of affairs, and whether such a transformation affects the nature of the wrongdoing at issue. If transforming violent domestic relationships into violent non-domestic relationships is an intrinsically valuable state of affairs, then it at least stands a chance of being a value which is directly relevant to the project of ending domestic violence, and thus prosecutorial actions which achieve this consequence stand a chance of being deemed effective prosecutorial actions. So, is it intrinsically valuable to transform violent domestic relationships into violent non-domestic relationships? Some would presumably say yes, based on their belief that domestic relationships, especially marriages, are inherently oppressive to women and thus worthy of abolition as a social form.[53] This belief seems to rely on the view that the transformation of a domestic relationship into non-domestic relationship is intrinsically valuable. Others, however, would likely disagree. Some authors such as Linda Mills, for example, are concerned to maintain domestic relationships intact despite ongoing violence, thereby suggesting a commitment to the view that the transformation of such relationships from domestic to non-domestic is not itself valuable.[54] Neither extreme seems satisfying. Surely there is value in ending violent domestic relationships if doing so ends the violence; but the actual value at issue appears to be nothing more than the value of eliminating or lessening the violence. The transformation of the domestic relationship appears to serve merely as a contingent mediator toward this actual value. So the question remains: is it valuable to end violent domestic relationships even if doing so does *not* decrease the violence?[55] My inclination is to say no, ending violent domestic relationships by making them into violent non-domestic relationships is not independently valuable; rather, whatever value can be realized here arises

---

[53] S Firestone, *The Dialectics of Sex* (New York: William Morrow & Co, 1970).

[54] For example, Linda Mills endorses the value of maintaining some domestic relationships despite ongoing violence. L Mills, *Insult to Injury: Rethinking our responses to intimate abuse* (Princeton: Princeton University Press, 2003) 5.

[55] Notably, whilst ending violent domestic relationships is correlated with a decrease in violence over the long term, it often leads to a short-term increase in violence, coined 'separation assault'. R Fleury, C Sullivan, and D Bybee, 'When ending the relationship does not end the violence: Women's experiences of violence by former partners' (2000) 6 *Violence Against Women* 1363; K Roberts, 'Women's experience of violence during stalking by former romantic partners: Factors predictive of stalking violence' (2005) 11 *Violence Against Women* 89; C Humphreys and R Thiara, 'Neither Justice nor protection; Women's experiences of post separation violence' (2003) 25 Journal of Social Welfare and Family Law 195; M Mahoney, 'Legal images of battered women: Redefining the issue of separation' (1991) 90 Michigan L Rev 1.

parasitically from the contingent success that ending the domestic relationship may have as a mediator in ending the violence. If this intuition is correct, then a domestic-violence prosecution should not be deemed effective simply in virtue of having the consequence of transforming a violent domestic relationship into a violent non-domestic relationship, because such transformation is not valuable.

Let us assume, however, that my intuition on this matter is incorrect and that it *is* intrinsically valuable to transform violent domestic relationships into violent non-domestic relationships. In other words, if a prosecutor succeeds in causing the partners in a domestically violent relationship (Alex and Barbara) to split up, then she has achieved a valuable state of affairs. However, in order to control for this one particular conceptual element of domestic violence (domesticity) we must also assume that the violence continues unabated in this relationship. So, for example, whilst Alex previously beat Barbara, his wife; Alex now beats Barbara, his ex-wife. Given our operative assumption, the latter is a more valuable state of affairs:[56] all other things being equal, it is better (so the argument goes) that batterers and victims not remain in domestic relationships with one another. If this claim is correct, have we now succeeded in identifying a second kind of value that is relevant to the project of ending domestic violence? I believe the answer to this question is no, on the basis that the transformation of a violent domestic relationship into a violent non-domestic relationship (even if valuable) does not affect the nature of the wrongdoing at issue. In other words, the kind of wrongdoing Alex commits against Barbara remains similar in all salient respects, irrespective of whether Alex and Barbara remain in an on-going domestic relationship with one another.[57]

(b) Domestic violence in its strong sense

Turning to the question of which values are relevant to the project of ending domestic violence in its strong sense, the answer is: those values which contribute to the project of eliminating violence that both occurs within a domestic context *and* tends to sustain or perpetuate patriarchy. Initially, we might think that contributions to this project can be realized by eliminating or lessening any one of the three elements of domestic violence in its strong sense: violence, domesticity, or patriarchy. In other words, we might seek to remove the violence from the domestic, remove the domestic from the violence, or leave the violence and the domestic intact but remove the patriarchy.

The first two options (removing the violence from the domestic and removing the domestic from the violence) were discussed above in detail. It was concluded that eliminating or lessening the violence in domestic relationships *is* indeed a value that contributes to the project of ending domestic violence, and thus

---

[56] This assumption runs against my intuition, as noted above.
[57] For this reason then, the expansion of statutory definitions of domestic violence to include both current and former partners strikes me as wholly justified. See n 51 above.

generates reasons which ground the effectiveness of domestic-violence prosecutorial action in cases of domestic violence in its weak sense. It bears noting here
that the same point holds equally true for cases of domestic violence in its strong
sense. So, in other words, prosecutorial actions which have the consequence of
eliminating or lessening the violence in domestic relationships count as effective
domestic-violence prosecutorial actions in *all* cases of domestic violence (both
strong and weak). Conversely, however, it was concluded that eliminating or lessening the number of domestic relationships in which violence occurs does *not*
generate reasons which ground the effectiveness of domestic-violence prosecutorial action vis-à-vis domestic violence in its weak sense. Again, this same point
holds equally true for domestic violence in its strong sense, so that we may now
conclude that prosecutorial action which has the consequence of eliminating or
lessening the number of domestic relationships in which violence occurs does not
count as effective domestic-violence prosecutorial action in any case whatsoever.

This brings us to the final element, which arises only in the context of domestic
violence in its strong sense: patriarchy. In addressing this element, we will take
the three questions above out-of-order and ask, first, whether a state of affairs
in which patriarchy is eliminated or lessened from domestically violent relationships is an intrinsically valuable state of affairs; second, whether that state
of affairs affects the nature of the wrongdoing at issue (domestic violence in its
strong sense); and third, whether domestic-violence prosecutorial actions can
realize that state of affairs.

First, if the account of patriarchy-as-wrong provided in Chapter 7 is plausible,[58]
there is good reason to suspect that a state of affairs in which patriarchy is
eliminated or lessened from domestically violent relationships is an intrinsically
valuable state of affairs. Thus, even if eliminating or lessening patriarchy has no
further valuable knock-on effects, the mere fact that patriarchy has been eliminated or lessened is itself intrinsically valuable. Of course, it is entirely possible
that eliminating or lessening patriarchy will *also* have valuable consequences. We
might find, as empirical researcher Michael Smith has demonstrated, that reducing levels of patriarchy has the consequence of reducing violence in domestic relationships.[59] However, we might also find just the opposite: reducing patriarchy
might actually lead to an *increase* in violence in domestic relationships. For example, Kersti Yllo's empirical research has demonstrated that violence in domestic
relationships tends to rise when patriarchy declines, suggesting the possibility of
violent backlash as a consequence of women's equality gains.[60] Smith's and Yllo's

---

[58] See Chapter 7, section D.
[59] M Smith, 'Patriarchal ideology and wife beating: A test of a feminist hypothesis' (1990) 5
Violence and Victims 257. Ironically, reducing patriarchy may also be consequentially valuable insofar as it may benefit men's health. D Stanistreet, C Bambra, and AJ Scott-Samuel, 'Is patriarchy the
source of men's higher mortality?' (2005) 59 J of *Epidemiology and Community Health* 873.
[60] K Yllo, 'Sexual equality and violence against wives in American states' (1983) 14 *J of
Comparative Family Studies* 67.

apparently inconsistent empirical findings illustrate a seeming contradiction in the social-science literature regarding the consequential effects of reducing patriarchy: sometimes it reduces violence in domestic relationships, and sometimes it has the backlash effect of increasing such violence.[61] However, my point here is that irrespective of its consequences, eliminating or lessening patriarchy retains intrinsic value.

Second, a state of affairs in which patriarchy is eliminated or lessened affects the nature of the wrongdoing at issue. Specifically, it contributes to the project of ending domestic violence in its strong sense by eliminating or lessening one of its conceptual elements (patriarchy); thereby transforming the kind of wrongdoing at issue from domestic violence in its strong sense into domestic violence in its weak sense.[62] This point rests upon two claims discussed in Chapter 6: first, that there is a salient distinction to be drawn between domestic violence in its weak sense and domestic violence in its strong sense; and second, that this distinction rests on relevance of patriarchy to a proper understanding of domestic violence. Moreover, we can now observe that the transformation from domestic violence in its strong sense to domestic violence in its weak sense is a transformation both in *kind* and *quality*: domestic violence in its strong sense is not merely a different kind of wrongdoing from domestic violence in its weak sense; it is also *ceteris paribus* more wrongful than domestic violence in its weak sense.[63]

Finally, we must ask whether domestic-violence prosecutorial actions can realize a state of affairs in which patriarchy is eliminated or lessened. If my previous arguments are plausible, then again, the answer is yes. Notably, prosecutorial action may realize this valuable state of affairs either consequentially or intrinsically. For example, as discussed above with respect to Sunstein's work, prosecutorial actions may spark a 'norm cascade' or 'norm bandwagon' which has the consequence of eliminating or lessening patriarchy.[64] Moreover, prosecutorial action may bear an intrinsic relationship to this valuable state of affairs insofar as the actions successfully reconstitute the character of the state (and community) as less patriarchal *ceteris paribus*. This point will be considered further below. For now it will suffice to note that we have identified the second kind of domestic-violence prosecutorial action which can properly be deemed effective: prosecutorial actions which realize the value of eliminating or lessening patriarchy.

---

[61] For a review of the empirical literature, see DB Sugarman and SL Frankel, 'Patriarchal ideology and wife-assault: A meta-analytic review' (1996) 11 *J of Family Violence* 13.

[62] Indeed, even if patriarchy is not entirely eliminated, its lessening at very least transforms the kind of wrongdoing at issue from domestic violence in its strong sense into something closer to domestic violence in its weak sense.

[63] This is not to say that all acts of domestic violence in its strong sense are more wrongful than acts of domestic violence in its weak sense. The limitation of *ceteris paribus* is meant to control for variables (other than the tendency of the act to sustain or perpetuate patriarchy) that might be relevant to the quality of the wrong, such as the degree of injury, etc.

[64] Sunstein (n 27 above).

(c) The value of disaggregating two kinds of domestic violence

In order to realize the elimination or lessening of patriarchy, it is necessary for domestic-violence prosecutors to disaggregate domestic violence in its strong sense from domestic violence in its weak sense. Prosecutorial actions can realize the value of eliminating or lessening patriarchy, but realizing this valuable state of affairs requires domestic-violence prosecutors to disaggregate these two kinds of domestic violence when engaged in prosecutorial action. In what follows, we will not consider the consequential relationship between prosecutorial action and this valuable state of affairs, but instead we will concern ourselves with the intrinsic value of prosecutorial actions vis-à-vis the elimination or lessening of patriarchy.

First let us consider the expressive value that can be realized through disaggregated domestic-violence prosecutorial actions. Prosecutorial pursuit actions which target domestic violence in its strong sense for particularly aggressive prosecution realize the intrinsic value of expressively denouncing patriarchy. Indeed, aggressive prosecution policies that fail to draw this distinction will fail to express the denunciation of patriarchy in virtue of their failure to disaggregate the types of wrongdoing being targeted. Such blanket (non-disaggregated) prosecutorial actions typically succeed in denouncing only violence in domestic relationships generally, thereby merely targeting the type of wrongdoing at issue in domestic violence in its weak sense (the wrongfulness of violence) and leaving the extra wrong which is constitutive of domestic violence in its strong sense (the wrongfulness of patriarchy) undenounced. Moreover, aggressive prosecutorial actions that fail to disaggregate domestic violence in its strong and weak senses often send the further disvaluable message that victims who engage in what Johnson calls 'violent resistance' are equally as culpable as batterers who engage in domestic violence in its strong sense.[65]

Prosecutorial non-pursuit actions that disaggregate the two kinds of domestic violence and, in comparison, decline to target domestic violence in its weak sense (eg, by dismissing pursuant to victims' requests in such cases) also realize the intrinsic value of expressively denouncing patriarchy, when coupled with the type of prosecutorial pursuit actions described in the previous paragraph. Engaging in non-pursuit actions in cases of domestic violence in its weak sense when, for example, victims request dismissal, in effect treats such cases as morally

---

[65] M Johnson, 'Conflict and control: Images of symmetry and asymmetry in domestic violence' (2006) 12 *Violence Against Women* 1003. For critique of non-disaggregated prosecutorial actions, see Coker (n 12 above); J Zorza, *Mandatory Arrest: Problems and possibilities* (New York: National Center on Women and Family Law, 1994) 16. Attempts to address this critique through educating police to identify and arrest the primary aggressor quite simply miss the point of the critique insofar as they continue to focus on the violence-based wrongdoing rather than patriarchal-based wrongdoing. M Finn and others, 'Dual arrest decisions in domestic-violence cases: The influence of departmental policies' (2004) 50 *Crime and Delinquency* 565.

equivalent to generic violence (wherein criminal charges are typically dismissed upon a victim's request[66]).

Treating domestic violence as morally equivalent to generic violence has been a popular, but I believe misguided, strategy in anti-domestic-violence advocacy. Typically, the call for law enforcement to 'take domestic violence seriously' has been understood as both (1) a call for the implementation of no-drop policies and victimless prosecutions in domestic-violence cases[67] and (2) a call to treat domestic-violence cases similarly to cases of generic violence.[68] In fact, however, treating domestic-violence cases similarly to cases of violence between strangers in public (ie, generic violence) would entail *rejecting* no-drop policies and victimless prosecutions in domestic-violence cases, since victims' non-cooperation is widely taken as sufficient grounds for dismissal in the vast majority of generic assault cases.[69]

As such, the call for law enforcement to 'take domestic violence seriously' is, I believe, better understood as a call for prosecutors to treat domestic-violence cases (or at least some domestic-violence cases) *differently* from how they would treat generic violence cases. By treating some domestic-violence cases the same as generic violence (eg, by dismissing pursuant to victims' requests), such prosecutorial non-pursuit actions express that there is nothing particularly special that requires a more aggressive response in such cases. On the other hand, by treating other domestic-violence cases *differently* from generic violence by, for example, refusing to dismiss pursuant to victims' requests, such prosecutorial pursuit actions express that there *is* something special about *those* cases which *does* require a more aggressive response. If the distinction between the former and latter group maps onto the distinction between domestic violence in its weak sense and strong sense respectively, then the combination of these disaggregated prosecutorial actions thereby expressively denounces patriarchy: the extra ingredient which marks the difference between domestic violence in its strong and weak senses and makes domestic violence in its strong sense particularly worthy of denunciation.

This discussion demonstrates that disaggregated prosecutorial actions can realize the intrinsic (expressive) value of denouncing patriarchy. But can such expressive actions realize a state of affairs in which patriarchy is eliminated or lessened? Does expressively valuable prosecutorial action contribute to the project of ending domestic violence in its strong sense? Put yet another way: are

---

[66] A Cretney and others, 'Criminalizing assault: The failure of the offence against society model' (1994) 34 British J of Criminology 15.

[67] Ellison (n 19 above).

[68] K Laster and R Douglas, 'Treating spousal violence "differently"' (2000) 7 *International Review of Victimology* 115. See also, Ellison (n 19 above) 769, arguing that 'a useful symbolic purpose' is served when prosecutors send a 'message to perpetrators that violence between intimate partners in private is taken as seriously as violence between strangers in public'.

[69] Cretney and others (n 66 above).

domestic-violence prosecutions effective in virtue of their expressive value in denouncing patriarchy?

As a matter of contingency, the answer may be yes; which is to say that domestic-violence prosecutorial actions may be effective in virtue of the contingent, consequential effects realized by their expressively valuable denunciations of patriarchy.[70] But, here we are concerned not with the *consequential* relationship that may exist between prosecutorial action and the valuable state of affairs in which patriarchy is eliminated or lessened. Rather, we are instead concerned with the intrinsic relationship that may exist between prosecutorial action and this valuable state of affairs. In other words, we are concerned with the intrinsic value of prosecutorial actions vis-à-vis the elimination or lessening of patriarchy.

So, are prosecutorial actions which expressively denounce patriarchy the kinds of actions that ground the effectiveness of domestic-violence prosecutions in virtue of the *intrinsic* value of the prosecutorial actions? Perhaps surprisingly, I conclude that they are not: for merely denouncing patriarchy does not (absent contingencies) eliminate or lessen patriarchy. Rather, in order to realize the elimination or lessening or patriarchy (absent contingencies), the denunciation must be *habituated*; for it is only through habituated action in opposition to a wrongful character trait that one can thereby reconstitute the relevant character trait in contradistinction to that wrong.[71] It follows that non-habituated prosecutorial actions that expressively denounce patriarchy will not be effective in reconstituting the character of the state (and community) as less patriarchal/more feminist (although they will, of course, still be expressively valuable).

If, however, such prosecutorial action *is* habituated, then the state's (and possibly the community's) character is thereby intrinsically, non-contingently reconstituted as less patriarchal/more feminist. In other words, habituated feminist prosecutorial actions reconstitute the state (and community) as more feminist: *ceteris paribus* such actions create a feminist state (and feminist community). It follows that prosecutorial actions which realize the intrinsic value of reconstituting the character of the state (and community) as less patriarchal contribute to the project of ending domestic violence in its strong sense and therefore ground the effectiveness of such prosecutorial actions.

We can now therefore refine our account of the second kind of effective domestic-violence prosecutorial action. Above, we observed that prosecutorial actions which realize the value of eliminating or lessening patriarchy are properly deemed effective. Now, we can explain an additional wrinkle to this point, namely that prosecutorial actions can realize this value either consequentially *or* intrinsically. When prosecutorial actions realize this value consequentially, they do so as a matter of contingency. When prosecutorial actions realize this value intrinsically, however, they do so as a matter of reconstituting the character of

---

[70] See discussion of Sunstein at text to n 27 above.
[71] See Chapter 3, p 57 and Chapter 4, pp 72–5.

the state (and community) as less patriarchal/more feminist *ceteris paribus*. In the latter case, such prosecutorial actions are properly deemed effective irrespective of any contingencies.

The UN Special Rapporteur on Violence against Women, Yakin Ertürk, in her 2006 report to the Commission on Human Rights regarding states' due-diligence obligations to eliminate violence against women, emphasizes the relevance of intrinsic value in domestic-violence prosecution:

> [P]rosecutors working on cases of domestic violence have the potential and the obligation to change the prevailing balance of power [between men and women] by taking a strong stance to disempower patriarchal notions. Interventions at this level may have both consequential effects in that condemnations of patriarchy can lead to changes in socio-cultural norms, as well as intrinsic effects, in that prosecutors ... can be considered to be the 'mouthpieces' of society, and strong statements condemning violence against women made on behalf of society through the ... prosecutorial services will make that society less patriarchal.[72]

Ertürk's report marks an important development in our understanding of what 'effective' prosecution of domestic violence means. Specifically, by recognizing the intrinsic relationship between the prosecution of domestic violence and the lessening of patriarchy, the Special Rapporteur highlights a significant aspect of prosecutorial effectiveness in such cases. In commenting on this link, Ertürk cites my previous work, republished here as Chapter 6, in which I distinguish domestic violence in its strong sense from domestic violence in its weak sense. The argument of this book employs this disaggregated account of domestic violence and explains its relevance to the intrinsic value of lessening patriarchy through domestic-violence prosecutions. In this sense, this book thereby serves as an explanation and defence of Ertürk's observations regarding the prosecution of domestic violence.

4. The value of a feminist state

The preceding argument explains the sense in which domestic-violence prosecutors can create a more feminist state and defends the further claim that such actions constitute the 'effective' prosecution of domestic violence. But why does it matter whether domestic-violence prosecutors can create a more feminist state? Moreover, why should we think of this project as something that particularly concerns domestic-violence prosecutors as opposed to other government officials?

The reason why domestic-violence prosecutors should create a feminist state and why this project is of particular relevance to domestic-violence prosecution is

---

[72] Report of the Special Rapporteur on violence against women, its causes and consequences, Yakin Ertürk, *Integration of the Human Rights of Women and the Gender Perspective: Violence against women*, 'The due diligence standard as a tool for the elimination of violence against women' UN Doc E/CN.4/2006/61 (20 January 2006) 20.

that these prosecutions are *ripe* for such action—which means that they present opportunities both to improve the state's moral character and (thereby) to transform the moral quality of the wrongdoing being targeted by the prosecutions. Many types of government action present opportunities to reconstitute the state's moral character in valuable ways. Habituated actions extending social welfare to the disadvantaged, for example, might constitute the moral character of the state as generous; and brave actions habituated by National Guard members in the course of responding to a natural disaster might constitute the moral character of the state as courageous. Furthermore, sometimes the (re)constitution of the state's character will affect the moral quality of wrongdoing that is targeted by the criminal law.

Some criminal wrongs are constituted in part by wrongful structural inequalities which correspond to character traits in that society. The same physical action, say punching someone in the nose, can have a different moral quality depending upon the character of the society in which the action takes place: the nature of the wrong constituted by that action is sometimes (at least in part) dependent upon the character of the society in which the action occurs. If a society's character is constituted in part by structural inequalities, those inequalities can ground (at least in part) the quality of (at least some) of the moral wrongs which occur in that society.

It should be obvious by now that I think domestic violence is one such wrong: specifically, that the moral quality of domestic violence (in its strong sense) is grounded in part on the structural inequality of patriarchy. But domestic violence is not the only such wrong. For example, the moral quality of rape is, I believe, also constituted in part by the patriarchal character of society,[73] just as the moral quality of gay-bashing is constituted in part by the heterosexist character of society and the moral quality of race-hate crimes are constituted in part by the racist character of society. Prosecutorial actions in all of these kinds of cases have the potential to reconstitute the character of the state in morally valuable ways which can affect the moral quality of the wrong being prosecuted—which is to say that all of these types of prosecutions are ripe for reconstitutive state action: domestic violence and rape prosecutions are ripe for non-patriarchal (feminist) action; gay-bashing prosecutions are ripe for non-heterosexist action; and race-hate crime prosecutions are ripe for anti-racist action.[74]

Domestic-violence prosecutions are particularly are ripe for feminist action for at least two reasons: (1) they frequently present issues of patriarchy; and (2) such

---

[73] To this extent, then, I believe that accounts of the wrongness of rape which omit the role of patriarchy are therefore incomplete. Eg, S Shute and J Gardner, 'The wrongness of rape' in J Horder (ed), *Oxford Essays in Jurisprudence* (4th edn, Oxford: OUP, 2000). Compare, MM Dempsey and J Herring, 'Why sexual penetration requires justification' (2007) 27 OJLS 467.

[74] It is assumed herein that the character of a state is at least in part constitutive of the character of the community which grounds the moral quality of the types of wrongdoing under consideration, but recall the possibility that prosecutorial action may also reconstitute the character of the community directly. See discussion in Chapter 3.

cases call upon prosecutors to take a position to endorse, ignore, or denounce patriarchy as instantiated in those cases. The first condition sets the stage for habituation, so that if the prosecutors' response to the second condition is consistent (eg, if they consistently denounce patriarchy), they will thereby (re) constitute the character of the state as more feminist *ceteris paribus*.

Of course, not all government actions are equally ripe for feminist action. Some government actions are not ripe because they do not present issues of patriarchy frequently enough to ground the officials' responses as habituated responses to patriarchy. The water commissioner for the City of London, for example, is not typically called upon to address issues concerning patriarchy in the course of his work. And so even on the odd occasion when he is called upon to respond to patriarchy qua water commissioner (ie, qua state actor), he is not well positioned to habituate this response and will therefore inevitably fail to reconstitute the character of the state with respect to patriarchy one way or the other. There is, however, nothing particular about being a water commissioner that makes all of this true—it all depends on the social context in which government agents act. Compare the actions of the water commissioner in the Darfur region of the Sudan, where women and girls are regularly gang-raped by militias while going to collect water.[75] Acting in the role of water commissioner in that situation *does* regularly present issues of patriarchy. Whatever his response is to the water shortage, it will have implications for the patriarchal character of the state of Sudan. He can either fail to address the connection between water shortages and rape, thereby strengthening the patriarchal character of the state, or he can act to address the water shortage in a way that condemns the wrongness of rape as an act of patriarchal dominance, thereby reconstituting the character of the state as less patriarchal.

Domestic-violence cases likewise present prosecutors with a context for state action that is particularly ripe for reconstituting the character of the state. For example, domestic-violence prosecutors are frequently in a position to exercise discretion which disaggregates domestic violence in its strong sense from domestic violence in its weak sense, by making distinctions in deciding which cases to charge, which ones to pursue aggressively, and which ones to dismiss upon the victims' requests. By habitually basing their discretionary actions (at least in part) on the relevance of patriarchy to constituting the wrongdoing at issue, the prosecutors thereby habitually denounce the particular wrong of patriarchy and thus reconstitute the character of the state as less patriarchal *ceteris paribus*.

This point brings us full circle to our motivating question: what should public prosecutors do when victims withdraw their support for the prosecution of domestic-violence cases? The answer to this question, we can now see, has an additional wrinkle. When victims withdraw their support for the prosecution of

---

[75] Médecins Sans Frontières, 'The crushing burden of rape and sexual violence in Darfur' <http://www.doctorswithoutborders.org/publications/reports/2005/sudan03.pdf> accessed 5 January 2009.

domestic-violence cases, prosecutors should first be concerned to do that which is morally permissible (justified); but once that requirement is satisfied, prosecutors should do that which makes their prosecution of domestic violence more effective. One way in which to make the prosecution of domestic violence more effective, it has been argued, is to disaggregate their responses to victim withdrawal cases so as to differentiate cases of domestic violence in its strong sense from cases of domestic violence in its weak sense. By habituating a disaggregated response to these cases, and thereby treating domestic violence in its strong sense as especially worthy of denunciation in light of its tendency to sustain and perpetuate patriarchy, prosecutors can reconstitute the character of their state (and community) as less patriarchal—thereby contributing to the project of ending domestic violence in its strong sense.

C. Conclusion

This chapter has employed the accounts of value and reason set forth in Part II of the book and the conceptual analyses set forth in Chapters 6 and 7 to shed light on our motivating question: what should public prosecutors do when victims withdraw their support for the prosecution of domestic-violence cases? In response to this question, we have considered issues of both justification and effectiveness. In sum, the answer to our question can be stated as follows: within the realm of justifiable (permissible) prosecutorial action, public prosecutors should respond in a way that constitutes the effective prosecution of domestic violence.

With respect to the effective domestic-violence prosecutions in particular, this chapter has demonstrated why it is important for prosecutors to make a distinction between domestic violence in its strong sense and weak sense in their practical reasoning (and to act on the reasons generated by this distinction): because this is one important way in which the state (and community) speaks to the wrongness of patriarchy, habituates that denunciatory expression, and thereby reconstitutes its character as less patriarchal *ceteris paribus*. This point, however, should not be taken to suggest that prosecution is the *only* way that a state (or community) can speak to the disvalue of patriarchy. Indeed, there are many ways that a state (or community) can denounce and/or condemn patriarchy. This matter will be explored further in the concluding chapter, but first we will examine some the implication of the argument developed thus far in considering the rights and duties of domestic-violence victims.

9

Victims and Prosecutions

This chapter considers the rights and duties of domestic-violence victims with respect to participating in the prosecution of domestic-violence cases. It should be noted at the outset that the exploration undertaken in this chapter concerns the question of moral rights and duties, not legal rights and duties. In other words, I am not offering a doctrinal account of the rules and principles which actually govern various legal systems with respect to victims' rights and duties in criminal proceedings. Rather, I am merely offering a partial account of some of the considerations which should feature in a determination of what such legal rights and duties should be.[1]

This chapter proceeds in four parts. First, it revisits and expands upon the distinction briefly sketched in Chapter 5 between 'reasons to do it yourself' and 'reasons to help someone else do it' in order to identify the kinds of reasons which might ground a better understanding of the rights and duties of victims in the context of criminal prosecutions. Second, it considers the nature and scope of victims' rights to participate in domestic-violence prosecutions. Third, it considers whether victims ever have a duty to participate in domestic-violence prosecutions, and finally, whether that duty justifies prosecutorial enforcement through such legal mechanisms as compelling victims to testify.

A. Four Kinds of Reason Generated by Wrongdoing

As argued in Chapter 5, wrongdoing generates four kinds of reasons for action, depending on the role of the actor and whether the actions are a direct or indirect response to wrongdoing. In what follows we will consider two distinct roles actors

---

[1] I take it as given that the question of moral rights and duties normally should precede the question of legal rights and duties. So, for example, if victims do not have a moral right to participate in criminal prosecutions, there would be little point in affording them a legal right to do so. However, of course, affording a legal right to participate may ground a moral right to do so which would not otherwise have existed; and this moral right might then provide the grounding required for the continuance of the legal right. I will assume in this chapter that no such pre-existing legal rights exist. Similarly, if victims do not have a moral duty to participate in criminal trials, it would likely be unjustifiable to impose upon them a legal duty to do so. An existing legal duty to participate might of course ground a moral duty to do so (if, for example, there were a general moral obligation to obey the law, or the victim has specifically promised to obey the law), but unlike the case of pre-existing legal rights, pre-existing legal duties would not ground the sorts of moral duties that might then justify the continuance of the legal duty.

might occupy in responding to wrongdoing: an actor may respond to wrongdoing qua victims and/or qua member of the community. Therefore, we will consider distinctly both the actions of *victims* in response to wrongdoing, and the actions of the *community* in response to wrongdoing. Moreover, we will consider both direct and indirect responses to wrongdoing. Direct responses to wrongdoing will be understood to include actions which denounce, condemn, deter, etc, the wrongdoing. Indirect responses will be understood to include actions which support another actor in his, her, or their direct response to the wrongdoing. The distinction between direct and indirect responses to wrongdoing is based on the dual assumptions that both kinds of response to wrongdoing can realize distinct values. It is uncontroversial that denunciation, condemnation, deterrence, etc, of wrongdoing are valuable activities, and the sorts of consequential and intrinsic values that can be realized through these activities were examined in detail in Chapter 4. Perhaps more controversially, it will be assumed that supporting another person or group of people in their pursuit of such valuable activities is *also* valuable, albeit in a distinct way.[2] It is valuable, as I shall say, as an *indirect* response to wrongdoing.

The distinctions drawn above are fairly easy to illustrate in the following hypothetical. Imagine a group of people standing in a lift waiting for the doors to close. As John and Mary step onto the lift before the doors close, John is clearly enraged and staring daggers at Mary, who looks quietly at the floor. John turns to Mary, grabs her arm tightly and says accusingly, 'Don't think I didn't see that guy looking at you, you filthy whore. I don't know why I ever married you, you slut.' Assuming John and Mary are not practicing a play, I will take it as given that John's conduct constitutes an instance of wrongdoing. Specifically, I intend the hypothetical to illustrate an instance of domestic violence in its strong sense.[3] Now consider three stages of possible responses to John's conduct, each of which illustrates different sorts of reasons generated by wrongdoing. In stage one, Mary shrugs her arm away from John's grip and says, 'Get your hands off me, you paranoid jerk.' In stage two, the other people in the lift respond to Mary's actions by showing that they support what she has done: smiling warmly, offering her a supportive 'thumbs-up', etc. Now imagine that John flies into a further rage and moves to grab Mary's arm once again. At this point, stage three, other people on the lift respond to John's actions by physically restraining him and saying things such as, 'Hey, calm down, cut it out…what's the matter with you?!' If we grant that the people in the lift constitute a community in some sense,[4] then the three stages of this hypothetical can be charted as follows:

---

[2] This assumption is consistent with John Gardner's and Timothy Macklem's observation that '[e]verybody's personal engagement with valuable activities is in principle everybody's business'. J Gardner and T Macklem, 'Reasons' in J Coleman and S Shapiro (eds), *The Oxford Handbook of Jurisprudence and Philosophy of Law* (New York: OUP, 2004) 458.

[3] See Chapter 6 on the distinction between domestic violence in its strong and weak sense.

[4] Clearly, the people in the lift do not constitute a community in its fullest sense. For an illuminating discussion of the normative ideal of community, see RA Duff, *Punishment, Communication and Community* (Oxford: OUP, 2001) 42–6. The type of community I have in mind is more along

Table 1

	VICTIM	COMMUNITY
DIRECT	Stage One: Mary condemns and attempts to deter John's wrongdoing	Stage Three: Other people in lift denounce and attempt to deter John's wrongdoing
INDIRECT		Stage Two: Other people in lift support Mary's direct response to John's wrongdoing

Up to this point in the story, we can identify three kinds of value realized by the actions of the various parties, and the first-order reasons for actions to which these values give rise.[5] First, when Mary responds directly to John's wrongdoing, she realizes the kinds of value we previously identified in Chapter 4 as expressive and telic, insofar as she is condemning John's conduct and attempting to deter it. In what follows we will limit our focus to expressive value in order to simplify our illustration of the point at issue. By condemning John's wrongdoing, Mary realizes expressive value akin to truth-telling: *ex hypothesi* it is true that John *was* acting like a paranoid jerk and, since there is value in truth-telling, it follows that there is value to be realized through the actions of anyone expressing this truth about John's conduct.[6] In principle, anyone who can express this truth can realize this value—and we will return to this point below. For now, however, consider the kind of expressive value which Mary in particular can realize by condemning John's wrongdoing. Because Mary stands in a particular role vis-à-vis John's wrongdoing—specifically, she stand in the role of victim—she is able to recognize a unique expressive value when she condemns his actions. I will refer to this expressive value as 'standing up for oneself'. This kind of value is emphasized by authors such as George Fletcher when he conceptualizes violent crimes as acts of domination, by which the offender establishes his dominance over the victim.[7] Now, of course, there is much that can be said regarding the dominance

---

the lines of what Ronald Dworkin labels a 'de facto model' of community: one in which its members treat their membership 'as only a de facto accident of history and geography'. R Dworkin, *Law's Empire* (London: Fontana, 1986; reprint Oxford: Hart, 1998) 209. Specifically in our lift hypothetical, this particular community came together in virtue of the accident of history and geography by which each of them came to be in the lift before the doors closed on this particular occasion.

[5] Note that the kinds of reason identified here do not purport to be a complete account of the reasons generated by John's wrongdoing. One obvious omission includes the kinds of reason which apply to John, which would have him denounce, condemn, deter, etc. his own wrongdoing. Such reasons may be particularly relevant in considering restorative justice approaches to domestic violence.

[6] See Chapter 4, section B.2 ('Expressive value').

[7] G Fletcher, 'Domination in wrongdoing' (1996) 76 Boston University L Rev 347; G Fletcher, 'The place of victims in the theory of retribution' (1999) 3 Buffalo Criminal L Rev 51, 57. This

which exists in a particular offender-victim relationship and indeed in society more generally even *before* any violent crime has occurred, especially with respect to domestic violence. Putting that point to the side for a moment, however, and granting Fletcher's point that violent crimes either create (or at least sustain and perpetuate) such dominance, we can see how actions taken by the *victim* when she condemns the wrongdoing realize a particular kind of expressive value. By standing up for *herself* against John's violence and abuse, Mary realizes a value which no one else can realize: a value grounded in self-respect, courage, self-mastery, refusal to be dominated, etc. Given that Mary can realize this value through her action, she has a reason to do so. Of course, it does not follow that Mary necessarily *should* do so all things considered, but if the normal correspondence thesis holds, then Mary at least has a first-order reason to stand up for herself by condemning John's wrongdoing.[8]

Second, when other people on the lift support Mary's direct response to John's wrongdoing by smiling warmly at her, offering her a supportive 'thumbs-up', etc, they realize different kind of expressive value.[9] This value is best understood as indirectly related to John's wrongdoing, for it is not a direct condemnation of his conduct. The expressive value realized by this small kindness is instead directed primarily at Mary. I will refer to this expressive value as 'fellow feeling'. By responding to Mary as they do, the people in the lift demonstrate that they are supportive of her response to John's conduct. It is a way for the other people in the lift to express empathy, sympathy, or compassion toward Mary. Moreover, their conduct is a way of extending a sense of community membership and belonging to Mary: a way of saying she is not alone, but instead belongs to a group of people who support her and applaud her efforts to stand up for herself.[10] In virtue of the fact that the people on the lift can realize this value, they have a reason to do so.[11] Again, it does not follow that they necessarily *should* do so all things considered, but assuming the plausibility of the normal correspondence thesis,

---

theme also runs through theories of punishment which claim that criminal punishment corrects the unfair advantage offenders gain through their crimes. Eg, J Finnis, *Fundamentals of Ethics* (Oxford: Clarendon, 1983) 128–9.

[8] See Chapter 5, section B ('The Normal Correspondence Thesis').

[9] Again, for the sake of simplicity, we will limit our considerations here to the expressive values at stake and will not consider whether the kindness showed to Mary also realized other sorts of value such as telic and/or consequential value.

[10] Notably, through such actions, the people on the lift take a step toward transforming their community from a mere 'de facto' model to a more normatively ideal community. See n 4 above.

[11] Note the importance of the condition that the people in the lift *can* realize this value. If this condition were not met, then they would have no reason to act so as to realize the value of fellow-feeling. For example, imagine that one of the people in the lift is John's ex-wife, Sue, who previously warned Mary that John was a paranoid, violent jerk and that she would come to regret marrying him. Mary rejected Sue's advice and has considered her an enemy ever since. After Mary responds to John, Sue catches her eye and offers a warm smile and 'thumbs-up'. Sue's actions, we shall assume, are intended with sincere empathy. In light of their history, however, Mary interprets Sue's actions as mocking and derisive. Thus, instead of expressing a sense of fellow-feeling, Sue's actions (albeit unintentionally) express something more along the lines of 'I told you so'. The realization of

then the people on the lift have at least a first-order reason to express fellow-feeling with Mary by supporting her actions in standing up for herself against John's wrongdoing.

Third, when the people on the lift take direct action against John, by denouncing his conduct and restraining him from further violence, they realize another distinct kind of expressive value.[12] In many respects, this value is akin to the value which Mary realized earlier when she condemned John's wrongdoing, insofar as it takes John's wrongdoing as its direct object. By accusing John of wrongdoing, the people on the lift realize an expressive value which places them in direct opposition with John. No longer are the other people on the lift merely standing on the sidelines, cheering on Mary as she stands up for herself; rather the other people are now standing alongside Mary in opposition to John, offering their own direct denunciation of John's conduct. I will refer to this expressive value as 'calling to account'. As Duff and others have observed, the realization of the value of 'calling to account' is a core function of the criminal justice process: the process by which the political community, through its prosecutors, calls alleged wrongdoers to account for their alleged wrongdoings.[13] The people in the lift can (and do) realize the value of calling John to account by responding accusatorially when he lashes out again at Mary.[14] Since they can, through their actions, realize this value, it follows from the normal correspondence thesis that they have at least a first-order reason to do so.[15] With these matters clarified, we can now represent three distinct kinds of reason for action which are grounded, either directly or indirectly, in John's wrongdoing:

Table 2

	VICTIM	COMMUNITY
DIRECT	Reason to 'stand-up for oneself' against wrongdoer	Reason to 'call wrongdoer to account'
INDIRECT		Reason to express 'fellow-feeling' with victim

expressive value is therefore susceptible to lack of correspondence between speakers' intentions and audience uptake. JL Austin, *How to Do Things with Words* (Oxford: OUP, 1962).

[12] Again, for the sake of simplicity, we will limit our considerations here to the expressive values at stake, although it seems clear from the hypothetical that the peoples' conduct also realized the consequential value of (at least temporarily) incapacitating John.

[13] RA Duff and others, *The Trial on Trial, Vol 2: Judgment and calling to account* (Oxford: Hart, 2006) 3–10.

[14] Of course, it is also true that they could have realized this value previously, by calling John to account for his initial wrongful actions.

[15] See Chapter 5, section B. Again, this point does not imply that all things considered, they should do so.

It will not have gone unnoticed that the title of this section promised an account of *four* kinds of reasons generated by wrongdoing, and as yet we have only unpacked three. The fourth kind of reason for action is that which the *victim* has to *support the community* in calling the wrongdoer to account. This kind of reason was not thrown clearly into view in our lift hypothetical, because in that example all of the members of the relevant community had adequate grounds to call John to account based on their own personal observations (for *ex hypothesi*, they all witnessed his wrongdoing). So, while the lift community was able to pursue its valuable project of calling John to account without relying on Mary's assistance, the broader political community outside of the hypothetical lift would not be able to pursue such a project without either Mary's assistance *or* the assistance of the other people on the lift. Imagine, for example, that as the doors of the lift open, a police officer just happens to be standing waiting for the lift and he sees John being restrained. The police officer inquires, 'What is going on here?' At this point, the officer is keen to embark on an investigation which might enable him (as a representative of the broader political community) to engage in just the sort of valuable project of 'calling to account' which the members of the lift community had already begun.[16] As noted earlier, I assume that supporting another person or group of people in their pursuit of valuable activities is itself a way to realize a distinct value.[17] By telling the police officer what happened, the people in the lift support the broader political community is pursuing its own valuable project of calling John to account. In supporting this project, the people in the lift demonstrate their membership within the broader political community: they express what I will refer to as 'good citizenship'. Given that everyone in the lift can realize this value (by assisting the police officer's investigation), it follows that they all have a first-order reasons to tell the police officer what happened.[18]

[16] In other words, the values being pursued in the criminal justice system are ones that can be realized through the *community's* actions when it engages in a *direct* response to wrongdoing. My claim is therefore fundamentally different from one which believes that the criminal 'charge that is brought against an accused person is essentially a complaint *by the individual victim* and then regulated through the criminal process' (emphasis added). SE Marshall, 'Victims of crime: Their station and its duties' (2004) 7 *Critical Review of International Social and Political Philosophy* 104, 112. Note that the quoted passage is not endorsed by Marshall. Indeed, her later works are explicitly consistent with my understanding of such proceedings as actions by which the *community* (not the victim) calls the defendant to account. See, eg, S Marshall with RA Duff and others, *The Trial on Trial: vol Three* (Oxford: Hart, 2007). Compare Marcus Dubber's account of the criminal process, in which he claims that 'the modern prosecutor ... regards herself as the representative of the victim ...'. M Dubber, 'The criminal trial and the legitimation of punishment' in RA Duff and others (eds), *The Trial on Trial, vol 1: Truth and due process* (Oxford: Hart, 2005) 96; M Dubber, *Victims in the War on Crime: The use and abuse of victims' rights* (New York: New York University Press, 2002). In sympathy with Dubber, my claim is that if the modern prosecutor indeed views herself in this light, she is incorrect to do so: rather, her role is better understood as that of state (community) representative, for it is 'the state, not the victim who takes up arms against the defendant'. Ibid 202. See also, Chapter 3, section A.2 above.

[17] See n 2 above.

[18] The link here depends as well on the plausibility of the normal correspondence thesis. See Chapter 5. In what follows, we will focus on the victim's reasons for supporting the broader political

Outside of hypothetical lifts, of course, things are more complicated in the real world. Especially regarding domestic violence, it is typically the case that few if any other witnesses to the violence exist aside from the victim. Thus, in typical cases of domestic violence, the political community's pursuit of the valuable project of denouncing wrongdoing requires the victim's assistance for, without her providing information (at very least), the community will not know what conduct should be called to account.

Now that we have filled in the last piece of our puzzle, we can revise our table to reflect four distinct kinds of reasons for action which are grounded, either directly or indirectly, in John's wrongdoing.[19]

Table 3

	VICTIM	COMMUNITY
DIRECT	Reason to 'stand-up for oneself' against wrongdoer	Reason to 'call wrongdoer to account'
INDIRECT	Reason to serve as 'good citizen'	Reason to express 'fellow-feeling' with victim

Our analysis of four kinds of reasons for action generated by wrongdoing has thus far emphasized reasons grounded in expressive values. Given the one-off nature of the lift hypothetical used to illustrate our analysis, there was no opportunity to consider what affect the opportunity for habituation might have on the sorts of reasons under consideration. However, before leaving our analysis, we will take up this question directly and ask what kind of *constitutive* values can be realized by habitually acting for the reasons identified in Table 3.

First, consider the habituated actions of victims directly responding to wrongdoing. If a person habitually stands up for herself when victimized by wrongdoing, what trait does she constitute in her character through her actions? Well, it all depends. Assuming her response achieves the virtuous mean by standing up for herself on the right occasions in the right way, her habituated actions will constitute in her character traits such as courage and self-respect. Second, consider the habituated actions of a community indirectly responding to wrongdoing by supporting the victim's valuable project in her direct response. Again, assuming the community achieves the virtuous mean

community's valuable project of denouncing wrongdoing. However, as the hypothetical illustrates, such reasons can in principle apply to anyone who is in a position to support that project. These sorts of reasons, as they apply to other people, explain community members' first-order reasons to serve as witnesses at trial, to serve as jurors, to pay taxes to support well-functioning court systems, etc.

[19] Again, these four kinds of reason are not meant to suggest a closed list.

in its habituated actions, it will constitute in itself the character trait of being a compassionate society, one which is supportive of its members when they have been wronged. Third, consider the habituated actions of a community directly responding to wrongdoing. The character traits at issue here are tricky to identify, but I wish to suggest that the substance of these traits are parasitic upon the character of the wrongdoing at issue. So, for example, if a community habitually acts directly against violent wrongdoing, it thereby constitutes in itself a less violent character. Similarly, if a community habitually acts directly against racist wrongdoing, it thereby constitutes in itself a less racist character. And, of course, as I have argued previously, if a community habitually acts directly against patriarchal wrongdoing, it thereby constitutes in itself a less patriarchal (more feminist) character.[20] Finally, the habituated actions of a victim indirectly responding to wrongdoing by supporting the community's valuable project of calling the wrongdoer to account constitutes in her character traits which I will call 'civic virtue' and 'community-mindedness': traits which are the hallmark of one concerned to be an engaged and responsible member of her community.

With this additional wrinkle now in view, we can formulate a final table which demarcates not only the four kinds of reasons for responding to wrongdoing which concern us here, but also the corresponding character traits which may be constituted in the victim's or community's character by habitually acting upon the kinds of reasons we have identified.

Table 4

	VICTIM	COMMUNITY
DIRECT	Reason to 'stand-up for oneself' against wrongdoer; character traits of courage, self-respect	Reason to 'call wrongdoer to account'; character trait in opposition to the character of the wrongdoing at issue (eg, feminist)
INDIRECT	Reason to serve as 'good citizen'; character traits of civic virtue, community-mindedness	Reason to express 'fellow-feeling' with victim; character traits of compassion, supportiveness

In the next two sections, we will put the above analysis to work in addressing the questions of whether domestic-violence victims have a (moral) right to participate in the prosecution of their batterers, and whether victims have a (moral) duty to do so.

---

[20] It is assumed that in order to constitute these valuable character traits, it would be necessary for the community to achieve the virtuous mean in its habituated actions.

B. Do Victims Have a Right to Participate in Prosecutions?

In what follows, I will assume the plausibility of what is typically referred to as the 'interest theory' of rights.[21] The gist of this theory is simply that rights are justified by the interests of the rights-holder. So, if a victim has a right to participate in the prosecution of her batterer, it is because she has an interest in doing so. The notion of an interest, as I understand it here, does not equate to mere desire; rather it will be assumed that someone might have a right which she does not desire and indeed would be quite happy to forfeit. In other words, I am assuming the existence of inalienable rights. Thus, while a victim's desires can be relevant to determining her interests (and thus her rights), I will assume that her interests are not coterminous with her desires.[22] Earlier I said that if a victim has a right to participate in the prosecution of her batterer, it is because she has an interest in doing so. However, it does not follow from the fact that a victim has an interest in participating in the prosecution her batterer that she therefore necessarily has a right to do so. Rather, a victim has a right 'if and only if *ceteris paribus*... [her] interest is a sufficient reason for holding some other persons to be under a duty'.[23] Whether another person has such a duty depends upon the relevant circumstances at issue: for the 'dynamic aspect of rights', as Raz correctly observes, means that rights have the 'capacity to generate new duties with changing circumstances'.[24]

Applying the above considerations to the question of whether victims have a right to participate in the prosecution of their batterers, we may draw the following preliminary conclusion: victims have a right to participate in the prosecution of their batterers if, and only if, *ceteris paribus* their interests are a sufficient reason for holding some other persons to be under a duty. Any number of people might qualify as the 'other persons' who may be held to be under a duty vis-à-vis a victim's right to participate. For example, if we conceive of victim participation in terms of their testifying at trial and focus on whether the defendant has any duties, we might frame the question as follows: *ceteris paribus* are victims' interests in testifying at trial sufficient for holding defendants to be under a duty

---

[21] This theory of rights is sometimes referred to as a 'benefit' theory of rights, and the 'interest' or 'benefit' theory of rights is typically taken as standing in opposition to a 'choice' or 'will' theory of rights. Specifically, the version of interest theory of rights I assume here is inspired by a Razian account of moral rights, as developed in chapter 7 of J Raz, *The Morality of Freedom* (Oxford: OUP, 1986).

[22] As Bill Edmundson has correctly pointed out, when used as a justificatory account of rights (as I do here), the choice theory of right is best understood as a species of an interest theory: 'Interest Theory simply tells us that rights are justified by their serving to protect and further the interests of individuals... Choice Theory can be viewed as a specification of the interest rights serve— namely, the interest in exercising autonomous choice.' WA Edmundson, *An Introduction to Rights* (Cambridge: Cambridge University Press, 2004) 127.

[23] Raz (n 21 above) 166. Internal parentheses omitted.

[24] Ibid 186.

not to prevent victims' testimony? Presumably, under most conceivably circumstances, the answer would be yes. An argument of this sort would go some way toward justifying laws which prohibit defendants from intimidating victims into not testifying at trial. Based on this line of thought, therefore, we can conclude that victims do have a right to participate in prosecutions (at least in this limited sense).

Of course, the right we have identified above is not the broad claim of rights which normally motivates debates regarding victim participation in prosecutions. Typically the claim is for a right to a much more expansive and engaged form of participation. To understand this difference, we might draw a distinction between three types of victim participation in prosecutions: (1) informative; (2) advisory; and (3) authoritative. The traditional role of victim as witness represents the paradigm of informative participation. In this type of participation, the victim serves merely to provide the tribunal with information regarding the offence at issue; her opinion on matters such as whether to charge an offence, what level of offence to charge, whether to plea bargain, what level of sentence to impose, etc, is neither sought nor considered by the prosecutors or judges. Advisory participation, however, entails some degree of consideration by the police, prosecutors and/or judges of the victim's opinion on such matters.[25] The practice of allowing victims to present victim impact statements at sentencing nicely illustrates both the distinctions between and the joining together of these two types of participation. In some US jurisdictions, for example, victim impact statements are an accepted means by which victims can advise the judges in sentencing; while in the UK, victim personal statements (as they are called) are meant merely to provide information to the tribunal, not advice.[26]

The broadest rights claim that can be made with respect to victim participation in prosecutions is a claim for a right to authoritative participation: consisting either of participation as a party to the litigation, with legal standing to decide whether charges will be brought (or dismissed) and whether plea bargains will be permitted (or denied); or as a non-party who nonetheless has the power to control the exercise of prosecutorial discretion. Authoritative participation is considerably

---

[25] The recently enacted Crime Victims' Rights Act, which amends US Federal Criminal Procedures, reflects an expansion of victims' participation in federal prosecutions from informative participation to advisory participation. Pub L No 108–405, § 102(a), 118 Stat 2260, 2261–2 (codified as amended at 18 USC §3771 (Supp 2006)); PG Cassell, 'Treating crime victims fairly: Integrating victims into the federal rules of criminal procedure' [2007] Utah L Rev 861. Advisory participation seems in alignment with the sort of 'victim participation model' of criminal justice envisioned by Douglas Beloof in DE Beloof, 'The third model of criminal process: The victim participation model' [1999] Utah L Rev 289, insofar as the 'the public prosecutor retains control over critical decisions and retains central responsibility for the prosecution', ibid 299. However, Beloof's suggestion that victims should be afforded 'the opportunity to engage in voir dire selection, opening statement, questioning and calling witnesses, objecting to evidence, and closing argument' suggests something closer to authoritative participation, discussed below. Ibid 321.
[26] L Zedner, *Criminal Justice* (OUP, 2004) 145–6, 184–5. See also, S Bandes, 'Empathy, narrative, and victim impact statements' (1996) 63 University of Chicago L Rev 361.

more expansive and engaged than mere participation as a legal party to the prosecutorial proceedings. Indeed, while several jurisdictions afford the victim a
formal role at trial, whether as a *partie civile* or as an auxiliary prosecutor,[27] no
modern legal systems officially sanction authoritative participation by the victim.
As Thomas Weigend observes:

> even where the victim has a comparatively well-protected position at the trial, he never
> plays a leading role. Since criminal justice has been taken out of the hands of the private
> victim by the modern state, the trial is not mean to provide a forum for the victim to state
> his case or to obtain redress for the immaterial damage he has suffered.[28]

While Weigend is correct to observe that no modern jurisdiction recognizes *de
jure* authoritative participation by the victim, numerous jurisdictions permit
de facto authoritative participation at least with respect to the issue of whether
charges should be dismissed. In domestic-violence cases in particular, it remains
commonplace for prosecutors to treat victims' requests to dismiss as authoritative directives to dismiss. By this, I mean that prosecutors treat the victims'
requests as a binding, content-independent reason for action, rather than merely
a weighty consideration to be taken into account along with all other relevant
considerations.[29]

However, our concern is not with whether victims have been provided a *legal*
right to participate authoritatively in the prosecution of their batterers, but
instead whether victims have a *moral* right to do so. In other words, are victims'
interests in authoritatively participating in the prosecution of their batterers a sufficient reason *ceteris paribus* for holding some other persons to be under a duty?
To answer this question, we must first identify who the 'some other persons'
might be. Presumably, in order to serve the interests of victims to participate
authoritatively in the prosecution, the 'other persons' must be in a position to give
binding, content-independent effect to the victims' requests in the prosecution.
Given the structure of modern criminal legal systems, the 'other persons' at issue
are therefore either judges or prosecutors. In asking whether victims have a right
to authoritative participation, in other words, we are asking whether there is sufficient reason (grounded in the victims' interests) to impose a duty upon judges
to grant victims' requests authoritative effect in the litigation, or to impose a duty
upon prosecutors to defer to victims' requests as binding, content-independent
reasons for action.

What interests of the victim might ground a right to authoritative participation? We can explore this question by further unpacking the notion of the

---

[27] See Chapter 1, pp 8–9.
[28] T Weigend, 'Why have a trial when you can have a bargain?' in Duff and others (n 13 above)
216.
[29] On authoritative directives as providing binding, content-independent reasons for action,
see generally, S Shapiro, 'Authority' in J Coleman and S Shapiro (eds), *The Oxford Handbook of
Jurisprudence and Philosophy of Law* (Oxford: OUP, 2002).

victims' authoritative participation and identifying the values that can be realized through such action. Authoritative participation by the victim places her firmly in the driver's seat of the prosecution: through her actions, she calls the shots as to whether charges are brought, whether charges are dismissed, etc. In other words, the victim's authoritative participation provides a context in which the *victim* can *directly* respond to the wrongdoing. Direct responses by victims to wrongdoing indeed realize important values. Returning to the analysis set forth above in section A, we identified values of this kind which are potentially of tremendous importance. By directly responding to the wrongdoing at issue, victims act upon values that are fundamental to one's dignity and self-worth. By acting on the reasons they have to stand up for themselves, they realize these important values and, if their actions are habituated, the victims constitute in themselves highly valuable character traits, such as courage and self respect.

So, we may safely conclude that the interests of victims in authoritatively participating in the prosecution of their batterers are weighty interests indeed. Yet, are these interests sufficient to ground a duty in judges or prosecutors to grant victims' requests authoritative status? Well, it all depends. Given the dynamic aspect of rights, the correct question is not 'are victims' interests *always* sufficient to ground such a duty?' but rather, 'are there some occasions on which victims' interest will be sufficient to ground such a duty?' If, for example, a legal system existed in which victims were not provided with any adequate means to realize the kinds of values at stake when they directly respond to wrongdoing (ie, the value of standing up for themselves), it may be conceivable to ground a duty for judges and prosecutors to grant victims' authoritative participation in criminal prosecutions.

However, by granting authoritative participation rights to victims, judges and/ or prosecutors would be placed under duties which would fundamentally alter the nature of the proceedings. No longer would criminal prosecutions be brought on behalf of the State, the People, Regina, etc, and if such labels remained, they would be effectively meaningless in understanding the sorts of values realized through criminal prosecution. Criminal prosecutions would no longer be a setting in which the political community calls the defendant to account; where the community responds directly to the wrongdoing. Rather, the criminal trial would be transformed into a setting in which victims respond directly on their own behalf.

These considerations suggest that victims do not have a right to authoritative participation, at least not in legal systems which have a fairly well-functioning tort system or alternative means by which victims may realize the kinds of value at stake when they directly respond to wrongdoing. Authoritative participation by victims in criminal prosecutions does serve important victim interests, but they are interests that are better served in other contexts. For, if the victim's right to authoritative participation in criminal prosecution is recognized, it will come at the cost of effectively dismantling the very system in which victims claim a right to participate.[30]

C. Do Victims Have a Duty to Participate in Prosecutions?

It is commonly thought that domestic-violence victims have a moral duty *ceteris paribus* to participate in criminal prosecutions by, for example, testifying at trial against their batterers. Typically, this claim does not extend to any absolute duty to participate, and indeed it is widely recognized that victims (especially those who face threats of violence) can justifiably refuse to participate. Still, the notion that victims have at least a prima facie duty to testify has been relatively uncontroversial, while academic discussion has focused instead on the justifiability of enforcing that duty through legal mechanisms such as subpoenas, contempt of court, and material witness warrants. I wish to challenge the accepted wisdom that victims have even a prima facie duty to testify at trial, at least with respect to many sorts of criminal prosecutions. With respect to domestic-violence prosecutions in particular, I wish to offer an argument which will hopefully go some way toward dampening the zeal of those who favour enforcing such a duty against victims who refuse to participate. My argument proceeds in three steps. First, I consider and reject two arguments which conclude that victims have a duty to participate in criminal prosecutions. Second, I consider (and find more plausible) a third kind of argument in support of such a duty: an argument grounded in the interests that communities have in victims helping to hold defendants accountable. Finally, in section E, I consider the separate question of whether victims' duties to participate can be justifiably enforced through mechanisms such as subpoenas, contempt of court, and/or material witness warrants. I conclude that while such measures may be justifiable in some domestic-violence prosecutions, they do not form part of an effective *feminist* domestic-violence prosecution strategy.

In what follows, I will focus specifically on the question of whether domestic-violence victims have a duty to participate in criminal prosecutions of their batterers by testifying at trial. Clearly there are other duties of participation which we might consider, such as a duty to sign a criminal complaint against the defendant, a duty to approve charges, a duty to serve as a party to the litigation, etc. Yet, for the reasons considered above regarding victims' rights to participate in prosecutions, it seems implausible to suggest that victims would ever have a duty to engage in such activities. Moreover, we will not consider in detail the duty victims may have to participate in prosecutions merely by being cooperative: ie, by not requesting dismissal, by being helpful and pleasant in providing information during investigations, etc. While prosecutors and courts may have

---

[30] For arguments along a similar theme, see M Hildebrandt, 'Trial and "fair trial": From peer to subject to citizen' in A Duff and others (n 13 above) 32–5.

some interest in victims cooperating in this sense, insofar as such cooperation facilitates the ease of bureaucratic administration entailed in any prosecution, that interest strikes me as wholly insufficient to ground any duty on the part of victims to 'play nice'. Certainly, of course, victims (and others) have a duty not to *interfere* with just prosecutions by, for example, engaging in witness tampering or jury intimidation; but this duty is not specific to victims nor is it best understood as a duty to participate.

1. On promises and fair play

In this section, we will consider and reject two arguments which might be thought to ground a domestic-violence victim's duty to testify at the trial of her batterer. The first is grounded in the assumption that domestic-violence victims are obligated to participate because they have promised to do so.[31] This argument shares the same basic logical structure as social-contract theories of political obligation, and it suffers from the same weaknesses.[32] The major premise of such arguments state that people have a duty to do that which they have promised to do. The minor premise states that victims have agreed (implicitly or explicitly) to participate in the prosecution their batterers. The conclusion states that therefore victims have a duty to participate in the prosecution of their batterers. While the logic is valid, the argument remains unsound on the whole for, since there is little reason to believe that victims typically do anything like promise to participate in the prosecution of their batterers, the minor premise is false. As Kent Greenawalt has correctly noted in criticizing similar arguments regarding the supposed general duty to obey the law:

One can be obligated in the way promissory theory assumes if one has made a promise or engaged in a promise-like act, and the promise is not undercut by duress or some other vitiating condition.[33]

In the domestic-violence cases, victims have typically neither explicitly promised to participate, nor have they engaged in a promise-like act to participate which might ground an implicit promise-based argument that they have such a duty. It is occasionally suggested, however, that victims' requests for police assistance constitute an implicit promise to participate in the eventual prosecution of their batterers. Withdrawal in such cases is viewed by some as the victim reneging on her implicit promise to cooperate with the prosecution. However, of course, calling

---

[31] The point is often phrased in terms of consenting, but I decline that usage here in light of my belief that the normative function of consent is limited to generating exclusionary permissions for those to whom consent is granted, and thus does not even have the potential to generate duties. MM Dempsey and J Herring, 'How consent works' (forthcoming). By limiting the major premise to instances of promising, its plausibility remains intact.

[32] See generally, K Greenawalt, *Conflicts of Law and Morality* (Oxford: OUP, 1987) 62–93.

[33] Ibid 64.

for assistance at the time of a battery is not tantamount to an implicit promise to participate in any eventual prosecution. It is better understood as merely a request for assistance: assistance to which each member of the community is entitled without offering any further consideration such as a promise to cooperate with future law enforcement action. Occasionally, victims do engage in conduct such as signing a criminal complaint against their batterers, and such conduct is more easily (but still incorrectly) construed as a promise to participate in the prosecution. At best, a victim's signature on a criminal complaint should be construed as an agreement that the defendant should be charged with a criminal offence: this act should not be understood to commit the victim to any particular form of participation in the ensuing prosecution.

It is of course possible for a domestic-violence victim to make an explicit promise to participate in the prosecution of the defendant. A criminal complaint form could easily incorporate language of explicit promising, such as: 'I understand that by signing this complaint, I hereby promise to participate in any prosecution of the named suspect for the offence described herein, including but not limited to testify against the suspect at any criminal proceedings based on this complaint.' However, even where such a form is signed (and thus an explicit promise is made), the second of Greenawalt's conditions will typically not be satisfied in domestic-violence cases, since the victim's promise is likely secured under duress or some other vitiating condition.[34] Undoubtedly, promises secured shortly after the battery would be invalid on these grounds and thus would not serve as an adequate basis for claiming that the victim has a duty to participate in the prosecution.[35] In order for such promises to give rise to a duty, the promise would have to be made after the victim had been provided with the sort of comprehensive support envisioned by Carolyn Hoyle's and Andrew Sanders' 'victim empowerment' model of domestic-violence prosecution; so that it would be certain that the victim's promise was motivated by her desire to commit herself to participating rather than a desire to secure the safety and community support to which she is entitled in any event.[36] Overwhelmingly, victims are not provided with such comprehensive and effective support in domestic-violence cases. As such, given the typical lack of any explicit promise to participate and the vitiating conditions which typically attend any such promises, the argument that domestic-violence victims have a promise-based duty to participate in criminal prosecutions fails.

A second form of argument in defence of the claim that domestic-violence victims have a duty to participate in trials by testifying against their batterers is grounded in conceptual claims regarding the communicative nature of criminal

---

[34] Greenawalt (n 32 above).

[35] This point is consistent with Hoyle's and Sanders' 'victim empowerment' model of the criminal justice system's response to domestic violence. C Hoyle and A Sanders, 'Police response to domestic violence: From victim choice to victim empowerment?' (2000) 40 British Journal of Criminology 14.

[36] Ibid.

proceedings and normative claims regarding the value of fair play. This form of argument is not exclusively directed to domestic-violence cases or indeed even to duties of victims in particular. Rather, the claim defended is a general one which extends to all members of the community who call the defendant to account. The argument as developed by Duff and others conceives of criminal prosecution as a communicative process through which the defendant is called to account to the community for his alleged wrongdoing. Upon being called account, so the argument goes, the defendant has a duty to participate in the criminal proceedings. As a matter of fair play, the victim should also therefore be understood to have a duty to participate. Importantly, however, the victim's duty in this regard is no different than the duty owed by other witnesses and other concerned community members:

[I]f we think it important that...the accused should have to answer in person to the charge that he faces; and if, as we suggest, this is because what he is charged with is a wrong for which he must answer to the polity as a whole, through this criminal court: it must also be important that other members of the polity with a role in the trial—as witnesses, as judges, or as jurors—should face him in person. There would be a clear contradiction in calling on you to answer in person to us, but refusing to face you ourselves.[37]

The fair-play argument contains a grain of truth insofar as it links the duty of participation to the values that can be realized through the criminal process. However, the argument as framed is overly broad because it fails to specify *which* members of the community should be expected to face the defendant in court. If the whole community (polity) is calling the defendant to account, then why should we limit the category of community members who have a duty to appear to face the defendant in person? Why should we not conclude that every member of the community has a duty to participate?[38] Presumably the point behind the fair-play argument is that anyone whose testimony is *necessary* to establishing the defendant's guilt should be thought to have a duty to appear in court and face the defendant personally, which explains why the argument extends not only to victims, but to all witnesses. This move in the argument, however, raises the further question of *which* witnesses' in-court testimony *should* be considered necessary for the prosecution. When, for example, are concerns about the admission of hearsay evidence substantial enough to ground the determination that a particular witnesses' in-court testimony is necessary for the prosecution? As we shall see below, the answer to this question will depend on a variety of considerations

[37] RA Duff and others (2007) (n 16 above) 118. See also SE Marshall, extending this form of argument to a duty of victims (and other witnesses) to report crimes as well as testify at trial. Marshall (n 16 above) 113–14.

[38] Historically, community-wide participation in criminal trials was the norm, while even today such methods for quasi-criminal proceedings are being resurrected (albeit not without significant problems). P Clark, 'Hybridity, holism and traditional justice: The case of the Gacaca courts in post-genocide Rwanda' (2007) 39 George Washington International L Rev 765. For a historical analysis of the criminal trial, see RA Duff and others, (2007) (n 16 above) 17–53.

which are better illuminated if we pursue a different method of grounding the victims' duty to participate.

2. Interest-based duties

In this section, we consider a more plausible form of argument in defence of the claim that domestic-violence victims have a duty to participate in criminal prosecutions. This argument is grounded in the interest theory of rights and the account of duties to which it gives rise.[39] Employing the interest-theory framework, we may determine whether a victim has a duty to testify by asking whether any person (or group) has an interest (or interests) which *ceteris paribus* is (are) sufficient reason for holding the victim to have such a duty. This inquiry can be broken into three steps. First, we ask whether victims' testimony against the defendant would serve the interests of some person or group of people. Next, we ask whether those interests are sufficient to ground a duty for victims to testify. If so, then at this point, we may conclude that the relevant interest-holders have a right to have victims testify against the defendant. However, given the dynamic aspect of rights discussed above, we have not yet determined whether a victim in any particular instance has a duty to testify. In order to resolve this matter, we must further inquire as to which (if any) conditions will defeat the interests of the would-be rights holder and thus block the formation of a duty on the part of victims to testify. According to this approach, any plausible claim regarding a victim's duty to participate in the prosecution of her batterer must be grounded in an account of the *interests* which her participation will serve.

To simplify matters, let us focus our attention on the community as the potential rights-holder.[40] First we must identify what, if any, community interests can be served through victims' testimony against their batterers. The most obvious answer is that victims' testimony will serve the community's interests by facilitating the conviction of guilty defendants. But of course, this is not a complete

[39] See nn 21–4 above and surrounding text. I do not mean to imply that all duties are best conceived as interest-based. Promising, as the previous discussion demonstrates, may ground a duty to do that which one has promised to do—but it does not necessarily follow that the promisee has an interest sufficient to ground that duty. J Raz, 'Promises and obligations' in PMS Hacker and J Raz (eds), *Law, Morality and Society: Essays in honour of HLA Hart* (Oxford: Clarendon Press, 1977). The problem we found with promise-based arguments above was not that promises do not ground duties (indeed, I believe they typically do), but rather that in the case of domestic violence, victims do not typically promise to participate and, if they do, the normative force of the promise is typically vitiated by duress or the like.

[40] It is possible to imagine that other parties' interests might ground such a duty for the victim. For example, the victim's testimony may serve important interests of her children (ie, their interest in safety, etc), and we may conclude both that the children have a right to have their mother testify against her batterer and, further, we may conclude that the children's interests ground a duty for the victim to testify. However, as we are concerned primarily with whether prosecutors would be justified in enforcing the victim's duty to testify, we will limit our attention to whether the community (as represented by the prosecutor) is the relevant interest-holder.

answer, for the value of prosecution is not merely the consequential one of securing conviction. Rather, as discussed at length in Chapter 4 there are a myriad
of consequential and intrinsic values that can be realized through criminal
prosecutions.[41]

Importantly, through her testimony, the victim can serve the community's
interest in realizing expressive values of denouncing the defendant's wrongdoing (ie, calling him to account). Moreover, if the particular case at issue is part
of a habituated response by the community acting against the wrongdoing of
domestic violence in its strong sense, the victim's testimony may also serve the
community's interest in reconstituting its character in a valuable way. Specifically,
by making it possible for the community to target domestic violence in its strong
sense, victims' testimony can make an important contribution to the community's valuable project of reconstituting its character as less patriarchal (more
feminist) *ceteris paribus*. As explained in section A of this chapter, the fact that
the victim *can* contribute to this valuable project generates first-order reasons for
her do to so. The question we face now, however, is whether the victim has more
than a mere first-order reason to support her community's valuable project in this
regard, but whether she has a *duty* to do so.

Continuing our interrogation of whether the victim has such a duty, we
must now consider whether a community's interests in (inter alia) convicting
the defendant, expressively denouncing his wrongdoing, and reconstituting its
character as less patriarchal (more feminist) are sufficient to ground a duty for
victims to testify.[42] Clearly, it all depends. It depends on, among other considerations, the likely consequences of his prosecution and conviction—eg, will
he be deterred from or spurred on toward committing further violence? Also, it
depends on what kind of wrongdoing has been committed and thus, how much
expressive value there is in denouncing (calling him to account for) this kind of

---

[41] Moreover, it should of course be noted that the victim's testimony is sometimes not necessary to convict (eg, when there are independent eyewitnesses who are willing and able to testify).
Indeed, sometimes when the victim testifies *against* her batterer, the case is *less* likely to result
in conviction than when she recants or refuses to testify. During one particular trial term as a
domestic-violence prosecutor, I secured convictions in all of the 'victimless' prosecution jury trials
I brought forward, but failed to secure convictions in two cases where the victims testified against
the defendants. In speaking with the jurors following the trial, I learned that they disbelieved the
victims' testimony in these cases (or at least failed to believe it beyond a reasonable doubt), in part
because the defendants and victims were engaged in on-going divorce proceedings, one of which
involved a child custody dispute. Apparently, in the cases in which the victims testified against
the defendants, the jurors thought that the victims were lying in order to secure better bargaining
position in the divorce proceedings; whereas in cases in which the victims recanted (ie, testified *for*
the defendants), the jurors thought that the victims were lying in order to protect themselves from
further attack or to protect their partners. Either way, the jurors were receptive to the thought that
the victims were lying, and thus securing victim testimony against a defendant should not necessarily be thought of as the best way to secure a conviction. For an interesting analysis of the problem
of women's perceived lack of credibility as witnesses, see K Mack, 'Continuing barriers to women's
credibility: A feminist perspective on the proof process' (1993) 4 Criminal Law Forum 327.

[42] The reference here to consequential, expressive, and constitutive values is not meant to suggest
that these present a closed list. See Chapter 4 for further discussion of the array of values at issue.

wrongdoing. It further depends on whether this particular case is part of a larger project by the community, through its prosecutors, to reconstitute its character as less patriarchal (more feminist). Presumably, by making contributions to the realization of each of these valuable projects, the victim's testimony will serve substantial community interests. We may therefore tentatively conclude that (in the right kinds of cases at least) the community's interests are indeed sufficient to ground a duty for victims to testify against their batterers.

It is worth pausing a moment to reflect on which kinds of cases will be more likely to ground a community's right to have a victim testify against her batterer. Consider a given community's rights in two separate cases. The first case involves domestic violence in its weak sense, while the second involves domestic violence in its strong sense. Assuming all other relevant facts of the cases are identical, it follows from the argument set forth above that the community is more likely to have a right to the victim's testimony in the second case, particularly if that prosecution forms part of a habituated feminist prosecutorial response to domestic violence. This conclusion follows because the values which the community realizes through the prosecution of domestic violence in its strong sense are greater *ceteris paribus* than those which it realizes through the prosecution of domestic violence in its weak sense.

Moreover, consider which one of two different communities—one less patriarchal, one more patriarchal—is more likely to have a right to victims' testimony in cases of domestic violence in its strong sense. Assuming that all other relevant facts remain identical and provided that the prosecutions form part of a feminist habituated prosecutorial response to domestic violence, it is more likely that the *more* patriarchal society will have a right to the victims' testimony in such cases. The prosecution of domestic violence in its strong sense makes possible the realization of significant expressive and constitutive values in both societies, but *ceteris paribus*, the more patriarchal the society, the more opportunity there is for feminist prosecutions to serve significant community interest. Thus, since the interests served through the victims' testimony will be greater in more patriarchal societies, it is more likely that those communities will have a right to the victims' testimony.

It follows from the above that in at least some kinds of domestic-violence cases, the community may have a right to have the victim testify against her batterer. However, it does not yet follow that any particular victims actually have a duty to do so. Again, the dynamic aspect of rights means that we must further inquire as to which (if any) conditions will defeat the interests of the would-be rights holder and thus block the formation of a duty on the part of victims to testify. The sorts of conditions which might block the formation of a victim's duty to testify should be fairly obvious and non-controversial. Conditions, for example, regarding victims' safety, would undoubtedly block the formation of such a duty. Thus, no matter how great the community's interests may be in having victims testify against their batterers, it follows that victims have no duty to testify under conditions which jeopardize their safety. If, however, the victims' safety is equally in jeopardy irrespective of whether she testifies, the duty to do so may arise.[43]

We can see clearly now how the approach outlined above differs in significant respects from what we might call a benefit or gratitutde theory of victims' duties to participate in prosecutions. In discourse regarding political and legal obligation, benefit or gratitude theories claim that subjects' duty to obey is grounded upon their duty of gratitude which arises in response to the benefits which the polity bestows upon them.[44] Since communities bestow a benefit upon victims by taking up their cause by prosecuting their batterers (so the argument goes), victims have a gratitude-based duty to help support such prosecutions by testifying against the defendants. Under the theory defended above, however, the community's prosecution of the defendant is not understood in terms of a benefit bestowed upon the victim, but rather as a distinct project, pursued by and on behalf of the community. The community's prosecution of the defendant is not understood as something that the community kindly does on the victim's behalf:[45] rather, it is understood as something the community does on its own behalf, in response to the distinct reasons which it has to respond to the defendant's wrongdoing.

D. Against Enforcement

We have identified a particular kind of domestic-violence prosecution in which it may be said that victims have a duty to testify against their batterers. A prosecution in which the victim's testimony can realize values which serve substantial community interests and in which no conditions defeat its formation will ground a duty on the part of the victim to testify against her batterer. Given the arguments set out previously, it is most likely that such a duty will arise in cases where the violence at issue is serious and on-going, where prosecution is likely to reduce the violence, where the violence has a tendency to sustain and perpetuate patriarchy (ie, where it constitutes domestic violence in its strong sense), and where the prosecution is part of a habituated feminist response to domestic violence. Where

---

[43] This line of thought may go some way toward justifying the practice of compelling witness testimony in organized crime cases, with the thought here being that the witnesses' safety is equally in jeopardy whether he testifies or not. Typically in domestic-violence cases, it is thought that victims' testimony against their batterers will *ceteris paribus* increase their risk of facing further violence, although no studies exist to support this common-sense view. On a related topic, there is data to support the conclusion that leaving a violent domestic relationship significantly increases victims' risk. See Chapter 8, n 55.

[44] CH Wellman and AJ Simmons, *Is there a Duty to Obey the Law?* (Cambridge: Cambridge University Press, 2005) 119.

[45] Nor is it understood as something the community has stolen from the victim. Cf N Christie, 'Conflicts as property' (1977) 17 British Journal of Criminology 1.

these conditions are met, we may conclude that the victim indeed has a duty to participate by testifying at trial.

However, the fact that victims may have such a duty does not mean that prosecutors (or anyone else) would be justified in enforcing that duty against them. In order to explore this line of thought, we must first explain what is meant by enforcement. There are a number of ways a prosecutor might secure a victim's testimony at trial and not all of them are properly understood as enforcement. The least problematic way to secure a victim's testimony is simply to ask her to attend court and testify. Indeed, this measure is so morally unproblematic that it is appropriate to use in any justified prosecution, even when the victim has no duty to testify. The prosecutor's request simply provides the victim with (another) first-order reason to testify: it does not purport to obligate her in anyway and there is no threat of sanction attached if she refuses the request. Of course, for these very reasons, mere requests to attend court and testify are unlikely to persuade a reluctant victim to testify. Beyond mere requests, therefore, the prosecutor (or a victim-witness liaison representing the prosecutor's office) may attempt to persuade the victim to attend court and give testimony, emphasizing to the victim the reasons she has for doing so and the values that can be realized through her testimony. This approach, which we might colloquially call 'laying on a guilt trip', presents a legitimate option in cases where the victim has a pre-existing duty to testify. Moreover, it has the benefit of not threatening sanctions if the victim fails to comply.[46]

By enforcement, I mean to refer to measures used in an attempt to persuade the victim to testify which threaten sanction if the victim fails to comply. Use of such measures by prosecutors present a significant moral problem and call for independent justification. In other words, it will not suffice for a prosecutor to threaten sanctions against a victim for refusing to testify and then attempt to justify making that threat simply by reference to the fact that the victim has a duty to testify. Indeed, it may very well be the case that the victim does have a duty to testify, but that fact alone will never provide sufficient justification for the prosecutor threatening sanctions if she refuses to do so. Rather, any argument which seeks to justify enforcement measures by prosecutors against victims who refuse to testify must be based on an account of the exceptionally strong interests which the victims' testimony will serve. Examples of justifiable enforcement against witnesses, for example, can be found in organized-crime prosecutions, where the community's interest in incarcerating the most dangerous repeat offenders goes some way toward justifying the practice of forcing witnesses to testify.[47]

[46] To increase the effectiveness of either of these measures, of course, it will be advantageous to treat the victim with the proper respect, to provide adequate victim support and information, etc. Not only are such measures likely to increase the chance that the victim will opt to testify, but will realize independent values of the sort which motivate the 'therapeutic jurisprudence' literature. See Chapter 8, pp 166–7.

[47] In some cases, another consideration justifying enforcement measures is the option witnesses are provided with to enter witness-protection programmes. It follows that if such programmes were extended to domestic-violence victims, this provision might, in some cases, render enforcement

So what measures count as enforcement? Let us consider four enforcement measures that were available to prosecutors to secure witness testimony at trial during my tenure as a prosecutor:[48] (1) serving the victim with a subpoena which commands the victim to appear in court and give testimony upon threat of contempt of court; (2) filing a petition against the victim requesting that she be held in contempt of court for refusing to comply with a subpoena; (3) requesting a material-witness warrant directing law-enforcement officers to arrest the victim and bring her to court; and (4) bringing a motion before the court to have a victim who refuses to testify held in contempt of court and imprisoned until she agrees to testify. Clearly these measures are ordered in terms of the level of justification called for by each. Indeed, the first option, issuing a subpoena, may be a case which stands at the borderline of what counts as enforcement and thus would call for little if any special justification over and above the victim's duty to testify. The final option in comparison, that of having a victim imprisoned until she testifies, calls for a degree of justification which, in my view, is likely never to be satisfied in a domestic-violence case.

As a prosecutor, I routinely issued subpoenas for victims in domestic-violence cases, but I never sought to have them enforced by the court when the victim refused to appear and/or testify. At the time, I conceived of subpoenas as a more formal version of a request to testify, rather than as a command to testify backed by threat of sanction. Clearly, I now recognize that I misconceived the nature of my practice and failed to consider the need for justification to which this practice gave rise. If I had been guided by the arguments as I now understand them, I would have issued subpoenas only in select cases: specifically, those cases which I judged (hopefully correctly) to be cases of domestic violence in its strong sense, and where the risk of violence would be decreased by securing the victim's testimony.[49] In such cases, it is likely that the victims would have had a duty to testify (as that duty is conceived above), and that duty may have sufficed to justify my issuing subpoenas to those victims. I phrase the above point conditionally ('may')

---

justifiable. Of course, witness-protection programmes will not typically be feasible in domestic-violence cases since there is often strong reason (either actual or perceived) for the victim to maintain contact with the defendant. As such, it is not suggested here that witness-protection programmes can be easily mapped onto domestic-violence cases so as to justify enforcement measures against victims. Rather, my point is simply that in cases where such measures would be appropriate and welcomed by the victim, they should be made available and, if they are utilized effectively, their use may go some way toward justifying enforcement measures.

[48] Specific mechanisms for enforcement will vary across jurisdictions, both in terminology and procedural requirements (eg, England has changed its terminology from witness subpoena to witness summons). It is hoped that the illustrations above will draw out some general considerations which apply across jurisdictions.

[49] There is, of course, always a risk of getting these evaluations wrong, due to a lack of empirical data upon which to make the evaluation, a failure to exercise feminist practical wisdom in disaggregating cases of domestic violence in its strong and weak sense, and/or a lack of will to do so. For further discussion, see MM Dempsey, 'Toward a feminist state: What does "effective" prosecution of domestic violence mean?' (2007) 70 MLR 908, 932–3.

because of my belief that subpoenas stand at the conceptual borderline of what counts as enforcement.

Whether subpoenas count as an enforcement measure depends in part on the bureaucratic and procedural context in which they are issued. The matter comes down to a question of which arm of government, in practice, retains control over whether to enforce the subpoena. If the prosecutor retains discretion over enforcement, then the mere issuance of a subpoena is not properly conceived of as an enforcement measure; whereas if the court takes it upon itself to enforce subpoenas, then their issuance does count as enforcement.

The following case illustrates this distinction well. In my early days of pursuing 'victimless' prosecutions, there were many occasions on which victims who had been served with subpoenas failed to appear for trial. When this occurred, I would routinely request a continuance of the trial until the following month, so that my office might locate the victim and encourage her to testify at that time.[50] For the first couple months, the judge granted these motions to continue. However, the court's docket was quickly backlogged with old cases that had been continued from previous months being added to the ever-expanding number of new cases being filed. Under the former policies, the cases which had been continued would simply have been dismissed due to the victims' lack of cooperation; whilst under the revised policies, however, these cases were still being pursued. Not surprisingly, the day came when yet another request for continuance was made, but the court denied my motion. The case in question had already been continued from the previous month and, despite continuing efforts, we had been unable to convince the victim to testify. While I earnestly presented the prosecution's motion to continue, the judge perused the court file and noticed paperwork indicating that the victim had been served with a subpoena to testify. The court denied my motion to continue, declaring that the case would be resolved that day one way or another. Then, the judge directed a sheriff's deputy to locate the victim and bring her to the courtroom to testify. I must admit, I panicked: if the victim was not located until after the court adjourned for the day, she would be held in jail for the night to await trial, which would commence the next day. Even if she was located before the court adjourned, she would still be arrested by the deputy, treated like a criminal, perhaps even restrained or placed in handcuffs if she resisted. It was clear things had gone terribly wrong and I had to do something to stop the enforcement of the subpoena. Despite my strenuous objections to the court's enforcement of the subpoena, the deputy was directed to be on his way. As he began to walk from the courtroom, I caught his eye and motioned for him to wait while I admitted defeat: 'Your Honor, the People move to dismiss on condition that the victim subpoena not be enforced and no contempt proceedings be brought against her.'

---

[50] Trials in Champaign County were conducted in monthly one-week trial terms, so typically a request for a continuance meant that the case would be continued until the following month.

The judge, having achieved his goal of moving along a clogged docket, granted the motion. So in the end, there was no trial and the defendant went free—but at least the victim was not arrested.

This example illustrates the sense in which subpoenas can be transformed from a quasi-enforcement measure (when the prosecutors retain power to enforce them and never opt to do so), into a full-blown enforcement measure (when court exercise their power over non-complying victims). In the end, I struck an implicit deal with the judge before whom I prosecuted domestic-violence cases: I kept his docket from getting too clogged, and he never enforced another subpoena against a victim in one of my cases. It follows that my use of subpoenas might potentially have been justifiable, provided I had restricted their use to cases where the victim had a duty to testify. In the event, of course, I issued victim subpoenas indiscriminately and thus, enforcement measure or not, my use of victim subpoenas was overbroad and therefore unjustified.

The above arguments against enforcing domestic-violence victims' duties to testify against their batterers suggest that such measures are very likely to be unjustified in most cases and thus impermissible. However, the argument allows for the possibility that some enforcement measures may be justifiable in the right kinds of cases: specifically, in cases where the violence at issue is serious and on-going, where prosecution is likely to reduce the violence, where the violence constitutes domestic violence in its strong sense, where the prosecution is part of a habituated feminist response to domestic violence, and where (in addition to the foregoing) exceptionally strong community interests will be served by the victim's testimony.[51] In such cases, enforcement measures may be justifiable.

This approach to the question of whether it is appropriate to enforce a victim's duty to testify is notably distinct from approaches which claim that uniform enforcement measures against victims are justifiable in order 'to take the burden off the victim'.[52] Undoubtedly, in cases where the victim wants the prosecution to go forward but does not want the defendant or others to perceive her as supporting the prosecution, enforcement measures *do* take the burden off the victim. However, there is little reason to think that such cases (which I have previously referred to as 'performative withdrawal' cases) constitute all, or even a majority, of victim withdrawal cases on the whole.[53] In cases of sincere (ie, non-performative) victim withdrawal, enforcement measures do not take a burden off the victim but instead place a heavy burden on a victim who sincerely does not desire state intervention. Oftentimes, intervention in the form of continued prosecution is nonetheless justifiable and indeed can form part of an effective feminist prosecution strategy; but one should not kid oneself into thinking that enforcement measures directed against sincerely uncooperative victims are beneficial to those victims.

[51] For example, the defendant is not only a domestic batterer but also an extremely violent repeat offender who had killed or seriously injured in the past and is likely to do so in the future.

[52] C Hanna, 'No right to choose' (1996) 109 Harvard L Rev 1849, 1866.

[53] See Chapter 1, pp 17–20.

Following from this point, it is important to note that that even where enforcement measures are justified (and thus permissible), it does not follow that such
measures form part of an effective feminist domestic-violence prosecution strategy.[54] In order to form part of an effective feminist domestic-violence prosecution
strategy, the prosecutor's actions must serve the value of reconstituting the state
(and community) as less patriarchal (more feminist).[55] Insofar as enforcement
measures aimed at securing the victim's testimony enables the habituated targeting of domestic violence in its strong sense by prosecutors, these measures have
the potential to serve this value. However, pursuit of this value in this particular way (through enforcement directed at victims) is likely to be self-defeating;
since the use of enforcement measures directed against domestic-violence victims
itself has a strong tendency to sustain and perpetuate patriarchy.[56] Such measures tend to replicate, in the relationship between the victim and the state, the
very same patriarchal qualities which feminist prosecutorial action is meant to
oppose. Thus, enforcement measures directed against domestic-violence victims
are counterproductive to the feminist project envisaged here, because such measures are antithetical to the cultivation of a feminist character in the state and the
community more generally.

E. Conclusion

This chapter has set forth a conceptual analysis of the values that can be realized
by various responses to domestic violence, and has specified four kinds of reason
grounded in the realization of these values. Moreover, this chapter has outlined
four sorts of character trait which can be cultivated by habitually acting for those
reasons. With this analysis as grounding, the chapter proceeded to consider both
the rights and duties of domestic-violence victims with respect to participation
in the prosecution of their batterers. As to the question of whether domestic-
violence victims should be understood to have a moral right to participate in
prosecutions, a tripartite distinction was drawn between informative, advisory,
and authoritative participation. While informative and advisory participation
rights were accepted as non-controversial, the claim that victims have a right to
authoritative participation in criminal trials was rejected on grounds that such
participation would fundamentally alter the nature of criminal proceedings, ren-
dering them more akin to civil proceedings in which the victim (as opposed to

[54] On the distinction between justified and effective prosecutorial action, see Chapter 8.
[55] Ibid.
[56] Specifically, such measures have a tendency to sustain and perpetuate patriarchy insofar
as they are typically grounded in a misconception of women's attributes, needs or interests (sex
discrimination) or a failure to value women (sexism). It is not suggested that such measures are
typically grounded in misogyny. For an analysis of patriarchy as a structural inequality consisting
of social forms characterized by sex discrimination, sexism, and/or misogyny, see Chapter 7.

the community as a whole) directly calls the wrongdoer to account. Finally, this chapter considered whether victims should be thought to have a moral duty to participate in criminal prosecutions by testifying at trial against their batterers. An argument was advanced that victims may indeed have such a duty, at least in cases where their testimony will realize important values which serve substantial community interests, such as reducing serious violence, expressively denouncing and condemning patriarchy, reconstituting the state and community's character as less patriarchal (more feminist), etc, and where a duty to testify would not be defeated by other considerations, such as jeopardizing victim safety.

However, it was further argued that prosecutorial enforcement of this duty through legal mechanisms such as subpoena enforcement and contempt of court is unlikely ever to be justified, and even where justified, is self-defeating to the project of feminist prosecution defended in this book. This final point echoes the concerns expressed by Linda Mills in her critique of mandatory prosecution strategies in domestic-violence cases when she warns, '[f]eminist political practice—even in the name of gender warfare—should not mimic patriarchy through . . . the use of threat tactics . . . '.[57] Despite the general tenor of the arguments in this book running counter to the arguments set forth by Mills in her work on domestic violence generally, we have reached a point at which agreement may be found: prosecutorial enforcement measures taken against domestic-violence victims to secure their testimony has a tendency to sustain and perpetuate patriarchy, thereby defeating the project of feminist prosecutorial action more broadly. Thus, prosecutors cannot reconstitute their states (or communities) as more feminist if they habitually resort to using enforcement measures against victims.

[57] L Mills, 'Killing her softly: Intimate abuse and the violence of state intervention' (1999) 113 Harvard L Rev 550, 568.

10

Conclusion

In this chapter, I step back from the main arguments of the book and consider broader questions regarding prosecution and criminal law more generally. In the introductory chapter, I identified some of my personal and academic reasons for choosing to write a book on domestic-violence prosecution. At this point I wish to revisit my choice, in order to provide a more fully developed justification for spilling so much ink on this topic. I will approach this task first by attempting to justify my focus on prosecution as a response to domestic violence, as opposed to other forms of organized social response to domestic violence both outside and inside the criminal justice system. Second, I will address the critique that the criminal law is too blunt an instrument to address problems such as domestic violence adequately. Finally, I will consider whether reconstituting a society as less patriarchal through habituated feminist prosecutorial action is likely to result in a consequential backlash effect. In other words, I will address the substantial work that the phrase '*ceteris paribus*' has done in limiting the strength of my claims throughout the book, and consider the likelihood that all else will not remain equal.

A. Why Prosecution?

Prosecution is not the only way that a community can speak to the disvalue of patriarchy, so why have I been at pains to focus on prosecutorial action in this book rather than considering a wider ambit of possible responses to domestic violence? It is true, of course, that many (perhaps all) of the values I have identified can be realized through actions other than prosecutorial actions. A community could, for example, establish a non-criminal forum in which specific cases of alleged domestic violence were adjudicated, with no imposition of conviction or threat of punishment. The denunciation of patriarchy could instead take a more declaratory form, and this forum would provide a proper context for realizing the kinds of expressive and constitutive values I have discussed in this book. As a dense social form, patriarchy cannot be effectively denounced in generalities; rather, its effective denunciation requires that it be addressed in its particularities. Since a non-criminal community forum can address each instance of domestic violence on a case-by-case basis, it could therefore achieve the particularity required to effectively denounce patriarchy and thus avoid the problem of generality that would accompany other kinds of responses to patriarchy, such as passing a general legislative declaration which denounces patriarchy.

The question of what counts as patriarchy can only be answered by drawing (sometimes fine, not to mention contentious) distinctions in the fact patterns of numerous cases where patriarchy presents itself. Through the practice of drawing these distinctions in case after case, a picture of patriarchy develops—a picture akin to the narratives that are rich with layers of meaning and which, as noted by Raz, are a key source of knowledge regarding such matters.[1] As this picture of patriarchy develops, it shapes our understanding of its social forms—and the drawing of this picture creates a context for moral dialogue regarding the nature of these social forms, creating a space in which they can be laid bare and reconstituted. If the dialogue includes a process of denouncing the wrongness of patriarchy, then the process of reconstitution will *ceteris paribus* produce a progressively more valuable social form out of the old. Since a non-criminal community forum can in principle address each instance of domestic violence on a case-by-case basis, it could therefore achieve the disaggregation, and thus specificity, required to denounce patriarchy—and, therefore, serve many of the same functions currently served by criminal prosecutions.

This point suggests that I am not opposed in principle to non-criminal responses to domestic violence, such as community restorative justice programmes; and indeed I am not, provided that such responses draw the kinds of distinctions between domestic violence in its strong sense and domestic violence in its weak sense that enable actors in these systems to denounce patriarchy and habituate their denunciation directly on behalf of the community. This last clause is crucially important; for in order to be confident that these forums are capable of reconstituting the character of the community, I would want to ensure that their actions denounced and condemned patriarchy directly on behalf of *the community* itself, rather than merely *helping the victim* to engage in such denunciation and condemnation. This concern echoes my earlier discussions regarding the importance of distinguishing between reasons to do something yourself and reasons to help someone else do it.[2] In those discussions, I explained and defended the claim that it is *only* when the community calls the wrongdoer to account *directly to the community* that the community expresses its *own* denunciation of the wrongdoing. If a restorative justice forum simply provides a way for *victims* to hold offenders accountable to themselves (victims), rather than a way for the community itself to hold offenders accountable directly to the community, then such a forum risks being rendered incompetent to reconstitute the character of the community.

---

[1] J Raz, *The Morality of Freedom* (Oxford: OUP, 1986) 310–1, 350.
[2] See Chapter 5, section D and Chapter 9, section A.

These concerns justify (to some extent) my focus on the criminal justice system, but why pick out prosecution as my focus, as opposed to say, policing? It is true, of course, that a state (and community) can speak to the disvalue of patriarchy directly through policing actions, and these actions satisfy some of my concerns above. Certainly, for example, police officers' individual case-by-case responses to domestic violence satisfy the requirement of specificity discussed above, and the police can be understood as state (and community) actors in much the same way that prosecutors can. Yet, it is more questionable whether police actions taken in response to domestic-violence offences are the kinds of responses required to reconstitute a community as non-patriarchal (feminist). For, in order for actions to reconstitute a character as feminist, those actions must *oppose* patriarchy: they must denounce it, or condemn it, etc. It is not clear that police actions can count as these kinds of action, for it might be thought that the core function of the police is to maintain order and *investigate* alleged offences, *not* to denounce or to condemn.[3] If the police were called upon qua police to make decisions regarding accusation (ie, to denounce or refuse to denounce), then we might understand the police function as capable of reconstituting the character of the state as more or less feminist through their habituated responses in domestic-violence cases; but arguably the police are not called upon qua police to make such decisions. Therefore, although the police qua police might be engaged in habituated actions that speak to patriarchy in the proper way in terms of specificity and state/community representation, their actions may nonetheless be inadequate to the task of reconstituting the character of the community as feminist because their engagement with patriarchy is by and large evaluatively neutral.

Finally, why have I not focused on *judicial* action in domestic-violence cases as opposed to prosecutorial actions? Judicial action, like prosecutorial action, is case-specific and thus able to respond to the dense social form of patriarchy; and (perhaps to an even greater extent than prosecutorial action) we may conceive of judges acting as representatives not only of the state but also their communities.[4] Moreover, judicial action in response to domestic violence is capable of producing the kind of response to patriarchy (condemnatory) that is required to constitute a feminist character in opposition to patriarchy. It seems, therefore, that all of the values I have identified with respect to prosecutorial action are equally realizable in the context of judicial action.

---

[3] This account is consistent with the traditional model of police action as distinct from prosecutorial action, discussed in Chapter 3, text to n 28. Admittedly, this account may rest on an oversimplification which understands police charging decisions as instances of police acting qua prosecutors. The traditional account leaves unresolved the question of whether police arrest action constitutes denunciation rather than mere order-maintenance or investigation and I will not seek to resolve this issue here.

[4] In other words, the political legitimacy conditions outlined in Chapter 3, at the text to n 17, are perhaps more likely to be satisfied in the relationship between judge and community, than in the relationship between prosecutor and community.

But two points bear noting. First, prosecutorial actions speak to the disvalue of patriarchy in an importantly different way than do judicial actions: prosecutorial actions denounce, whilst judicial actions condemn. This distinction is crucial since, as noted earlier, denunciation kicks off a moral dialogue, whereas condemnation ends it.[5] Whilst both denunciation and condemnation are in principle the kinds of responses that are capable of reconstituting character in opposition to patriarchy, denunciation is the more effective of the two due to the nature of patriarchy as consisting of dense social forms. As compared to denunciation, condemnation is a blunt instrument.[6] Condemnation, particularly the type realized through the criminal justice system's process of conviction which places often disparate types of wrongdoing into the same category, fails to attend to the myriad of 'shared beliefs, folklore, high culture, collectively shared metaphors and imagination, and so on' embedded within the dense social forms which constitute the structural inequality of patriarchy.[7]

This point echoes my earlier reference to Dan Kahan's work on the problem of sticky norms, where I noted Kahan's claim that it is crucial to engage in a moral dialogue of denunciation with respect to some wrongs, rather than merely offering blanket condemnations. As Kahan explains it, the problem of sticky norms arise 'when the prevalence of a social norm makes decision-makers reluctant to carry out a law intended to change that norm'.[8] Kahan believes that by taking a softly-softly approach to changing these norms (what he calls 'gentle nudges') rather than a sledgehammer approach (which he labels 'hard shoves') we can better encourage law enforcement decision-makers to carry out laws intended to change these socially entrenched norms.[9] I do not wish to endorse Kahan's thesis as a whole. In particular, my sense of the matter with respect to domestic violence is that it has oftentimes been the law enforcement decision-makers themselves (eg, prosecutors) who have been most eager to engage in hard-shoving against norms that sustain and perpetuate patriarchy. My point in referencing Kahan's work is, rather, merely to highlight my agreement with his claim that blanket condemnations will often fail 'to make sticky norms come unstuck'.[10] Particularly when dealing with norms that reinforce dense social forms, unsticking such norms requires attention to the complex social meanings and symbols that constitute the social forms at issue. Thus, denunciation is a better tool than condemnation when it comes to accomplishing this task.

The second point that bears noting is that condemnatory judicial actions are only made possible because prosecutorial pursuit actions bring cases before the courts for conviction and sentencing. So, to some extent, the ability of judges to realize the values at stake in this book are dependent upon prosecutorial action. Of course,

---

[5] See Chapter 4, text preceding n 32.

[6] The blunt instrument critique will be considered further below.

[7] Raz (n 1 above) 311; see also discussion in Chapter 7.

[8] D Kahan, 'Gentle nudges vs Hard shoves: Solving the sticky norms problem' (2000) 67 U of Chicago L Rev 607, 607.

[9] Ibid.   [10] Ibid 608.

if judges engaged in conviction and sentencing without prosecutions, they could indeed speak to the disvalue of patriarchy in a manner that was similar in all important respects to the account I have provided of prosecutorial action. But in that case, the judge's action in *selecting* defendants for conviction and punishment can be understood as a form of prosecutorial action itself—albeit a form of prosecutorial action engaged in by the person we call judge (ie, judge acting qua prosecutor).[11]

Before leaving the comparison between prosecutorial action and judicial action, it is worth considering the characterization of judicial action as condemnation. Understanding judicial actions as a form of condemnation suggests an exclusive focus on judges in their post-conviction sentencing role. However, judges play an important role in the administration of criminal cases long before the question of sentencing arises. In their pre-conviction role, judicial actions are not condemnatory (nor for that matter denunciatory) but are instead normatively inert. When judges engage in actions such as setting court dockets or ruling on pre-trial motions, their actions qua judge are not condemnatory of the alleged wrongdoing before them. As such, these actions are not the kinds of response required to reconstitute the character of the state (and community) as feminist. It is not until the judge is called upon to sentence the defendant post-conviction that the judge qua judge properly engages in the kind of condemnatory response that can potentially reconstitute the character of the state (and community) in opposition to patriarchy. For example, consider the difference between a prosecutor's actions in assigning cases to a Domestic Violence Unit, as compared to a judge's actions in assigning a case to a Domestic Violence courtroom. The prosecutor's action is best understood as at least partially denunciatory: a way of taking these cases more seriously, treating them more aggressively, or at least recognizing them as involving distinct type of wrongdoing. In comparison, the judge's actions are not best understood in this way. It is not for the judge, at that stage, to take a normative position vis-à-vis any aspect of the case—thus her decision (if it is indeed hers) to assign the case to the Domestic Violence Court should be based on considerations of administrative efficiency rather than on considerations regarding a perceived need to take those case more seriously, treat them more aggressively, or even recognize them as involving a distinct type of wrongdoing.

B. Criminal Law: A Blunt Instrument?

My argument in this book may be thought to reflect naïve optimism in the role that the criminal justice system can and should play in creating a just society. It is, of course, an oft-heard claim in arguing against such optimism that the

---

[11] For example, the cartoon character Judge Joe Dredd can be understood to function in a variety of roles, only some of which are properly understood as providing a context for judicial action. Whilst police investigate and judges adjudicate, prosecutors move a case from one stage to the other (or decline to move the case from one stage to the other). Without prosecutors (or someone functioning in a prosecutorial role, call him or her what you will), there can be no judicial action.

criminal justice system is a 'blunt instrument'.[12] In one sense this observation is surely true, but only trivially so. After all, the criminal justice system is a legal system—that is, a rule-based system[13]—and it is in the nature of rules to apply generally across more than one situation. However, it should be noted that this point is consistent with Carole Smart's sceptical observation that 'law is not *simply* "a set of tools or rules that we can bend into a more favourable shape"',[14] for as Celia Wells has noted, the law 'sits in a framework that . . . is sustained by webs of practices and beliefs that perpetuate micro cultures'.[15] So, of course, the criminal justice system is not simply a rules-in-the-books system, but is simultaneously a rules-in-action system.[16] In both senses then, when dealing in rules, one is necessarily dealing with somewhat blunt instruments: instruments that by their very nature smooth over distinctions by generalizing across similar cases.

However, if the rules are well designed and well implemented, this smoothing-over process will not obscure too many rationally salient distinctions—although inevitably it may obscure some, and that might just be the price we pay for dealing in rules. If dealing in rules helps us better to comply with the reasons that apply to us than we would do if we were left to our own devices, then we are better off dealing in rules.[17] Everyone except for philosophical anarchists will concede that well-designed and well-applied rules *can* provide this service,[18] and all but those who are slavishly authority-abiding will recognize that many times rules *fail* to provide this service. So whilst the criminal justice system is a blunt instrument in this sense, this version of the critique hardly packs much of a punch unless one is prepared to abandon rule-following altogether.

It seems then that the 'blunt instrument' critique of the criminal justice system must be meant to communicate something more than a mere anarchistic scepticism about the ability of rules to justifiably guide our conduct. Indeed, a far more successful use of the 'blunt instrument' critique is made by those who concede that the criminal justice system may be well suited to guiding our behaviour in some areas where rationally salient differences are few and far between. As the

---

[12] C Stokinger, 'Symposium: Women, children and domestic violence: Current tensions and emerging issues' (2000) 27 Fordham Urban LJ 565, 663; D Coker, 'Enhancing autonomy for battered women: Lessons from Navajo peacemaking' (1999) 47 UCLA L Rev 1, 57 58; L Mills, 'On the other side of silence: Affective lawyering for intimate abuse' (1996) 81 Cornell L Rev 1225, 1262.

[13] HLA Hart, *The Concept of Law* (2nd edn, Oxford: Clarendon, 1997); J Raz, *The Concept of a Legal System* (Oxford: Clarendon, 1970).

[14] C Smart, *Law, Crime and Sexuality* (London: Sage, 1995) 129, cited in C Wells, 'The impact of feminist thinking on criminal law and justice: Contradiction, complexity, conviction and connection' [2004] Crim L Rev 503, 508.

[15] Wells (n 14 above) 508. My point here is similar to Wells', except that I wish to emphasize the way in which these webs of practices and belief perpetuate *character traits* rather than what Wells refers to as 'micro cultures'.

[16] On the distinction between law-in-the-books and law-in-action, see R Pound, 'Law in books and law in action' (1910) 44 American L Rev 12.

[17] J Raz, *Ethics in the Public Domain* (Oxford: OUP, 1994) 214.

[18] R Wolff, *In Defence of Anarchism* (New York: Harper & Row, 1970).

sceptical argument regarding the issue at hand here goes, domestic violence is simply not one of those areas: it is too fully packed with rationally salient distinctions to be an appropriate object of the law's ruliness. These sceptics would willingly concede, for example, that the criminal justice system has a legitimate role to play in responding to parking violations and traffic offences, because there is little chance of obscuring rationally salient differences between such cases when smoothing over the distinctions between them through the application of rules. But in cases of domestic violence, they contend, the application of the criminal law is bound to obscure rationally salient differences during the smoothing-over process, because these cases are so intricately fine-grained that it is virtually impossible to design and implement a set of rules that will properly address all of their rationally salient features.

Phrased this way, the 'blunt instrument' critique is not an indictment of rule-governed systems in general or even of the criminal justice system generally, but is instead a critique grounded in the particularly nuanced, complex structure of the wrongdoing at issue in cases of domestic violence.[19] This second version of the 'blunt instrument' critique is compelling. The structure of wrongdoing in domestic-violence cases is, admittedly, complex. Indeed, it was due to this complexity that I was moved to write Chapters 6 and 7 of this book—and even those chapters required a significant deal of glossing over of salient distinctions.[20]

In most instances of domestic violence there are a myriad of intricately woven, rationally salient considerations that ought not to be ignored by anyone hoping to address these cases adequately. Surely, anyone concerned to apply to these cases the kind of rule-based guidance provided by the criminal justice system should remain alive to the possibility that they have misapprehended the nature and quality of the wrongdoing at issue in any given case. For example, a prosecutor must be open to the possibility that she has mistaken a case of domestic violence in its strong sense for domestic violence in its weak sense, or vice versa. Further, one must remain alive to the possibility that she has misjudged the justifiability and/or effectiveness of the chosen prosecutorial action in any given case by, for example, being willing to reconsider the scope, nature, and likelihood of the various values and disvalues that may be realized in virtue of her actions. There's no denying it, prosecuting domestic violence justifiably and effectively is a tall order—and prosecutors are bound to make mistakes that will have real costs, both in theoretical terms of prosecutorial effectiveness and in material terms of peoples' safety, liberty, and well-being. So, there is plenty reason to be wary of how we use the tool of domestic-violence prosecution, and we should proceed with caution.

---

[19] Similar critiques have been offered against the criminal justice system's response to rape cases. See N Lacey, 'Unspeakable subjects, impossible rights: Sexuality, integrity and criminal law' (1998) 11 Canadian J of L and Jurisprudence 47.

[20] For example, I said almost nothing about child abuse as a form of domestic violence nor about same-sex domestic violence.

But not surprisingly perhaps, I think it would be a mistake to allow this healthy dose of caution to paralyse prosecutorial actions in domestic-violence cases. Yes, the criminal justice system is a blunt instrument, but the natural tendency of rules to obscure rationally salient distinctions can be mitigated, even in complex cases like domestic violence, through the exercise of fine-grained prosecutorial discretion in accordance with feminist practical reason. After all, domestic-violence prosecutors are frequently called upon to exercise their discretion in making the very sorts of fine-grained decisions which ameliorate the obscuring effects of rule-governed systems. If they exercise their discretion in accordance with feminist practical reason, they will meet the principal concerns raised by the second, more plausible 'blunt instrument' critique. The upshot of all of this is that we do not need to abandon criminal prosecution as a potentially valuable and effective response to domestic violence: rather, we simply need more feminist prosecutors making the types of fine-grained decisions that will enable us to 'cash the cheques written by the state's progressive feminist policies'.[21]

C. *Ceteris Paribus?*

A central claim of this book is that if we lived in a feminist society, the meaning and nature of domestic violence would radically change. Admittedly, we should not expect a post-patriarchal world to be a wholly non-violent utopia: violence would likely still occur. Indeed, something understood as 'the domestic sphere' would likely survive as well, so there is at least some reason to believe that domestic violence in its weak sense would still exist in a post-patriarchal world. However, one thing would certainly be different: patriarchy would have ended—and thus the very concept of domestic violence in its strong sense could no longer exist, for such domestic violence cannot exist in a society without patriarchy.[22] Throughout this book, my claims regarding the ability of prosecutorial action to reconstitute the character of the state (and community) as feminist have been carefully limited by the phrase *ceteris paribus* (all things remaining equal). It is now time to own up to the likelihood that all things will *not* remain equal. Below, I consider both how seemingly successful individual cases can have disastrous consequences, and the possibility that the broader project of feminist prosecution may spark a backlash effect.

---

[21] G Brodsky and S Day, 'Women's human rights in an era of conservatism: Stories from Canada' Conference speech at Encountering Human Rights: Gender/Sexuality, Activism and the Promise of Law, University of Kent Law School, 5 January 2007.

[22] This point is a conceptual one, of the sort not directly amenable to scientific empirical testing.

1. How good cases go bad

Feminist prosecution of domestic violence can, of course, have many different sorts of consequences: some valuable, some disvaluable. Indeed, even a single case can realize both consequential value and disvalue. The case of *People v. Williams*, introduced in Chapter 1, illustrates this point well. As previously mentioned, the prosecution of David Williams was the first 'victimless' prosecution case brought to trial in Champaign County following the creation of a specialized domestic-violence prosecution unit and introduction of pro-prosecution policies. The victim, Linda Williams, first cooperated with the investigation, but she then requested dismissal and refused to appear at trial. Finally she did appear at trial, but when she took the witness stand, she recanted her prior statements and pleaded with the jury not to convict. Nonetheless, after a short deliberation, the jury convicted David Williams on all counts.

In the hour immediately following announcement of the jury's verdict, the prosecution in *People v. Williams* realized both considerable consequential value and, unfortunately, quite considerable consequential disvalue as well. One important consequential value realized by this prosecution occurred during the lunch break following announcement of the jury's verdict. After being convicted, David Williams was taken back to the jail to eat lunch along with the other inmates awaiting trial that day. As it happened, he ate his lunch seated next to James Darcy, another defendant awaiting trial on domestic battery charges. As overheard by a sheriff's deputy assigned to guard the inmates, Williams asked Darcy what he was in for, and Darcy explained that he was about to go on trial for battery against his girlfriend. Williams wished Darcy good luck in his trial and explained that he had just been convicted for battery against his wife. Darcy laughed in response to Williams' bad fortune and confidently explained that his trial would not turn out the same way. 'There's no way I'm gonna get convicted...My girl's testifying *for* me—she's gonna tell everyone I didn't do a thing.' Williams laughed as he explained to the confident Darcy, 'Ya, well, my wife just did that for me—and I got convicted on both counts!' When court reconvened immediately following the lunch break, Darcy plead guilty.

While all of this was occurring, however, different and more troubling events were unfolding in the parking lot outside the courthouse. It would not be an exaggeration to say that Linda Williams was unhappy with the jury's verdict. She was furious with me personally, the victim-witness liaison with whom I worked on the case, every member of the State's Attorney's Office, the judge who presided over her husband's trial, and more important to what follows, each member of the jury who convicted him. Linda focused her anger on one juror in particular, a young woman roughly about her age, whom Linda had apparently expected would sympathize with her plight and thus vote for acquittal. Following announcement of the jury's verdict, a distraught Linda followed this juror out to her car and accosted her. Linda yelled at the juror and demanded to know how she could have voted to convict David. As the juror tried to make her way past Linda to her car, Linda continued to follow her, yelling threateningly and blocking her way. A bailiff who observed these events took Linda into custody, and she was later charged with juror intimidation. Upon being convicted for this offence, Linda was sentenced to three years in prison.[23] Her young children were now left with neither parent to care for them, while both she and her husband David served their prison sentences arising from this case.[24]

As the Williams case aptly demonstrates, it is impossible to predict all of the positive and negative consequences which will flow from any given prosecutorial action. Such anecdotes do not, of course, justify the conclusion that prosecutorial action should not be taken in cases of victim withdrawal. Indeed, if the analysis of prosecutorial action set forth in Chapter 3 is plausible, then the decision to dismiss such cases is itself best understood as a form of prosecutorial action: namely, prosecutorial non-pursuit action. Non-pursuit action, just as pursuit action, comes with its own set of risks, and there is little reason to suppose that routine non-pursuit of such cases will have greater consequential value than prosecutorial pursuit actions will have. Certainly prosecutors should attempt to limit the risk of negative consequences arising from 'victimless' prosecutions,[25] but the risk of such consequences should not dissuade prosecutors from bringing these cases to trial.

2. The risk of backlash

In addition to the possibility that any individual case will have negative consequences, there exists a risk that feminist prosecutions will spark a more general backlash in society. The difficulty with such a backlash is that it may, on the whole, cause others to change their behaviour in ways that make the state (and community) *more* violent and *more* patriarchal. At present, patriarchy informs many societies' most cherished social forms, such as family structures and patterns of heterosexual intimacy. Prosecutorial action that concertedly opposes patriarchy will, of course, threaten the continued existence of these social forms as they currently exist. As many people derive much of their lives' meaning from their participation in these forms, they have reason to be wary of, if not adamantly opposed to, feminist prosecutorial actions. Thus, members of the community may come to resent feminist prosecutorial actions, which they perceive

---

[23] Linda's long sentence was due in part to the fact that she had previous felony convictions.

[24] To be clear, David's prison sentence was not directly due to his conviction in this case, but rather was due to the fact that his conviction in this case led to his parole being revoked in an unrelated felony case.

[25] Following the Williams' trial, for example, we instituted a policy of having court bailiffs accompany jurors safely to their cars in cases where the victim was likely to be upset with the jury's verdict. Fortunately, this procedure eliminated any further cases of jury intimidation by enraged victims.

as a threat to their way of life, and this resentment may further entrench the patriarchal character of the society. It follows from these observations that much, perhaps all, of what I have offered in terms of conceptual analysis and normative argument in this book is subject to being irrelevant if too much else was to remain unequal. So, in that sense, I make no apologies for my frequent use of the phrase '*ceteris paribus*', but at the same time, I recognize the profound extent of the limitations which frame what I have claimed here.

A somewhat more satisfying response to these concerns may be found in an analogy with the issue of multiculturalism. Perhaps patriarchy, which exists within one's own state or community, should be approached as one should approach different social forms arising in other cultures. Generally, the fact that people in a given society derive meaning from their participation in particular social forms means that the social forms at issue are entitled to tolerance. This point reflects the basic tenet of political liberalism that we should not seek to change a people's way of life simply because it is different from ours. Tolerance, however, even within a liberal framework, has its limits. Some social forms existing in other cultures should *not* be tolerated. As Raz observes, social forms which 'systematically frustrate the ability of people, or groups of people, to fulfil or give expression to an important aspect of their nature' are not entitled to tolerance, even by a liberal polity.[26] Indeed, in serious enough cases, the tendency of these social forms to oppress people within the society may justify their suppression.[27]

Thus, despite the fact that some people may derive significant meaning from their participation in patriarchal social forms, that fact alone does not mean that patriarchy should be tolerated. This much follows from Raz's observations regarding multiculturalism. What Raz fails to address in his discussion, however, is how we to respond if the attempt to dismantle oppressive social forms backfires. Presumably, we should not allow a temporary backlash to forestall our continued efforts; for since we cannot predict the future, the possibility exists that any given experience of backlash is merely temporary and will eventually be surpassed by a transformation in the society which will enable all members to lead valuable lives. It follows then that irrespective of whether feminist prosecutorial action generates a backlash of consequential violence or increased patriarchy, and irrespective of whether dismantling patriarchy jeopardizes existing social forms in which individuals currently find meaning and identity in their lives, patriarchy is still worth fighting.

D. Conclusion

This book has presented one vision of how patriarchy might be fought through feminist prosecutions. In sum, it has presented a picture of how feminist prosecutions

---

[26] Raz (n 17 above) 185.   [27] Ibid.

can contribute to the project of reconstituting our states and communities as less patriarchal. It has argued that the effective prosecution of domestic violence consists in a particular kind of prosecution: one that contributes to the project of reconstituting our society as non-patriarchal, thereby creating a world in which domestic violence in its strong sense no longer exists. It is hoped that this book has presented a plausible (albeit partial) account of how prosecutorial action can assist in the realization of these goals; how feminst prosecutions can move us a few steps closer, to paraphrase Catharine MacKinnon, toward a feminist state.[28] The moral of the story, if there is one, is that we need not reject criminal prosecution as a viable feminist project in the fight against domestic violence and patriarchy more generally. Rather, I hope this book has provided reason to believe that feminist engagement with the criminal justice system is a potentially valuable path to the creation of a more feminist state, a more feminist community, and the end of domestic violence as we know it.

[28] CA MacKinnon, *Toward a Feminist Theory of the State* (Cambridge, Harvard University Press 1989).

Bibliography

BOOKS AND ARTICLES

Acorn, A, 'Surviving the battered reader's syndrome, or: A critique of Linda G Mills' *Insult to Injury: Rethinking Our Responses to Intimate Abuse*' (2005) 13 UCLA Women's LJ 335.

Adams, C, 'Deterring domestic violence: Prospects for heightened success in the "victimless" prosecution of domestic violence cases' (2000) 11 J of Contemporary Legal Issues 51.

Alcoff, LM, 'Racism' in A Jaggar and IM Young (eds), *A Companion to Feminist Philosophy* (Oxford: Blackwell, 2000).

Alexander, L, 'What we do and why we do it' (1993) 45 Stanford L Rev 1885.

Alfieri, A, 'Prosecuting race' (1999) 48 Duke LJ 1157.

—— 'Prosecuting violence/reconstructing community' (2000) 52 Stanford L Rev 809.

—— 'Retrying race' (2003) 101 Michigan L Rev 1141.

—— 'Color/identity/justice: Chicano trials' (2005) 53 Duke LJ 1569.

Arendt, H, *On Violence* (London: Allen Lane, 1970).

—— 'Collective responsibility' in J Bernhauer (ed), *Amor Mundi: Explorations in the faith and thought of Hannah Arendt* (Boston: Lancaster, 1987).

Ashworth, A, 'Punishment and compensation' (1986) 6 OJLS 86.

—— *Principles of Criminal Law* (Oxford: OUP, 2005).

—— and M Redmayne, *The Criminal Process: An evaluative study* (3rd edn, Oxford: OUP, 2005).

Asmus, M, Ritmeester, T, and Pence, E, 'Prosecuting domestic abuse cases in Duluth: Developing effective prosecution strategies from understanding the dynamics of abusive relationships' (1991) 15 Hamline L Rev 115.

Audi, R, *The Good in the Right* (Oxford: Princeton University Press, 2004).

Austin, J, *The Province of Jurisprudence Determined* (Indianapolis: Hackett, 1832, reprint 1998).

Austin, JL, *How to Do Things with Words* (Oxford: OUP, 1962).

Baldwin, J, 'Understanding judge ordered and directed acquittals in the Crown Court' [1997] Crim LR 536.

Bandes, S, 'Empathy, narrative, and victim impact statements' (1996) 63 University of Chicago L Rev 361.

Baron, M, 'On the alleged repugnance of acting from duty' (1984) 81 J of Philosophy 197.

—— 'On admirable immorality' [1986] Ethics 558.

—— 'Justifications and excuses' (2005) 2 Ohio State J of Crim L 387.

Bartlett, K, 'Feminist legal methods' (1990) 103 Harvard L Rev 829.

Bartowski, J, 'Debating patriarchy: Discursive disputes over spousal authority among evangelical family commentators' (1997) 36 J for the Scientific Study of Religion 393.

Beloof, DE, 'The third model of criminal process: The victim participation model' [1999] Utah L Rev 289.

Bentham, J, *An Introduction to the Principles of Morals and Legislation* (New York: Prometheus Books, 1781, reprint 1988).

Bergan, RK, *Issues in Intimate Violence* (Thousand Oaks, CA: Sage, 1998).

Berk, R, 'Mutual combat and other family violence myths' in D Finkelhor and others (eds), *The Dark Side of Families: Current family violence research* (Beverley Hills, CA: Sage, 1983).

Bird, R, *Domestic Violence: Law and practice* (5th edn, Briston: Jordan, 2006).

Bix, B, 'Conceptual questions and jurisprudence' (1995) 1 Legal Theory 465.

Blake, M, and Ashworth, A, 'Some ethical issues in prosecuting and defending criminal cases' [1998] Crim LR 16.

Boyd, S, *Challenging the Public/Private Divide: Feminism, law and public policy* (Buffalo: University of Toronto Press, 1997).

Braithwaite, J, *Markets in Vice, Markets in Virtue* (New York: OUP, 2005).

—— *Restorative Justice and Responsive Regulation* (New York: OUP, 2005).

Broadie, S, and Rowe, C, (trans), *Aristotle's Nichomachean Ethics* (Oxford: OUP, 2002).

Brownlee, ID, 'The statutory charging scheme in England and Wales: Towards a unified prosecution system' [2004] Crim LR 896.

Brownlie, I, *Principles of Public International Law* (5th edn, Oxford: OUP, 1988).

Buel S, 'Obstacles to leaving, aka, why abuse victims stay' [1999] Colorado Lawyer 19.

Buzawa, E, and Buzawa, C, *Domestic Violence: The criminal justice response* (Newbury Park: Sage, 1990).

Canary, D, and Emmers-Sommer, TM, *Sex and Gender Differences in Personal Relationships* (Guildford Press, 1997).

Case, MA, 'Reflections on constitutionalizing women's equality' (2002) 90 California L Rev 765.

Cassell, PG, 'Treating crime victims fairly: Integrating victims into the federal rules of criminal procedure' [2007]) Utah L Rev 861.

Cassidy, M, 'Character and context: What virtue theory can teach us about a prosecutor's ethical duty to "seek justice" ' (2006) 82 Notre Dame LR 635.

Chang, R (ed), *Incommensurability, Incomparability, and Practical Reason* (London: Harvard University Press, 1997).

Choongh, S, *Policing as Social Discipline* (Oxford: Claredon, 1997).

Choudhry, S, and Herring, J, 'Righting domestic violence' (2006) 20 Intl J of Law and the Family 95.

Christie, N, 'Conflicts as property' (1977) 17 British J of Criminology 1.

Clark, NL, 'Crime begins at home: Let's stop punishing victims and perpetuating violence' (1987) 28 William and Mary L Rev 263.

Clark, P, 'Hybridity, holism and traditional justice: The case of the Gacaca courts in post-genocide Rwanda' (2007) 39 George Washington International L Rev 765.

Clark, S, ' "Who do you think you are?" The criminal trial and community character' in RA Duff and others (eds), *The Trial on Trial, volume 2: Judgment and calling to account* (Oxford: Hart, 2006).

Coady, CAJ, 'The idea of violence' (1986) 3 J of Applied Philosophy 3.

Coker, D, 'Enhancing autonomy for battered women: Lessons from Navajo peacemaking' (1999) 47 UCLA L Rev 1.

Coker, D, 'Crime control and feminist law reform in domestic violence law: A critical review' (2001) 4 Buffalo Crim L Rev 801.

—— 'Race, poverty, and the crime-centered response to domestic violence' (2004) 10 Violence Against Women 1331.

Crenshaw, K, 'Demarginalizing the intersection of race and sex: A black feminist critique of antidiscrimination doctrine, feminist theory, and antiracist politics' [1989] U of Chicago Legal Forum 139.

—— 'Mapping the margins: Intersectionality, identity politics, and violence against women of color' (1991) 43 Stanford L Rev 1241.

Cretney, A, and Davis, G, 'Prosecuting domestic assault' [1996] Crim LR 162.

—— and others, 'Criminalizing assault: The failure of the offence against society model' (1994) 34 British J of Criminology 15.

Crispin, K, 'Prosecutorial ethics' in S Parker and C Stamford (eds), *Legal Ethics and Legal Practice: Contemporary issues* (Oxford: Clarendon, 1995).

Cruz, JM, '"Why doesn't he just leave?" Gay male domestic violence and the reasons victims stay' (2003) 11 J Men's Studies 309.

Currie, D, 'Violent men or violent women: Whose definition counts?' in RK Bergan (ed), *Issues in Intimate Violence* (Thousand Oaks: Sage, 1998).

Das Gupta, S, 'Just like men? A critical view of violence by women' in M Shepard and E Pence (eds), *Coordinating Community Responses to Domestic Violence* (Thousand Oaks: Sage, 1999).

Davis, K, *Discretionary Justice: A preliminary inquiry* (Baton Rouge: Louisiana State University, 1969).

de Beauvoir, S, and Parshley, HM (trans), *The Second Sex* (New York: Alfred Knoff, 1953).

Dekeseredy, W, '(Review) *Insult to Injury: Rethinking our responses to intimate abuse* by Linda G Mills' (2004) 44 British J of Criminology 621.

—— and Schwartz, M, 'Measuring the extent of woman abuse in intimate heterosexual relationships: A critique of the conflict tactics scales' (February 1998) National Resource Center on Domestic Violence <http://www.vawnet.org/ DomesticViolence/ Research/VAWnetDocs/AR_ctscrit.pdf> accessed 3 November 2008.

Delgado, R, and Stefancic, J, 'Why do we tell the same stories? Law reform, critical librarianship and the triple helix dilemma' (1989) 42 Stanford L Rev 207.

Dempsey, MM, 'What counts as domestic violence? A conceptual analysis' (2006) 12 William and Mary J of Women and the Law 301.

—— 'Toward a feminist state: What does "effective" prosecution of domestic violence mean?' (2007) 70 MLR 908.

—— *Prosecution, Reason and Value: Considering domestic violence* (DPhil thesis, University of Oxford, 2007).

—— and Herring, J, 'Why sexual penetration requires justification' (2007) 27 OJLS 467.

—— 'Sharing reasons for criminalization? No thanks . . . already got 'em!' in P Robinson, K Ferzan, and S Garvey (eds) *Criminal Law Conversations* (OUP, forthcoming).

Dickson, J, *Evaluation and Legal Theory* (Oxford: Hart, 2001).

—— 'Interpretation and coherence in legal reasoning' (2005) Stanford Encyclopedia of Philosophy <http://plato.stanford.edu/entries/legal-reas-interpret/> accessed 26 August 2008.

Dobash, RE, and Dobash, R, *Violence Against Wives: A case against the patriarchy* (New York: Free Press, 1979).

—— and —— 'Community response to violence against wives: Charivari, abstract justice and patriarchy' (1981) 28 Social Problems 563.

—— and —— 'The context-specific approach' in R Finkelhor, R Gelles, and G Hotaling (eds), *The Dark Side of Families: Current family violence research* (Beverly Hills: Sage, 1983).

—— and —— 'The nature and antecedents of violent events' (1984) 24 British J of Criminology 269.

—— and —— 'The response of the British and American women's movements to violence against women' in J Hanmer and M Maynard (eds), *Women, Violence and Social Control* (London: MacMillan, 1987).

—— and —— *Women, Violence and Social Change* (London: Routledge, 1992).

—— and —— *Rethinking Violence Against Women* (Thousand Oaks: Sage, 1998).

—— and —— 'Separate and intersecting realities: A comparison of men's and women's accounts of violence against women' (1998) 4 Violence Against Women 382.

—— and —— 'Women's violence to men in intimate relationships: Working on a puzzle' (2004) 44 British J of Criminology 324.

Dressler, J, 'New thoughts about the concept of justification in the criminal law: A critique of Fletcher's thinking and rethinking' (1984) 32 UCLA L Rev 61.

Dubber, MD, *Victims in the War on Crime: The use and abuse of victims' rights* (New York: New York University Press, 2002).

—— ' "The power to govern men and things": Patriarchal origins of the police power in American law' (2004) 52 Buffalo L Rev 1277.

—— 'The criminal trial and the legitimation of punishment' in RA Duff and others (eds), *The Trial on Trial, vol 1: Truth and due process* (Oxford: Hart, 2005).

Duff, RA, *Trials and Punishment* (Cambridge: Cambridge University Press, 1986).

—— 'Choice, character, and criminal liability' (1993) 12 Law and Philosophy 345.

—— 'Penal communications: Recent work in the philosophy of punishment' (1996) 20 Crime and Justice 1.

—— *Punishment, Communication and Community* (Oxford: OUP, 2001).

—— and Marshall, S, 'Communicative punishment and the role of the victim' (2004) 23 Criminal Justice Ethics 39.

—— 'Who is responsible? For what? To whom?' (2005) 2 Ohio State J of Crim Law 441.

—— and others (eds), *The Trial on Trial, vol 1: Truth and due process* (Oxford: Hart, 2005).

—— and others (eds), *The Trial on Trial, vol 2: Judgment and calling to account* (Oxford: Hart, 2006).

—— 'Criminal responsibility: Municipal and international' (draft) Presented at the Oxford Jurisprudence Discussion Group (4 May 2006).

—— and others, *The Trial on Trial, vol 3: Towards a normative theory of the criminal law* (Oxford: Hart, 2007).

Dworkin, A, *Woman Hating* (New York: Plume, 1974).

—— *Letters from a War Zone* (Chicago: Lawrence Hill Books, 1993).

Dworkin, R, *Taking Rights Seriously* (London: Duckworth, 1978).

—— *Law's Empire* (London: Fontana, 1986; reprint Oxford: Hart, 1998).

Editors, 'New state and federal responses to domestic violence' (1993) 106 Harvard L Rev 1528.

Edmundson, WA, *An Introduction to Rights* (Cambridge: Cambridge University Press, 2004).

Edwards, S, *Policing 'domestic' violence: Women, the law and the state* (London: Sage, 1989).

Edwards, S, and Halpern, A, 'Protection for the victim of domestic violence: Time for a radical revision?' [1991] J of Social Welfare and Family Law 94.

Ehrenreich, N, 'Subordination and symbiosis: Mechanisms of mutual support between subordinating systems' (2002) 71 U of Missouri Kansas-City L Rev 251.

Elliot, FR, *Gender, Family & Society* (London: MacMillan, 1996).

Ellison, L, 'Prosecuting domestic violence without victim participation' (2003) 65 MLR 834.

—— 'Responding to victim withdrawal in domestic violence prosecutions' (2003) Crim LR 760.

Epstein, D, 'Effective intervention in domestic violence cases: Rethinking the roles of prosecutors, judges and the court system' (1999) 11 Yale J of L and Feminism 3.

Epstein, D, Bell, ME, and Goodman, LA, 'Transforming aggressive prosecution policies: Prioritizing victims' long-term safety in the prosecution of domestic violence cases symposium: Confronting domestic violence and achieving gender equality: Evaluating battered women and feminist lawmaking' (2003) 11 American Univ J of Gender, Social Policy and the Law 465.

Faragher, T, 'The police response to violence against women in the home' in J Pahl (ed), *Private Violence and Public Policy* (London: Routledge, 1985).

Farber, D, and Sherry, S, *Beyond All Reason: The radical assault on truth in American law* (Oxford: OUP, 1997).

Farmer, P, 'On suffering and structural violence: A view from below' (1996) 125 Daedalus 261.

Feeley, MM, *The Process is the Punishment* (New York: Russell Sage, 1979).

Feinberg, J, 'The expressive function of punishment' in *Doing and Deserving: Essays in the Theory of Responsibility* (Princeton: Princeton University Press, 1970).

—— *Harm to Self* (Oxford: OUP, 1984).

Filmer, R, *Patriarcha: Or, the natural power of kings* (London: Chiswell, 1680).

Finkelstein, C, 'Excuses and dispositions in criminal law' (2002) 6 Buffalo Crim L Rev 317.

Finn, M, and others, 'Dual arrest decisions in domestic violence cases: The influence of departmental policies' (2004) 50 Crime and Delinquency 565.

Finnis, J, *Natural Law and Natural Rights* (Oxford: Clarendon, 1980).

—— *Fundamentals of Ethics* (Oxford: Clarendon, 1983).

—— 'Natural law theories' (2007) Stanford Encyclopedia of Philosophy <http://plato.stanford.edu/entries/natural-law-theories/#HumPerNotLawCreButProPoi> accessed 26 August 2008.

Firestone, S, *The Dialectic of Sex* (New York: Morrow, 1970).

Fisher, S, 'In search of the virtuous prosecutor: A conceptual framework' (1988) 15 American J Crim Law 197.

Fletcher, G, *Rethinking Criminal Law* (Boston: Little Brown, 1978).

Fletcher, G, 'Domination in Domination in wrongdoing' (1996) 76 Boston University L Rev 347.

—— 'The place of victims in the theory of retribution' (1999) 3 Buffalo Crim L Rev 51.

Fleury, R, Sullivan, C, and Bybee, D, 'When ending the relationship does not end the violence: Women's experiences of violence by former partners' (2000) 6 Violence Against Women 1363.

Ford, D, 'Prosecution as a victim resource: A note on empowering women in violent conjugal relationships' (1991) 25 Law and Society Rev 313.

—— and Regoli, MJ, 'The preventive impact of policies for prosecuting wife batterers' in E Buzawa and C Buzawa (eds), *Domestic Violence: The criminal justice response* (Thousand Oaks: Sage, 1996).

Fredman, S, *Discrimination Law* (Oxford: Clarendon, 2002).

Frye, M, *The Politics of Reality* (Trumansburg, NY: Crossing Press, 1983).

Gallagher, V, *The True Cost of Low Prices: The violence of globalization* (Maryknoll: Orbis, 2006).

Galligan, D, *Discretionary Powers: A legal study of official discretion* (Oxford: Clarendon, 1986).

Galtung, J, 'Violence, peace and peace research' (1969) 6 J of Peace Research 167.

Gardner, J, 'Justification and reasons' in A Simester and A Smith (eds), *Harm and Culpability* (Oxford: Clarendon, 1996).

—— 'Crime: In proportion and perspective' in A Ashworth and M Wasik (eds), *Fundamentals of Sentencing Theory: Essays in honour of Andrew von Hirsch* (Oxford: Clarendon, 1998).

—— 'On the general part of criminal law' in RA Duff (ed), *Philosophy and the Criminal Law: Principle and critique* (Cambridge: Cambridge University Press, 1998).

—— 'The virtue of justice and the character of law' [2001] Current Legal Problems 1.

—— 'The mark of responsibility' (2003) 23 OJLS 157.

—— 'The wrongdoing that gets results' (2004) 18 Philosophical Perspectives 53.

—— 'Law's aim in law's empire' in S Hershovitz (ed), *Exploring Law's Empire* (Oxford: OUP, 2006).

—— and Macklem, T, 'Reasons' in J Coleman and S Shapiro (eds), *The Oxford Handbook of Jurisprudence and Philosophy of Law* (Oxford: OUP, 2002).

Garner, J, 'Evaluating the effectiveness of mandatory arrest for domestic violence in Virginia' (1997) 3 William and Mary J of Women and the Law 223.

Gavison, R, 'Feminism and the public/private distinction' (1992) 45 Stanford L Rev 1.

Gelles, R, *The Violent Home* (Newbury Park: Sage, 1974).

—— *Intimate Violence in Families* (3rd edn, Thousand Oaks: Sage, 1997).

—— and Straus, M, *Intimate Violence* (New York: Simon & Schuster, 1988).

George, R, *Making Men Moral* (Oxford: Clarendon, 1993).

Givertz, H, 'An anatomy of violence' in S Stanage (ed), *Reason and Violence: Philosophical investigations* (Oxford: Basil Blackwell, 1974).

Goodmark, L, 'Law is the answer? Do we know that for sure? Questioning the efficacy of legal interventions for battered women' (2004) 23 Saint Louis U Public L Rev 7.

Gratzer, T, and Bradford, J, 'Offender and offense characteristics of sexual sadists: A comparative study' (1995) 40 J of Forensic Science 450.

Green, L, 'The duty to govern' (2007) 13 Legal Theory 167.

—— 'Pornographies' (2000) 8 J of Political Philosophy 27.

Green, S, *Lying, Cheating, and Stealing: A moral theory of white-collar crime* (Oxford: OUP 2006).

Greenawalt, K, *Conflicts of Law and Morality* (Oxford: OUP 1987).

Griffin, L, 'The prudent prosecutor' (2001) 14 Georgetown J of Legal Ethics 259.

Grillo, T, 'Anti-essentialism and intersectionality: Tools to dismantle the master's house' (1995) 10 Berkeley Women's LJ 16.

Hampton, J, 'The moral education theory of punishment' (1984) 13 Philosophy and Public Affairs 208.

—— 'Punishment, feminism, and political identity: A case study in the expressive meaning of the law' (1998) 11 Canadian J of L and Jurisprudence 23.

Hanna, C, 'No right to choose: Mandated victim participation in domestic violence prosecutions' (1996) 109 Harvard L Rev 1849.

—— 'Because breaking up is hard to do' (2006) 92 Yale LJ Pocket Part <http://www.thepocketpart.org/2006/10/12/hanna.html> accessed 1 September 2008.

Harel, A, 'Why only the state may inflict criminal sanctions: The case against privately inflicted sanctions' (2008) 14 Legal Theory 113.

Harris, A, 'Race and essentialism in feminist legal theory' (1990) 42 Stanford L Rev 581.

Harris, J, *Violence and Responsibility* (London: Routledge, 1980).

Hart, HLA, *The Concept of Law* (2nd edn, Oxford: Clarendon, 1994).

Hartley, CC, 'A therapeutic jurisprudence approach to the trial process in domestic violence felony trials' (2003) 9 Violence Against Women 410.

Hawkins, K, *Law as Last Resort: Prosecution decision-making in a regulatory agency* (Oxford: OUP, 2002).

Hendy H, and others, 'Decision to leave scale: Perceived reasons to stay in or leave violent relationships' (2003) 27 Psych Women Q 167.

Herman, B, 'On the value of acting from the motive of duty' (1981) 90 Philosophical Rev 359.

Hester, M, and N Westmarland, *Tackling Domestic Violence: Effective interventions and approaches* (Home Office, 2005).

Hetherington, T, *Prosecution and the Public Interest* (London: Waterlow, 1989).

Higgins, T, 'Anti-essentialism, relativism, and human rights' (1996) 19 Harvard Women's LJ 89.

Hildebrandt, M, 'Trial and "fair trial": From peer to subject to citizen' in RA Duff and others (eds), *The Trial on Trial, vol 2: Judgment and calling to account* (Oxford: Hart, 2006).

Hill, A, and others, 'Sexual sadism and sadistic personality disorder in sexual homicide' (2006) 8 J of Personal Disorders 671.

Holmes, E, 'Anti-discrimination rights without equality' (2005) 68 MLR 175.

Hook, S, 'Ideologies of violence' in S Hook (ed), *Revolution, Reform and Social Justice* (Oxford: Basil Blackwell, 1976).

hooks, b, *Feminist Theory: From margin to center* (Cambridge: South End Press, 1984).

Hoyle, C, *Negotiating Domestic Violence: Police, criminal justice and victims* (Oxford: OUP, 1998).

—— and Sanders, A, 'Police response to domestic violence: From victim choice to victim empowerment?' (1998) 40 British J of Criminology 14.

Hudson, B, 'Restorative justice and gendered violence: Diversion or effective justice?' (2002) 42 British J of Criminology 616.

Hume, D, 'Of national characters' in E Miller (ed), *Essays: Moral, political and literary* (rev edn, Indianapolis: Liberty, 1985).

—— *A Treatise on Human Nature* (4th edn, London: Penguin, 1985).

Humphreys, C, and Thiara R,, 'Neither justice nor protection: Women's experiences of post separation violence' (2003) 25 J of Social Welfare and Family Law 195.

Husak, D, 'Why criminal law? A question of content' (2008) 2 Criminal Law and Philosophy 99.

Hutchinson, DL, 'Identity Crisis: "Intersectionality," "multidimensionality," and the development of an adequate theory of subordination' (2001) 6 Michigan J of Race and Law 285.

—— 'New Complexity Theories: From theoretical innovation to doctrinal reform' (2002) 71 U of Missouri Kansas-City L Rev 431.

Jaspers, K, *The Question of German Guilt* (New York: Ashton, 1961).

Jeschenk, HH, 'The discretionary powers of the prosecuting attorney in West Germany' (1970) 18 American J of Comparative L 508.

Johnson, A, 'Defending the use of narrative and giving content to the voice of color: Rejecting the imposition of process theory in legal scholarship' (1994) 79 Iowa L Rev 803.

Johnson, D, 'The organization of prosecution and the possibility of order' (1998) 32 Law and Society Rev 247.

Johnson, H, 'Rethinking survey research on violence against women' in RE Dobash and R Dobash (eds), *Rethinking Violence Against Women* (Thousand Oaks: Sage, 1998).

Johnson, M, 'Patriarchal terrorism and common couple violence: two forms of violence against women' (1995) 57 J of Marriage and the Family 283.

—— 'Conflict and control: Images of symmetry and asymmetry in domestic violence' in A Booth, A Crouter, and M Clements (eds), *Couples in Conflict* (Hillsdale, NJ: Lawrence Erlbaum, 2001).

Jones, A, *Next Time She'll be Dead* (Boston: Beacon Press, 2000).

Jukes, A, *Why Men Hate Women* (London: Free Association Books, 1993).

Kagan, S, *The Limits of Morality* (Oxford: OUP, 1991).

Kahan, 'Gentle nudges vs Hard shoves: Solving the sticky norms problem' (2000) 67 U of Chicago L Rev 607.

Keenan, P, 'The new deterrence: crime and policy in the age of globalization' (2006) 91 Iowa L Rev 505.

Kelly, H, 'Rule of thumb and the folklaw of the husband's stick' (1994) 44 J of Legal Education 341.

Kelly, L, 'Disabusing the definition of domestic abuse: How women batter men and the role of the feminist state' (2003) 30 Florida State U L Rev 791.

Kerr, RM (ed), *Blackstone's Commentaries on the Laws of England* (London: John Murray, 1862).

King-Reis, A, 'Crawford v Washington: The end of victimless prosecution?' (2005) 28 Seattle U L Rev 301.

Korsgaard, C, 'Two distinctions in goodness' (1983) 92 Philosophical Rev 169.

—— 'Teleological ethics' in E Craig (ed), *Routledge Encyclopedia of Philosophy* (London: Routlegde, 1998) <http://www.rep.routledge.com> accessed 14 November 2008.

Krug, P, 'Prosecutorial discretion and its limits' (2002) 50 American J of Comparative L 643.

Kwan, P, 'Jeffrey Dahmer and the cosynthesis of categories' (1997) 48 Hastings LJ 1257.

LaBelle, B, 'Snuff: The ultimate in woman-hating' in L Lederer (ed), *Take Back the Night* (New York: William Morrow, 1980).

Lacey, N, *State Punishment: Political principles and community values* (International Library of Philosophy, Routledge, 1988).

—— 'Theory into practice? Pornography and the public/private dichotomy' in A Bottomley and J Conaghan (eds), *Feminist Theory and Legal Strategy* (Oxford: Blackwell, 1993).

—— 'Unspeakable subjects, impossible rights: Sexuality, integrity and criminal law' (1998) 11 Canadian J of L and Jurisprudence 47.

LaFave, W, 'The prosecutor's discretion in the United States' (1970) 18 American J of Comparative L 532.

Landes, J (ed), *Feminism, the Public and the Private* (Oxford: OUP, 1998).

Laster, K, and Douglas, R, 'Treating spousal violence "differently"', (2000) 7 International Review of Victimology 115.

Laufer, W, 'The rhetoric of innocence' (1995) 70 Washington L Rev 329.

Leigh, L, 'Private prosecutions and diversionary justice' (2007) Crim LR 289.

Lemon, N, *Domestic Violence Law* (St Paul: West, 2001).

Levin, R, 'The administrative law legacy of Kenneth Culp Davis' (2005) 42 San Diego L Rev 315.

Levit, N, 'Theorizing the connections among systems of subordination' (2002) 71 U of Missouri Kansas-City L Rev 227.

Lewis, HD, 'Collective responsibility' (1948) 24 Philosophy 3.

Lewis, R, 'Making justice work: Effective legal interventions for domestic violence' 44 British J of Criminology 204.

Little, A, 'Balancing accountability and victim autonomy at the International Criminal Court' (2007) 38 Georgetown J of Intl L 363.

Lloyd, G, *The Man of Reason: 'Male' and 'female' in western philosophy* (Minneapolis: University of Minnesota Press, 1984).

—— 'Rationality' in A Jaggar and IM Young (eds), *Blackwell's Companion to Feminist Philosophy* (Oxford: Blackwell, 2000).

Locke, J, *Two Treatises of Government* (London, 1821; reprint Cambridge: Cambridge University Press, 1991).

Loseke, DR, Gelles, RJ, and Cavanaugh, MM, *Current Controversies on Family Violence* (Thousand Oaks: Sage, 2005).

Luban, D, *Lawyers and Justice: An ethical study* (Princeton University Press, Princeton 1988).

Luna, E, 'Principled enforcement of penal codes' (2005) 4 Buffalo Crim L Rev 515.

MacCormick, N, *Legal Reasoning and Legal Theory* (Oxford: Clarendon, 1978).

—— *HLA Hart* (London: Edward Arnold, 1981).

Mack, K, 'Continuing barriers to women's credibility: A feminist perspective on the proof process' (1993) 4 Criminal L Forum 327.

MacKinnon, CA, *Feminism Unmodified* (Cambridge: Harvard University Press, 1987).

—— *Toward a Feminist Theory of the State* (Cambridge: Harvard University Press, 1989).

—— 'Reflections on sex equality under law' (1991) 100 Yale LJ 1281.

MacKinnon, CA, 'Points against postmodernism' (2000) 75 Chicago-Kent L Rev 687.
—— *Sex Equality* (New York: University Casebook Series, Foundation Press, 2001).
—— *Are Women Human? And other international dialogues* (London: Harvard University Press, 2006).
Macklem, T, *Beyond Comparison: Sex and discrimination* (Cambridge: Cambridge University Press, 2003).
Madison, J, *A Lynching in the Heartland: Race and memory in America* (New York: Palgrave, 2001).
Mahoney, M, 'Legal images of battered women: Redefining the issue of separation' 90 Michigan L Rev 1.
Mahoney, P, L Williams, and C West, 'Violence against women by intimate relationship partners' in C Renzetti, J Edelson, and RK Bergan (eds), *Sourcebook on Violence Against Women* (Thousand Oaks: Sage, 2001).
Malavet, P, 'Outsider citizenships and multidimensional borders: The power and danger of not belonging' (2005) 52 Cleveland State L Rev 321.
Margolin, G, 'The multiple forms of aggressiveness between marital partners: How do we identify them?' (1987) 13 J of Marital and Family Therapy 77.
Marshall, S, 'Victims of crime: Their station and its duties' (2004) 7 Critical Review of International Social and Political Philosophy 104.
—— and Duff, RA, 'Sharing wrongs' (1998) 11 Canadian J of L and Jurisprudence 7.
Martin, K, Vieraitis, L, and Britto, S, 'Gender equality and women's absolute status: A test of the feminist models of rape' (2006) 12 Violence Against Women 321.
Matsuda, M, 'Pragmatism modified and the false consciousness problem' (1990) 63 Southern California L Rev 1763.
McConville, M, Sanders, A, and Leng, R, *The Case for the Prosecution* (London: Routledge, 1991).
Meares, T, 'Rewards for good behavior: Influencing prosecutorial discretion and conduct with financial incentives' (1995) 64 Fordham L Rev 851.
Merry, SE, *Human Rights and Gender Violence: Translating international law into local justice* (London: University of Chicago Press, 2005).
Midgely, C, *Sisterhood and Slavery: Transatlantic antislavery and women's rights* (British Abolitionism and Feminism in Transatlantic and Imperial Perspective, Proceedings of the Third Annual Gilder Lehrman Center International Conference at Yale University, 25–28 October 2001).
Mill, JS, 'On the subjection of women' in R Wolheim (ed), *Three Essays: On Liberty; Representative Government; The Subjection of Women* (Oxford: OUP, 1975).
—— *Utilitarianism* (Indianapolis: Hackett, 1861, reprint 1979).
Miller, S, *Victims as Offenders: the paradox of women's violence in relationships* (London: Rutgers University Press, 2005).
Mills, L, 'On the other side of silence: Affective lawyering for intimate abuse' (1996) 81 Cornell L Rev 1225.
—— 'Killing her softly: Intimate abuse and the violence of state intervention' (1999) 113 Harvard L Rev 550.
—— *Insult to Injury: Rethinking our responses to intimate abuse* (Oxford: Princeton University Press, 2003).
—— 'Intimate violence as intimate: The journey and a path' (2003) 9 Cardozo Women's LJ 461.

Moore, M, *Placing Blame: A theory of criminal law* (Oxford: Clarendon, 1997).

Mordini, N, 'Mandatory state interventions for domestic abuse cases: An examination of the effects on victim safety and autonomy' (2004) 52 Drake L Rev 295.

Morley, R, and Mullender, A, 'Hype or hope: The importation of pro-arrest policies and batterers' programmes from North America to Britain as key measures for preventing violence against women in the home' (1992) 6 Intl J of L and the Family 265.

Nicolson, D, and J Webb, *Professional Legal Ethics: Critical interrogations* (Oxford: OUP, 1999).

Nussbaum, M, 'Human functioning and social justice: In defense of Aristotelian essentialism' (1992) 20 Political Theory 202.

—— *Sex and Social Justice* (Oxford: OUP, 1999).

O'Donovan, K, *Sexual Divisions in Law* (London: Weidenfeld and Nicolson, 1985).

Ogden, DRH, 'Prosecuting domestic violence crimes: Effectively using rule 404(B) to hold batterers accountable for repeated abuse' (1998–1999) 34 Gonzaga L Rev 361.

Packer, H, *The Limits of the Criminal Sanction* (Stanford: Stanford University Press, 1968).

Parton, C, 'Women, gender oppression and child abuse' in VACS Group (ed), *Taking Child Abuse Seriously: Contemporary issues in child abuse theory and practice* (London: Unwin Hyman, 1990).

Pateman, C, *The Sexual Contract* (Stanford: Stanford University Press, 1988).

Pence, E, and Paymar, M, *Power and Control: Tactics of men who batter* (Duluth: DAIP, 1993).

Petit, P, 'Consequentialism' in P Singer (ed), *A Companion to Ethics* (Oxford: Blackwell, 2000).

Pharr, S, *Homophobia: A weapon of sexism* (Inverness, CA: Chardon Press, 1988).

Pound, R, 'Law in books and law in action' (1910) 44 American L Rev 12.

Rawls, J, *A Theory of Justice* (revised edn, Cambridge: Belknap, 1999).

Raz, J, *The Concept of a Legal System* (Oxford: Clarendon, 1970).

—— 'Promises and obligations' in PMS Hacker and J Raz (eds), *Law, Morality and Society: Essays in honour of HLA Hart* (Oxford: Clarendon Press 1977).

—— *The Authority of Law* (Oxford: OUP, 1979).

—— 'Legal principles and the limits of law' in M Cohen (ed), *Ronald Dworkin and Contemporary Jurisprudence* (London: Duckworth, 1984).

—— *The Morality of Freedom* (Oxford: OUP, 1986).

—— *Practical Reason and Norms* (2nd edn, New York: OUP, 1999).

—— *Ethics in the Public Domain* (Oxford: OUP, 1994).

—— *Engaging Reason* (Oxford: OUP, 1999).

—— 'Incorporation by law' (2004) 10 Legal Theory 1.

—— 'The problem of authority: Revisiting the service conception' (2006) 90 Minn L Rev 1003.

Réaume, D, 'Comparing theories of sex discrimination: The role of comparison' (2005) 25 OJLS 547.

Reece, H, 'The end of domestic violence' (2006) 69 MLR 770.

Regan, D, 'Authority and value: Reflections on Raz's *The Morality of Freedom*' (1989) 62 Southern California L Rev 995.

Rich, A, 'Compulsory Heterosexuality and Lesbian Existence' (1980) 15 Journal of Women's History 11.

Richman, D, and others, 'Panel discussion: The expanding prosecutorial role from trial counsel to investigator and administrator' (1999) 26 Fordham Urban LJ 679.

Richman, D, and Stuntz, W, 'Al Capone's revenge: An essay on the political economy of pretexual prosecution' (2005) 105 Columbia L Rev 583.

Roberts, K, 'Women's experience of violence during stalking by former romantic partners: Factors predictive of stalking violence' (2005) 11 Violence Against Women 89.

Robinson, P, *Criminal Law Defences* (St Paul: West, 1984).

—— and Darley, J, 'Does criminal law deter? A behavioural science investigation' (2004) 24 OJLS 173.

Robson, R, 'Lavender bruises' (1990) 20 Golden Gate U L Rev 567.

Rogers, J, 'Restructuring the exercise of prosecutorial discretion in England' (2006) 26 OJLS 775.

Russell, D, *The Politics of Rape* (New York: Stein and Day, 1975).

—— *Rape in Marriage* (2nd edn, Bloomington: Indiana University Press, 1990).

Sack, E, 'Battered women and the state: The struggle for the future of domestic violence policy' [2004] Wisconsin L Rev 1657.

Sanders, A, 'Personal violence and public order: Prosecution of domestic violence in England and Wales' [1988] Intl J of Sociology of L 359.

—— and Young, R, 'From suspect to trial' in M Macguire, R Morgan, and R Reiner (eds), *Oxford Handbook of Criminology* (Oxford: OUP, 2002).

—— 'The ethics of prosecution lawyers' (2004) 7 Legal Ethics 190.

Saunders, D, 'Wife abuse, husband abuse, or mutual combat? A feminist perspective on the empirical findings' in K Yllo and M Bograd (eds), *Feminist Perspectives on Wife Abuse* (Newbury Park: Sage, 1988).

Scales, A, 'The emergence of feminist jurisprudence: An essay' (1986) 95 Yale LJ 1373.

Schatzki, T, 'Structuralism in social science' (1998) Routledge Encyclopedia of Philosophy Online <http://www.rep.routledge.com/article/R036?ssid=467079195&n=2#> accessed 13 April 2007.

Schauer, F, *Playing by the Rules* (Oxford: Clarendon, 1991; reprint 2002).

Scheffler, S (ed), *Consequentialism and its Critics* (Oxford: OUP, 1988).

Schmidt, J, and Sherman, L, 'Does arrest deter domestic violence?' in E Buzawa and C Buzawa (eds), *Do Arrests and Restraining Orders Work?* (Thousand Oaks: Sage, 1996) 54–82.

Sen, A, 'More than one hundred million women are missing' (20 December 1990) New York Review of Books.

Shapiro, S, 'Authority' in, J Coleman and S Shapiro (eds), *The Oxford Handbook of Jurisprudence and Philosophy of Law* (Oxford: OUP, 2002).

Sherman, L, *Policing Domestic Violence: Experiments and dilemmas* (New York: Free Press, 1992).

—— and others, 'The variable effects of arrest on criminal careers: The Milwaukee domestic violence experiment' (1992) 83 J of Crim L and Criminology 137.

Sherman, N, *The Fabric of Character: Aristotle's theory of virtue* (Oxford: OUP, 1989).

Shute, S, and Gardner, J, 'The wrongness of rape' in J Horder (ed), *Oxford Essays in Jurisprudence* (4th edn, Oxford: OUP, 2000).

Siegel, R, 'The rule of love: Wife beating as prerogative and privacy' (1996) 105 Yale LJ 2117.

Slote, M, *Goods and Virtues* (Oxford: Clarendon, 1983).

Smart, C, *Law, Crime and Sexuality* (London: Sage, 1995).

Smart, J, and Williams, B, *Utilitarianism: For and against* (Cambridge: Cambridge University Press, 1973).

Smith, A, 'Can you be a good person and a good prosecutor?' (2001) 14 Georgetown J of Legal Ethics 355.

Smith, M, 'Patriarchal ideology and wife beating: A test of a feminist hypothesis' (1990) 5 Violence and Victims 257.

Smith, P, 'Discrimination and disadvantage in feminist legal theory: A review of Deborah Rhode's justice and gender' (1992) 11 Law and Philosophy 431.

Stanage, S, 'Violatives: Modes and themes of violence' in S Stanage (ed), *Reason and Violence: Philosophical investigations* (Oxford: Basil Blackwell, 1974).

Stanistreet, D, Bambra, C, and Scott-Samuel, AJ, 'Is patriarchy the source of men's higher mortality?' (2005) 59 J of Epidemiology and Community Health 873.

Stanko, E, 'Unmasking what should be seen: A study of the prevalence of domestic violence in the London Borough of Hackney' in E Edna and K Laster (eds), *Domestic Violence: Global responses* (Bicester: AB Academic Publishers, 2000).

Stark, E, 'Insults, injury, and injustice: Rethinking state intervention in domestic violence cases' (2004) 10 Violence Against Women 1302.

—— *Coercive Control: How men entrap women in personal life* (New York: OUP, 2007).

Steinmetz, S, 'The battered husband syndrome' (1977) 2 Victimology 499.

Stokinger, C, 'Symposium: Women, children and domestic violence: Current tensions and emerging issues' (2000) 27 Fordham Urban LJ 565.

Straus, M, 'The conflict tactics (CT) scales' (1979) 40 J of Marriage and the Family 75.

—— 'Injury and frequency of assault and the "representative sample fallacy" in measuring wife beating and child abuse' in R Gelles and M Straus (eds), *Physical Violence in American Families* (New Brunswick, NJ: Transaction, 1990).

—— 'The controversy over domestic violence by women' in XB Arriaga and S Oskamp (eds), *Violence in Intimate Relationships* (Thousand Oaks: Sage, 1999).

—— and R Gelles, 'Societal change and change in family violence from 1975 to 1985 as revealed in two national surveys' in M Straus and R Gelles (eds), *Physical Violence in American Families* (New Brunswick, NJ: Transaction, 1990).

——, ——, and Steinmetz, S, *Behind Closed Doors: Violence in the American family* (Garden City: Bantam, 1980).

—— and others, 'The revised conflict tactics scales (CTS2): Development and preliminary psychometric data' (1996) 17 J of Family Issues 283.

Stubbs, J, 'Beyond apology? Domestic violence and critical questions for restorative justice' (2007) 7 Criminology and Crim Justice 169.

Sugarman, DB, and Frankel, SL, 'Patriarchal ideology and wife-assault: A meta-analytic review' (1996) 11 J of Family Violence 13.

Suk, J, 'Criminal law comes home' (2006) 116 Yale LJ 2.

Sunstein, C, 'Social norms and social roles' (1996) 96 Columbia L Rev 903.

Tadros, V, 'The distinctiveness of domestic violence: A freedom based account' (2005) 65 Louisiana L Rev 989.

Thornton, M (ed), *Public and Private: Feminist legal debates* (Melbourne: OUP, 1995).

Tolany, SE, and Beck, EM, *A Festival of Violence: An analysis of Southern lynchings, 1882–1930* (Urbana: University of Illinois Press, 1995).

Tuerkheimer, D, 'Crawford's triangle: Domestic violence and the right of confrontation' (2006) 85 North Carolina L Rev 1.

von Hirsch, A, *Past or Future Crimes: Deservedness and dangerousness in the sentencing of criminals* (Manchester: Manchester University Press, 1986).

Vorenberg, J, 'Decent restraint of prosecutorial power' (1981) 94 Harvard L Rev 1521.

Waites, K, 'The criminal justice system's response to battering: Understanding the problem, forging the solutions' (1985) 60 Washington L Rev 267.

Walby, S, *Theorizing Patriarchy* (Oxford: Blackwell Publishers, 1990).

Wanless, M, 'Mandatory arrest: A step toward eradicating domestic violence, but is it enough?' [1996] U of Illinois L Rev 533.

Weigend, T, 'Why have a trial when you can have a bargain?' in RA Duff and others (eds), *The Trial on Trial, vol 2: Judgment and calling to account* (Oxford: Hart, 2006).

Weissman, D, 'The political economy of violence: Toward an understanding of the gender-based murders of Ciudad Juárez' (1995) 30 North Carolina J of Intl L and Commercial Regulation 795.

Wellman, CH, and Simmons, AJ, *Is there a Duty to Obey the Law?* (Cambridge: Cambridge University Press, 2005).

Wells, C, 'The impact of feminist thinking on criminal law and justice: Contradiction, complexity, conviction and connection' [2004] Crim L Rev 503.

Wells-Barnett, IB, *On Lynchings* (Amhurst: Humanity Books, 2002).

Westen, P, 'The empty idea of equality' (1982) 95 Harvard L Rev 537.

Wills, D, 'Mandatory prosecution in domestic violence cases: The case for aggressive prosecution' (1997) 7 UCLA Women's LJ 173.

Wolff, R, *In Defence of Anarchism* (New York: Harper & Row, 1970).

Yllo, K, 'Sexual equality and violence against wives in American States' (1983) 14 J of Comparative Family Studies 67.

—— 'Using a feminist approach in quantitative research' in R Finkelhor, R Gelles, and G Hotaling (eds), *The Dark Side of Families: Current family violence research* (Beverly Hills: Sage, 1983).

—— 'Political and methodological debates in wife abuse research' in K Yllo and M Bograd (eds), *Feminist Perspectives on Wife Abuse* (Newbury Park: Sage, 1988).

—— 'Through a feminist lens: Gender, power and violence' in R Gelles and D Loseke (eds), *Current Controversies on Family Violence* (Thousand Oaks: Sage, 1993).

—— and M Bograd, *Feminist Perspectives on Wife Abuse* (Thousand Oaks: Sage, 1988).

Young, IM, *Inclusion and Democracy* (Oxford: OUP, 2002).

—— *On Female Body Experience: 'Throwing like a girl' and other essays* (New York: OUP, 2005).

Zacharias, F, 'Specificity in professional responsibility codes: Theory, practice, and the paradigm of prosecutorial ethics' (1993) 69 Notre Dame LR 223.

Zedner, L, *Criminal Justice* (Oxford: Clarendon, 2004).

Zlotnick, D, 'Empowering the battered woman: The use of criminal contempt sanctions to enforce civil protection orders' (1999) 56 Ohio State LJ 1153.

Zorza, J, 'The criminal law of misdemeanor violence (1970–1990)' (1992) 83 J of Crim L and Criminology 46.

—— *Mandatory Arrest: Problems and possibilities* (New York: National Center on Women and Family Law, 1994).

MODEL CODES AND POLICIES

American Bar Association Code of Professional Conduct.
Crown Prosecution Service, *Code for Crown Prosecutors* (2004).
Crown Prosecution Service, *Policy for Prosecuting Cases of Domestic Violence* (2005).
US Model Code of Professional Responsibility.

REPORTS

Amnesty International, 'Mexico: Killings and abductions of women in Ciudad Juarez and the city of Chihuahua—The struggle for justice goes on' (20 February 2006) <http://www.amnestyusa.org/document.php?id=ENGAMR410122006> accessed 29 August 2008.
Dempsey, MM, *The Use of Expert Witness Testimony in Domestic Violence Cases* (CPS 2004).
Ertürk, Y, 'The due diligence standard as a tool for the elimination of violence against women', *Report of the Special Rapporteur on Violence Against Women, its Causes and Consequences: Integration of the human rights of women and the gender perspective: Violence against women,* UN Doc E/CN.4/2006/61 (20 January 2006).
HMCPSI, *Violence at Home* (2004).
Sanlon, J, Cassar, A, and Nemes, N, 'Water as a human right?' (IUCN Environmental Law and Policy Paper No 51, UNDP 2004).

NEWSPAPER REPORTS

'Editorial' *Daily News* (New York, 14 June 2005).
Bindel, J, 'Terror on our streets' *Guardian* (London, 13 December 2006) <http://www.guardian.co.uk/suffolkmurders/story/0,,1970938,00.html> accessed 14 July 2007.
Broder, JM, and Madigan, N, 'Michael Jackson cleared after 14-week child molesting trial' (New York Times, online version, posted 14 June 2005) <http://www.nytimes.com/2005/06/14/national/14jackson.html> accessed 3 November 2008.
Schenk, M, 'Aggressively pursuing abuse cases at issue' *News-Gazette* (Urbana, IL, 13 July 1997) <http://www.news-gazette.com/search/archives/aggressively pursuing abuse cases at issue.htm> accessed 27 April 2007.

SPEECHES AND PRESENTATIONS

Brodsky, G, and Day, S, 'Women's human rights in an era of conservatism: Stories from Canada' presented at University of Kent Law School conference 'Encountering human rights: Gender/sexuality, activism and the promise of law' (London, 5 January 2007).

Index